Tim Clayton is the award-winning author of a number of books on navel and military history, including *Trafalgar, Tars* (winner of the Mountbatten Literary Award 2008) and *Finest Hour*, the bestselling book that accompanied the landmark BBC1 television series.

SEA WOLVES

The Extraordinary Story of Britain's WW2 Submarines

TIM CLAYTON

LITTLE, BROWN

First published in Great Britain in 2011 by Little, Brown
This paperback edition published in 2012 by Abacus

A CIP catalogue record for this book
is available from the British Library.

ISBN 978-0-349-12289-2

Typeset in Bembo by M Rules
Printed and bound in Great Britain by
Clays Ltd, St Ives plc

Papers used by Abacus are from well-managed forests
and other responsible sources

MIX
Paper from
responsible sources
FSC® C104740

Abacus
An imprint of
Little, Brown Book Group
100 Victoria Embankment
London EC4Y 0DY

An Hachette UK Company
www.hachette.co.uk

www.littlebrown.co.uk

To Bill King who inspired me to write it

Contents

The Norwegian Campaign

70°
10°
0°
10°
20°

FINLAND

Narvik

Arctic Circle

ATLANTIC
OCEAN

Trondheim

SWEDEN

NORWAY

Gulf of Bothnia

60°   Shetland Is.

Bergen

Oslo

Orkney Is.

Scapa Flow

Larvik

Stavanger
Obrestad
Egersund
Kristiansand

Lillesand
The Skaw

Tobermory

NORTH
SEA

Skagerrak

Dundee   Montrose
Ardrishaig   Dunoon
Rothesay   Aberdour
Campbeltown   Rosyth
Londonderry

German declared
mined area

Kattegat

DENMARK   Copenhagen

Baltic Sea

Blyth

Horns Reef

Barrow

British declared
mined area

Heligoland

Kiel

Birkenhead

Immingham

Cromer

Wilhelmshaven

GERMANY

GREAT
BRITAIN

Harwich

London

Plymouth   Portsmouth

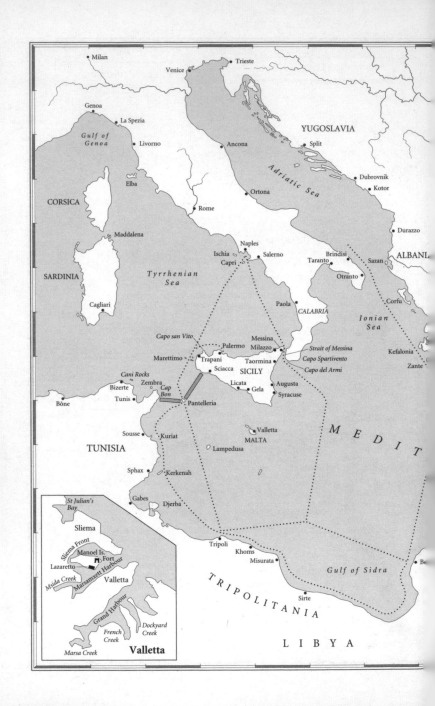

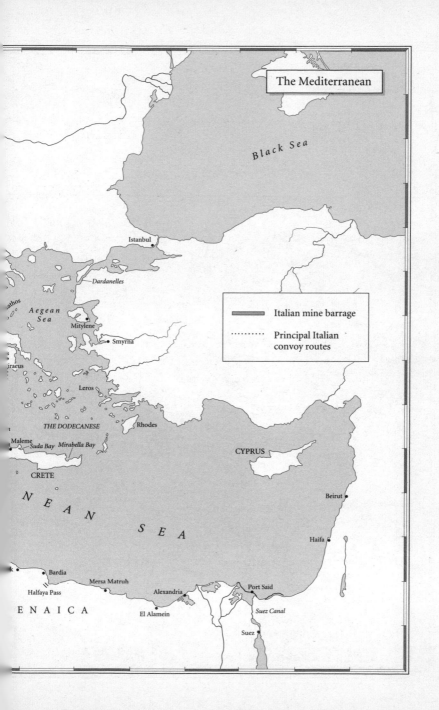

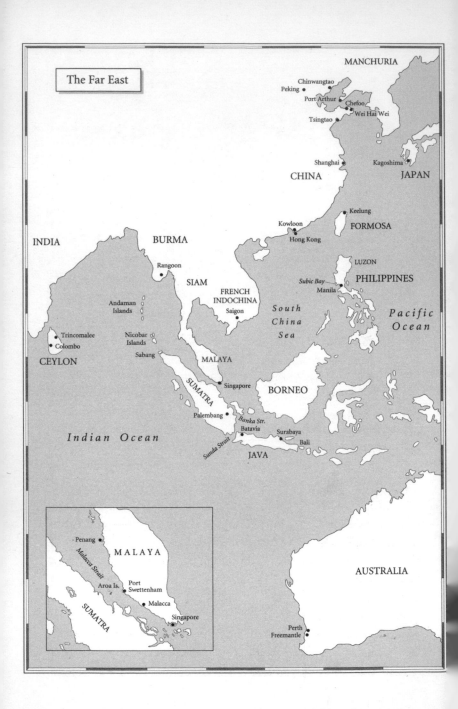

Prologue

PERSEUS

On the seabed in 171 feet of water off the village of Mavrata, near the south-eastern tip of the Greek island of Kefalonia, lies His Majesty's Submarine *Perseus*. There is a crack in the port bow, but otherwise the wreck looks intact, though encrusted with sea creatures and inhabited by fish. A Greek diving team has filmed it and you can watch the results on the internet. The eeriest of the films shows the rusty interior of the after torpedo compartment and of the control room, where the engine telegraphs can be seen set at 'Stop' and 'Half Ahead'. The camera tastefully avoids the human bones that litter the compartment.

To the trained eye there is nothing particularly odd about the submarine, except that the hatches are open. By 1941 war orders required all hatches except the one above the control room to be clamped shut from the outside, because experience had proved that they sometimes lifted and let in water when a submarine was depth-charged.

Early in December 1941 the submarine *Perseus* was patrolling off Italian-controlled Kefalonia. She had sixty-one men aboard, of whom at least two were passengers. Lieutenant Nicolaos Merlin was, ostensibly at least, on his way to Alexandria to take command of a Greek submarine, while Leading Stoker John Capes was returning to his own submarine, *Thrasher*, after attending a court hearing in Malta where he stood accused of having destroyed a Maltese horse-drawn carriage in a motor car accident in 1940.

Perseus was one of the large patrol submarines built for the China Fleet in 1928 out of heavy brass and steel; she was spacious and comfortable by submarine standards, with robustly elegant wooden fittings, although she was beginning to show her age. Her skipper was Commander Edward Nicolay, a 34-year-old veteran with high standards and a short temper. In the last eight months he had sunk an impressive ten ships for a total of just over 15,000 tons. They had left the Lazaretto at Malta on 26 November and on 4 December he had added to his total with the 3300 ton Italian merchant *Eridano* off Lefkada.

Two nights later they were on the surface off Kefalonia. It was a dark, windy, moonless night. Nobody knows what they were doing there but it is possible that they were so close to the coast because they were preparing to land an agent, and the presence in the boat of Nicolaos Merlin, whose mother was Kefalonian, reinforces the suspicion. It was normal for a collapsible canoe, or folbot, to be stored in the torpedo space forward, from where it could be brought to the surface through the wide torpedo hatch in order to be launched.

What is certain is that *Perseus* hit a mine. The anchor of an Italian mine is still there, close to the wreck. The position of the engine telegraphs and the angle of the rudder suggest that at the last second the submarine's lookouts saw it and attempted to avoid it. But they failed.

As a stoker, the passenger John Capes had found a berth right aft behind the stokers' mess, in an empty torpedo rack in the machinery space. It was as comfortable a berth as any in a submarine and the warmth from the nearby engines and motors was welcome in December. Almost above him as he lay in his 'comfortable torpedo tray browsing over elderly letters' was the after escape hatch. He had woken up for the rum issue, having 'saved some rum tots in my private blitz [bottle]. Tots kept me awake at night so I saved them for our return to harbour.'

Out of nowhere 'a devastating explosion rocked the boat from stem to stern. My makeshift bed reared up throwing me in a complete somersault.' The submarine listed to starboard and went almost vertically downwards. 'The bows hit the bottom with a nerve shattering jolt, the boat hung poised for a moment, standing on her head. Then the stern, where I was, fell back settling on the sea bed.' The impact created a two-metre crater in the sandy mud. When she finally settled it was stern down with a thirty-degree list to starboard. As he landed, Capes hit the hydroplane control wheel in the centre of the compartment, then fell on to the bulkhead of the stokers' mess. As the submarine righted itself he slithered downwards, badly bruised and in pain, but not seriously injured.

When he came to himself and realised he was alive but in danger, his first thought was to find out who else had survived. 'No time for pains now. How about the chaps in the engine room?' Every pipeline and valve in the after end and rear compartments were broken. All lighting failed within fifteen seconds of the explosion. He 'groped for the torch near the escape hatch. "Thank Heaven", I thought, it was in its position, and it worked! The powerful rays pierced the dank foggy air already beginning to stink of paint.' The increased air pressure had burst drums of oil and paint that were stored there. He walked up the slope toward the bows through the stokers' mess deck, and through the next bulkhead to the motor room. In there the electricians 'had apparently been killed by falling on live switches'. As he went into the engine room he saw that 'half of the cylinder heads at the front end of the engines had sheared off from the studs, with the operation gear hurled against the engine room forrard.' The engines were not going to be working again. Then he realised that the next bulkhead door had not been shut deliberately. 'No clips had been secured. It must have been slammed by the first blast of the explosion, and was now held in place by water . . . It was creaking under the great pressure. Jets and trickles from the rubber joint seeped through.'

Capes had found five other stokers clinging on to life. He was fully alive to the drama. 'Our plight was one of vital horror. The water was rising in the engine room bilges and we were surrounded by the mangled bodies of a dozen dead. *Perseus* had become a cold steel tomb surrounded by the relentless sea.' The sea temperature in this spot is only 50° F in July and with the machinery no longer creating heat the temperature soon dropped. Feeling cold, Capes characteristically 'thought of the rum in my blitz bottle. That would warm us up all right. I nipped back aft, had a stiff livener and handed the bottle round for a swift pick-me-up.' He guided or dragged his badly wounded comrades to the escape hatch in the stern compartment ('No time to be fussy about wounds'). Now training took over. He knew that they had to put on Davis Submerged Escape Apparatus (DSEA) survival sets, let down the canvas trunking around the escape hatch, and flood their compartment until the pressure inside was equal to the pressure outside in the open sea. Then he had to open the hatch, if by luck nothing had fallen on it to jam it. Even were it to open the chances of survival looked slim. The depth gauge, if it was still working, showed just over 270 feet. Their DSEA sets were designed for depths of less than 100 feet and he had never heard of anyone escaping from deeper water. But, he said to himself, 'If death was going to claim me it would not be without a fight.'

It took half an hour to drag three wounded shipmates to the after escape compartment. In the torchlight he 'gave them another noggin of rum each and had two myself. Liquor at least kept out the damp cold for the moment.' Something like an hour had passed since the explosion and if he was to escape it had to be soon. The fumes, oil and pressure were killing them. Water with a filthy scum on it was running through the engine room. There wasn't much more time. With some difficulty he shut the 'after water-tight door, isolating us in the stern compartment'. Then he broke the seals of the four lockers and strapped rubber escape sets on his companions. The DSEA sets consisted of a rubber lung, worn on the chest, a small bottle of high pressure oxygen across the stomach, a nose clip, goggles and a tightly fitting mouthpiece with an adjustable rubber band. By the time he had the sets strapped on, the atmosphere in their small space was becoming foul. He 'lowered the collapsible canvas trunk from a recess fitted around the escape hatch, and secured it by lashings to the deck. At the top of the trunk inside was the escape hatch, with four nuts holding four large clips securing the hatch firmly on the rubber seating joints all round the rim.'

He found the valve in the starboard bilge to flood the compartment from the sea, knowing from his training that 'the water would rise around the escape trunk, leaving a small space of air considerably compressed. This would stop the water rising further. Then we would have to insert our mouthpieces, duck down under the water coming up into the trunk and then out into the open sea through the escape hatch.' The spindle on the valve was bent and he couldn't shift it. For a moment he panicked: they were trapped. He had to find a way to flood the compartment quickly before they all froze to death. He wondered about the torpedo tubes, but he couldn't let water in through those without the hydraulic telemotor system. Then he thought of the underwater gun. 'That was it! Thank god we were in the compartment with the gun.' Housed under their compartment, it was used to send smoke signals to the surface. With its four-inch bore it would let in water rapidly. 'The water was rising steadily, the only chance was to flood quickly, release the hatch and leave without a minute's delay.' Capes splashed down to the gun and opened the breech. He 'tried the sluice valve gently and could feel the thrust of water entering. It increased to a steady whirl as the sea gushed in and then steadied, the air space round the hatch diminished rapidly. Here it came ... the sea that would save us, drown us or freeze us to death.'

Johnny 'Choppa' Capes was five foot ten, dark, and educated at Dulwich College. This made him an unusual stoker, well-spoken when he chose to be. His father, a civil engineer and archaeologist, had left his mother and gone to live in Alexandria. 'Choppa' loathed authority and didn't hesitate to show it. He joined the navy unusually late, at twenty-five, as a stoker second class and went into submarines as soon as he could, which was three years later. People who served with him noted his extreme fondness for women and rum. Those who went ashore with Capes got into frequent scrapes but found that he was a stalwart companion in a tight spot. He continued in the navy after the war, enjoying a great reputation as a yarner. Many of his contemporaries didn't believe his tale of his escape from *Perseus*.

Elements within the account do seem exaggerated. He claimed that the boat was 270 feet under water when its depth was actually 171 feet – although, according to Greek diver Kostas Thoctarides, a depth gauge incorrectly shows the depth of 270 feet that Capes recalled. Capes also claimed to have done all he could for five other injured stokers, but some who heard his story suspected that he was suppressing a darker episode of panic and struggle to escape. There are no human bones in the compartment from which the escape was made, so Capes either pushed the others out, as he said, or he was always alone there.

The study of the wreck made by Thoctarides has, however, proved most details in Capes's story to be correct, while his efforts to locate the positions of the bodies of the crew may further reveal the truth of what happened that night.

He ducked down through the paint scum, groped for the bottom rim of the escape trunk, braced himself against the deck and dragged himself upwards. He found his head above water in the little pocket of air in the air lock below the hatch. He unscrewed the vent cock in the centre of the steel lid. The air whistled out and the slimy water rose above his face. His teeth were chattering. He applied all the force he could muster to the tommy bar in the tube spanner to undo the nuts. They came away easily. As the last nut dropped he gave a mighty heave and the hatch flew wide open. A giant bubble of air escaped. He clung to the top rungs and rim of the hatch. He lost his mouthpiece, but recovered it and stuffed it back in place. Breath came again, and a few bubbles from the lung streamed upwards.

He rubbed his goggles and dipped into the trunk for the last time. Coming out of the hatch, he felt overhead for the jumping wire, but it had snapped and was gone. He flashed the torch around but could only see a few feet of steel deck. He let go and the buoyant oxygen lifted him rapidly upwards. The pain became intense, his lungs and body bursting. Dizzy with agony, he realised he was rising too quickly and unrolled the apron of the DSEA set to slow his ascent. He saw a tethered mine about fifteen feet away. He burst to the surface, wallowing in the swell. The ascent took about a minute and a half. He reckoned it was about 1½ hours since the explosion.

Following drill, he shut off the mouthpiece of his DSEA set and made the oxygen bag into a kind of lifebelt. He removed the nose clip and lifted his goggles to have a good look round. The sea was choppy, whipped up by the wind, hardly ideal for swimming. He could see no sign of any other survivors. Only one of his companions had stood much chance of making it to the surface. Some distance away, he saw a ribbon of white bobbing about on the wave crests. It appeared to be a broken line of cliffs. He flashed SOS with the torch in that direction but got no response.

The night air was refreshing but the water was very cold. He started to swim. The torch was a dead weight so he dropped it. The will to live kept him going, now on his back, now breast stroke, resting frequently. Gradually the cliffs became clearer and a high mountain, looming in the background, came into view. 'My mind, body and whole being were concentrated on one thing only ... the shore.' Finally, he could see a low pebbly beach, almost within reach. The wind dropped as he came beneath the cliff. His foot struck a rock. He dragged himself over more rocks and on to pebbles. 'Face down, head on hands, I lapsed into oblivion.'

When Capes woke, the sun was high in the sky. Cautiously looking round, he could see an Italian sentry in the distance, standing on the cliff looking out to sea. Then he heard voices. Two men were slithering down a cleft out of sight of the sentry. 'In fierce whispers they asked "Inglese? Inglese?"' He nodded. 'They signalled me to stay put and ran back up the cleft like mountain goats.' Later, other villagers arrived with a gourd of ouzo and a jacket, trousers and khaki overcoat.

That night they put Capes on a donkey and took him up the cliffs to the house of Gerasimos Vallianos in Mavrata. The villagers were worried that he was a spy. They contacted Helen Cosmetatos, an Englishwoman who belonged to the Kefalonian resistance, and she interrogated him to make sure that he wasn't an Italian plant. She gave him a postcard on which he wrote, 'All well, Hawtrey' (his middle name), addressing it to Emsworth 369, his mother's telephone number. Amazingly, some months later, long after she had been told that her son was presumed dead, the postcard reached her.

Capes was taken to Hionata on foot and then to Rozata by car, then into the hills at Pharouklata and Kourouklata. He moved over and over again, spending time both at Helen Cosmetatos's house and with Gerasimos Razis, mayor of Argostoli. According to Capes's debriefer's report, Razis proved very helpful both then and over a period of many months.

'My life became one of desperation and boredom, mingled with the ever present fear of capture; and of course the reprisals taken against the people sheltering me would be obvious ... Clandestine flights through the rugged countryside constantly took place.' Much of his time was spent alone in the hills with a donkey named Mareeka, loaned to him on condition that he promised not to eat her. Only once was he ever spoken to by an Italian sentry, and then he was merely asked for a match. He handed it over in the stony silence that the villagers normally reserved for Italians.

Finally, after he had been in hiding for eighteen months, another woman, Cleo Pollatos, came to tell him he was leaving and took him to the house of Nikos Vandoros at Agia Irini, where he was shown a note from Major Michael Parrish. 'Milo, a weather-beaten fisherman, slouched into a small unoccupied house I had been taken to the previous night. His small half decked schooner, only 25 feet long, was intended to carry me to freedom.' Milo, known to Capes's debriefer as Captain Milton, was actually Captain Militiades Houmas, who belonged to Parrish's secret flotilla, run by MI9. His caique *Evangelistria* carried out sixty-five smuggling and rescue missions for the British.

Milo picked up Capes from a secluded bay and after a windy six-day voyage, dropped him at Smyrna. "'Ianny," cried Milo. "Quick, take a swim and wash. Somebody important is coming to see you."' Capes was 'struggling back into my old clothes as a launch came alongside. On her deck stood a neat figure in glistening tropical whites, waving a flask of brandy. The British Consul himself, immaculate to the monocle! "Oh my poor boy! How do you feel?"'

1

FIRST BLOOD

'We was dozing right in Fritz's front dooryard with the gauges at sixty feet,' recalled one of the crew of *E9*, Max Kennedy Horton's submarine. It was their first patrol in 1914. They had been sent into the Heligoland Bight, where the Ems, Weser and Elbe reach the sea, and *E9*'s patrol area included the island of Heligoland itself, one of the German fleet's bases. Horton had taken his submarine into its harbour and, finding nothing there, had rested it on the seabed to wait.

'Commander Horton, Mr Chapman, and the navigating officer were playing bridge,' continued the submariner. 'Most of the hands were lying down reading. We could hear enemy ships scuttling about overhead, when sudden like I hears something clang against us away for'ard.' It was unnerving because one week into the war, they didn't know what weapons and secret devices the enemy might have. This, though, sounded like a sweep, designed to locate underwater objects, and it was feeling its way along *E9*'s hull, baffled only by the jump wire that was supposed to prevent such devices from hooking on.

The submariner was listening intently, waiting for explosions, 'when I hears the captain say, "Your play, Chapman." Mr

Chapman, I noticed, was a bit interested in this here row up for'ard too.' The submariner followed the sound of the wire creeping along the hull, visualising its progress. It slipped and scraped along the bow, scratched over the jump wire, reached the periscope standard and 'after what seemed like a couple of weeks' finally cleared the stern. 'Just as it did Mr Chapman says, "Sorry, Horton old chap, but you are down one trick doubled." The captain laughs. A nasty laugh, it seems to me. "Don't you believe it, Chapman," he says. "You revoked just when the wire hooked on. You forfeit two tricks." Then he turns to the navigating officer, who was keeping score, tells him what to put down, and says, "Bridge, gentlemen, is a game you've simply got to keep your mind on if you ever hope to play it well."'

About a month later, at dawn on 13 September, Horton surfaced in thick fog six miles south-west of Heligoland harbour. As the fog began to clear he took *E9* to periscope depth, and on his first look round he saw the light cruiser *Hela* emerging from a patch of mist. He closed to 600 yards, fired two torpedoes and dived. Both torpedoes hit. Horton came to periscope depth to see the cruiser listing. Shelled by destroyers, he dived, then came up again to look. The cruiser had gone and trawlers were picking up survivors. *E9* was hunted all day, and at night as he tried to run his engines to charge the batteries that powered his boat underwater, he was repeatedly forced to dive. But he got away and returned to Harwich in triumph, entering port flying a little Jolly Roger.

This was the very first time a British submarine had sunk a ship. The dangerous economy of the situation was obvious. Traditionally, a bigger, more powerfully armed ship sank a smaller one and was invulnerable against it. Destroyers did not sink battleships, but submarines might. In this modest case a boat of 667 tons with a crew of 30 sank a ship of 2000 tons with a crew of 178. Horton's boat received a bounty of £1050 from a country grateful to have a success at a time when the war was going badly. It may have been then that Horton decided that thirteen was his lucky number, or perhaps the daring young gambler had already embraced the number that others feared.

Another pattern was also established – the cool sang-froid of the submariner who concentrated on his card game, oblivious to the efforts of the enemy to destroy him. It is significant that these paradigms were established by Horton, because it was Horton who as Admiral Submarines guided British submariners through the crucial years of the Second World War.

Max Kennedy Horton was a difficult personality. He was ambitious and determined but not ingratiating. He would not charm his way to advancement by flattering superiors, but he was ruthless. 'Most conversations about this much-discussed man, although prefaced with sincere tributes to his quality as a great sailor, were followed very often with a "but".' Horton was tough, competitive, selfish and cruel, but extremely effective in whatever he undertook. And he was cool.

Horton joined the nascent Submarine Service in October 1904. He was the son of a stockbroker and his Jewish mother was the daughter of another. He began life at Rhosneigr in Anglesey where his father had bought a hotel with shooting rights after losing money in a slump. Max and his elder brother D'Arcy had few friends, since their neighbours spoke Welsh and regarded them as foreigners. At the age of nine Max told his mother that he wanted to go into the navy, inspired by dreams of travel and adventure. He passed the exams to Dartmouth, the Royal Naval College, easily since he was an excellent mathematician. He won the middleweight boxing prize and played First XI football, though at Dartmouth the sport was a minor one. He loved mechanical things and was very keen on the technical side of naval training.

The newly invented submarine offered a world of intricate, futuristic machinery, possibilities for independence, new ideas and early command. At twenty-two he found himself in charge of *A1*, a new submarine that had already been sunk in a collision.

But he chafed at authority, or at least at authority he did not respect. An early confidential report had him:

> *Good* at his boat and *bad* socially.
> Made very good attacks in A.1. Always supposed to be very good at the engine.
> A boxer and footballer – desperate motor-cyclist.
> Troublesome in the mess – insubordinate to First Lieutenant.
> Bad language – but extremely intelligent.

In 1906 Bernard Acworth became Horton's first lieutenant in *C8*. 'In those early days,' he wrote, 'the Submarine Service was, in many respects, a nest of pirates in the eyes of the old-established and austerely disciplined Navy, and there is no denying that Max K., when safely back from one of those submerged exercises which, in peacetime, cost so many submarines and lives, was the most notable pirate of all.'

Having gambled their lives by day, submariners played for high stakes in the evening. 'Max K.'s reputation as a poker-player was second only to his credit for coolness and sobriety as a submarine commander,' noted Acworth. Another shipmate recalled ruefully that he was 'a past master at snooker and poker and made quite a bit of money that way. His luck was extraordinary and he backed it.' Like many other submariners he loved motor bikes. 'It was on an old twin-Minerva,' wrote Acworth, 'if I remember rightly, that he raced Bertie Herbert down Butser into Petersfield, and to his intense surprise and disgust was beaten.'

After a day of exercise south of the Isle of Wight, the C-class submarines regularly raced each other into harbour and 'the mechanical skill of her artificers, and the general efficiency of the boat were to some extent judged by the outcome of these competitions'. Acworth reckoned Horton's 'almost childish love of "getting in first," by one means or another, was typical of him'. *C8* often did win and 'Horton was credited with almost legendary powers with early petrol engines', but in fact *C8*'s successes were achieved chiefly through more devious ingenuity. By 'cutting down the fields of the main electric motors to a point at which they reinforced the engines by discharging heavily as motors, instead of charging up the batteries as dynamos', Horton found extra power and speed. Such a thirst for technical knowledge and hands-on interest in oily machinery gained the Submarine Service its nickname of 'The Trade'. It was no place for a gentleman. It involved far too much specialisation, knowledge and getting one's hands dirty.

Acworth also credited Horton with helping to establish 'that form of discipline which, generally speaking, has characterised the Submarine Service for fifty years – a combination of ruthlessness towards any form of incompetence or slackness in the performance of duty, and a warmhearted and very real fraternity among all ranks and ratings who live in more intimate contact with one another than in any class of ship, naval or mercantile'. This inclusive discipline was an utterly crucial feature that made the service unusually efficient and unusually attractive to serve in.

Women found Horton immensely appealing. A Russian beauty, hired by pro-German Russians to poison him, fell for him instead, and eventually escaped from Russia using as a passport Horton's signature, engraved on his gold cigarette case. Horton was very successful in disrupting German operations in the Baltic and became a popular hero there. He got on very well with his Russian colleagues. In 1915 the Admiralty ordered his return but the chief of the Russian naval staff requested that he should remain in the Baltic as senior naval officer. The Second Sea Lord drily demurred: 'I understand Commander Horton is something of a pirate and not at all fitted for the position of S.N.O. in the Baltic.'

The Jolly Roger that Horton flew to celebrate the sinking of the *Hela* had not gone down well at the Admiralty. On sinking his second ship he flew two. When he ran out of space for little pennants he designed a big pirate flag, with a white bar marked on it for each ship sunk. The sailors and the press loved it, but the

Sea Lords disapproved. When they sent him home, the British Ambassador at St Petersburg himself protested that Horton 'gets on particularly well with the Russians which requires special qualifications, and his experience in the Baltic is also valuable. Would it not be possible to allow him to remain?' The answer was no and Horton returned to England, dressed in a full-length sable coat and chain-smoking Russian cigarettes.

Before 1914 the submarine had been an unknown quantity, the stuff of the new literary form known as science fiction. It vied with the aeroplane as the weapon of the future, the threat to the status quo. Britain, with her innumerable busy merchant ships and her imposing array of cruisers and battleships, was especially vulnerable to submarines. The French embraced submarines as soon as the invention of the torpedo gave underwater craft a weapon that threatened surface ships. They began to develop a submarine fleet that might finally accomplish their long-cherished dream of destroying British economic might by picking off merchant vessels. With Jules Verne, author of *Twenty Thousand Leagues under the Sea*, a leading enthusiast, they envisioned a future where unseen and undetected vessels cleared the seas of British ships.

Once the French adopted submarines, the British felt that they must also have some. But they did not buy them with enthusiasm. The Parliamentary Secretary of the Admiralty 'took the view that it was wise not to be unprepared in regard to these inventions' but confessed that he hoped submarines 'shall never prosper'. The Controller of the Navy added emphatically, 'I call them underhand, unfair, and damned un-English' and threatened to hang enemy crews as pirates. The British master of science fiction, H.G. Wells, sought to calm the unease inspired by his Gallic rival. Submarines, he noted, were 'practically blind' underwater, and he couldn't see 'any sort of submarine doing anything but suffocate its crew and founder at sea'.

Within a year the periscope was invented, so submarines were no longer blind. The first British submarines took part in the fleet manoeuvres of 1904 and Admiral Jacky Fisher wrote of 'the immense impending revolution which submarines will effect as offensive weapons of war'. Jules Verne agreed. Writing on the 'Future of the Submarine' in the American magazine *Popular Mechanics*, he remarked that

> I followed very carefully the experiments made lately during the French maneuvers in the Mediterranean, and during the maneuvers of the English fleet, and I was very much struck by the accuracy with which the submarines of both fleets managed to slip in, strike, and get away in safety. Imagine hundreds of these vessels with their deadly freight ... it seems that my fading eyes are destined to behold sickening carnage in the unequal contest of the improved submarine machine with the heavy battleship, whose days are numbered.

In 1905 Fort Blockhouse at Gosport became the base for British submariners. At first the little petrol-driven submarines had very limited range and it was difficult to envisage a more enterprising role for them than guarding harbours. But the diesel-driven D-boats introduced from 1910 offered new possibilities. *D1* was the first submarine to have a radio and now it seemed possible to the planners that the new boats might make effective scouts. Their commanders had more ambitious ideas. In an exercise in 1912 two submarines separately sailed up the Firth of Forth avoiding 'enemy' patrols and caught the opposing fleet at anchor. Geoffrey Layton 'sank' his own depot ship anchored at Rosyth and soon afterwards Max Horton in *D6* 'torpedoed' two 'hostile' warships there.

Despite this clear lesson, First Lord of the Admiralty Winston Churchill maintained that 'no one seriously contemplated hostile submarines in time of war entering the harbours of either side and attacking ships at anchor', and so consequently no one thought of fortifying fleet anchorages against submarines. On his way back to his own base at Harwich, Horton surfaced close to a battle cruiser and claimed to have sunk her too, but such claims were derided. The indignant, older, senior commanders of the large surface units consistently denied that they had been sunk, claiming that their guns had picked off submarines long before.

Still nobody knew what would happen in a real war. One officer wrote to the *Daily Mail* predicting that 'as the motor has driven the horse from the road, so has the submarine driven the battleship from the sea'. In *The Times* he suggested that Britain should stop building battleships and instead devote resources to submarines and aircraft. He predicted that battleships at sea would be in great danger from submarines so that in a war each side would keep its battleships in a safe harbour. He considered that it would no longer be possible to bombard a hostile port that was adequately guarded by submarines and predicted that the enemy's submarines would come to Britain's coast and sink everything in sight. Five admirals went into print to oppose his views, one of them being the founder of the Submarine Service.

Then war broke out. On 5 September 1914 a German submarine lurked at the entrance to the Firth of Forth and torpedoed the light cruiser HMS *Pathfinder*. She sank so fast that the Admiralty thought she must have hit a mine, but one of the twelve survivors from her crew had seen the periscope of a submarine and the track of a 'tinfish'. On 22 September German submarine skipper Otto Weddigen sighted three British cruisers. From 500 yards he hit the *Aboukir*. The *Hogue* stopped to pick up survivors and Weddigen reloaded. He sank her and then turned his stern torpedoes on to the *Cressy*. Again, a lookout saw the 'tinfish' coming but the ship could only avoid one of them, and as a result 1459 men and boys were killed. The stark reality of this destruction, which inflicted more British casualties than the Battle of Trafalgar, 'made the world realise for the first time the ferocious menace of the submarine.' By 7 October His Majesty's Grand Fleet had retreated from Scapa Flow, now deemed insecure, to Loch Ewe – and then, when a U–boat (a German submarine or *Unterseeboot*) was sighted there, back to Lough Swilly in Northern Ireland.

From the beginning it was common to attribute a successful attack to the captain. The reason for this was simple. 'When a submarine is submerged her captain alone is able to see what is taking place; the success of the enterprise and the safety of the vessel depend on his skill and nerve.' It was an amazingly responsible job and most commanders of submarines were very young. Horton got his first command at twenty-two. While the pay was also very high, it was the chance to command a boat so early that was the attraction for most officer recruits. 'In my opinion good handling of a submarine needs a finer blend of eye, training, and leadership than any of the other arts of war,' wrote Charles Gordon Brodie, known as 'Seagee'. 'There are other examples of one-man control over a weapon of delicate or massive concentration of power which provide peak moments of experience,' he continued, comparing an attack in a submarine to landing an aircraft or turning a convoy, but he reckoned that a successful submarine attack beat them all. 'The submariner must know more about his machine than the airman, and more of the men who share in the handling of it than the Commodore of a convoy ever can.'

The captain manoeuvred into position, and he aimed and chose the moment to fire. But he didn't press the trigger. Success depended on 'the prompt, precise execution of the men under his command'. A submarine crew was a team, and while the captain might be the only one who could see what was going on, his attack could be spoiled by a failure on the part of anybody else in his boat.

The same was true of survival. A mistake from any single crewman could endanger everyone else. 'In submarines', Max Horton used to repeat like a mantra, 'there is no margin for mistakes, you are either alive or dead.' Generally, the crews were hand-picked men with a high standard of technical proficiency. Discipline was different in submarines. There were still officers and men and there was a social and professional gulf between them, but they were also close and bonded as in no other sphere of naval life. Just after the war a submarine officer wrote:

There is a Democracy of Things Real in the boats which is a very fine kind of Democracy. Both men and officers in a submarine know that each man's life is held in the hand of any one of them, who by carelessness or ignorance may make their ship into a common coffin; all ranks live close together, and when the occasion arises go to their deaths in the same way. The Fear of Death is a great leveller, and in submarines an officer or a man's competency for his job is the only standard by which he is judged.

Carelessness and ignorance were not tolerated and inefficient crewmen quickly left a boat.

The successful commander, then, had to know his machine inside out. He had to have a perfectly disciplined and dependable team of men to execute his orders instantly and perfectly and he had to have a demanding blend of aggression, judgement and skill to know when to make an attack and how to carry it out successfully. This was an art that had to be improvised. For the first submarine commanders there was no guidebook – they invented the rules. There was no previous experience to refer to, so they had to develop their own tactics. They needed to be independent thinking, self-reliant, self-sufficient, technically minded masters of machinery, adventurous and highly disciplined. Rudyard Kipling tried to explain the mysteries of the new service to the general public in his *Tales of the Trade*, a series of articles first published in *The Times* in 1916:

the Trade lives in a world without precedents, of which no generation has had any previous experience – a world still being made and enlarged daily. It creates and settles its own problems as it goes along, and if it cannot help itself no one else can. So the Trade lives in the dark and thinks out inconceivable and impossible things which it afterwards puts into practice.

From the beginning the Trade attracted strong characters and colourful personalities. Recruits were often unconventional people and they showed it by cheerfully disregarding uniform. One of the most attractive was Ernest Leir, soon known as 'the Arch Thief'. The motto of his submarine, *E4*, 'We need no Lead', allegedly referred to an incident where 300 tons of Admiralty lead ballast had been disposed of at a substantial profit. But Leir was typical of the Trade in his flair for mechanical improvisation: during the war he solved communication problems by contriving a very long radio aerial by attaching the wire to a kite. His most publicised wartime performance was to rescue a whaler's crew who had been abandoned while picking up German survivors. When their destroyer was chased off by a German cruiser Leir popped out of the water and took them all aboard, together with some specimen Germans, leaving the other Germans with water and biscuit in the whaler. Other submarine heroes of the war included Geoffrey Layton, whose boat was attacked by German destroyers after it ran aground in neutral Denmark in a much-publicised incident.

By general consent the top British ace of the First World War was Martin Nasmith. 'Nasmith was one of the most popular officers in the British submarine service. A medium-sized man, built and conditioned like a quarterback, extravagantly admired by his crews, affable and sociable in the ward room', wrote a junior officer. He did indeed look like an American quarterback: powerfully and sturdily built with strong arms and chiselled, handsome features. In fact, though, his game was rugby and he was a centre three-quarter. Brodie, slightly junior to Nasmith at Dartmouth's Royal Naval College, known as HMS *Britannia*, worshipped him as a hero from the day in 1898 when 'I as a humble "new" first saw him, at rugger, battling for the "threes" through a crowd of "niners". In the *Britannia* "news" were worms to be trodden on, "threes" were worms that had begun to turn, and "niners" were superior beings enjoying in their fourth term brief privileges, before starting afresh as "warts" in a gunroom at sea.'

Nasmith was a fanatic. Admirers wrote of his 'strength of character and sheer single-minded zeal', of 'an almost ferocious insistence on efficiency'. Before the war he was put in charge of training at Fort Blockhouse – a key appointment. While in that role he invented crude instruments to calculate deflection angle and approach courses during a submarine attack. Until then commanders had had to trust to their own judgement.

Nasmith left his training post to take command of *E11*. He was lucky to have a fine first lieutenant in Guy D'Oyly Hughes and in 1915 they conducted an epic patrol in the Sea of Marmora that made *E11* famous. It began in the normal manner for a trip through the long, narrow and heavily guarded Dardanelles: 'The voyage was not unusual. Only seven hours when the crew's nerves were like taut piano wires.' Nasmith sank a battleship and penetrated the harbour of Constantinople but the episode that resonated most with submariners was his ruthless treatment of the radio operator who could not mend his set when it failed to work at a crucial moment:

I consider a man of this type more deserving of the death penalty than the unfortunate individual who, from work and fatigue, drops asleep at his post of duty. Personally, I think I could forgive the man who fails in his duty because he falls victim to his outraged nature. But a man who accepts a post of importance as the member of a submarine's crew knowing, as this man must have known, that he was not fully capable of meeting any emergency that might arise, either as a result of enemy action or ordinary wear and tear on his equipment, is a menace to his shipmates and a traitor to his cause.

It was in this way that Nasmith and his colleagues set the tone for the Trade: 'all for one and one for all' produced pride and camaraderie, but it might not have been effective had not the captain admitted in all humility, 'I am ashamed to confess that, owing to my own inefficiency I am unable to tell this man how the repair should be made.' Nasmith prided himself on knowing his equipment inside out but he had not mastered the new-fangled radio. The point of these first war parables was that every-one must be master of his own job, each should also know the other's, but the captain in particular must be master of all.

These British aces had their share of glamorous success, but it was the German commanders who made the submarine a weapon of terror. Great War propagandists created a distinction between 'good' submarines and 'bad' U-boats that persisted throughout the Second World War, when all enemy submersibles were evil U-boats.

From February 1917 Germany declared an unrestricted cam-paign against all merchant shipping moving within a wide area around Britain. From February to June sinkings averaged 650,000 tons per month, with another 100,000 tons of seriously damaged ships needing repair. Many neutrals quickly decided to stay at home. Losses in April were terrible and at that moment the collapse of Britain and its war effort 'began', as Churchill put it, 'to loom black and imminent'. The Germans had expected that their move against shipping might bring the USA into the war against them, but they hoped to force the British to sue for peace first. They promised their people peace by August 1917.

Rear-Admiral William Sowden Sims, US Navy, arrived in Britain on 9 April 1917, four days after the USA declared war. He was told that German submarines were winning the battle and that Britain could not last longer than November or December. Sims was a great advocate of convoys as an aggressive strategy and promised American destroyers to make it possible. During May eighteen destroyers arrived from the States; there were seventy-nine in Europe by 1918. The convoy system was introduced in May and extended gradually during 1917.

Slowly it had an effect. U-boats redeployed away from west-ern approaches and towards the coasts, so in December coastal convoys were introduced. U-boat losses mounted steeply, and although machines could be replaced, trained crews and experienced leaders became fewer. Attacks became harder to execute. Instead of destroyers patrolling empty oceans for U-boats, the U-boats now came to them. Destroyers kept boats under water so they couldn't use their guns and had to expend their small stock of torpedoes. Better American hydrophones hunted them more efficiently. Depth charges were used more frequently, and sometimes more effectively. Britain survived November and December and disappointment led to discontent in Germany. The U-boats were never exactly defeated, but eventually the war was won elsewhere.

The German naval staff anticipated that the war might end before they achieved their ultimate goal. A memorandum sent to the Kaiser in January 1916 already envisaged a further war. Its closely reasoned analysis dealt with the ends and means of a war based on U-boats such as Germany was to fight in 1917, but it looked further into the future. The ultimate goal, 'apart from destroying the English fleet', was to 'reduce [Britain's] total economy in the quickest possible time'. To do this Germany would 'cut off all trade routes to and from the British Isles', cripple all British ships and all neutral ships trading with Britain, and 'by means of air attack, disrupt the trade and commerce in the British Isles, showing its population quite mercilessly the stark realities of war'. The U-boats could no longer be based only in Germany:

> Most important for the carrying on of the U-boat campaign in the North Atlantic would be bases in the Faroes and in the Azores and also on the Spanish coast. Bases in these places would reduce considerably the lines of approach for U-boats and facilitate greatly the task of blockading the British Isles. One cannot tell at this point in time whether, when peace is declared, the Faroes and the Azores may be acquired and whether in the next war it will be possible to obtain the use of Spanish ports for our purposes . . .

The memorandum went on to discuss the deployment of U-boats against American harbours and in the Indian Ocean, concluding that this would depend on the future development of U-boats and the possession of suitable bases and must remain 'a question for the future'. The plan envisaged that 'our U-boat fleets must be so numerous that a decisive victory is not only certain but can be achieved quickly'.

The onslaught of 1917 was to be merely a foretaste of a greater onslaught to come 'in the next war'. For Germany the submarine was still the weapon of the future.

2

SENIOR SERVICE

With the war to end all wars over, there was a reasonable hope that years of peace might stretch ahead. The Royal Navy remained the largest in the world, the senior service of the British Empire's armed forces. It was steeped in tradition. In its past lay Drake, Hawkins and Raleigh, Vernon, Anson, Hawke and Boscawen, Rodney, Howe and Nelson. It policed a vast, worldwide network of trading posts and colonies and safeguarded line after line of commercial ships, from sleek, modern luxury liners to humble colliers. Even in peacetime it provided about 100,000 jobs. To boys the navy still offered the prospect of travel, adventure and excitement.

Many naval officers came from naval families. Hugh Haggard's father was a naval captain at the time Hugh himself was ushered towards the navy. Hugh's great-uncle was Rider Haggard, the novelist of imperial adventure, author of *She* and *King Solomon's Mines*. Hugh followed his father's career: for the tall, gangling boy there seemed 'hardly any way out'.

Bill King came from a similarly privileged dynasty. His redoubtable grandmother Cecilia was a celebrated yachtswoman married to a shipping magnate. General Martel, equally celebrated for his work with tanks, was his uncle. His father worked on balloons for the army and was closely involved with flying machines before his death on the Western Front in 1917 as a sapper colonel. Bill's mother sent him to a boarding prep school and then discussed with friends what she should do next. Asked if he would like to join the navy, Bill was eager. He loathed his prep school and looked forward to Dartmouth. 'The Navy sounded jolly and romantic. Well versed in the exploits of Drake and Nelson I visualized a salty fresh-air future for myself, punctuated with exciting sea fights if only one had the luck of a war or so.'

The corrupt old days when family connection got untrained youths into a ship were over. The Royal Naval College at Dartmouth provided theoretical instruction for fledgling officers. However, in some ways it made entry to the officer class even more exclusive. The fees for Dartmouth were exorbitant and only affluent middle-class parents could afford to send their children there. The first step for a child who wished to become an officer was a journey to London to undergo a medical examination in a government building in Tothill Street near Westminster Abbey. Candidates who passed the medical examination travelled to London again a couple of months later to sit the entrance examination for Dartmouth, held in a hotel near Bedford Square. Between papers representatives of Messrs Gieves, the naval outfitters, pounced on candidates to measure them up for uniforms. Academic standards were not prohibitively high, but it was perfectly possible to fail the exam.

Each term about fifty thirteen-year-olds arrived at Kingswear station and then took a ferry across the Dart to the college. That group, the 'term', became the basic unit for about three and a half years. Ruling them was a term chief petty officer, a benign father figure, with a term officer assisted by a term cadet captain and a cadet captain. These last were prefects in their final year. Each term had its own room, known as a gunroom after the place midshipmen berthed in eighteenth-century warships, and members of the term had to pass the gunrooms of senior terms at the run. Hugh Mackenzie went to Dartmouth in the Anson term of 1927. His father was a doctor and he grew up near Inverness in the Scottish Highlands. He had classic Scottish pale skin and his red hair soon won him the nickname 'Rufus'. His term officer, though kind and approachable, was only interested in team sports. In Mackenzie's third year Tony Kimmins took over, a naval pilot who at Dartmouth started to write plays and to act, and later became a film producer and director. Kimmins wrote and directed most of George Formby's comedies. He allowed his pupils more freedom. Team games were no longer compulsory and Mackenzie pursued his love of ornithology and photography. When Mackenzie arrived the captain of the college was the famous submariner Martin Nasmith, VC, who had changed his name to Dunbar-Nasmith in 1923.

Under the captain there was a naval staff of twenty-eight. This included eight term officers, along with an engineer commander assisted by three lieutenants (E) who taught marine engineering in the workshops and machine shops. Four former chief petty officers with fantastic depth of knowledge taught seamanship. There was a fleet of rowing boats, whalers and cutters on the Dart and cadets were encouraged to use these as much as possible in the summer months to practise seamanship on a small scale. Three officers taught navigation and one taught electronics. Then there was the academic staff under the headmaster. Most of the boys' time was taken up with maths, history, English, geography, science, modern languages and, of course, sport. The Blue Book each term listed staff and cadets.

The college placed great emphasis on the value of team sport and life was always easiest for a talented rugby player such as Nasmith had been. Small, slight boys like King and Mackenzie were usually less at ease. The navy was a serious force in sport and it found places for a lot of boys of international standard in major sports, beginning with rugby. King became a long-distance runner.

Mackenzie enjoyed Dartmouth, though he never won a prize

or colours or became a cadet captain: 'the discipline and constant rushing to and fro presented no problems.' King was less forgiving. For him it 'was run like a Japanese prisoner-of-war camp and I hated it'. In the morning 'we were taught to leap from our beds at a bugle note, scamper to the wash-room for a cold shower and race down stone corridors to the dining hall,' he wrote. 'We washed, brushed teeth, ate, dressed and prayed to the stop-watch.' In the mornings and evenings the boys 'huddled over desks, studying if not learning'. King thought it a brutal regime: 'The old tradition of inculcating immediate response by beatings remained. For many years no seaman had been flogged, but for embryo officers aged thirteen to eighteen this procedure was incessantly used as incentive as well as deterrent. The avoidance of flogging became the motive power of one's life.'

But with canings delivered 'for such sins of omission as leaving a button undone, or folding socks the wrong way', it was impossible to escape every time. Inevitably, at one time or another you found your name 'in the evening roll-call which drew shivering boys out of the dormitory to the ministrations of a grinning cadet-captain.'

Dartmouth ended with final passing-out exams in seamanship, history, French, engineering, mathematics, navigation and science. This was followed by a passing-out dinner, in Mackenzie's case at the Criterion restaurant in London.

This system produced about 150 cadets annually. They were joined by a much smaller number of 'Special Entry Cadets' who came direct from public school at eighteen. Some of these had for one reason or another missed out on Dartmouth. Others decided late to join the navy or opted for a broader education. Tony Miers, whose father was killed in 1914 commanding what was left of the Cameron Highlanders during heavy shelling, went to Wellington, the school founded to educate the orphaned sons of army officers.

The fledgling officers were appointed to ships – usually battleships or cruisers, since these had by far the largest crews. King found himself in the brand-new HMS *Nelson* in the company of a royal prince and other aristocrats. Six months later he became a midshipman and was transferred to the much older battleship *Resolution*, where, though eighteen and an officer on board ship, he was still punished for 'any forgetfulness or a fault in routine while on watch' with a humiliating thrashing. This 'ritual necessitated walking through the ship clad in pyjamas to the jeers of one's friends and the amazement of marine sentries who, coming from poorer homes, could hardly be expected to guess at the training of England's young gentlemen'. At the time King was being trained, senior officers were just beginning to question the wisdom of corporal punishment as a means of instilling discipline, but King's contemporaries 'took for granted the routine which allowed us to command grown men in the morning and be thrashed by the sub-Lieutenant in the afternoon'.

During King's time in *Resolution* the nineteen-year-old public schoolboys among the midshipmen rebelled and the captain decided that they should be immune henceforth, but it was many years before corporal punishment for Dartmouth cadets and junior midshipmen was abolished.

That was not the end of the sadism either. George Simpson, whose miniature stature – five foot two – earned him the lasting nickname 'Shrimp', left a harrowing account of life in a gunroom in 1917.

If the sub-lieutenant shouted 'breadcrumbs' it meant that a conversation was about to take place which warts must not hear, so all warts stopped their ears with their fingers. If the sub-lieutenant then said 'O.K. cancel breadcrumbs' and you took your fingers out of your ears you got a dozen with a dirk scabbard across the backside for listening. Fingers must be kept in the ears until a senior snottie came and removed them.

If the sub-lieutenant of the mess wished to remove anybody from the mess he would shout 'Dogs of War' whereupon all warts would growl. He would then order 'Out Mr X' and all warts in the gunroom at the time would eject Mr X, and if he resisted hotly the sub-lieutenant might add 'debag Mr X' and he would be ejected without his trousers.

These were the least dangerous and humiliating of the 'evolutions' which sub-lieutenants justified as naval tradition, although nothing like this occurred in the much less idle eighteenth-century navy. Between bouts of organised sadism in the gunroom, midshipmen were taught further lessons in engineering and navigation and gained experience around the ship. According to Simpson, 'What happened to me and my contemporaries as midshipmen was immensely important in those impressionable years, it was also the main reason why I and many others sought the refuge of submarines as a career and blessed our choice.'

Even the more reticent Mackenzie recalled that 'the treatment meted out to us strengthened my evolving prejudice against "big ship" life and so had a lasting effect on my future.' Nevertheless, he 'could not subscribe to the view that gun-room life in those days was harsh, certainly not in the three great battleships of which we had direct experience. Hard, yes, but not harsh ... Only once in my nearly three years in gun-rooms can I recollect a midshipman being punished by being caned.' Mackenzie was younger and perhaps the custom was disappearing, or perhaps he was luckier in his ships.

In *Resolution* Mackenzie found himself under Captain Max Horton. Having attained a senior position, Horton had dropped his dashing, piratical persona and now wore a mask of austere severity. Discipline in *Resolution* was very tight. Ostensibly in order to endow his midshipmen with self-confidence (and perhaps to get to know them), Horton had one of them report to him at noon each day with an account of what was going on in the ship and in their current geographic location, as well as of any major recent world events. Mackenzie found the experience terrifying but character-building.

Like Mackenzie, King enjoyed touring the Mediterranean, visiting Greek ruins, climbing the mountains. And for the glory of his battleship he continued his running career, winning a large silver cup as champion of the Mediterranean Fleet.

After three years at sea the midshipmen had to undergo an oral examination in seamanship to qualify for promotion to sub-lieutenant. The marks gained affected the date of eventual promotion to lieutenant with 900/1000 needed for a first-class pass. In the autumn of 1933, Mackenzie's Anson term intake of 1927 reassembled at the Royal Naval College, Greenwich, for sub-lieutenants' training courses. Six months were devoted to mathematics, physics, English, general and naval history and French. Nearly every sub-lieutenant possessed a clapped-out old banger in which to visit London whenever possible. After two terms the group moved on to Portsmouth for courses in the Gunnery, Torpedo, Navigation and Signals Schools. During that summer they had to state a preference for future specialisation. The choices were gunnery, torpedo, navigation, anti-submarines, signals, the Fleet Air Arm or submarines.

Most naval ratings also joined the service as boys. Charles Anscomb was born in 1908 in the Great Lakes in Canada, where his father was a self-employed builder. They returned to England when Charles was six, after which he became fascinated with the ships in the Pool of London. He wanted to travel and see the world and finally tried to join the navy when fourteen. The recruiting officer told him he was too young and suggested the Marine Society. Established in the eighteenth century with the purpose of training penniless orphans for the sea, this charity had become a way to join the navy early. Anscomb's training at Warspite (which was not the battleship but a former hotel at Tilbury) resembled King's, only the food was worse. 'You had your allotted place at the mess table and never sat anywhere else,' he recalled bitterly. 'You were not allowed "ashore", you could never get a decent wash, and you were constantly and brutally bullied by the older boys. For a lad from a good home it was bloody misery.' Anscomb did not yet realise that it would turn out to be good preparation for the brutal discipline of the navy. 'After a week of it I had had enough. I tried to escape. When they caught me and brought me back to the ship I was strapped over the horse and given the arsing of all arsings.' After this beating Anscomb decided to buckle down and make the best of the training he was offered. Subsequently he became a convert, not to sadistic beating but certainly to the need for strict discipline.

The normal route for those who joined the navy was to sign up at age fifteen or sixteen for twelve years' service and then spend at least nine months at one of the boys' training establishments. The most terrifying of these was HMS *Ganges* at Shotley in Suffolk, where up to two thousand boys were trained at any one time. Each day began with the boys climbing up a huge mast, swarming over the yard arm and down the other side. Like Dartmouth, *Ganges* combined conventional schooling with nautical attainment. Boys learned the skills of seamanship: ropes, knots, splices, guns, boats and sailing.

Norman Drury, the son of a farm labourer, grew up in a little weatherboarded cottage in Herne Hill, Kent. His schoolteacher inspired him to join the navy and he arrived at Shotley just after the general strike in 1926. The new entry was a 'Nozzer' and his first task was to sew his name on his kit over the temporary version with which it had been stamped. After about three weeks of square bashing, washing and cleaning he left the Nozzers' mess and went to class. If he did well he could progress to advanced seamanship or communications. Drury chose communications and started learning Morse and flags. He did well at his exam too, but then caught scarlet fever and had to drop two classes.

The alternative to *Ganges* was the smaller HMS *St Vincent* at Gosport with capacity for about 800 boys. Fred Buckingham went there in 1929 after leaving school at fourteen and spending two years in a factory. On arrival they were met by a man in naval uniform carrying a large cane. 'His first words were: "Have any of you got any cigarettes?" Some of them had, and offered him one. "Right – hand them over." This having been done he then said: "From now on anyone found smoking will get six of the best from this," as he swished his cane.' They soon got used to naval discipline. 'It has been said that a midshipman is the lowest form of animal life but that was said by someone who had never been a "Boy 2nd Class",' wrote Buckingham. 'You just can't get any lower than that.' The general style was similar to Dartmouth:

We were ordered around from morning till night. Everything had to be done 'At the Double'. We seemed to be running from 5 a.m. until 8.30 p.m. Bedtime at 8.30 for lads of 15 to 17, but by God we were ready for it. The last order before hopping between the blankets (remember no sheets) was: 'Say yer prayers.' We all knelt at our beds to obey the last order for the day. One lad who remained standing was pounced on by the duty Petty Officer. 'I don't say prayers,' said the boy. 'What's that got to do with it?' said the PO. 'Get on yer knees and go through the motions.'

Buckingham elected to specialise in communications and after a few weeks of general training he started a twelve-week course, intending to become a signalman. He felt at a disadvantage because 'most of the boys in my signal class had been to grammar or secondary schools so were way ahead', but he found he caught up. In the end he decided to plump for wireless telegraphy, partly because 'winter was approaching and I found that I much preferred sitting in a warm classroom trying to read Morse to standing on a windswept parade ground in sub-zero temperatures trying to read semaphore'. He also preferred the petty officer telegraphist instructor, 'a cheerful tubby', to the yeoman of signals who 'went out of his way to make life as miserable for us youngsters as he appeared to find it himself'.

Ben Skeates went to *St Vincent* in 1935, and in the same year Jack Howard and Jim Thomsett went as boys to *Ganges*. Ratings, like officers, often came from naval families and Mrs Thomsett's four brothers had all fought in the navy in the Great War. Like his elder brother Harry, who had joined already, Jim Thomsett's 'one desire was to go in the navy' so he joined as a boy at sixteen and was an able seaman three years later, adapting easily to life in the battleship *Warspite*. Jack Howard came from a Sheffield family of seven boys and one girl. Jack's elder brother Leslie did the standard thing in Sheffield and went to the steelworks, but Jack wanted something different. Jack was small and slight, only five foot one when he arrived at *Ganges*, but at least that made climbing the mast easier. He went on to the 'mighty' *Hood*, Admiral Geoffrey Layton's flagship at Malta and the pride of the Royal Navy. When officially a man, rated ordinary seaman, he was still only five foot five, but now sported a tattoo of a sailor with flags on his right arm.

Skeates, similarly, had no family naval background. He grew up in Hampshire, where his father found employment as a painter and decorator on Lord Eldon's estate at Longwood. After leaving school Ben got a job with an electrician in Winchester. When they ran out of electrical work and transferred him to plumbing, he went down to the naval recruiting office in Southampton because he had always wanted to join the navy.

The sadistic discipline came as something of a shock to him too. He never forgot the day when Class 239 was ordered to climb the mast in threes without boots. If the class of thirty were not down in three minutes they were marched at the double into the mess deck. After the officer of the day had said Grace, 'the two lads detailed to bring the breakfast in did so, and then they were ordered to throw it in the garbage bin; that day we would get no breakfast.' On another occasion one boy became 'panic stricken at the top and had to be brought down in a bosun's chair. The Instructor (a Gunnery P.O.) then went up to him and grabbed his two nipples and twisted them.' This instructor also supervised swimming, sailing and showering. 'If you hesitated at swimming you were pushed in and when you came out of the shower you invariably received a whack across your backside with his whistle chain.' Eventually he went too far and was sent back to Whale Island, the gunnery school in Portsmouth Harbour. Not everyone in the navy was sadistic, but when in 1931 First Lord A.V. Alexander tried to reduce the corporal punishment inflicted on seaman boys, the investigative committee concluded that 'caning is by far the most suitable punishment for boys'.

Having finished their shore training, the boys were sent to sea. Anscomb went first to HMS *Ajax* and then to HMS *Danae*. There, under Captain Bertram Ramsay, later mastermind of Dunkirk, they became shipmates. Anscomb appreciated Ramsay's sense of discipline, but he 'soon found that I was nothing but a number for a holystone. The *Danae* was the cleanest general-service ship I ever served in, and we boys did our full share towards making her decks snow-white and her brasswork mirror-bright.' He explained that 'a holystone is so called because you only ever use it when you are on your hands and knees in an attitude of prayer. A big holystone is a "bible", a small one a "prayer book".' He spent every morning on hands and knees, 'a "prayer book" in either hand, rubbing, rubbing, rubbing those endless decks'.

Anscomb admired the *Danae* as a fast and beautiful cruiser but observed that she was built for guns, not for men. Hundreds of them tried to use a tiny washroom. The messes were cramped and the food was ruined by the cooks. They did half a day's schooling until they passed the educational test; then they progressed through the naval ratings, from ordinary seaman to able. At that stage they kept watches and occasionally steered the ship.

The engineers were a special branch of the service with a different career pattern. They left school at sixteen and then applied for an apprenticeship which lasted four and a half years. You had to sit an exam to become an engine room artificer (ERA) apprentice, being tested in science. Joel Blamey, generally known as 'Joe', completed his apprenticeship in 1925 and was drafted to the battleship *Valiant*. He took passage in the *Royal Oak* where he had a miserable time, and then in the submarine tender *Adamant*, which acted as a practice target and recovered torpedoes for the 1st Submarine Flotilla. *Adamant*'s engineers were a happy bunch and life there contrasted favourably with *Royal Oak*. As a group the engineers were highly trained technicians who generally knew more about mechanics than officers did.

It was not quite impossible to make the jump from seaman to officer, although there was not a great deal of mobility – far less than there had been in the eighteenth century. There was a mechanism for promotion called the 'Mate scheme', which had been introduced in 1912 and produced several hundred officers during the First World War. Officers recruited this way, however, did not become lieutenants until the age of twenty-eight or twenty-nine, unlike the 22-year-olds from Dartmouth, and the title 'mate' tended to stigmatise its holders. In 1930 First Lord Alexander set up a committee to investigate means to facilitate transfer from the forecastle to the quarterdeck, instructing his colleagues to bear in mind Lord Justice Darling's quip that 'Justice is open to all – like the Ritz'. The Sea Lords opposed this bid to introduce grammar school boys to the quarterdeck with the time-honoured objection that 'the men of the Lower Deck ... give greater respect to what is known as the Officer Class than to other officers drawn from their own ranks'.

The committee replaced the title 'mate' with that of 'acting sub-lieutenant' and lowered the age at which able seamen might seek promotion, measures which became fully effective in 1933. Between 1932 and 1936 eighteen executive officers, fifteen engineers and two marines were commissioned this way. It was hardly a shattering influx and the reason why soon became apparent: candidates had to prepare for the professional and educational examinations in their own time, while simultaneously performing normal duties as able seamen, which was quite a challenge. In 1937 a special course was introduced and thirty-one candidates came through it in the first year. One of the first to benefit from the new scheme, swotting for the exams in his own time, was Leslie Bennington. Bennington joined the navy as a fifteen-

year-old Boy 2nd Class in 1927 and took the exam as an able
seaman, much to the admiration of a Liverpudlian shipmate
named Stanley Hawkey.

For Hawkey and others without the means, ambition, determination or intelligence to take Bennington's route, even if they
wanted to, life in the navy was a gradual process of finding out
what you liked and didn't like. Charles Anscomb was able and
clever and was rising up the ladder towards becoming a petty officer. He had his share of the travel he had joined for, toured the
Mediterranean and visited China. He particularly enjoyed a four-
month cruise around Malaysia. 'I was learning my job and keen
to make a success of it,' he wrote. 'I liked the life in general,' but
he reached the conclusion that he was instinctively a 'small ship'
sailor.

> The strict discipline and formality of life in a big ship may suit
> some men whose minds are set that way, but if you don't take
> easily to a cast-iron discipline imposed arbitrarily from with-
> out, with no allowance made for individual initiative, if you
> long to succeed in your own way and make your mark as an
> individual, if you don't like being ordered about by a bugle, if
> you are fed up with being a number for a holystone and want
> to be treated as a man with a name of your own, then a cruiser
> or a carrier or a battlewagon is no good for you. If you're a
> pirate by nature you must go in a small ship – sloop, destroyer,
> sweeper, submarine, it doesn't matter, as long as she's one of
> the little ones.

In China he worked out which type of little ship he wanted
to serve in. The fleet went into action against pirates operating
near Hong Kong. He helped to land marines but the *Danae* saw
no pirates. It was the little ships that actually got into action. He
and his mates were especially 'thrilled and excited by the very
gallant and dashing "cutting out" expedition carried out by
Lieutenant-Commander Halloran in submarine *L4*'. The SS *Irene*

had been captured by the pirates, and *L4* was sent to intercept her, which she did with brilliant seamanship and audacity. 'I never saw the *L4*, but I didn't need to. The picture my imagination painted of that gun snout rising with a rush of foam out of the oily black water and slamming a warning shot across the *Irene*'s bows made my heart beat faster. *This* was what I had been looking for. This was where the action lay – *under* the water. I could hardly wait to get my request in – "To transfer to submarines".'

Eventually, Norman Drury, Stanley Hawkey, Jack Howard and Ben Skeates all made the same decision.

3

THE SUBMARINE BRANCH

On the face of it, requesting a transfer to submarines was an odd decision to make. Submarines were conspicuously dangerous. Eleven sank before the First World War began, sixty were lost in the four years of war and twelve went down accidentally between 1919 and 1932. These figures included only the subs that had actually sunk, omitting explosions and other accidents that killed submariners without destroying the boat. Submarines were dangerous enough in peacetime. It was obvious that in any new war they would be in the front line, heavily engaged and regarded as expendable. They would be much more dangerous to serve in than ordinary ships.

Stoker Syd Hart was considered a bit of a daredevil in his Lancashire village. 'Tha's not so lung to live,' they said after he roared in on his motorcycle, sardonically calculating his life insurance: 'I've putten a tanner a wick on thee.' A tall, athletic, cheerful blond, he had joined the navy and sailed in surface ships in the Mediterranean. It is hardly surprising that he had a few second thoughts about his latest act of bravado. 'During that tedious train journey,' he wrote, 'I had ample time to wonder why in God's name I'd elected for the Submarine Service. Or why my eleven travelling companions had made the same choice?' The lure of adventure and the chance to 'cut a dash' by belonging to this elite, hazardous service were the main factors in his choice, along with the near certainty of seeing action, fulfilling 'a wish to get back at a potential enemy who would be only too eager to wreak havoc with our merchant shipping, by which Britain could mainly hope to survive in freedom, if the threatened war should come'.

Hart joined the service in 1939, when he was twenty-three and war was looming. He recalled that 'as a child of seven I'd played submarines on my mother's old-fashioned wringer, using the screw-down top as a periscope, whilst boys of my own age played engine driver.' To get involved in fighting in the way that small ships did and big ships didn't was a powerful motive when it looked like there was going to be a war. This combined with Charles Anscomb's awareness that in peacetime, too, volunteering for submarines was the surest way to avoid battleships. Anscomb did admit afterwards that money had also played a part in his decision to volunteer.

Norman Drury certainly joined for the money, which in 1932 was very tight. He knew a little about submarines because he had spent a year in 1929 as part of the ship's company of the submarine depot ship *Titania* out in China and Japan, where they were monitoring Japanese radio messages. By joining he doubled his daily rate of pay. An able seaman's 3s. 3d. became 5s. 3d. with an extra 1s. when at sea in a submarine. Pay increased with rank, and included bonuses for time in the rating and for various extra accomplishments and considerations. To a chief petty officer's 7s. 6d., basic submarine pay added 2s. 6d. a day, with an extra 1s. 3d. when part of a commissioned crew, and a further 1s. 3d. 'hard layers' when actually sleeping at sea. With all allowances in, submariners were paid rather less than double what ordinary mariners received. They argued that they went through clothes much faster than general service ratings so that they were barely in pocket by the change, but few submariners wasted good clothes on life in a submarine.

For officers the considerations were similar. Hugh Mackenzie reckoned that there were only two ways to avoid battleships: the Fleet Air Arm or submarines. He quite fancied flying but 'various personal reasons persuaded me not to pursue this'. That left submarines. 'I had little knowledge of them, but the attractions of possible early command, of an independent way of life, and influenced by what I had seen of submarine officers during my previous three years at sea, all combined to sway me in this particular direction.'

There is a myth that all submariners were volunteers. This was never true, even in peacetime. At frequent intervals, sometimes after fatal accidents but especially during periods of rapid expansion, sufficient volunteers were lacking and people were conscripted. This was what happened to Bill King: 'I did not want to specialise, but when it came to my time there were no volunteers for submarines, and the Admiralty said, you, you and you, right turn, quick march. Not one of us wanted to go into submarines. That was 1931.' A few years earlier Ronnie Mills had met the same fate. The son of a wine shipper from Putney, he had 'no idea' why he had been sent into the navy. He chose to specialise in navigation but was sent into submarines. Later, the same happened to Arthur Hezlet. Born in Pretoria, the son of a Northern Irish army officer, he 'wanted to be a gunnery officer but the navy hadn't any volunteers for submarines at the time so they had to choose whoever they could'.

Mills, King and Hezlet all changed their minds. Mills said, 'I wasn't very pleased rather naturally, but after I had been in for my first three years I appreciated the extra pay that I was getting and I was thinking of getting married and one thing and another and I thought I had better stay on.' Hezlet reckoned that 'there were two great advantages of serving in a submarine. One was that your pay nearly doubled. As a lieutenant you were paid 13s. 6d. a day. You got six shillings extra for submarines and three shillings for every night you slept in them, so you were very substantially better off than anyone in general service. The other was that you got a very early command, generally at about the age of twenty-eight. So after a little while in submarines I said, "Kindly transfer my name onto the volunteers. I will stay now I'm here.'" Conscripts had to stay for three years, volunteers for five. King, like the others, was still in submarines fifteen years after conscription.

Much the same was true of engineers. West Countryman Jack Pook was conscripted around 1938 and was delighted with the result. He had joined the navy at sixteen in 1928 and four years later found himself one of thirty bored ERAs in the battleship *Rodney*, where everyone was moaning about pay and conditions. He found submarine life 'so much happier, so much closer; there is not so much red tape'. People in his previous ships had despised submariners as 'dirty, smelly and undisciplined'. He soon agreed that submariners were grimy, oily and sweaty, and neither the 'strictness of difference between officers and ratings' nor the strictness of dress was the same as he had been used to. But for him there was 'far more discipline in a submarine' because it was the real discipline of personal responsibility – 'an awful lot of self-discipline and this is one of the things that makes it an attractive service'. Every engineer counted in a submarine. You had to get on with the job rather than wasting time on rubbish.

Joe Blamey was twenty-one when he was drafted into the expanding Submarine Service in 1926. It was a little over a year since he had completed a four and a half year apprenticeship as an ERA. The draft didn't trouble Joe much one way or the other, but his mother was not so pleased. The family lived at St Budeaux, almost in sight of the Devonport dockyard where, a few days after Joe picked up his draft from the office, *H29* sank alongside the wharf. The chief ERA was killed along with several civilian dock workers, one of whom was a neighbour who had been to school with Joe. That was Monday 9 August. The following Friday (the 13th) Joe left for Fort Blockhouse.

From Portsmouth Harbour station the recruits took a motor launch to the fort that guarded the western side of the entrance

to the harbour on the seaward side of Haslar Creek. A haphaz-
ard collection of accommodation blocks and workshops clustered
around the old fortress. The ancient depot ship HMS *Dolphin*, a
converted merchant vessel tied up alongside, contained the offices
of Admiral Submarines and accommodation for trainee officers.
Rating trainees slept on dry land, together with spare submarine
crew, the crews of about eight or ten submarines that comprised
the 5th Flotilla, and the flotilla captain and his staff.

Blamey's course lasted only three weeks and consisted of lectures on submarine construction and machinery, together with
practical lessons at sea in one of the little H-boats, like the
recently sunk *H29*. The weather was poor and the little submarines rolled and pitched appallingly. This, aggravated by the
noise and the smells of diesel and battery gas, meant the trainees
spent their sea hours being sick. For Blamey 'it was hard to imagine ever caring for this life, but working hard between bouts of
nausea I learned as much as possible about the main and auxiliary machinery, and the method of diving'. He also learned how
to do things in an emergency, 'such as the hand operation of normally power operated equipment'.

Sub-lieutenant Ben Bryant arrived at the fort just a year later.
His car had had a puncture and he was late – too late to drive his
girlfriend home, so he dropped her at a hotel in Fareham and
drove through Gosport and over the drawbridge into the base.
He found a dance in progress. The hall porter escorted him to his
accommodation in HMS *Dolphin*, whose 'cabins had been condemned as unfit for human habitation, which meant that they
were suitable only for sub-lieutenants'. Eight years later Hugh
Mackenzie reckoned that 'an oilskin over one's bunk was essential in wet weather'.

Next day, after reporting to the captain in full dress including
sword, Bryant's teaching began. He found himself back with
friends from Dartmouth. Born in India, Bryant had just returned
from visiting his family in Belgium. At over six foot and around
thirteen stone, he made a useful forward in any rugby team,

though his abilities paled in comparison with those of some of his contemporaries. Big, burly Hugh 'Hairy' Browne played hooker for Ireland. John 'Tubby' Linton, an abrasive Welshman, played in the front row for the navy. In the year above them Geoffrey 'Slasher' Sladen was soon, in 1929, to win caps for England.

The teaching was conducted in wooden huts outside the walls of the fort. Ben Bryant was taught most of his classes by a chief petty officer torpedo gunner's mate (TGM), with engineering and wireless taught by specialists. The instructors had great practical experience and it was the practical that they emphasised. The course for officers lasted four months. It wasn't strenuous, partly, Bryant thought, because half his class were conscripts rather than volunteers. They were interested in the work, and talked 'shop' a lot during dinners and games of auction bridge or liar dice. Between lectures there was plenty of opportunity for sport, or in Bryant's case for clandestine meetings with girlfriend Marjorie, from whose house he had been banned. When it came to the final exam their wireless tutor, aware that his class had been less than conscientious, took the precaution of revealing the questions in advance.

There was one other group undergoing training at Blockhouse. While Ben Bryant's class was getting its introduction to submarines, Shrimp Simpson, four years Bryant's senior, was one of four lieutenants taking the three-month course to qualify for submarine command.

After 1929 the navy adopted the Davis Submerged Escape Apparatus as an aid to escaping from submarines that had been sunk. A deep water tank was constructed outside Fort Blockhouse to simulate the circumstances in which people would find themselves in a sunken submarine. Passing a test in which successful candidates rose calmly to the surface from a flooded submarine compartment became the prerequisite for qualification in submarine training. It proved a useful means of identifying people who were liable to panic. Around this time the staff increased and theory was modernised, but there were no drastic changes later in the thirties. Charles Anscomb and Norman Drury in 1932 faced essentially the same procedures and challenges as Stanley Hawkey and Syd Hart, who qualified later.

Anscomb came with a group that was almost entirely volunteer and determined to do well. 'Uneasy speculation about the various horrible rumours we had heard about the programme ahead of us formed the main topic of conversation on the train to *Dolphin* from Chatham.' From the harbour station they took a boat. Hart's ride across the harbour was chilling: 'Our shining oilskins did serve to keep out the rain and slashing spray, but the bitter cold was marrow-piercing.' Fort Blockhouse eventually came in sight, exciting but forbidding. Once more the doubts crowded into his head, but 'on the wind-swept jetty my eyes focused on the three submarines tied up alongside: one O class, an H class, and, nearest to us, *L26*. Sight of her dispelled every last doubt from my mind; my ambition to become a submariner quickened into certainty.'

The trainee mess was not reassuring: 'Here the whole topic of conversation was submarines, submarines, submarines,' Hart recalled. 'Never was so much shop discussed outside working hours ... We felt rank outsiders, not because anybody treated us that way, but because the world we found ourselves in was so utterly alien to the one outside Fort Blockhouse.' It all seemed so very technical compared with general service, with the discussion among the advanced trainees at night in the mess revolving around Kingston valves, master blows and main vents, conducted with an assurance that Hart found daunting. 'Those who had been in a training submarine told us what they had been put through and what they had been shown, and I was flabbergasted that anyone could absorb so much complex knowledge. I would never make it.'

On his first night Hart quickly located the bar and thought he had found 'a sort of seaman's paradise'. He couldn't believe how much money was being spent, 'and a pleasing impression of opulence quickly helped us forget the cold and the rain outside'. As they turned in that night, 'the general run of conversation amongst us potential submariners was concerned mainly with the abounding wealth of the Fort Blockhouse occupants.'

They passed a thorough medical, and Anscomb lapped up a speech telling them that the service wanted only those with real quality and initiative. He flaunted his new white sweater and hat band around town, just slightly nervous that he might not keep them. Then he was shown round a submarine: 'Cautiously, hearts thumping in excitement, we climbed down the ladder, into a confusion of wheels, valves, engines, periscope, and saw for the first time the tiny cramped world we would be living in if we passed our tests.'

But they still had to pass. First up was the escape test, with two days to practise. The first morning they got used to the DSEA sets in the classroom, wearing goggles, a breathing bag fed with oxygen, a mouth piece and a nose clip, and a rubber 'apron' which could be unrolled and was used to slow down the escaper's ascent to the surface in order to prevent 'the bends' – the formation of gas bubbles within body tissues owing to the rapid decrease in pressure.

In the afternoon 'we were due to go down into some twenty-five feet of water from the tank top'. They climbed down a ladder to the bottom of the tank to get used to breathing underwater. At twelve feet the pressure on the ears became painful, but 'painted in red letters on the tank's side were the words: "Blow your ears here!"' Breathing down the nose relieved the pressure. They spent fifteen minutes on the bottom.

Next morning the trainees practised the complicated escape drill and in the afternoon came the test. 'When it came our turn to take the test we checked and re-checked nervously,' Anscomb recalled. 'My heart was pounding. Would I make it? If I wanted to be a submariner I *had* to.' Once again he recalled the drill, 'Set on and properly secured to the body. Mouthpiece in. Exhaust cock to breathing bag shut – all air in the bag was sucked out of it through the mouth and exhausted through the nose to ensure a bag full of clean air. Bag empty. On nose clip. Open oxygen supply. Ready to go.'

Hart was equally nervous as he and two others entered the pressure equalisation cell. His instructor, who was in the compartment with them, ordered one of them to open the 'sea' valve. 'In came the water flooding over our feet, creeping above our ankles, then past our knees. The air, being compressed by the intake of water, was playing havoc with our ears – every few seconds we went through the drill of blowing them, as practised during the first dive.' When the water reached their waists it stopped rising, air pressure and water pressure being exactly equal. Then the escapees loosened the tie bars and unrolled the canvas escape trunking around the hatch above down to below water level, and lashed it with ropes to various valves in the compartment to make a tunnel. The instructor fitted his oxygen mask, crawled under the edge of the canvas tube, climbed up the escape ladder and released the stop valve to open the vent in the escape hatch door above. The air trapped in the top of the trunk rushed out and the sea took its place, filling the trunk completely.

'I was scared now,' recalled Anscomb. 'For a second I thought I was going to choke – open the exhaust valve! Then the officer opened the escape hatch, I simply waited my turn and went out, rising slowly to the surface through that cool, silent green world. It was over. I had passed.' It proved a fairly simple matter to push the hatch fully open, and slowly ease up through to the outside. Hart also had his moment of doubt: 'Imagination worked strange freaks in my feelings, but there was nothing for it but prompt Service obedience.' Afterwards they had to make a second ascent without the instructor, doing the things that he had done themselves.

The speed of ascent to the surface was controlled by using the rubber apron as a brake. If you went up too fast you experienced 'the bends'. From any great depth this could be fatal, so resisting the temptation to escape fast and learning to rise gradually was vital. Of the dozen in Anscomb's class, only two failed and were drafted back to general service. All of Hart's class passed.

Once through this test the trainees underwent an intensive course of lectures, combined with practical experience afloat. Different teachers did things different ways. On Hart's first visit to a submarine he wasn't allowed to touch anything, just to watch and listen. He was still apprehensive about his ability to master the complex machinery, and the first impression of pipes, valves, electric wiring, switches, pressure gauges and junction boxes put his mind 'in a bit of a whirl: would it ever learn the individual details of such intricate, baffling mechanism?' As the fore-hatch was slammed shut and they moved into the tube, the 'atmosphere grew thick like that of a crowded bar parlour'. They walked on in silence, while 'the snap of perfect efficiency on every hand made us feel ham-handed like so many raw recruits.'

Edward Young was similarly dumbstruck and bewildered when he was first led aft along the passageway of *Otway*. Young, in May 1940, was one of the first Royal Naval Volunteer Reserve (RNVR) officers to be allowed to train for submarines. He had been working in publishing and had designed the Penguin logo for Allen Lane. Now he was in another world.

The fore-hatch led into the seamen's mess. Forward was reload torpedo stowage space and the torpedo tubes themselves, the domain of the torpedo gunner's mate. These two-ton, self-propelled bombs were the submarine's main armament. They could be set to run at different depths and different speeds to a maximum range of about five miles. Their delicate machinery required constant maintenance. Going aft they passed the petty officers' mess, the ERAs' mess, and the ward room where the officers slept. Above these was the gun that was the submarine's second weapon. Then, amidships, came the captain's cabin and the control room with the two periscopes, a high-powered bifocal one forward for searching and a thinner, less conspicuous one aft for making attacks. There was the machine for calculating attack angles, the plot table for navigation and the steering and depth-keeping controls. Also in the control room was the so-called main blowing panel – actually a mind-boggling maze of pipes, dials and valve wheels that controlled the input of air and water to the various tanks. Next, going aft, was the wireless telegraphy office with radios to broadcast and receive messages and underwater listening gear, and a tiny galley for the cook.

Underneath these compartments amidships were the three battery tanks, each containing 112 cells, each cell one foot square, four feet high and weighing eight hundredweight, so each battery weighed forty-five tons. These provided electrical power for the motors and other equipment. Then came the engine room which, with two massive fifty-ton diesels going, became a raucous 'madhouse of brass and steel and frantically moving pieces of machinery'. Next came the motor room, flanked by panels of switches, ammeters and voltmeters with the motors themselves under the floor, and then the stokers' mess which would be Hart's home. Behind that was a compartment containing the compressor and steering gear. All of these spaces were crammed with bewildering machinery.

Young was surprised first of all by the size of the submarine. He had expected something smaller. The hull was wider than a London tube train and in most places you could stand upright and walk about comfortably on decks covered with brown corticene, a non-slip linoleum. The lighting was bright and in the messes there were wooden bunks and cupboards and curtains, pin-up girls and green baize tables. In the ward room, First Lieutenant Bill Jewell introduced himself and suggested they go up to the bridge while the submarine left harbour. As they entered the control room their eyes boggled at 'the appalling concentration of levers, valves, wheels, depth-gauges and other mysterious gadgets'. Then they climbed a brass ladder into the conning tower and another on to the bridge.

Looking down they saw the sea washing over the bulging saddle tanks, while on the perforated casing seamen in white jumpers stowed away the mooring ropes and wires. Jewell explained that it was the air in the saddle tanks that kept them afloat. When they wanted to dive the air would be let out of the vents that they could see along the tops of the tanks. The moment the engines started the conning tower became a wind tunnel as they sucked in air. Young climbed down into the control room and was startled when the klaxon sounded to announce a dive. As a flurry of orders was issued 'he began to feel a little sick'. Then he realised that the boat was already under water without his having noticed. There was a slight bow-down angle. Everything became peaceful. The engine noise had stopped and the motors were inaudible. 'We had stopped rolling: even at this shallow depth the swell seemed to have lost its effect. The change from the noisy, turbulent surface world to this sub-marine peace amazed and delighted me. My stomach began to recover.'

Soon he had another treat. After taking a careful look round himself, the skipper, 'Jumbo' Watkins, invited Young to use the periscope. It took him some time to position his eyes in the right place, then he got a clear picture of the sea. As waves broke on the top lens, it blurred and cleared again. He moved the handles to turn the tall column of bronze and saw the Isle of Wight. The field of vision was remarkably wide. Lieutenant Watkins showed him how a twist of one handle increased the magnification to high power – four times normal vision – bringing the Needles right up close. By twisting the other Young could look up at the clouds or down at the sea. Watkins explained that this allowed them to scan the sky for aircraft. Young found that he loved the whole experience, but neither of his fellow trainees was quite so enthusiastic, one having suffered a strong sense of claustrophobia.

Anscomb was given an experienced submariner as guide, and each of his class in turn operated the wheels that moved the rudder to steer the boat to port or starboard and the hydroplanes – essentially horizontal rudders – that steered it up or down. Then they 'learned to operate the valves controlling the water in the ballast tanks as though the submarine were actually below the surface'. As they did so their experienced mentors explained 'the technical mystery of water pressure and the method of pumping water out of the submarine's ballast tanks against the greater pressure of water around her so that she would dive'.

Next time the trainees dived and controlled the boat themselves, so busy at their stations that they hardly noticed they were underwater. Hart had more leisure to analyse. As he watched the depth gauge he felt no sense of atmospheric pressure but rather 'a curious feeling as if we were descending into an unnatural world where nothing was quite as it had been'. He chuckled to himself as he thought how his folks would be doubling their stake on his life insurance if they only knew what he was doing now.

The next weeks, as Ben Skeates recalled, 'involved intensive training, in every aspect of the workings of a submarine: the light and electronics, asdic, echo sounders, hydrophones, and the mechanical, high and low pressure air lines for moving the internal water ballast around during trimming, diving and surfacing'. Gradually, to each of them, the meaning of each valve, stop valve and wheel became clear. They learned about the motor room, the engine room, the control room, the torpedo compartment and tube space. Last, but by no means the least difficult, was the 'heads' or toilets. Finally, they sat an exam, preceded by a practical in which Anscomb nervously took control of the hydroplanes controlling the angle of the dive. He was apprehensive but in the event he scored 90 per cent.

For the specialists there were further courses. Norman Drury was sent from the wooden huts of Fort Blockhouse to the wooden huts of HMS *Osprey*, home of the anti-submarine school at Portland. There he learned the mysteries of Anti-Submarine Detection (ASD), or asdic as Churchill later called it. Apparently, Churchill coined the word in Parliament in 1939 and the *Oxford English Dictionary* asked for an explanation. The Admiralty claimed it was an acronym of the Allied Submarine Detection Investigation Committee, though there is no record that any such committee ever met.

This was the discovery that many believed had put submarines out of business. From a destroyer the ASD machine sent out pulses of ultrasonic sound waves in a cone-shaped beam. When these hit a dense object like a submarine they were reflected and the echoes were picked up. The time elapsed from sending the beams gave the range and their direction the bearing of the invisible target. The only missing co-ordinate was the depth, but in the First World War submarines had only operated at shallow depths and nobody had anticipated the need to place a submarine vertically.

The sound pulses were clearly audible, so submarines could use asdic in its passive role: they listened for asdic-armed destroyers that were attacking them. In theory submarines could also send out sound beams to find enemy vessels, but the weakness of this was that the enemy would hear the pulses and could usually escape faster than the submarine could attack. Subs could also use asdic pulses for discreet underwater communication. The pulses could be heard locally but could not be picked up further away as radio transmissions might be. Asdic was also useful for navigation in narrow spaces, where continuous transmission could locate rocks or even mines.

Norman Drury joined *H32*, which in 1926 had been the first submarine to be equipped with asdic. The asdic transmitter was fitted in a dome. In *H32* this was a copper dome on the upper casing; later submarines had the dome underneath. When submerged Drury would rotate the oscillator by hand, while the receiver was an ancient French one. It was all very primitive.

After passing his command course, Shrimp Simpson was also sent to *Osprey* where he commanded *H49*. He found working with the scientists and officers there 'first class training for developing cunning in avoiding asdic location by the use of tide rips, other shipping, depth, and holding trim stopped'. He learned the importance of knowing the terrain, but generally found it easy to dodge asdic-armed destroyers, especially with the help of his own asdic: 'The impression I gained at first hand during 1928 was that the anti-submarine specialists and scientists could never make asdic into more than a close range and unreliable location device, whereas its introduction to the submarine would vastly improve the efficiency of that vessel in both attack and escape.' In Simpson's view the new discovery made the submarine more dangerous, not less.

For officers, appointments were offered to candidates in the order of passing out. In theory those who did best in the exam could choose the best appointments. In practice the rugger players were distributed among the Blockhouse flotilla so that they could continue to play for the service and the navy. Thus Linton and Browne became 'Blockhouse Loungers' and remained with the 5th Flotilla until 1932. Sladen, similarly, stayed at home to play for England. This left the foreign fields clear for intelligent, hard-working submariners who were not good at rugby. Mackenzie found himself with a choice and it was not difficult to make: 'The Fourth Submarine Flotilla on the China Station was the dream of every young officer: "old China hands" never ceased to sing the praises of the Far East.'

4

THE CHINA STATION

It was a disconcerting fact that all these people were training to use a weapon that the Admiralty said it wanted to abolish. In 1919 Britain had tried to get submarines outlawed by the Treaty of Versailles but France refused, arguing that the submarine was the appropriate weapon of the weaker naval power. Indeed, in *La Revue Maritime* in 1920 a French officer went so far as to argue that Germany had been absolutely justified in using submarines against commerce. He was then appointed principal lecturer on the French senior officers' course. When the French rejected the British proposal to abolish submarines at the Washington Conference in December 1921 and demanded a minimum of 90,000 tons of submarines for themselves, the British delegate quoted from this article and provoked fury, contributing to glacial relations between Britain and France. The King was one of those who urged most strongly 'the total abolition of submarines'. He also worried about air bombardment by the French.

Royal sentiment, impressed on successive Prime Ministers, was one reason why the Admiralty continued to advocate the abolition of submarines throughout the 1920s and right up to the London Naval Conference of 1935. Long before then it became perfectly clear that abolition was impossible since the French, and later the Japanese and Italians, were determined to have submarines. The British position remained contradictory; while arguing for abolition in full knowledge that the argument was futile, Britain maintained a substantial submarine fleet. The fleet would have been larger had not the Treasury repeatedly refused to spend money on boats that the Admiralty was proposing to abolish. In the background, idealists strove for disarmament, and money was in short supply.

It did not help that some senior submariners were unconvinced of their own weapon's continuing potency. Shrimp Simpson's view that asdic was of more use to the hunted than it was to the hunter was not widely shared. Most people believed far too complacently that asdic had mastered submarines. In 1928 the respected Great War veteran Seagee Brodie lectured the Royal Naval War College on 'Frightfulness – the post-war view'. 'Frightfulness' encompassed unrestricted submarine warfare, poison gas and the bombing of civilians. The old submariner reassured his audience: 'I do not believe in the submarine as a dominant weapon, though it may cause losses against the best screened ships, and must never be ignored.' He continued:

> Although submarines may have improved in various directions, and may have the benefit of air reconnaissance in future, I think the pendulum has swung very markedly against them.
>
> Detection devices have vastly improved, and the complete immunity enjoyed by a well-handled submarine against all attack unaided by a mishap or remarkable luck, will never recur. The numbers and the standard of efficiency required to produce decisive results against shipping are prohibitive. I consider the submarine menace against our commerce definitely dead as a decisive factor.

Brodie concurred with the prevailing wisdom that terror bombing was the weapon of the future, and thought the use of poison gas inevitable and no more abominable than any other weapon. But the veteran submariner believed that asdic had conquered submarines. It is hardly surprising that others underestimated them.

The confidence placed in asdic by senior naval figures was one reason why there was no exercise between 1919 and 1939 to test the protection of a slow-moving convoy against submarine attack. Germany showed no sign of wishing to rejoin battle with the Royal Navy, and in view of Britain's treaty obligations it would have been difficult to explain an exercise in which British submarines attacked merchant ships. Nevertheless, some sort of practice in defending merchant convoys might have been useful.

Instead, submariners were trained to fight warships. The anticipated theatre of war was the Far East and the enemy was Japan. As early as 1919 Admiral Jellicoe identified 'Japan as the nation with which trouble might conceivably arise in the future'. Until the Washington Conference of 1921 the Royal Navy had always reckoned to match its power to the combined strength of its two nearest rivals. At Washington it surrendered its traditional dominance, accepting parity with the US Navy and a 5:3 ratio over Japan. Should Japan attack Britain in alliance with a European power the navy no longer had enough warships for superiority on both fronts.

No aspect of war against Japan was neglected. Plans for minelaying were worked out in 1926. Fleet exercises examined the problems entailed in protecting fast military convoys designed to reinforce Singapore's defence against a Japanese attack. An exercise in the Aegean in 1925 studied the difficulties that might be faced around the Malacca Strait. Another in 1928 simulated a Japanese attack on Hong Kong, which had to be relieved before the Japanese conquered Singapore. Unless or until the Royal Navy's full force could be deployed against Japan, Britain would be locally the weaker power and in that case the submarine was its natural weapon.

The Admiralty convinced the government that the only way to challenge a Japanese battle fleet north of the Philippines was with submarines. The submarines built in the 1920s – the O, P and R classes – were designed to hold off a Japanese attack until Britain could reinforce Singapore. At 280 feet long and 1500 tons, they were big and had a long range. The first three, *Oberon*, *Oxley* and *Otway*, proved too slow, unstable and electronically unreliable and were quickly relegated to training. Six better Os were finished in 1928–9 and the six P class and four R class submarines completed in 1929–30 were essentially similar. Their job was to attack and destroy Japanese warships and large troop convoys. It was to these brand new submarines and their brand new mother ship *Medway* that those submariners fortunate enough to be sent to the China station reported.

Medway was designed to be a submarine depot ship – the first time the Royal Navy had placed such an order. Previous depot ships had all been converted from merchantmen or liners and had proved more or less unsatisfactory. *Medway* had excellent workshops and excellent accommodation and submariners loved her. Launched in 1928, she sailed for China in 1929 to replace *Titania* and her L class boats with the six new O class submarines. She remained on the China station until April 1940. The P and R class boats followed her to China. *Poseidon* sank in an accident in 1931, leaving the flotilla fifteen strong. With one or two always refitting or detached there were usually twelve alongside. This meant that *Medway* was home to about 800 submariners plus her own substantial complement of staff, sailors, engineers and spare crew.

These 1920s boats were futuristic and extremely complicated electrically. *Rainbow* had power loading for the six forward torpedo tubes. Hugh Mackenzie found that in action this 'turned the fore-ends into a nightmare of strumming wires and whizzing torpedoes'. The noisy and accident-prone automated system took seventeen and a half minutes to reload a salvo. However, the boats were solidly built of steel and brass and very comfortable to live in. Equipped for the China Seas, they had twelve-foot refrigerators running the length of the seamen's mess and were fitted with air conditioning, although it was noisy and inefficient. They dived slowly but they could dive deep. They were well armed and reasonably fast. One serious defect was identified. They carried their oil fuel in riveted external tanks which leaked after prolonged battering. As Anscomb remarked, 'Sooner or later with all riveted tanks the oil fuel leaked out and rose to the surface. A submarine leaving that sort of visiting card in wartime would not live long.'

Ben Bryant joined the flotilla in 1931 and eventually became first lieutenant of *Perseus*. By then he had married his girlfriend. They left their baby and nanny with Bryant's parents and, like other service families, took rooms in a hotel in Kowloon. It was a pleasant life: in the morning Marjorie would throw her evening dress out of the window with a cry of 'Amah!' and the laundress would catch the floating gown to iron it ready for the next party. Bryant's friend John Linton was first lieutenant of *Oswald*. Ronnie Mills came out as first lieutenant of the newly built *Proteus*. Bill King, rather younger, arrived in Hong Kong in 1932 as torpedo officer of *Orpheus*.

These privileged young men all spoke with the clipped upper-class accent familiar from wartime films: the voice of Noël Coward in *In Which We Serve*. Most would have shared the views of Lieutenant Desmond Martin on Coronation Day in 1937: 'Isn't England, the Empire and all it stands for a wonderful thing? . . . In the mess before the King spoke they played "God Save the King"; we all stood up and stood still too. This may sound funny to you but the last thing a Naval Officer will do is outwardly to show his feelings . . . ' A stiff upper lip and poker face were *de rigueur* in public.

The first sight of Hong Kong was unforgettable. The beautiful peak of the island and the hills of the mainland were a backdrop to vibrant, pulsating activity. The sexiest streamlined passenger liners, ocean-going cargo ships under every flag, little coastal steamships armed against piracy, bustling ferries, hundreds of junks and what looked like thousands of sampans seemed to cover the surface of the water entirely. The sampans were home to Chinese families; the man in the stern smoking, while the woman paddled the boat with a child strapped to her back. Most women and many men wore the traditional waist-length pigtail. Women coolies dressed uniformly in a black shirt, wide hat, knee-length pants and wooden sandals. The British communicated with the Chinese in pidgin English – 'makee plenty quick' – which the Chinese seemed to prefer and English sailors quickly learned. The relationship between them was generally cordial and friendly.

The flotilla was there to exercise and train. Its one serious job was to send a single submarine at a time to patrol Bias Bay against pirates. Charles Anscomb in *Pandora* had been inspired to join submarines by a daring victory over pirates, but to his disappointment there were no dramatic rescues while he was there. Pirates were still very active in all Chinese waters, attacking coastal shipping and seizing prisoners, but when David Luce of *Osiris* was kidnapped the navy tamely paid a large ransom to free him.

For the officers especially 'Hong Kong was wonderful'. One reckoned 'I was much better off as a sub-lieutenant in Hong Kong than I was really for the rest of my life . . . Everything was very cheap. I had a polo pony; I had a speedboat; a Chinese servant.' There was racing on the Happy Valley flat course, steeplechasing at Fanling on the mainland and some officers rode with the Fanling hunt. Then there were cocktail parties at which hostesses devised exotic drinks beyond the standard Manhattans, Martinis, Sidecars and White Ladies. The social life was hectic and there were plenty of girls to chase. At this time King was rebelling against his privileged background, made a cult of toughness and ignored girls. When the boats were in dry dock for a refit the officers lived in flats on the Peak at the summit of the island by the old cable car station. King would end an evening by running up the flights of steps that climbed 1300 feet from the dockyard to the cable station. *Orpheus*'s officers could do it in twenty minutes.

The submariners made their own occasional contributions to Hong Kong social life. There was an annual children's party for which in 1938 George Colvin wrote the orders 'in best Colvin style'. He was one of the most articulate submarine officers, the son of a well-known journalist, with a brother, Ian, who was then the deeply anti-Nazi correspondent of the *News Chronicle* in Berlin. For his party 'Jimmies' (first lieutenants) were to dress up as pirates and dispense doubloons. Rule three was: 'Flying speed is essential. Bar opens at 11 am. as usual and if you can't be a convincing pirate by zero hour you haven't been trying.' Rule six: 'Do not breathe on the little beasts.' The result, according to Ian Anderson of *Olympus*, was 'a grand party; the children seemed to enjoy it too, and only two were sufficiently frightened to have hysterics'. Anderson was the son of a Glasgow doctor and had joined submarines the year before. Rugby was very much at the centre of his life and he was an important player in the Scottish team that won the international tournament at Hong Kong that autumn.

For engineer Joe Blamey the cost of getting his wife Clare to Hong Kong was prohibitive. Being recently married and, like Anderson, a top-class sportsman, Blamey didn't go in much for wine, women and song. He found that the Chief Petty Officers' Club in the dock had reasonably priced English beer and billiards. Then he discovered and joined the China Light and Power Recreational Club in Kowloon. This had two tennis courts, a badminton hall, table tennis tables and billiards. Next door was the German Club where returned tennis balls were received without a smile.

For those who did like the night life, Hong Kong was rich in entertainment for ratings as well as officers. Stoker John 'Choppa' Capes left a description of a run ashore. He and his oppo 'Scouse' put together a kitty of $100HK (about £6) and caught the last launch to the jetty steps, Hong Kong side. Approaching the Fleet Club, they fought their way through 'the inevitable wave of girls from the age of ten upwards, screaming "Me first time piece".'

After a few pints of draught Youngers, they 'proceeded to Loo
Kwoc for a couple of noggins in the sea food bar to look over the
talent. Got the eye from a couple of White Russians, off-white
camels.' Choppa reckoned they looked much too attractive to be
true, especially in the dock area of Wanchai, and talked Scouse
out of 'shackling up' by mentioning 'China chafe'.

They popped out of the side entrance and extricated themselves from the 'wave of struggling humanity persistent in their
entreaties', just as a tram approached and slowed down for them
to jump in. It was 'not what any ordinary person would recog-
nise as a tram, being a kind of double-decker framework in the
last possible state of desperation and dilapidation perched on two
pairs of bogey wheels, groaning and screaming in protest as worn
out wheels and track provide motive power. No glass windows
of any kind are allowed. Will not blow over in normal typhoons.
Upper deck having a horrifying sway and lurch in all conditions
and weathers.' They jumped off at the dockyard canteen, in a
more central district out of the slums. The tombola was in full
swing, 'packed humanity tiered up the walls, a tense, highly per-
spiring mob ... After four games, hoarse anguished whisper in
my lughole "sweating!"' Seconds later Scouse had some winnings. 'Any winnings always splitters. Half in the kitty. Myself
having the most experience and years always keep the kitty, now
augmented by $64 (HK).'

They left the dockyard canteen quickly. 'In any Eastern grot,
on the winning side motto is "Instant Scapa".' They walked
down to the ferry jetty and caught the Kowloon harbour ferry
boat, which looked like a Mississippi river steamboat. Kowloon
was on the mainland side of Hong Kong harbour, with the
Chinese border only a dozen miles away. It was 'more Yankeefied
and more exotic generally'. They visited the Bar B.Q., owned by
two retired US Navy old sweats. It had 'superior EWO draught
and bottled', although the 'speciality in this glittering sin palace
[was] "Panther's Piss", a genuine North Chinese bottled beer
from Macao'.

Choppa and Scouse were 'in naval parlance, "Ballroom centipedes"'. Next door to the Bar B.Q. was Dreamland, a small dance hall. 'The attraction was exotic camels in cheongsam ball gowns, 10 dances for one dollar, as an introduction to possible further interesting athletics.' Scouse was quickly 'wrapped round his favourite, Ah-Sin, very statuesque, and thoroughly warmed up now, about midnight'. Choppa 'sneaked back for further liquid refreshment and a quick look in at the Savoy Ballroom.' He saw that Suzy was in great form and decided not to barge in. About an hour later he winkled Scouse out of Dreamland and they took a rickshaw each to the Kowloon ferry. On reaching the Hong Kong side they decided that oysters might settle the stomach, since the renowned seafood of Jimmy's Kitchen was close at hand with oysters at $10 a dozen. After a few of these they took rickshaws to the China Fleet club and enjoyed a 'comfortable doss' till 7 a.m., when they drank tea and took the 7.30 liberty boat back to the *Medway*.

In the summer the fleet left steamy Hong Kong and sailed north to Wei Hai Wei. Until they handed it back to the Chinese in 1930, the British had rented a large territory in Shantung province. After 1930 they retained a lease on the island of Lui Kung Tao, where they had established a naval base. It was 1300 miles north of Hong Kong, on the same latitude as Malta, and enjoyed a delightful summer climate. The harbour was in the relatively sheltered channel between the island and the mainland.

Wei Hai Wei offered little to lovers of nightlife, but it was a paradise for sportsmen and here the fleet's sporting rivalries were played out. The island contained a few bungalows which were rented by senior officers. There was one hotel, taken over by the wealthier officers who could afford to have their wives with them. Marjorie Bryant and the pregnant Nancy Linton took up residence there in 1932. Each room had a veranda, a bathroom with a thunder box and an earthenware bath, which was filled by coolies from four-gallon kerosene tins suspended on a pole. The Officers' Club was all-male except on Fridays when there was dancing, so there was little for the women to do except play tennis and drink. Living 'in each other's pockets', the women regularly fell out with each other and the atmosphere around the hotel and on Fridays at the club was often a little tense.

For those officers, such as Hugh Mackenzie, who liked to shoot game, there was very fine duck and snipe shooting on the mainland in a chain of lagoons ten to fifteen miles east. Migrating birds rested in Shantung province after crossing the Yellow Sea and for a few weeks they were plentiful wherever fields of soya beans alternated with strips of maize.

For the ratings there was a NAAFI canteen by the huge sports ground with six bowling alleys. It had cheap British beer, cheap British food and plentiful fruit. Few women were in evidence, though; even the canteen staff was male. There was a lot of organised sport. Tubby Linton had left *Oswald* by the time Joe Blamey joined her, but navigator Jumbo Watkins and the engineer officer both played rugger for the navy in China, where submariners usually contributed about half the team. Blamey was also selected, and two of the crew were good enough to play for the flotilla. They met their match, however, in *Rainbow*, Hugh Mackenzie's boat. Though able to compete with her at rugby, they were hammered at any other sport. *Rainbow*'s highly competitive and abrasive first lieutenant, Tony Miers, 'was "well in" with the drafting staff and literally ruthless in the picking of his crew'. One of his able seamen confirmed that he was only taken on after claiming to play rugby, football and cricket well and to be willing to eat Miers for breakfast at boxing. Mackenzie passed Miers' test because they both came from Inverness, but he was also a top-class hockey player.

Miers was fiery and difficult, hard on junior officers and at war with his captain. Miers lost his temper easily and violently but was equally quick to apologise, generous and loyal. When push came to shove the honour of *Rainbow* came first. An aggrieved officer from *Phoenix*, coming to demand satisfaction after being sent off by referee Miers during a water polo match won by

Rainbow, shouted to the officer on deck, 'I say *Rainbow*, is your fucking first lieutenant aboard?' The officer on deck turned out to be the captain, who replied, 'No he fucking well isn't. Report to my cabin immediately.'

Exercises at Wei Hai Wei were as competitive as sporting fixtures. In 1932 Bill King's *Orpheus* was top submarine. 'When we won the torpedo-loading competition, which involves the complicated launching of six two-ton steel monsters into their tubes, we did the exercise in six minutes, the next best ship took twelve minutes. We also won the flotilla sports, rifle-shooting and Lewis-gun competitions. For trophies we ranked second to an aircraft-carrier.' By 1937 practice torpedoes had a special collision head so that it could be established whether or not they had hit a ship in an exercise. Submarines also practised with their powerful four-inch guns. The gun crew mastered putting ten rounds into a ten-foot-square target at 600 yards in a minute, beginning and ending with the boat beneath the surface. It was an exciting and popular test and the tactic had already proved successful against pirates. Crews became extremely good at this, having worked out the bearing before they surfaced so that the gunlayer was able to open fire as soon as he reached the gun. The flotilla gunnery cup was much coveted.

The Yellow Sea was an ideal exercise area with little passing shipping. Its one drawback was that asdic conditions were sometimes very poor. For submariners, however, this meant they could get on with practising torpedo drill and gunnery without being made to act as quarry for destroyers. Torpedoes were massively complicated and delicate pieces of machinery, each costing £3000. When fired in practice they were set to float. King lost one once, and although it was later recovered having washed ashore and been set up by Chinese peasants as a fertility totem in their temple, he never lost another. As a safety precaution, submarines were forbidden to dive by night during exercises. *Rainbow* was once sent on a mock war patrol, but Mackenzie spent it submerged by day and surfaced with navigation lights on.

He did, however, gain experience of the tedium and discomfort of crouching for hours at the periscope seeing nothing, while being boiled alive with no air conditioning. This was his only 'war patrol' before war broke out.

From Wei Hai Wei there were cruises to other nearby bases. The Germans had a concession at Tsing-tao where they had established a brewery. King's low point as a tough came when he was mugged there and woke up in the gutter with a bleeding head, treated by the multitude as just more trash by the side of the road. Visits to the US Navy's summer base at Chefoo, just forty miles west of Wei Hai Wei, were more common. Here, in contrast to the British base, there were abundant 'Russian bares' to service the sailors. The old Russian base at Port Arthur was now in the hands of the Japanese, along with the rest of Manchuria. Blamey played a game of rugby there and to his surprise was beaten; it turned out that the Japanese had imported their national team, trained specially for the visit. From Port Arthur King visited Harbin, a city with 50,000 Russians, mixed red and white, blending east and west, where he gorged on incredibly cheap caviar in exotic nightclubs.

From the port of Chinwangtao it was possible to take the train to Peking. King and Mackenzie both saw the Forbidden City and the Temple of Heaven, and muddy streets with low shops selling a fabulous range of goods. There were no cars, just masses of people, rickshaws, camels and donkeys. At night the teeming city was full of bars, restaurants, dance halls and innumerable white Russians selling everything, themselves included. They both made the excursion to the Great Wall. Only later did King realise that his pale dawns seen from holy mountains and chance encounters with barefoot philosophers were a last glimpse of a vanishing world.

The return voyage from Wei Hai Wei was usually combined with a longer cruise. Mackenzie visited Kagoshima in Japan and was bathed by Geisha girls who were fascinated with his red hair. Even the brothels there were hygienic and cheap. A receipt was anonymously preserved: '2 Girlie – 1 hour – 15 yen' (then £1 2s. 6d.). Keelung in Formosa proved much less welcoming and friendly than the Japanese mainland. Three sailors were beaten up and incarcerated for no very good reason. The highlight of Mackenzie's cruise came after the fleet split up. *Rainbow*'s officers were taken to a Dayak longhouse in Borneo. Served fabulous curry by slim and exquisitely beautiful topless girls, he wrenched his eyes away to see that all the pillars were decorated with shrunken human heads. King's voyage incorporated a visit to the Americans in Manila and a test march through the Malaysian jungle towards Singapore. King's party made ten miles a day, though in the official view the jungle remained impassable to troops.

Even the trip home offered potential for adventure. One enterprising group of submariners commissioned a yacht, the *Tai-mo-shan*, and sailed her back to England. Each put in £500, 'the boat cost £800 and we had a lot of money to fit her out and store her up.' They were entitled to three months' leave, and the navy's willingness to allow them the rest of the time on half pay was partly down to a little side project. On the way they were to examine the military potential of the Kuriles, a volcanic chain of islands stretching north-east from Japan for 700 miles. The aim was to find possible bases close to the Japanese islands for submarines or for detached parties with radio transmitters or radio intercept equipment 'in the event of hostilities against Japan or between Japan and America'. The islands were sparsely populated, usually shrouded in fog, and thought to have deep ports that might accommodate submarines or even warships.

In July 1933 *Tai-mo-shan* visited Nemuro on the tip of Hokkaido and her crew was interrogated. It was obvious that the Japanese had something to hide in the northern Kuriles. 'Pointing to the island of Paramushir they wanted to know how far off it we would pass and what day! What was our daily progress? And could they verify this from the log?' The Japanese navy prevented a night visit to Paramushir. The submariners learned little except that the Japanese had a secret. These foggy islands were where the Japanese fleet hid before Pearl Harbor.

The rest of their trip was pure pleasure – bar riding out a typhoon. They sailed across to Vancouver, then down to Los Angeles. 'There we were given a tour of the Hollywood studios and met Fred Astaire and Ginger Rogers. We were then towed through the Panama Canal by a Fyfe's banana boat and onwards to England.'

Bryant's journey home was also ominous. He booked a passage in 1934 in a German merchant ship: 'The German ships were the only ones on the Far East run with all white crews; they were government subsidised and in 1934 all the crew of S.S. Coblenz were already being trained for war.'

In 1935, on King's last trip to the mainland to shoot duck – not his favourite pastime – their regular sampan man, known as 'Tomato Face', remarked as he bent to the oar during the twelve-mile journey and contemplated the distant swamps, 'Two years, Japanese come.' He was right. In 1931 they had taken over Manchuria, the northern part of China; in 1937 they began to take over the whole, despite a long guerrilla war against Chinese resistance. Mackenzie left on a liner in 1937 for a voyage via Canada. The first stop was Shanghai, where they found the population streaming away carrying their belongings on foot or in rickshaws and handcarts. It was disconcerting and they hurried their departure. Two days later the Japanese attacked. Desmond Martin, Mackenzie's relief in *Rainbow*, was an orphan with wealthy cousins, who had trained as a merchant seaman but transferred to submarines in 1937 as the service expanded. On his last voyage as an officer in a liner he had fallen for an eighteen-year-old passenger, Joanna Dennistoun, and he wrote to her constantly, sending letters via Siberia 'as the Chinks and Japs shoot up any plane they see flying over Shanghai'. At Wei Hai Wei, he noted, 'the Chinese are making trenches and gun emplacements ready for the Japs.' Unfriendly brushes with Japanese warships became commonplace.

War was looming. From 1937 under Captain Claud Barry and 'Colonel' George Menzies the flotilla practised attacking in small divisions on the surface in 'wolf packs' of four. It was dangerous, and communication and split-second understanding became vital, but throughout the complex manoeuvres there was no accident. The 'Colonel' was a very popular senior officer and there was a great celebration when his promotion to captain was announced during the Peak Club fancy dress ball. Ronnie Mills was back in China in command of *Regent*. A talented cartoonist, he drew a fine joint portrait of his fellow COs, entitled 'Such Men as These'. In January 1938 they held an exciting fleet exercise simulating a Japanese attack on Singapore, in which for the first time they practised attacking and diving by night. In the light of experience, Desmond Martin suggested a way in which the normal submerged firing drill could be speeded up for surface attacks, and to his joy his suggestion was adopted.

When Anderson and Martin returned to Wei Hai Wei in 1938 they found the Japanese flag flying on the old Chinese headquarters, British flags flying from the cricket ground and golf course, buildings with Union Jacks painted on their roofs and an array of notices identifying 'British property'. Ashore were the same fruit stalls, the same shops and the same screaming rickshaw and sampan men as always, but the mood was uneasy. The Chinese were passively sulky, resentful of the order that they should bow low before all Japanese when passing them in the street. There were two Japanese submarines and a cruiser around. When a tiny Japanese officer with a gigantic sword appeared in *Medway*'s ward room, fifty officers sprang to attention followed by 'an awful stony silence and then someone offered him a cigarette and the tension eased'.

At the time of the Munich crisis in 1938 they were ordered to sea late at night, and Anderson ended up in the specially reopened bar. 'By this time (and it was 2.30 am after all) I was beginning to feel quite dramatic and heroic and excited (calm exterior of course, though), especially as the chaps left aboard seemed to regard us as going to our deaths and came up with offers of "Anything I can do, old man?" and "What about a last drink?", while Captain Barry was rushing round in a dressing gown ... with sheafs of orders in sealed envelopes in his hand.'

It turned out to be a false alarm, and another year passed during which the tension grew. Next year at Wei Hai Wei the sampan and rickshaw men were less helpful, while in town the Chinese 'looked depressed and sad and many shrank away from us, an entirely new state of affairs'. All naval families were evacuated to Hong Kong. Officers going shooting were suspected of gun-running to the guerrillas and the Japanese searched their sampans. There was a stand-off between a British cruiser and a Japanese one. In July the exercise period ended early and abruptly and the flotilla moved to Hong Kong. In August it moved again, to Singapore. Japanese marines landed in September.

The Chinese employed by the British paid the usual price for collaboration with imperialists. For rowing British officers to shoot wildfowl, the Japanese crucified Tomato Face; he died looking out across the lovely waters to where the snipe rested.

5

WAR CLOUDS

With the rise of the Nazis in Germany and Mussolini's fascists in Italy, trouble was also brewing in Europe. In 1935, thanks to the Abyssinian crisis, the possibility arose of immediate war against Italy, a country that was building a modern fleet with more submarines than anybody else. Britain was lagging behind. Having completed the submarines designed for China in 1930, the Admiralty turned its attention to minelayers based on the P design, to a new generation of huge submarine fast enough to operate with the fleet – the River class – and to small submarines intended for use in the shallower and confined waters of the North Sea and the Mediterranean – the S class. These boats had fuel tanks situated inside their pressure hull so they no longer leaked before the boat was in mortal danger.

Unfortunately, by 1935 there were only five operational S-boats. Charles Anscomb had already served in one of them, *Sturgeon*, launched in 1932 as the first British submarine with a disappearing gun. The gun retracted efficiently enough while diving, but as it rose while surfacing it took in so much water that the boat rolled, which made firing hopelessly inaccurate. While *Sturgeon* was altered, Anscomb left for the more spacious and comfortable *Pandora* and it was in this boat that he was redeployed in 1935 from China to face Italy. His job was originally first fore-endman, chief assistant to the torpedo gunner's mate who controlled the maintenance, loading and firing of the boat's principal weapons. In China Anscomb passed for petty officer and became second coxswain, which meant that his post in action was now on the hydroplanes, controlling depth.

At Malta *Pandora* moored beside the depot ship *Cyclops*, joining a flotilla commanded by Guy D'Oyly-Hughes. Hughes was 'a tall, cool, handsome chap, very able, very efficient, and very sure of himself'. The principal British naval base in the Mediterranean, Malta had the finest of harbours and a commanding position in the centre of the sea. It was so close to Sicily and the principal Italian harbours that it offered fantastic potential as an advanced base for submarines and other raiders, but the Admiralty worried that it could no longer be used as a wartime base for the fleet.

In its long history the island fortress had proved more than once how well it could stand up to attack from the sea. But there was a new worry now. How well could it stand up to attack from the air? Being such a short distance from enemy airfields, Malta was terribly vulnerable to air bombing and in the 1930s bombing terrified everyone. It was thought that nothing could deter bombers and that they would pulverise everything beneath them. In the event of war against Italy, Malta's harbours and the ships in them would quickly be destroyed.

However, D'Oyly-Hughes had an answer to this. He proposed cutting submarine shelters into the rock under Valletta from Marsamxett Harbour. The design provided docking facilities, maintenance, supply and living quarters for a flotilla of six submarines beneath 200 feet of rock. The stone was so soft that the project was quite easy to accomplish and the projected cost was that of a single submarine, £340,000. In this way the submarines and their support facilities would become invulnerable to air bombing and could continue to operate, however difficult life might become above ground. D'Oyly-Hughes told Shrimp Simpson about his plan when Simpson, then commanding *L27*, arrived with the older boats of the 2nd Flotilla. Simpson agreed that the way to use Malta was to turn it into a modern fortress of rock shelters, covered by fighters, with airfields and harbours bristling with anti-aircraft guns. Excavation of the submarine pens commenced.

As a practice exercise the submarines 'attacked' Grand Harbour to test the defences. 'The entrance to Grand Harbour was narrow and well guarded,' recalled Anscomb. 'To look at it you wouldn't say a submarine had the faintest hope of getting inside ... We got into Grand Harbour by disguising ourselves. Two miles outside the harbour we dived. On the periscope we mounted a small sail and "sailed" right through into the harbour submerged, with the captain conning the ship from the periscope standard, and surfaced alongside the flagship without being detected.' Anscomb found it a really useful exercise. 'The whole exploit called for some very accurate depth keeping on the part of the cox'n ... and myself, the second cox'n. It was invaluable training for me and I was very glad of it later on.'

Joe Blamey in *Oswald* remembered these exercises as the first in which he ever dived at night. Night diving in peacetime was strictly prohibited for reasons of safety, but with war possibly days away it was time to start practising. They also started to practise the 'crash dive' – getting under water as fast as possible. They had never done this before either – again for reasons of safety – but they began to get used to doing things fast and to reducing the time it took to submerge.

Bill King was rushed out to the Mediterranean in *Starfish*, but war did not materialise in 1935, and King received his promotion to first lieutenant, the next step on the career ladder. He was appointed to *Narwhal*, newest of the minelayers. She had a fine captain and crew and he loved her. On a summer cruise he walked across Mull with Hugh Mackenzie to catch the ferry for lunch with a Mackenzie family friend who owned the island of

Ulva. Mackenzie had recently met some German U-boat men at Gibraltar and was impressed with their professionalism and their friendliness. Their host, who had lost her husband in the First World War, found such benevolent views intolerable. She picked up her stick and threatened to beat them with it unless they woke up and began to regard Germans as dangerous. It was an episode that impressed both King and Mackenzie.

Soon after this, Mackenzie was appointed first lieutenant of *Seahorse* while King, succeeded as first lieutenant of *Narwhal* by Hugh Haggard, was called to take his 'perisher', the course that qualified him to command a submarine. Each officer spent a period as navigator and as torpedo officer of a boat. Usually, they would then become first lieutenant of something old and small and afterwards of something big and new. Finally, they took the Commanding Officers' Qualifying Course, formerly known as the 'Periscope School', from which the sardonic nickname 'perisher' for both the course and the candidate derived. Those who failed the course perished and returned to general service. You could not have a submarine commander who was incapable of making successful attacks.

King approached the ordeal with mixed feelings. The competitive side of him wanted to do well, but he had been forced into submarines and still 'cruisers and destroyers appealed to me far more'. To fail was hardly disastrous, since 'many excellent officers failed to pass this particular examination and went on to command bigger ships with great success.' To succeed required 'a certain eye and a certain flair which it is difficult to reveal until you are actually undergoing the course'. The lonely responsibility of making the calls that determined success or failure for a submarine was huge and it was very easy to lose confidence, believing that you did not have that eye and flair.

The first stage of the perisher took place in a small building that housed the mechanism known as the 'attack teacher' just beyond the escape tank, a short walk from Fort Blockhouse. Five or six candidates took each course, the courses being run by an experienced commander who would take charge of teaching for a year or two. One of the perishers was shut in a circular white box with a First World War vintage periscope. The box, which resembled part of a control room, could be turned at speed to simulate the movement of the submarine. The periscope looked out on to a scene in which ship models were mounted on a trolley on rails. The upper part of the building, reached by an outside stair, opened to allow the railway to extend some yards into the open air. The angle of the ship model and speed of the trolley could be altered according to orders delivered by the officer at the periscope and the counter-measures devised by the other candidates. Somehow, the perisher had to keep track of the respective positions of the imagined submarine and the model target. It was very easy to forget which way you were supposedly pointing and become 'lost in the box', unable to maintain a mental picture of the position of your submarine relative to the target and its escorts. The manoeuvres of the target and the submarine were followed on a plotting table from where the ship-bearing trolley was controlled. If the plotters succeeded in ramming the attacker they jumped up and down to signal his humiliation.

The attack teacher became more sophisticated later on and by 1942 the equipment was controlled by 'a team of charming and intelligent Wrens' under the direction of the equally charming Commander Teddy Woodward. Woodward, by then highly experienced in the ways of the enemy and the difficulties experienced in genuine attack, chose the target and its course of action. The perisher gave out orders for the submarine and the Wrens plotted everything on the chart table. It would begin with a Wren's voice, 'Control-room, control-room. You are a T-class submarine on patrol in the North Sea. Submarine's course one four five. Are you ready? Start the attack.' At the order 'Up periscope', a Wren unmasked the top lens to reveal 'the urgent sight of the *Scharnhorst* coming straight at me, or a merchant ship I cannot for the moment identify, or perhaps a U-boat whose angle on the bow is impossible at that range to judge'. At the end

of each attack everyone went upstairs to listen to Woodward pull
the candidate's tactics to pieces and analyse what had happened.

The second part of the course took place at sea in a real submarine. In 1935 this was the newly qualified Bryant's *H49*. The
perishers took turns to command the boat, manoeuvring it out
and then conducting attacks on a target ship. The practice submarine's commander had to hold himself back as the apprentices
got his boat into peril and only press the klaxon to dive if the
danger became acute. As Bryant noted, 'it was not difficult to get
the submarine into a position where it would get rammed by the
target; the way out of this trouble was to break off the attack and
go deep underneath it.' Each attack was recorded and analysed
afterwards. After a few weeks of practice the perishers began to
get used to manoeuvring and making estimations through the
periscope. They learned some of their own failings – a tendency
to under-estimate range might be revealed and remembered later
on when it mattered. Eventually the course examiner summoned
each candidate to his cabin and told him his fate.

Those who passed usually commanded one of the little 1919-
vintage H class training submarines for a few months, before
getting an appointment to a modern boat. Submarines regularly
made mock attacks on their depot ship but opportunities to practise attacks in simulated wartime conditions were rare. Shrimp
Simpson, who did a refresher course on the attack teacher in
1935, made his one and only practice attack on a capital ship the
following June. The 2nd Flotilla intercepted the battleships of the
Home Fleet as they sailed south from Scapa Flow with their protective screen of destroyers. The ideal range for a submarine
attack was 1000–1500 yards, within the destroyer screen which
was usually 2–3000 yards from the capital ships. The rules stated
that at over 1000 yards the submarine was to surface and signal
the target's course and speed. At under 1000 yards, it was to fire
a yellow signal flare but stay submerged until all ships were safely
past.

Simpson reckoned that these rules encouraged senior officers to discount and ignore submarine attacks. Determined that his attack should be noticed, he surfaced and signalled *Hood*'s course and speed from 250 yards off her beam. He saw with some foreboding that *Renown*, astern of *Hood*, had to alter course to ensure she missed him. As Simpson anticipated, his flotilla captain had to defend him against angry accusations of recklessness from the captains of *Hood* and *Renown*, but the commander-in-chief had been watching and judged that Simpson's attack had been safe. His assessment was, 'I adjudge *Hood* sunk. *L27* carried out a good attack of a type unsuited to peacetime exercises.'

These exercises were genuinely dangerous. The loquacious and energetic Hugh 'Dogberry' Dewhurst was captain of *Seahorse*, Hugh Mackenzie his first lieutenant and Joe Blamey chief engine room artificer when they took part in a similar exercise off the Firth of Forth. Dewhurst was penetrating the destroyer screen to make his attack when he took a quick all-round look with the attack periscope. 'I saw a look of horror flash across his face as he ordered, "Down periscope, Flood Q. Sixty feet. Shut watertight doors",' Mackenzie recalled. *Seahorse* had just begun to gain depth when there was a deafening roar overhead and a rumbling sound as the submarine shuddered slightly. Neither periscope could be moved. They were blind. They fired smoke candles, and after listening carefully, came to the surface. Both periscopes had been flattened. The destroyer *Foxhound* had not detected them with its asdic, had not spotted the periscope, and had very nearly sunk them by accident. They, for their part, had surfaced too early and had not identified the danger until it was very nearly too late.

Christopher Hutchinson, who qualified to command late in 1935, was another who regretted the lack of realistic exercise for submarines. He attributed this to the fact that several submarines had been lost in accidents related to exercises, so that for reasons of safety their participation in these simulations was limited. 'The captains of cruisers and battleships wanted as little to do with submarines as possible because they might be held responsible for any disaster' at a time when competition for promotion was intense. He found it incredible that submariners were never exposed to the sound of a depth charge, or schooled in how to survive a counter-attack. 'It was never drummed in to us that when you have finished an attack, as soon as you've fired you alter course to right or left so that destroyers can't follow the tor- pedo tracks. We were never taught to turn off course the moment you'd fired.' Hutchinson felt that 'the whole attitude towards submarines in peacetime was mistaken. They knew little about them, they cared less about them. They were things that got you into trouble. The wider navy rarely saw them in action.'

There was a general lack of understanding between sub- mariners and the main navy. The fact that the Admiralty was trying to abolish submarines to remove their potent menace to merchant ships in war, encouraged the British Submarine Service to fall back on its own resources. The image of submariners as dirty mechanics persisted, combining strangely with envy of their high pay and disapproval of their disregard for uniform and normal discipline. The danger that they posed to battleships com- pounded their unpopularity with the dominant gunnery branch, whose opinions submariners despised.

Non-submariners were alarmingly ignorant of the strengths and weaknesses of submarines. One reason for this was that whereas submarine officers were required periodically to serve in other types of vessel in order to keep in touch with developments elsewhere, the reverse was not the case. General service officers rarely served in submarines. In general service the only people with direct knowledge of submarines were former submariners who had gone on to other duties. In the end everyone came to regard the Submarine Service as 'a private navy', whose 'arcane mysteries were not for communication to outsiders – who in any case would not understand them'.

The naval staff consistently underrated the danger from sub- marines in their training exercises. Christopher Hutchinson remembered doing a tactical course at Portsmouth with a table- top war game. He manoeuvred his submarine into an attacking position 'and I fired four torpedoes at the *Hood* – I had previously served in *Hood* and knew how vulnerable she was. The umpires awarded me two hits on the *Hood* which reduced her speed by two knots. Two hits on the *Hood* would have had the crew swimming.' There were very few submarine specialists on the naval staff.

During this period the navy expanded steadily. It had contracted to under 90,000 men in 1932, but was up to 118,000 by 1938 and 129,000 in 1939. Including spare crews and those in training, submarine crews accounted for 270 officers and 2500 men. The general service crews of the depot ships and shore bases took the Submarine Service total to about 5000, but they were a tiny proportion of the whole. Rapid expansion of the navy depended on reservists as well as regulars. The Royal Naval Reserve (RNR) was for recently retired regulars and merchant seamen. There were 450 submariners in reserve, men who had left the navy after twelve years' service. Aston Piper was an officer in the merchant navy but the military navy appealed to him and he joined the Royal Naval Reserve as a midshipman. During a nine-month training course at Portland, learning asdic and the like, he 'did a day in a submarine and found it was most interesting work'. He decided to do the rest of his training in submarines and volunteered to join *Dolphin*, where he was pleased with what he learned. He was one of just twenty-three junior officers in reserve who were qualified in submarines.

The Royal Naval Volunteer Reserve catered for those without previous experience at sea. Jack Casemore grew up in Bromley, Kent. He left school at fourteen in 1935 and got a job as a messenger boy with the Field Press, eventually graduating to the editorial staff of the *Law Times*. In August 1938 he joined the RNVR, adding a year to his age. 'I knew there was going to be a war and it was about time the Germans were taught a lesson.' He did two weeks' training on the cruiser *Cumberland* and didn't enjoy it: 'there was so much bullshit on her, and as an ordinary seaman, you were the lowest of the low and the officers were gods. I promised myself there and then that, if possible, I would go for small ships where the officers were more human.'

In the Mediterranean the war clouds had never dispersed. Britain ducked out of a war over Abyssinia, but hardly had that threat receded when in 1936 civil war broke out in Spain. Both Italy and Germany backed the Nationalist rebels while Russia supported the Republican government. Many American volunteers helped the Republicans but powerful US corporations supplied the Nationalists. Britain was similarly divided. Senior naval figures were sympathetic to Franco's fascists, although much public opinion favoured the other side.

David Wanklyn, a solitary, conscientious, gangly youth two years older than Mackenzie who had also grown up in the Highlands, joined *Shark* late in 1936. Despite excellent exam results at Dartmouth, he had not enjoyed the choicest run of appointments and had missed out on China, but in the spring of 1937 Malta seemed a good second best. *Shark* spent only two days a week at sea and ashore it was a life of picnics, sailing and fishing for Wanklyn, a keen birdwatcher and photographer. That spring Wanklyn fell for Elspeth 'Betty' Kinloch. In the summer she returned home and *Shark* went with *Snapper* and *Sealion* to Gibraltar to protect British shipping against Spanish Nationalist submarines that everybody knew were really Italian. The S-boats exercised under the Atlas Mountains, chiefly playing 'clockwork mice', as submariners called their role when required to allow destroyers to practise hunting them with their asdic, and by spring 1938 were back in Malta.

The 1st Flotilla had a new captain in a brand-new depot ship, *Maidstone*. Philip Ruck-Keene was forty years old. From a clerical-naval family, he went to Haileybury and joined the navy late. 'He was a huge bull of a man with a ruddy countenance, bushy eyebrows and eyes so deep-set that it was impossible to see their colour,' wrote Bill King. 'He was a roarer. He roared with laughter, roared orders and roared his rage at any deviation from perfection. I found him hard as nails in resolve, flexible in action and, above all, realistic.' Bryant thought him 'the most forward-looking submariner between the wars'. To Simpson, four years his junior, Ruck-Keene was an old friend and mentor, his favourite sort of officer, not brought up at Dartmouth and not overburdened with veneration for tradition. 'He had a flair for knowing what mattered and putting things in their correct priority, and for cutting through time-wasting formality. He would tackle anybody or everybody who might be in a position to help, whilst rebuff or the annoyance of authority was flung off with a shrug.' Known as 'Ruckers', his preferred relaxation was rock-climbing. 'It's the greatest fun,' he told King, who loved walking up mountains, 'the only thing that ever makes me sweat with fear. You must try it ... '

One of Ruck-Keene's first acts was to tackle the Commander-in-Chief in the Mediterranean to allow night diving and night exercises without lights. These were things that Ben Bryant had never done before in all his eleven years in submarines, but while the 1st and 4th Flotillas trained for war, the home-based submarines lacked realistic preparation. Mackenzie, who was still with the Home Fleet, reckoned 'we were quite good at firing torpedoes and the technical side of how to conduct a patrol', but 'tactically, we had no training there'. He found it 'almost criminal that right up to the outbreak of war in any Fleet exercises, submarines were told to surface at sunset for safety reasons, and withdraw with navigation lights switched on until dawn. That was appalling – the enemy doesn't just withdraw from the war at sundown ... The Mediterranean submarine squadron had persuaded the C-in-C Med to alter the rules ... but, generally speaking, the old rule applied.'

Submariners preserved fond memories of Malta in those last two years before the war. There were weddings. A young lieutenant of *Clyde*, Ian McGeoch, had married the daughter of the vicar of Holy Trinity Sliema in December 1937. He was already engaged when he volunteered for submarines earlier in the year. The extra money had been one motive, although he was also keen on small boats and early command and 'had read most of the accounts of the operations of British submarines in WW1'. McGeoch was an enthusiastic theorist, and before Ruck-Keene took over he had already submitted a paper to the flotilla staff that advocated practising the firing of torpedoes at night. After the wedding ceremony, he walked with his bride through a tunnel formed by the raised swords of his colleagues in full dress. David Wanklyn was one of them, and in May Wanklyn and Betty followed McGeoch's example. 'There were dances at the club, parties night after night, bathing picnics by day and night, scandals and gossip, race meetings and games. The shadow of war caused no depression, Malta between the wars was gay, and gay it remained,' wrote Bryant, a spare officer in *Maidstone*.

The Treasury refused to complete D'Oyly-Hughes's underground submarine pens and, with Italian bombers minutes away, Malta was judged unsafe for the valuable *Maidstone*, so Ruck-Keene established a base in Fort Manoel, an old and largely derelict army barracks on Manoel Island in Valletta's second, smaller harbour. The submariners colonised Sliema, the town on the opposite side of their harbour from Valletta. The innumerable bars along the Sliema front were closest to them – only a short walk from the base, crossing the bridge that linked Manoel Island to the mainland and turning right along the waterfront. In the heart of Valletta itself was Strada Stretta, known to sailors as 'The Gut', with pubs, dancing and cheap food. Fat, jovial 'Malts' stood outside, shouting to passing gangs of sailors that their shipmates were already inside enjoying 'big eats', in order to draw them into the Lucky Wheel, the Egyptian Queen or the Silver Horseshoe (known as the 'Galvanised Donk'). All the bars had a good Maltese violinist playing classical music. The place had been a principal home to the Royal Navy for over a hundred years. British sailors liked Malta and for the most part Malta liked British sailors. There were clubs and canteens for every branch of the service.

In August 1938, at the time of Munich, the fleet mobilised for war. Marjorie Bryant returned to England and Ben took a flat in Sliema overlooking Lazaretto Creek. He shared it with Slasher Sladen, the rugby international, and Edward Bickford, who was in command of *Salmon*. Bryant himself had just taken over *Sealion*. Bickford was twenty-eight, four years younger than Bryant and five years junior to Sladen. Bill King, six months younger than Bickford, joined them after passing his perisher and being appointed to command *Snapper*. 'Bickie' was good looking, highly intelligent, energetic and determined. 'Drive on! Drive on! There is an eternity of rest to follow,' he urged them. He spent many wet winter afternoons marching along the windswept Dingli cliffs on the south of Malta, endlessly discussing tactics with Bryant. King found him 'a young man of unforgettable charm'. He became the group's spokesman. 'One day you will really need submarines,' Bickie told surface ship officers. 'If you neglect their proper training you won't have them for long.'

Exercises were more frequent now. They trained in stopping and searching merchant ships according to the requirements of maritime law. Should the merchant prove to be enemy property they were entitled to bring it into harbour as a prize. Shrimp Simpson, now captain of the minelayer *Porpoise*, took part in an exercise in which he repeatedly tried to stop and search a tanker before an RAF Anson responded to its distress call. Usually *Porpoise* failed even to get its boat into the water before the plane was overhead. The RAF's speed of response was impressive and Simpson feared that some people would conclude from these exercises that merchant shipping was safe within a hundred miles of the coast. He found the stop and search routine hopelessly impractical, and reckoned that since the Germans couldn't possibly succeed in arresting British ships by following the rules they would obviously break them.

In March 1939, with Captain S2 (the captain of the 2nd Submarine Flotilla) busy moving his headquarters into the new depot ship *Forth*, Simpson led the flotilla to Malta for the annual Mediterranean and Home Fleet combined exercises. Submarines were only involved in the last two exercises. Simpson drew up the orders for the first of these, in which five cruisers and thirty-six destroyers were to sail down a narrow channel while twelve submarines attempted to intercept them. Simpson reckoned *Thames* was so big she was likely to be detected, so he placed her alone to ambush the enemy as they entered the channel. After encountering *Thames* the enemy faced a sixty-mile blank in which Simpson hoped their asdic operators would get bored, before they reached his submarines deployed in two lines, four miles apart. On the day asdic conditions were very bad. *Thames* managed a successful undetected attack, and three hours later the other submarines all attacked. Only one was located and 'sunk' by the escort.

The second exercise pitted the submarines against the whole combined fleet. Simpson's opposite number in the 1st Flotilla, Willie Banks, planned this one, and sent in his S class submarines as a wolf pack on the surface at night. They fired red flares from Very pistols to represent torpedoes from ideal positions halfway inside the destroyer screen. Bickford 'torpedoed' the aircraft carrier *Courageous* with a full salvo and Bryant and King also distinguished themselves. According to Bryant, *Courageous* was adjudged to have lost a mere two knots in speed, while the ship that he 'torpedoed' refused to acknowledge any damage, her captain saying 'a submarine had no business to be on the surface, darkened, amongst the fleet at night.' The larger submarines had been held back from this night attack for fear of collision, so Simpson got no chance to attack. Next day fog caused the manoeuvres to be called off.

At the 'wash-up' conference at Gibraltar, Banks pointed out that the submarines had scored a hit rate of 22 per cent with their torpedoes. Rear-Admiral Destroyers admitted that even allowing for the bad conditions the screen's performance had been not only disappointing but alarming. Admiral Forbes fulminated that the war would be won with guns and Admiral Pound sat next to him saying nothing.

By now submariners had grown used to ignoring exercise adjudications in which their hits merely slowed targets down and they were sunk by destroyers they knew they had evaded. The staff worked only in the horizontal plane: if a destroyer positioned itself over a submarine it was adjudged to have sunk it. No allowance was made for depth, and since asdic could not pinpoint a target's depth this was a serious flaw. Bryant made his own private analysis of the results, obstinately believing that he and his colleagues had inflicted greater damage and had not been 'killed'. Had he believed what the staff said he would have lost all confidence in submarines and in any chance of surviving a real war.

Meanwhile, the submariners trained hard and played hard. Frequently, submarines were sent to Alexandria to be asdic targets for destroyers. Bryant found Alexandria 'a delightful place'. There was 'racing and golf at Smouha and the Sporting club, surfing at Sidi Bish, shooting on Lake Mazorin', and he 'used to hire a felucca to go fishing'. In the evening he played bridge with the keen-witted Levantine residents and 'round about midnight you would go off to one of the cabarets for which Alexandria was famous.' At the night clubs there were 'taxi dancers' of a most exclusive kind. 'Many were Hungarians, soignée to a degree, beautifully dressed, exceedingly decorative and inexorably expensive.' Paying for a dance was just the start – they wanted champagne, roses, toy monkeys ... Of course Bryant, a married man, was not interested in the ultimate prize. Nevertheless, he had a regular Hungarian friend at the Excelsior and took her to look at his submarine. She quickly aroused considerable curiosity in his messmates, who were 'leaning over the side and taking an unnecessary interest in our progress'. Once inside the sub, she had a fit of hysterical claustrophobia. Restraining her from bolting back up the ladder screaming (for fear of the joyfully hysterical reaction from his colleagues), Bryant forced a whisky down her throat and found to his inexpressible relief that it worked.

In Malta the three clubs, the Union, the Sliema Club and the

Marsa Sports Club, were much frequented, especially the Sliema's weekly dance on Saturdays. Ship's dances also occurred frequently and Admiral Geoffrey Layton's daughters Diana, aged twenty-five, and her eighteen-year-old sister Suzanne were usually invited. In those days it was customary for girls to go out with whoever asked them, with not much beyond the odd kiss permitted before an engagement was announced. Diana had several admirers. At first she was fond of the 'very smooth and attractive' Christopher Hutchinson, then serving in her father's flagship the *Hood*. But *Hood* went home in February and the morning the ship sailed the two girls walked to the end of the breakwater to wave goodbye. 'We were both in tears as the huge ship sailed past us, and many caps were waved in farewell. As she faded from sight, Diana turned to me, blew her nose, and asked: "Let me see: who are we going out with tonight?"'

The climax of Malta's social year was the carnival. At that time Diana's principal beau was Jimmy Prowse, who became first lieutenant of *Oswald*. Suzanne spent her time with the younger sub-lieutenants. Michael Kyrle-Pope, who became third hand of *Oswald*, was her favourite. Kyrle-Pope taught Suzanne to ride at the Marsa Club, they played squash and he joined family picnics and outings to race meetings and the opera.

Tension rose again in April when Italy annexed Albania. The fleet sailed to Alexandria, because Malta was considered too vulnerable to air attack from Italy. Admiral Layton decided the time had come for Diana to marry Prowse. Suzanne on the other hand received a surprise when Kyrle-Pope revealed he already had a fiancée in England, who eventually came out to Malta and married him in March 1940. Suzanne became engaged to an army officer and married him the following month.

Realising war was close, 'we all began cramming intensive enjoyment into the few weeks left,' recalled King. 'We went to sea at five each morning, dived, took part in an exercise, returned to an afternoon of golf, sun-bathing and squash, and in the evening we found swimming-pools, music and companions . . .

At midnight we had to be back on board so our evenings were conducted at a furious pace.' *Snapper* and *Salmon* were 'chummy ships' so Bickford was King's closest companion. 'We swam, laughed, drank together. The sun poured down. Our bodies turned mahogany, our ships grew ready. And well we knew the days were running out ...'

For the submariners back in Britain this last summer of urgent enjoyment was punctured by the *Thetis* disaster. Hugh Mackenzie was at a guest night dinner in Fort Blockhouse when he noticed senior officers silently getting up to leave. Quickly the whisper went round that *Thetis*, a new T class submarine crewed by several ex-Sharks who had followed their captain Sam Bolus into his latest command, had failed to surface after her trial dive in Liverpool Bay. Shrimp Simpson and his officers were also having dinner when Anthony Miers rushed in, ashen-faced. The competitive sportsman, now Staff Officer Submarines to the Home Fleet, told them *Porpoise* had to go to Liverpool at top speed. For David Wanklyn, now first lieutenant of *Porpoise*, it was old friends and shipmates who were in danger.

Syd Hart, finishing his submarine training course, found the atmosphere at Blockhouse was like having a severe illness in the family. Their anxious, 'Any news of the Thetis?' was answered by the headlines: 'Tappings heard by divers in Thetis!', then 'Faint tappings still heard in Thetis!', and finally 'All hope abandoned for 99 men still left in Thetis!' It was the first serious submarine accident since 1932.

It was an ominous reminder of the submarine crews' vulnerability, and this was just peacetime danger. War was imminent. Mackenzie had planned a holiday in France but suddenly foreign travel was banned. In Mackenzie's circle even the volunteers felt that 'we hadn't joined submarines to fight a war' and they calculated that 'our chances weren't going to be very good'. There were no gung-ho glory seekers among them. Mackenzie had formed a close friendship with Edward Tomkinson, who had just done his perisher and was at Blockhouse as instructional lieutenant, commanding one of the boats used by trainees. 'Tommo', tongue in cheek, gave them their orders: 'no medals, no tombstones'. It became their catchphrase. However, there were others among the professional sailors, like Bryant, for whom war meant 'the climax of all that for which I had been training for so many years ... This was the war I had been trained to fight; I was in command of my chosen weapon; no man could ask for more.' His Mediterranean flotilla felt especially well-prepared and confident.

In mid-August 1939 the 2nd Flotilla submarines were suddenly recalled to their base at Dundee. The minelayers *Cachalot* and *Porpoise* embarked torpedo warheads and sailed for Portsmouth, 'where we again embarked our mines, left the previous October after Munich'. Told to be ready to sail at midnight for Malta, Simpson went to get his sailing orders from Captain S5, a Great War veteran and Simpson's first CO. Cyril Coltart's 'slick cynicism' and 'outward flippancy' had always puzzled Simpson. On this occasion he was greeted with, 'Ah, Shrimp, how nice to see you, but I can't spare a moment now.' Coltart put on a sports jacket. 'I'm off to Bishop's Waltham. Since it is obvious that war is about to be declared I must deal with first things first, so I am off home to help my dear wife to "black out" our pet white rabbit, Alice. I had difficulty in finding the necessary black rinse, but I have it at last. I have written your sailing orders and I shall be back this evening. Come and see me at 10 pm.'

When Simpson returned, Coltart offered him a chair. 'At once I sensed that I was talking to quite a different man. All that veneer of inconsequential jollity was gone and I was talking to a person I had never guessed existed.'

Coltart began, 'I want to help you with all those things that come to mind from my war experience. From the time you clear the Solent the war has started for you. The Germans may not wait for any declaration of war and you may be sure their submarines are already on patrol. You must assume you are already liable to attack. Off every focal point such as Ushant, Finisterre, Cape St Vincent, zigzag and be instantly ready to dive. Use your week on passage to Malta so that you feel confident that you can meet any situation you can think of and in particular defeat air attack by swift diving.' Coltart continued to deliver sound practical advice for some time and then paused.

'After the last war I swore that if there was ever to be another I would be the officer who said, "And you might switch off the light."' Since Simpson was likely soon to be commanding a flotilla, Coltart advised him, 'I beg you to take some trouble over giving your commanding officers that encouragement and sympathetic understanding that will give them confidence in you and in your interest in their affairs when they are out on patrol.' He explained that the phrase 'You might switch off the light' had stuck in his mind in 1917. Boats then sailed from Blyth after midnight and captains had orders to report to Commander (S) before sailing:

I would go up to Shanks Willis's cabin in *Titania* and knock on the door, and knock at intervals of five seconds until there was a grunt of, 'Come in, who's that?'

'Coltart, sir.'

'What do you want?'

'I'm sailing for patrol in ten minutes.'

'Oh – where to?'

'Well, sir, you have told me to spend the next three weeks forty miles N.N.W. of Heligoland.'

'Oh, yes, an excellent patrol position – by the way what's the weather like?'

'N.E. gale blowing, sir. It's snowing rather hard and the visibility is 200 yards.'

'Oh, yes, well plug into it. I say, you might switch off the light!'

6

TOTAL GERMANY

As Simpson sailed *Porpoise* for Malta other submarines were already on patrol. Five boats, each at a distance of twelve miles from the next, formed a reconnaissance line stretching westward into the North Sea from Obrestad in the south of Norway to spot and intercept warships or U-boats leaving for the Atlantic. It should have been a Coastal Command job, but their Anson patrol aircraft did not have the range to fly to the Norwegian coast and back again. Consequently submarines had to cover the sixty miles of sea nearest Norway. Their orders were to report enemy warships, which they were not to attack if doing so might prevent them sending a report. *Sturgeon* was one of them. With his shipmates, Norman Drury had rushed to get war stores on board – torpedo warheads and live three-inch and machine-gun ammunition. On the last day of August they watched the liner *Bremen* sail by, pride of the German merchant fleet. She was the only ship they saw, because the German war-ships had already sailed.

'Colonel' George Menzies, until recently captain of *Regulus*, was driving Rear-Admiral Bertram Watson the 488 miles from Gosport to Corriemar House, Aberdour. He had learned a week earlier 'that my job will be to mess about on R.A. (S) [Rear-Admiral Submarines'] staff. What a fate; though the man is charming.' The charming Watson had at last completed arrangements to take over a new base, not far from the headquarters of the Home Fleet at Rosyth and convenient for liaison with the RAF Coastal Command Area HQ. His administrative staff remained at Fort Blockhouse.

Watson controlled his submarines under orders from Sir Charles Forbes, Commander of the Home Fleet, and with occasional injunctions from various other masters, notably First Lord of the Admiralty Winston Churchill and First Sea Lord Sir Dudley Pound. In September 1939 the most powerful flotilla under Watson's direct control was the 2nd with the depot ship *Forth* based at Dundee. This comprised 7 S class, the new T class *Triumph* and the old and unreliable *Oxley*, fresh from reserve. Two more T class would soon join after sea trials. A smaller 6th Flotilla under Jock Bethell was based on *Titania* at Blyth, consisting of three new U class, two ancient L class and the 1918-vintage *H32*. Watson had eight more H class training submarines, as well as *Sunfish* and *Oberon*, at Gosport, Portland and Sheerness, and twelve T class boats building, all attached to Cyril Coltart's 5th Flotilla.

The distant flotillas got their orders from the local commanders-in-chief. At Gibraltar were the large, fast *Clyde* and *Severn*. The 4th Flotilla at Singapore and Hong Kong was fifteen strong and the minelayer *Seal* was at Aden on her way to join it. At Malta the 1st Flotilla comprised two minelayers, 4 S-boats and 3 Os. The deployment anticipated the possibility that Japan might declare war and that Italy might follow suit.

One major British weakness was intelligence. In the First World War naval intelligence had been a great strength and cryptanalysis had contributed significantly to the defeat of the U-boats, but the intelligence department had been neglected since 1918. In 1939 the highly gifted John Godfrey was appointed Director of Naval Intelligence. He established an Operational Intelligence Centre

(OIC) under Jock Clayton to analyse and disseminate intelligence and recruited veterans of the Great War intelligence department to re-establish specialised units. The Government Code and Cipher School, based at Bletchley Park, was now in charge of cryptanalysis but its staff at the beginning of the war was small. A handful of the Bletchley Park naval section remained with the OIC for liaison. In August 1939 the OIC had a staff of thirty-six. It quickly expanded its facilities for DF (direction finding – the pinpointing of enemy radio broadcasts by taking bearings) and for 'Y' (listening in to enemy radio broadcasts) by recruiting Wrens and there was a sudden demand for German and Italian speakers. The organisation of intelligence eventually became highly efficient, but it started from a very small base and took considerable time to expand, improve its methods, make breakthroughs and win trust.

The most regrettable defect in intelligence was a lack of air reconnaissance. This had been the RAF's lowest priority. They did not even have the wherewithal to assess the effects of bombing, never mind provide the sort of evidence needed for naval operations. It was Godfrey, rather than the RAF, who invented a Photographic Reconnaissance Unit. Training in ship recognition was very limited. Coastal Command had been starved of resources for years and Admiral Forbes had no control over any planes except the sadly inadequate fighter-bombers of the Fleet Air Arm.

The Germans started several steps ahead. Their aerial reconnaissance was good and at the outset of the war, whereas the British had no insight into German naval codes, the German B-Dienst had penetrated the British naval cipher and was sometimes reading British communications quickly enough to use the knowledge operationally to attack or avoid British vessels.

On 3 September 1939 the Admiralty's first responsibility was to get to their ships the information that war had been declared. For those at sea this meant a coded radio broadcast. Messages were sent to the powerful transmission centre at Rugby. Even the commander at Singapore, sending a message to one of his boats, sent it enciphered by secure ocean cable to Rugby. Rugby broadcast at a routine time every four hours, so the message would reach the submarine at the next scheduled transmission, four hours at most after the time of origin (assuming nothing went wrong). The shore transmitting stations were powerful enough for a submarine to receive their messages while submerged, but they needed to be near the surface at periscope depth.

The declaration of war was timed to coincide with the routine transmission at 1100. So it was that Norman Drury was at his set in *Sturgeon* that Sunday morning, 'sitting there with the operator listening to Rugby calling, "All ships, all ships ... " and three minutes past eleven he made the call sign "All ships from Rugby. Most immediate. Total Germany, repetition Total Germany" and the time of origin was eleven o'clock'.

It did not go so smoothly in all boats. *Spearfish* had just been ordered to change her position and was running along on the surface, zigzagging just in case, on a crisp, clear day. Her captain was John Eaden, the son of a planter, who had lived as a small child among bananas and sugar cane in Dominica before prep school and Dartmouth and holidays with his grandparents, dogs and ponies. In China he had been a shipmate of Bill King in *Orpheus*. 'I had just remarked to my first lieutenant Donald Pirie that it was a lovely day and asked him if he could smell the scent of the pine woods off the Norwegian coast,' recalled Eaden, when they spotted bubbles off the starboard beam. For a moment they thought it was a porpoise, then Eaden ordered hard-a-starboard and a torpedo passed fifty feet ahead of them. For the British it was the first shot of the war. Eaden pressed the klaxon for a crash dive and was met in the control room by his petty officer telegraphist, who told him that an important signal had just arrived. *Spearfish* and *U20* stalked each other for some hours before losing contact. When he came home Eaden complained in a broadcast for the BBC that his signal had not been issued until 1117, seventeen minutes after the war had started.

Severn was on her way to Freetown to oppose German raiders

in the South Atlantic. Ian McGeoch was on the bridge and skipper Willie Banks was having a shower 'when the chief petty officer
telegraphist climbed the conning tower ladder and emerged, looking somewhat less glum than he usually did. In his hand was a pink
signal form which he gave to the officer of the watch. "We are
now at war with Germany, sir," he said. "I've informed the captain".' The excitement evaporated quickly. They spent four
months based at Freetown without sighting a German ship.

At Malta too there was frustration. They listened to the Prime
Minister's broadcast and waited in case the Italians joined in.
Bryant studied the static patrol 'billets' issued by the staff with disapproval. He wanted areas within which he could roam, not
immobility.

On the China station Alastair Mars had been playing tennis at
the United Services Recreation Club in Kowloon. A lieutenant
of well-manicured good looks, he had showered and was sitting
'over a whisky and soda when Signalman Cheale rang up from
the *Regulus* to inform me that hostilities had just commenced
against Germany but not Japan'. Peter Bartlett, captain of *Perseus*,
similarly,

> was in the Club having a drink when my first lieutenant tele-
> phoned to say that the signal 'TOTAL GERMANY' had been
> received, which meant that war was declared. I came back into
> the bar and told everyone present, but there did not seem to
> be much else to do but to go to a Chinese restaurant and have
> a good meal. The following morning the Commodore obvi-
> ously felt that, with the Commander-in-Chief maintaining
> wireless silence, it was up to him to do something, so we were
> all told to establish a patrol line east of Formosa, to try and
> intercept one of the German liners which had left Manila for
> Yokohama.

Aston Piper was chief officer in SS *Baltraffic* of the United
Baltic steamship line. Late in August the Admiralty flashed all

merchant ships, telling them not to return home as normal through the Kiel Canal but to use the Skagerrak. Having thus narrowly escaped internment Piper arrived back in Hull, where he found his fiancée Kathleen and a priority telegram instructing him to join *Dolphin*. First they went home to Harwich and got married. Four days later he reported to *Dolphin* and received instructions to join *Ursula* at Blyth as navigating officer. Royal Naval Reserve officers joining submarines were almost always made navigator, their navigational expertise usually being superior to that of young regulars.

Out at sea submarines glimpsed U-boats and trawlers and little else, but both sides began to suffer the teething troubles of war. The Germans had sent every available U-boat to sea and *U30* torpedoed the passenger liner *Athenia* on the first day. U-boats had orders to follow international law, which required them to stop and search merchant vessels, but *U30* mistook *Athenia* for an armed merchant cruiser. One hundred and twelve civilians died, including twenty-eight US citizens. More mistakes followed. On 6 September the RAF attacked both *Sturgeon* and *Seahorse*.

Then, a week into the war, came the Submarine Service's first kill. Pat Steel in *Triton*, fresh from her sea trials, was charging his batteries on the surface on a dark, drizzly night. He was about two miles from his billet off Obrestad, but four miles within his box. Each submarine had a square twelve miles wide to operate in, with their proper billet in the centre.

The officer on watch called Steel to the bridge because he could see a submarine. Coming from the bright light below, Steel could at first see nothing. Then he made it out. For a moment he wondered whether it might be his neighbour *Oxley*, but they had communicated earlier in the day and Steel had given *Oxley* his position and course. He manoeuvred himself into a firing position, readied two of *Triton*'s ten tubes and got the sights on. The signaller flashed the challenge in Morse with his Aldis lamp. After two repetitions there was still no answer. The signaller fired a rifle grenade which burst as three green flares. By now Steel was convinced the submarine was hostile and it was only a matter of time before it would torpedo *Triton*. He counted slowly to fifteen and fired. As the torpedoes sped towards the target, they could see something like a torch on the other bridge. Then the target exploded. Steel took a bearing and approached. 'Very soon we heard cries for help and as we came closer we actually heard the word "Help". There were three men swimming. I manoeuvred the ship to the best of my ability to close the men and kept Aldis lights on.' First lieutenant Jumbo Watkins and another officer attached lines to themselves, and dived into the oil to haul in Lieutenant Commander Bowerman and *Oxley*'s lookout. Lieutenant Manley was seen swimming strongly in the light of an Aldis and then suddenly disappeared. The other fifty-eight crewmen died in the boat.

Bowerman had only been called to *Oxley*'s bridge when the grenade was fired. Their own grenade failed to work and they were looking for another when the torpedo struck. Manley, the navigator, had been on watch. He told Bowerman he had answered the challenge, but Bowerman was not convinced and accepted Steel's version of events. *Oxley*'s recognition grenades were of 1917 vintage and proved unreliable. The enquiry into the loss of *Oxley* found that her navigation and watchkeeping were both at fault and exonerated Steel. The disaster was hushed up to prevent public outcry, but submariners soon knew. In future, boats on the 'Obrestad line' were placed sixteen miles apart.

Four days later in the grey dawn, as she set out from Dundee to begin a second spell on the Obrestad line, *Sturgeon*'s lookouts spotted a submarine on the surface in a position where no British submarine was supposed to be. David Gregory, *Sturgeon*'s tall Glaswegian captain, fired three torpedoes. The other submarine was in fact *Swordfish*. Leslie Bennington, the former able seaman, was on watch. He spotted *Sturgeon* and gave the order to dive and alter course without calling for the captain. The torpedoes passed over and exploded in shallow water. Flushed with enthusiasm, Gregory claimed a kill and was shocked when he was told what had happened. It was not his fault. The staff had neglected both to tell *Sturgeon* that *Swordfish* was inbound from patrol and to tell *Swordfish* that *Sturgeon* was outbound. *Swordfish* had had to alter course to avoid a British convoy and was not where she should have been. *Seahorse*, next to leave Dundee, was again bombed and missed by Coastal Command.

George Menzies confided his anxieties to his diary. In the first fortnight of fighting he noted down three separate complaints about the staff. Having started the war doing the job of aircraft, the service was now contending with orders which treated submarines as if they were fast surface ships. The staff of Sir Charles Forbes, Commander of the Home Fleet, ordered the 6th Flotilla out all at once and then brought them back all at once, so that for weeks there was nothing on patrol. Then they placed the crew at two hours' notice so they got no leave and couldn't carry out proper maintenance of their boats. Forbes's staff did not understand that submarines worked differently from surface ships, needing rolling reinforcement so that there were always some boats on patrol, and crews could rest when they were not at sea. Gradually, improvements were made. When close to base, submarines were escorted by surface ships to shield them from ramming by friendly ships and bombing by friendly aircraft. Finally, the order to report first and attack afterwards was rescinded.

The surface fleet too was having problems. With sublime confidence in the effectiveness of aircraft and asdic, someone had the inspired idea of sending aircraft carriers to hunt U-boats. On 14 September *Ark Royal* sent her antique Swordfish biplanes to answer a distress call from a merchantman. In dive-bombing the U-boat that had attacked the merchantman two of them were caught by the blast from their own bombs and crashed. Meanwhile, a second U-boat torpedoed the *Ark Royal* but the torpedoes missed astern and the U-boat was hunted down by the destroyer escort. Three days later the Germans had better luck. In very similar circumstances *Courageous* was torpedoed by one

U-boat while her Swordfish hunted another. She sank with the loss of 519 men and many of her 48 aircraft.

Churchill was a great enthusiast for hunting U-boats and so was veteran submariner Martin Dunbar-Nasmith, now in charge of the Western Approaches. Another idea they tried was to send out the trawler *Tamura*, commanded by former submariner William 'Tiny' Fell, backed by *H34*. The trawler was to lure a U-boat into attacking it with its gun and then *H34* would torpedo the U-boat. Remarkably, the ruse worked – except that *H34* missed.

By then the first British submarine had found out what it was like to be depth-charged. In the early weeks of the war the trawlers recruited by the Germans for anti-submarine work were unarmed. But by the third week in September the fishermen and their naval colleagues had received the very sensitive hydrophones developed by Germany, which worked best when stopped. With these they received a primitive echo-ranging device that could be used to home in once the hydrophones had got a bearing on a target. At the same time they were armed with guns and depth charges.

On 24 September Eaden and *Spearfish* became their first victims. Submariners had never had any practice with depth charges, so nobody knew what the sound or the experience would be like. The Obrestad line had been abandoned and the submarines sent further south. *Spearfish* had been ordered into the shallow water of Horns Reef, off the west coast of Denmark, to investigate a mysterious buoy which might mark a swept passage through the great defensive minefield known to Germans as the 'West Wall' and to the British as the 'Cabbage Patch'. In this area mysterious noises had been heard under water that nobody could identify. They went 'zump, zump, zump, zump, zump', like distant explosions. The sparkers called them 'North Sea farts'. They feared some sort of unknown anti-submarine device.

Soon after their dawn dive that Sunday *Spearfish*'s telegraphists picked up engine noise on their hydrophones. In the shallows they had had to raise their asdic dome and their basic hydrophones were not good. There was a loud explosion, so Eaden went to the bottom and lay still. They moved a little and there was another explosion. It became evident that *Spearfish* was being hunted, but they couldn't tell how far away the explosions were. In the early afternoon the enemy got excited by some false contact and dropped lots of charges. Then at 1720 Eaden heard something that sounded like a grapnel being dragged across the aft end. There was a bump on the after casing, a series of further bumps and a massive explosion.

This time there was more than noise. 'The whole ship seemed to spring inwards and then out again.' All the lights and the glass shades smashed and in the darkness there was the sound of spurting water and the hiss of escaping air. Eaden sat there for a moment expecting a wall of water, but the men posted astern reported bad leaks in the engine room but no immediate danger. After reading patrol reports from the First World War, Eaden had had wooden plugs of various sizes made for a moment like this, and the plugs saved them. Charges still came down but none so close. Then they stopped. Eaden handed out a tot of rum all round.

The air was foul. Several men were breathing heavily. They had violent headaches and it was difficult to think clearly. Eaden mustered the crew, congratulated them on their work and told them he was going to try to surface at 2030. There was a danger the ballast tanks might collapse when he blew them and when they reached the surface the trawlers might be waiting for them. The gun's crew readied themselves to fight and the stokers put the sensitive papers and code books under the bilge plates in the machinery room. They placed a demolition charge, angled two Mark VIII torpedoes to ninety degrees and prepared the others. The two oldest ratings were unconscious. Then Eaden blew the tanks. They held, *Spearfish* surfaced and the coast was clear.

However, she could barely move on her one sound electric motor. Her wireless wouldn't work and her periscopes were smashed. The hull was leaking badly, so there was no question of diving again and they were just north of Wilhelmshaven. By day-break Stan Peel and his engineers had repaired her two diesels and patched up the hull, while the sparkers had got the set to trans-mit. They sent a position and a report. Next day the RAF found her and destroyers reached her by midnight, with a much larger force behind. *Spearfish* reached Rosyth on 26 September and went into dock until early March.

Targets for the submarines were very rare. On 6 October *Seawolf* got off a distant shot at the *Nürnberg* but missed. Over the next three days a battle group led by the *Gneisenau* made a sortie. There were nine submarines in the area but they saw nothing. On 14 October David Gregory in *Sturgeon* fired three torpedoes at one of the little U-boats they called 'North Sea ducks'. He thought he had hit it, but once again he was wrong. Rear-Admiral Watson issued orders that U-boats were worth a full salvo of six torpedoes.

Then came the terrible news that a U-boat had penetrated Scapa Flow and sunk the *Royal Oak*. Faced with another humil-iation, First Lord Churchill was frustrated that British submarines were not even attempting anything so daring. Two Polish sub-marines had managed to make it through the narrows and the intensive German defences that guarded the entrance to the Baltic in order to escape to Britain, yet Watson dared not send his submarines to the Kattegat (the sea between Denmark and Sweden, leading to the Baltic), or so it appeared to the belliger-ent First Lord. At the end of the month a U-boat claimed to have hit the battleship *Nelson* with three torpedoes which, by amaz-ing good fortune, failed to explode. Asdic was not proving to be the wonder weapon it was supposed to be, and there were clearly not enough destroyers to guard capital ships.

During October Forbes, Watson and the Admiralty held dis-cussions about the use of submarines. Dunbar-Nasmith at Western Approaches wanted a flotilla of them to hunt U-boats. With pocket battleships on the loose in the Atlantic it was suggested that submarines might be attached to convoys to sink anything that attacked them. The Commander-in-Chief North Atlantic wanted submarines to watch the Spanish ports to which German merchant ships had fled. The Commander-in-Chief West Indies wanted submarines to sink raiders. The First Lord demanded attacks. Churchill wanted to cut the supply of iron ore from Sweden to Germany and he had a pet 'Plan Catherine' for battleships to blast through to the Baltic, followed by a flotilla of submarines to hunt in the sea where they had done so well in the Great War.

So the submarines were reorganised. The minelayers and S-boats had returned from Malta, although *Snapper* and *Porpoise* had to go into dock for repairs. A new 3rd Flotilla was set up at Harwich under Ruck-Keene and Simpson with eight S-boats. The Germans had started air raids and neither Dundee nor Blyth had anti-aircraft defences, so the 2nd and 6th Flotillas had retired to Rosyth. The 2nd now had five of the new T-boats plus the two Polish submarines, while Jock Bethell's 6th had *Sturgeon*, *Starfish*, *Swordfish* and *Seahorse*, three U-class and *L23*. Three minelayers were sent to Halifax, Nova Scotia for convoy duty. The 6th Flotilla was earmarked for 'Plan Catherine', but for now was ordered to try to interrupt the flow of iron ore. However, the restraints imposed for political reasons made the task more or less impossible, since the ships could only be stopped and searched if they strayed out of neutral waters.

Sturgeon sailed for her third patrol on 9 November. Off Heligoland they heard the eerie 'North Sea farts' that they suspected might be some acoustic ranging device. Then they saw three trawlers stopped, listening for them. Gregory decided the vessels were less dangerous when in motion, so to make them move he fired a torpedo at them and one blew up spectacularly. The *Gauleiter Telschow* was the first enemy ship, or rather boat, sunk by a British submarine in the Second World War. Next day *Scharnhorst*, *Gneisenau*, *Köln Leipzig* and three destroyers sailed past *Sturgeon* without being seen. The battle group was undetected until it sank the *Rawalpindi*. Every available submarine was placed to trap the Germans as they returned to port, but again they just sailed by.

This was the final straw for First Lord Churchill. He summoned Watson to a meeting with Forbes and Pound and gave him 'a rucking'. Watson was sacked. Menzies noted that 'it may have happened a little because of his good and correct disinclination to press the submarines in too quickly'. Conscious of the deficiencies of peacetime training, Watson felt his commanders and crews needed to learn before being given the deadliest missions. Churchill disagreed. What neither of them knew was that the Germans had broken the British naval codes and radio intercepts were sometimes revealing the positions of British submarines. *Scharnhorst*'s battle group was 'almost certainly' able to evade the waiting submarines because they knew where they were.

On 9 December Churchill wrote to Max Horton and offered him Watson's job. Horton was in the Orkneys commanding the Northern Patrol, which had also missed the raiders because the Germans knew his dispositions. Horton was delighted, writing to a friend, 'Always told you when things got bad I hoped they would send for me, and it looks like they have done it. I am so happy, happy, happy at the prospect of what lies ahead. I am almost falling over myself with excitement. I haven't forgotten all I knew and I hope to bring them luck anyway.'

Their luck was already changing. Early in November the ancient *Cyclops*, depot ship of the 3rd Flotilla, berthed at Harwich and Philip Ruck-Keene explained his plans to convert Parkeston Quay into a modern submarine base within three weeks. He had been told there was no labour available to make the base self-sufficient and that boats would have to go to Sheerness for repairs. He wasn't having that. The railway made available its workshops opposite the *Cyclops* and Ruck-Keene advertised for skilled labour for jobs 'of national importance', getting 1400 replies for 120 posts. He put Simpson in charge of entertaining the crews, ordering him to convert a warehouse into a theatre, get three billiard tables donated to a good cause, and arrange with cinemas and pubs a system for recalling seamen to their boat at one hour's notice. Ruck-Keene's beautiful niece Thelma came from London to be organising secretary. At the end of the month the crews of five S-boats moved in. *Salmon*, on her second patrol, became the test for Simpson's recall arrangements. At 10 p.m. on 2 December the cinemas and bars in Harwich called for *Salmon*'s crew to return on board immediately. An hour later *Salmon* sailed.

Two days after that the first lieutenant spotted what looked like a floating box, except that it didn't rise and fall with the waves. He called Edward Bickford and they agreed it was a U-boat. The attack angle was bad and Bickford eventually fired his salvo at 5000 yards, with one torpedo breaking surface and *Salmon* nose up. They regained trim in time to see a submarine blown 200 feet into the air. When *Sturgeon* had attacked the same U-boat a torpedo had run directly underneath. Bickford's were set to run at only eight feet below the surface. They were learning.

A week later *Salmon*'s asdic operator picked up HE – hydrophone effect, the sound of another vessel's engine – and through the periscope Bickie saw the *Bremen* crossing his stern 2000 yards away. She looked no different from when he had gone to America in her in 1933 and there was no sign of any weapons that would allow him to sink her. He surfaced and ordered her to stop, flashing 'K international' in Morse code with the Aldis lamp. *Bremen* ignored the signal and sped away. Bickford was about to fire across her bows when a German bomber forced him under.

Reckoning it dangerous to stay where he was, Bickford left his patrol area and struck lucky. If the Germans were basing their movements on the known position of British submarines this was just what he had to do. In any case, next morning his first lieu-tenant spotted a number of ships about seven miles away. It was an enemy battle group. A change of direction brought the cruisers in range and at 5000 yards Bickford fired a full salvo on a wide spread 'with the object of winging two ships rather than sinking one, hoping thus to provoke a fleet action'. He reckoned to have hit the *Leipzig* and possibly another. Once the counter-attacks had stopped and they were safely away he 'spliced the mainbrace' to celebrate.

Next day George Phillips in *Ursula* ambushed the same group. It was Aston Piper's first patrol as navigator and his fear was suppressed by his job of keeping a detailed record of exactly where *Ursula* was. Phillips fired at a cruiser and immediately went deep and into silent routine, with no speaking, and no walking on the metal plates. They heard two loud bangs and the asdic operator whispered that he could hear breaking-up noises. There was no counter-attack. Tense but elated, they retreated and signalled their success, which was announced immediately on national radio. Unfortunately, at the last second a destroyer had got in the way and saved what would have been the total destruction of *Leipzig*. But Bickford had damaged the ship so severely that she never fought again, and he also hit the *Nürnberg*, putting her out of action for months.

Thinking they had sunk two cruisers, at submarine head-quarters at Aberdour 'all was happiness' even though it was too late for Watson. American photographers surrounded Bickford on his return for an article in *Life* magazine. It was just what Churchill had been waiting for. For what was rightly termed an 'epic patrol', officers and men were generously decorated and promoted. Bickford was immediately made commander over the heads of thirty senior lieutenant commanders (including Bryant).

However, Bickford was not universally popular. When he reported the *Bremen* incident the Admiralty released the story for positive propaganda, but the British press was furious that Bickford had let *Bremen* go after the Germans had torpedoed *Athenia* and other ships, for by early December they had abandoned any pretence of abiding by international law. It was hard on Bickford, whose clear orders not to sink the *Bremen* conflicted with his own instincts. He told King, 'I itched, I just itched to torpedo her without surfacing – I'd travelled on the blooming ship as a passenger. I knew her the instant I saw her. Talk about *temptation*.'

In several submarines Christmas was spent at sea. *Sealion* had decorations up and the troops wore paper hats and raced clockwork cars over the battery boards. David Gregory put *Sturgeon* on the bottom of the sea at 100 feet to have a quiet day. He conducted a service and they sang carols. They received a signed Christmas card from the King and Queen. The ward room had brandy and donated some to the Christmas pudding, but they failed to set it alight because there wasn't enough oxygen.

On Boxing Day first lieutenant Leslie Bennington was on watch in his new boat *Triumph* on a dark night when he saw a mine floating just ahead. There was no time to avoid it, so he gave an order to turn in so as to take it on the bow, away from the pressure hull. He gambled that the safety arrangements would prevent the torpedoes detonating and by a miracle they didn't, though they were all lost or damaged. The forward bulkhead held and the radio worked well enough to get a message home. They limped off very slowly, running the pumps with a large section of the bow blown off. Just as an enemy bomber spotted them, Coastal Command Beauforts arrived on the scene and drove it off. They drove off another attacker before destroyers arrived to escort *Triumph* home. She spent the next months in dock but the crew survived.

They were the lucky ones. When Max Horton arrived at Aberdour on 9 January there was an air of gloom over the place. 'The Germans announced on Thursday at a press conference in Berlin that they had sunk a British submarine,' he wrote, 'and I am almost sure this is true. It happened the day before I joined, I think, and this is not the only cause of my anxiety either.' *Seahorse* became overdue the day after he arrived. *Undine* and *Starfish* followed on 12 January. The Germans announced their destruction and the capture of their crews on 16 January. Both had followed Gregory's example in ordering torpedo attacks on anti-submarine vessels. Thanks to a breakdown in communication *Starfish* had not actually fired; *Undine* missed. Both were hunted down in shallow water. *Seahorse*'s loss remains mysterious. She was possibly mined but the German 1st Minesweeping Flotilla claimed a kill after a long attack on an unidentified submarine on 7 January. Horton suspected the existence of some secret weapon or trap in the Heligoland Bight and stopped patrolling there.

The loss of half of one flotilla in a week was a terrible shock. Norman Drury could barely believe it: 'We had three submarines at sea and lost all three in one weekend, three from our flotilla and we lost the lot. We got a pep talk from Admiral Submarines who came over and said, "I promise you this won't happen again."' The officers were warned not to attack the small craft that the Germans were apparently using as bait – these being worthless targets, difficult to hit and dangerous if missed.

However, it is now known that the trawlers were not there by accident. They were ordered to those positions specifically and it is almost certain that this was on the basis of information gathered by the B-Dienst, the radio intercept service. The German secret weapon was intelligence.

7

FIRST PATROLS

What was it like? This was the question on the lips of Lancashire stoker Syd Hart and his fellow Triads when during October 1939 they arrived at the 2nd Flotilla depot ship *Forth*, moored off Rosyth. Soon after he finished his submarine training Hart was appointed to the *Triad*, which was being built by Vickers-Armstrong at Barrow. He was met off the train by coxswain Walter Holmes. His was a crucial role. As Charles Anscomb put it, 'If you're a submarine cox'n you're a bit of everything. Routine and discipline, victualling and first aid, they are all your province. You're not just a helmsman. You're a sort of cornerstone of the ship, a go-between linking officers and men.' As coxswain, Holmes was in charge of the welfare and discipline of the crew and had fixed Hart up with digs shared with a leading stoker, Gilbert Quick, a 35-year-old Bristolian. For Syd Hart and his fellow stokers, the war started in The Travellers, better known as The Submariner's Arms, in Dalton Road, Barrow. Nothing changed after Neville Chamberlain's announcement on 3 September except that 'maybe the drinks were consumed at a faster rate'.

Triad went through her trials. Arriving in *Forth* they heard from other crews 'hair-raising stories of crash-dives, of the resounding BRA ... M of bombs as their submarines had hurled themselves down into the depths, beating the bombs by seconds'.

Now their steaming kits were packed, they had loaded torpedoes, ammunition and vast stores of fresh and tinned provisions into the submarine from *Forth*, their newly built and fairly comfortable depot ship. They spent the last two hours on *Forth*'s mess-deck playing 'Shoot'. Second coxwain Frank Johnson, a 28-year-old from Harleston in Norfolk, handed out next of kin forms to be submitted at the Submarine Office before sailing. Stoker 'Geordie' Thompson filled in his home address as 'No place, Nr. Newcastle'. Then it was across the narrow gang plank from *Forth* to *Triad*, steaming kits through a narrow hatch and down through the engine room and the motor room to the stokers' mess right aft. Crammed with fifty-three bodies and their baggage, *Triad* looked 'like any London Tube at the rush hour'. The stokers readied the engine, although the submarine manoeuvred out of port on its electric motors, with coxswain Holmes at the wheel on the bridge doing the delicate steering out of the confined space and repeating verbal orders. Their order to start, 'Half ahead, both', came by telegraph, a hand-operated dial in the control room with pointers to the speeds slow, half or full, and ahead or astern. The telegraphs had repeaters in the motor room and engine room.

Lieutenant Commander Ronald Jonas's patrol orders gave him a detailed route, accounts of the whereabouts of British shipping and submarines and whatever enemy reports were available. Patrol positions were in lettered zones and details were provided of who would relieve whom. 'Friendly fire' incidents were very frequent – almost every boat avoided RAF bombs or over-enthusiastic attempts to ram at least once. Eventually submarines were given an escort out of coastal waters and thereafter sailed within a moving box, inside which friendly planes were told not to attack. The effectiveness of this system, however, was dependent on each party knowing its own location, and in the North Sea in murky winter that was rarely the case.

Once well out to sea the captain would order a trial dive to check the trim. The men went to diving stations, worked out by the coxswain and the first lieutenant after they had ascertained the skills and experience of their men when they first joined. At diving stations, with all the crew on duty, the best-qualified man always controlled each instrument; on normal patrol watch, with only a third of the crew on duty, it might be one of his two deputies. A man's 'action station', for fighting, might be different again, since he might be one of the guns' crew. To dive Coxswain Holmes took the fore planes, which controlled the angle of descent, and his deputy Johnson sat next to him in the control room at the wheel (or bar) that directed the after planes. In order to maintain the boat on an even keel, they both kept their eyes on a device like a spirit level, trying to maintain a bubble in the centre of the gauge. Behind them First Lieutenant Keith-Roach watched the depth gauges anxiously. The outside engine room artificer was at the diving panel, from where all the tanks were controlled.

The engine room was shut off and the diesels closed down. When the submarine was on the surface, the ballast tanks located in a bulge outside the pressure hull were filled with air. To dive, the vents were opened to replace the air with seawater. The captain pressed the klaxon twice and the lookouts piled down from the bridge. The officer of the watch came last, shutting the voice-pipe cock and the upper hatch. Jonas gave the orders, 'Open main vents, fore-planes hard to dive; both motors full ahead' and they slid below with fountains of spray from the tanks. 'As always, the same uneasy feeling attacked everyone, as always occurs after a submarine has been in port for several days.' *Thetis* was not long in the past, and the first dive was always worrying.

A T class sub aimed to get under water in thirty seconds. If the first lieutenant had miscalculated she might plunge rather sharply. This time it took just a little pumping and flooding of the forward and after tanks before 'she acquired a perfect trim', being level with 'neutral buoyancy'. Secure in the knowledge that *Triad* would dive safely when necessary, Jonas took her up again: 'Stand

by to surface, blow main ballast.' The outside ERA pushed water
out of the tanks with pressurised air to make the boat rise. The
swish of high-pressure air through the air-line into the main ballast tanks was clearly audible. At ten feet under, the captain
opened the lower hatch so that he, the signaller and lookouts
emerged on the bridge as the boat broke surface.

At first captains often employed only one lookout – the signalman, so that he could be ready to challenge or respond to
challenges from boats or aircraft. Good eyesight was an essential
qualification for his job. It was not long, however, before most boats
had four. Good captains worried and chivvied and harried their
lookouts, picking those seamen with the sharpest eyesight who
were not absolutely necessary elsewhere. In *Truant* Christopher
Hutchinson chose, in addition to signalman John 'Smithy' Smith,
a torpedoman and a couple of the gun's crew. One of King's lookouts was *Snapper*'s dependable coxswain, Bill Passant, and he always
kept one lookout staring into the sun for aircraft (which habitually
attacked out of the sun).

Initially, there were not enough binoculars and, according to
King, theirs were always getting flooded when the sea broke over
the low-trimmed hull. By putting a little water in the tanks they
could give the boat a very low profile, but it made life wetter.
King soon decided not to trim his boat low. He 'begged borrowed and stole binoculars' and even bought them from Bond
Street; the shop where his family always bought their racing
binoculars was eager to help. Ben Bryant wanted night binoculars. These had been considered unnecessary but, being ambitious
to survive, he bought some German ones out of his own pocket.

Night blindness was not yet understood – one of many unfortunate consequences of the lack of night exercises. At first
lookouts emerged from the bright light of the interior on to the
bridge and took some twenty minutes to get used to the light
without realising that they were relatively blind. Later, red lights
were introduced inside. King made his lookouts wear sunglasses
before going on watch.

Triad, like other T-boats, had five officers: the captain, first lieutenant, torpedo officer, navigator and a commissioned engineer. The captain stood no watch and was merely called to the control room or the bridge in emergency. Nor, usually, did the engineer. The other three stood watches during which they took charge of the boat, looked out through the periscope or with binoculars from the bridge and were responsible for everything, although they could call the captain at the first sign of trouble. In transit the officer of the watch used the periscope every half an hour to take an observation so as to fix the new position of the submarine on the chart. When on patrol at shallow depth he took a quick look round for a maximum of thirty seconds at least every five minutes. In action the first lieutenant was responsible for the trim – keeping an even keel at a given depth by adjusting the level of water in various tanks. Changes in water density and movement of men in the boat might upset the trim, so the officer of the watch had to keep a close eye on depth too. The first lieutenant also had his traditional naval role of organising the crew and generally making sure that the boat was in order, especially in harbour. The torpedo officer was responsible for the weapons, and the navigator for keeping track of both the boat's position and that of the enemy.

The engineer kept the boat watertight and moving. In *Triad* his department consisted of five engine room artificers, led by Chief ERA Buchanan, and seventeen stokers. They were responsible for all mechanical equipment, but the engines were their chief concern. The outside ERA, or 'outside wrecker', dealt with mechanical equipment outside the engine room with a senior stoker as his assistant. The rest of the crew belonged to the seaman branch. The communication staff, operating the radio office and the asdic in the control room, was led by a chief petty officer telegraphist with three assistants and a signalman who sent visual signals with Morse and semaphore. The torpedo gunner's mate was in charge of the torpedoes up front and had a crew of assistants. An electrical artificer was in charge of electrics and the motor room. Torpedomen were also qualified electricians. When dived at action stations, the coxswain and his deputy controlled the hydroplanes. Under normal circumstances these were looked after by seamen on watch, as was the helm.

The crew was divided into three watches (red, white and blue) and for most of the time a third of the crew would be on duty and the rest would be resting – if dived, preferably asleep in order to use as little oxygen as possible. The minimum personnel on duty when the boat was submerged was two men at the hydroplane wheels to keep the boat at the right depth; a helmsman to steer by gyro-compass; an ERA on the vent and blow panel and the lever which raised and lowered the periscopes; a leading torpedoman in the motor room to obey the speed telegraphs; a seaman listening through headphones to the hydrophones for the sound of approaching ships; and a stoker to operate the ballast pump and valves. Hart's watch in the engine room was shared with ERA Bert Hayward, whose father had died in a submarine in the First World War, and stokers Ingram and Thomas.

Anywhere remotely dangerous the boat dived at dawn and passed the day at periscope depth running at two knots on the motors, coming to the surface at dusk. *Triad* had to surface in order to recharge her batteries every night so that there was power for the motors the next day. Surfacing was also necessary to replenish the air supply. Surfacing at night was the most dangerous procedure. For the last twenty minutes before surfacing the submarine would go deep, because it was too dark to see properly through the periscope but not yet dark enough to be safe on the surface. To avoid any possibility of accidental collision a boat would dive below the depth of ships. Before it surfaced the asdic rating would listen hard for any noise that might betray an enemy waiting in ambush for them above. The lookouts scrambled on to the bridge the instant the boat broke surface. After they had searched carefully and reported all clear, the engines started up and the crew lit cigarettes as clean air flooded in. At first the submarine would move at modest speed on one engine, using the other to charge the batteries. The engines were enormously noisy, but the batteries were more or less silent, so there was a great contrast between the bumbling racket of progress on the surface and the silence of movement underwater.

Every four hours the telegraphists listened to the routine broadcasts from the Admiralty, transmitted via Rugby, checking especially for their own call sign. They could do this while underwater but they needed to be near the surface, and sometimes the officer of the watch had to stop the boat and point it in the right direction in order to get a decent signal. Instructions from the captain of the flotilla were broadcast in high frequency and received on the surface after the hydraulic aerial had been raised. Replying to a message was fraught with risk because the enemy could DF – direction find – a submarine's signal. It could be very difficult to make contact and the signals were sometimes picked up in Halifax, Nova Scotia, rather than in London and relayed to the Admiralty from there. Generally, submarines only broadcast important enemy sightings or an emergency request and then moved to a different position as quickly as possible.

Cooking was best done on the surface where a supply of air was available and there was some escape for smells, and unless the weather was bad it was more comfortable to eat up top. While surfaced it was usually permissible to smoke. For these reasons *Triad* turned night into day, with breakfast at 0700, dinner at midnight and supper at 0500. However, King in *Snapper* had breakfast after diving, lunch at midday and supper after surfacing, preferring the calm underwater to the rough seas above. *Triad* had a trained cook, but in the smaller S class 'someone had to be found and forced into the galley where he stood in an icy, wind-swept passage with men racing past him, freezing his backside and stewing his face over a small electric cooker.'

In theory submariners got the best of whatever food was available, but as usual, there was much to learn about the practicalities. Bread in a submarine became mouldy very quickly. First they put it in the oven to tune it up, then they cut off the mouldy bits, sprinkled it with condensed milk and baked it again. Finally they just ate the bits that weren't mouldy. The cook's job, in a situation where his pans kept sliding off his tiny stove, was so difficult that he seems generally to have commanded sympathy rather than resentment. The daily rum issue to the troops was usually given out just after surfacing. Gilbert Quick served it to the stokers, blacking his lip and doing an impression of Hitler as he did so. At the same time officers might have a bottle of beer or a tot of spirits.

Hart and his fellow stokers saw practically no daylight while at sea. 'Our only change of scenery during these eighteen days was a walk extending some eighty feet or so to the control room and back.' Their mess was a small compartment lined on three sides with two-tiered bunks, with folding tables in the middle. There were lockers for stowing kit. Most of the time, life in a submarine was simply boring – day after day with nothing seen. When not on duty – two-thirds of the time – the crew dozed, slept, read books or magazines, played cards (cribbage, bridge, rummy), played liar dice, played Monopoly, played the naval form of Ludo known as 'uckers', invented sweepstakes on anything they could think of . . . Anything to dispel the tedium.

Food was kept away from the engine room, but the stokers usually had one of the heads – the ship's lavatories – next to their mess. The proximity of the motor and engine rooms meant that the area was noisy but hot, which was a good thing in the North Sea in winter, but less attractive in the Mediterranean in summer. To some extent the smell of diesel oil drowned out the smell of the heads and other human odours.

In a large submarine there were four heads, one for officers, one for petty officers, one for seamen and one for stokers. In H class boats the only seat for ratings was in the open between the engines and anyone on it might have to move to let the staff through. In L class boats they moved it out of the gangway, but it was still public:

The position of the lavatory pan is merely aggravating to the seaman who has to walk the length of the ship in order to relieve himself, but to the stokers on the other hand, the sight of a seaman squatting in noisy operation, each time he lifts his eyes from the breakfast before him, incites a feeling of revulsion which he knows he must ignore. The stoker can, it is true, prevent operations during mealtimes – if he is vehement enough. But he must accept the fact that the first thing he may see, indeed will probably see, on waking from a deep sleep, is a slumped forward attitude of a squatter on a pan ...

Later boats had tiny cubicles two feet by two and a half, so it was not quite so bad for Hart. Before using the heads you had to ask permission from the officer on watch. He would check that there were no aircraft to see the bubbling sewage rising to the surface. Inside the cubicle was a very shallow pan with a bakelite seat and flap. Under a watertight flap at the bottom of the pan was a tank holding about one and a half gallons. Above the seat were pressure gauges, valves and an air bottle. By the seat was a lever about eighteen inches long. First you needed to make sure that the previous occupant of the cubicle had left everything as it should be. To empty the pan you lowered the flap on the seat and opened two valves to open a gap in the pressure hull and connect the tank with the sea. Then you charged the air bottle with pressurised air until its pressure was sufficiently greater than that of the sea outside. The experienced submariner would then put his foot on the lid of the pan and move the lever to no. 1 position, which opened the flap at the bottom of the pan. This could be a disastrous moment because if the previous user had neglected to vent the air pressure, and you forgot to have the pan down and your foot on it, the contents of the pan would be blown back in your face as you bent over the lever. This dire outcome was known as 'getting your own back'. Moving the lever to no. 2 position allowed seawater to flush the pan into the tank at the bottom. No. 3 position shut the flap at the bottom of the pan, and emptied the tank outboard by filling it with high-pressure air. Then, no. 4 position vented the air from the tank, to prevent blow back for the next user. Finally the lever was returned to the central position. All these difficulties 'made using the heads very unpopular, and a lot of the chaps used to hang on for a week or two if they could rather than use them. Betting on who could go the longest was common.'

Fresh water was in short supply so nobody shaved or washed much. There was no escape from shipmates. 'We grew to know each other's peculiarities,' wrote Hart: 'the way one man used his knife and fork, the way another made annoying noises when drinking tea, how this man's feet smelt – those little personal idiosyncrasies.' There were outbursts of temper but in happy boats the result was a close team. The S class boats, despite having a much smaller crew – thirty-nine against fifty-six – were much less comfortable. The same machinery was crammed into a much smaller space and even with imagination there was only room for off-watch crew to sleep. In these and smaller boats hot bunking was customary – men on watch took the bunks previously occupied by those off watch. No bunks were made for people over six feet tall, and giants like Hugh Haggard had to twist their legs or cut holes for their feet.

During most of the war submariners left harbour in uniform and returned in uniform. In between they dressed in whatever old clothes seemed suitable and rarely changed them. In the icy winter of 1939, those who were exposed to the weather on the bridge or in the wind tunnel between the conning tower hatch and the engines wore layer on layer, including balaclavas and seaboot stockings knitted and donated by charitable ladies. It was warmer and cosier beyond the engine room, where most stokers dwelt. There had been no great effort to discover clothes suitable for submariners – as usual in practical matters, the Germans were far ahead – although George Phillips won a lasting name for his submarine by inventing the relatively waterproof 'Ursula suit'. Over normal warm clothing King wore oilskin trousers and a rainproof golfing jacket and never took them off. Christopher Hutchinson got his nickname 'Jockey' by wearing riding breeches. Howard 'Boggy' Bone, the blunt, taciturn, efficient commander of *Tigris*, 'wore long woollen pants, thick socks, three sweaters, fur-lined flying boots and helmet and an oil-skin suit over all'.

Triad's first patrol was tame. Nothing was seen, the weather was unremarkable and there was merely the discomfort for a normal patrol of grime and smells. 'Once we were secured to moorings there was a dash to the parent ship for baths,' wrote Hart, 'a treat we had missed for eighteen mortal days.' Two to three weeks was a typical duration for these early patrols in home waters. Back aboard *Forth* they clipped and shaved their beards, although submariners who could grow convincing beards usually gave up and grew them. It was a delight to 'eat fresh bread after eating, first, green-moulded bread and then, during the last week, hard biscuits, and last, but best of all, to breathe fresh, pure air, air that had not been polluted by the conglomeration of scents bred in a submarine's interior – ah, this was bliss indeed!'

From November onwards, however, crews learned the real misery of life in submarines. Later on, experienced submariners came to describe patrols as '90 per cent boredom and 10 per cent cold fear'. That first winter they learned that cold fear was not only induced by the enemy. Long ago Queen Elizabeth had ordained that her sailors should pray for 'deliverance from the dangers of the sea and the violence of the enemy'. Nothing much changed at sea and the naval prayer was still in use. But in 1939 King reckoned that it should have been reversed: the danger from the enemy was nothing compared to the violence of the sea.

Coastal navigation was made extremely difficult because all the lights and buoys had been removed to make life harder for the enemy. After a while it became clear that the policy was doing more harm to the British than the Germans. With skies permanently overcast it was barely ever possible to get a sight of sun or stars for navigation. Each morning, having failed to shoot the sun,

'Drenched, frozen and unsure of our position we would climb down the conning tower, clip the hatches and dive to the strange stillness of 60 ft.' They dare not go any lower for fear of damaging the asdic dome on the bottom. Asdic could be used to take soundings and compare these with the charts – King bought fishing charts, which were more detailed than the Admiralty ones – but the risk was that the distinctive features on the seabed that fixed your position with certainty might be mined. Mines were a constant fear.

Fortunately, despite the dedicated efforts of both sides, those areas declared to be mined did not always have mines in them, as King discovered: 'One grey morning when the clouds finally parted, I stood on the bridge dodging to avoid the spray of each crashing wave and managed to keep the sextant dry enough to snatch a star-sight which gave us a clue to our peregrinations. We had been playing in the German-mined area for most of a week.' But in the constant gales many mines broke free from their moorings and might turn up anywhere, roaming the sea on the surface. It was one of these loose rogue mines that *Triumph* hit on Boxing Day when her bows were blown off.

The weather made life terrible for the lookouts. In *Sturgeon*, Norman Drury said, the officer of the watch and his two fellow lookouts were often up to their waist in water and it was bitterly cold. If your hands and face are freezing and your eyes weeping, 'Hutch' Hutchinson pointed out, it doesn't make for really good binocular work. Consequently, in these conditions the lookouts were changed frequently. Lookouts normally did one hour then went down to get warm. But it was so damp inside the submarines that nothing could be dried. In Bryant's *Sealion*, 'In rough weather, the decks were not only damp and covered with slime composed of upset food, bilge water and lub oil, but the deck head would drip condensation, so that the men had to cover themselves with an oilskin.' The lookouts put on wet clothes when off watch and then staggered up for another go. 'Mopping the spray off their half-flooded binoculars my look-outs resolutely poked their faces into the wind's teeth', wrote King, 'in case the impossible happened and a plane or funnel showed. One look-out struggling to keep the spray from pouring inside his collar remarked respectfully but pointedly, "The enemy wouldn't be such a bloody fool as to be out in this, sir."'

It became incredibly cold. By February 1940, Harwich harbour and much of the North Sea coast was covered in ice. At one point the RAF identified a German battle squadron at anchor and Bickford in *Salmon* was sent to investigate. They turned out to be trawlers covered in snow. Churchill telephoned Horton and said, 'I am not a religious man, Horton, but when I read your signal ordering *Salmon* to search under the ice I got down on my knees and prayed.' Horton told the story to Simpson: 'I much appreciated his keen interest but his knowledge of what was dangerous and what was not in submarine operations was naturally negligible.'

After Bickford's triumph in December Churchill had taken a personal interest in him. In February he invited him to lunch and, after the other guests had gone, sat him down with a brandy and a cigar and grilled him on current conditions and how to deal with U-boats. Churchill was impressed and suggested that Pound should have Bickford in the Admiralty plans division for a few months: 'This Officer seems to me to be very able, and has many things to say about anti-U-boat warfare which I trust will be gathered at the earliest opportunity.' Bickford, however, wanted to remain in active service.

Inevitably the weather caused damage to submarines buffeted by the waves above or 'down at 100 feet with the sub sliding backwards and forwards on the rocks'. In *Sturgeon* number one main vent began to leak and the outside ERA and a stoker went out on to the casing to repack it. Then the stern glands – the packing around the propeller shaft – started leaking and they had to raise the air pressure to keep the sea out. This had dire consequences. Their popular signalman Bill Penny, a bulky figure in sea boots, balaclava and sou'wester, with a towel round his neck, pulled the clips off the hatch to go on watch when they surfaced for the night, but 'the pressure was so great it just fired him out of the submarine and he went over the side'. They never found him.

A submarine was a relatively small boat with most of her bulk underwater. Consequently, when she was on the surface or just below it in bad weather life was horrible. 'She rolls violently sideways,' wrote King, 'a heavy, exhausting, waterlogged roll that diminishes the powers of the human mind and body. The diesel engines vibrated with incredible din and the nausea that some men suffered was quite pathetic.' During the day the amount of oxygen in the air diminished while carbon dioxide was breathed out. This made men pant, numbed their judgement, made them clammily cold. Before April the scientists provided trays of soda lime to absorb the carbon dioxide. For this to work properly the air needed to be forced through the lime, but because the trays could only be placed on the deck they improved the situation very little. Old or defective batteries produced nauseating gases that gave the men headaches. If seawater got into the batteries it produced highly dangerous chlorine gas, but the average cases were just unpleasant. Some complained of permanent 'submarine catarrh'. The horrible weather conditions combined with stress, which was at its worst in these early months when submariners' experience of the potential dangers was so limited. Some became ill: Bryant went down with jaundice in January.

Keeping the submarine at periscope depth – normally thirty feet – was almost impossible. King gave up and kept at sixty feet during the day in bad weather, listening on asdic. Even then there was a danger of breaking the asdic dome on the bottom. He could not stay at sixty feet permanently, however, as he had to come close to the surface for the radio every four hours. 'This ghastly see-saw usually ended in a break surface, floundering and flooding, followed by wild struggles to get down with propeller thrashing and precious battery capacity being wasted. Submarine crews are too busy or too exhausted to get on each other's nerves, but tempers did shorten in the futility of this struggle.'

One dark night a light on shore alerted them at the last second to the proximity of breakers ahead. The boat grounded just after King swung her round. A young stoker reached for his escape set. Arthur Cooper, the chief ERA, told him he could drop that because he could walk ashore from where they were. Each time the waves lifted the propellers off the sand King ran the motors, then stopped as the stern crashed on to the beach. John Bromage, the navigator, reminded King that the tide was falling. The engineer somewhat needlessly shouted in his ear, 'She'll fall apart soon, sir.' King could think of no other way but to keep going. 'Lift. "Full ahead," I would signal with the telegraphs. Drop. Crash. "Stop both motors."' King was filled with despairing thoughts of this ignominious end to his ship and his life. 'How the submarine held together I don't know. In my heart I had given up hope. I just didn't think survival possible. Nor could I get the crew off. They wouldn't walk. They'd drown.' He could barely believe it when the bumps became less frequent and then stopped.

In the same late-November storm Ronald Jonas had similar problems with *Triad*. When anywhere near periscope depth she 'took sickening nose-dives at a disconcerting angle. With screws screaming as they thrashed the air, our ship would slide under once more.' Next to Hart in the engine room, Stoker Thomas was violently ill yet continued to work through it, while the floor was covered with his vomit.

Several days later the storm was still raging. Hart was reading a novel in his bunk when, for no obvious reason, the boat stopped. From the engine room came a yell of 'Shut all watertight doors!' Hart slammed the door shut between the engine room and the stokers' mess, as sleeping stokers woke and asked what was going on. This was one of the more frightening situations a submariner could face. 'To be enclosed in a small compartment in a submersible, without knowing why, gives one a breathless suggestion of fear closely akin to panic.' The depth gauge showed they were still on the surface. Hart fought a strong urge to telephone the control room. Finally the phone rang. They were told to open the door and the engineer officer ran through to the hydroplane gear right aft. The hydroplanes were jammed hard to rise. They couldn't dive and the planes, smashed by the weather, were acting as a brake so they could only go slowly.

Jonas sent a wireless message for assistance and *Triumph* came to guard *Triad* until two destroyers arrived. They tried to tow *Triad* to Rosyth but gave up and took her instead to Stavanger, twenty-five miles away, where the laws of neutrality allowed her to go for repairs, after which the Norwegians escorted her out of territorial waters.

The moment they were ashore in England it was baths, drinks and leave for some. Officers crammed enjoyment into the brief time between patrols with either drink or sex as first priority, although some were attracted by the shooting on the frozen mudflats around Harwich. King, who now rated sex above drink, 'possessed a small green racing car which covered the miles to London in a remarkably short time, and once there one eagerly forgot submarines and their woes'. All too soon, slightly rested, it was back to the fray.

8

HORTON'S PURGE

Max K. Horton's style was very different from that of the charming Bertie Watson. 'He was a tiger to his staff, and we realised it within a few hours of his joining,' wrote one officer. 'But a tiger in whom we all had supreme confidence, and though he could and did bite hard when bites were needed, and though his growl was exceedingly fierce, to the trained ear that growl had a distinct note of friendliness on many occasions.' He was not a man you could be indifferent to. Shrimp Simpson reckoned 'people either cared deeply for Sir Max, or hated him'. Horton demanded competence: 'If a mistake were made and frankly confessed with full reasons for making it, Max would be as tolerant as anyone, provided the mistake was not made through slackness.' He hated people trying to conceal mistakes and 'woe betide any officer who tried to bluff that he had any more knowledge of a subject than he in fact had.' A ruthless campaigner against inefficiency, he worked hard and made his staff work harder, although he loathed unnecessary work. Like Churchill, he believed in taking action at once.

For several weeks, though, Horton watched and waited, feeling his way into the job. In February 1940 new orders were issued for Churchill's pet 'Plan Catherine'. Dudley Pound and his staff had finally persuaded the First Lord that the danger of losing major units of the fleet in forcing entry into the Baltic was too great, but as a sop to the politician's desire for aggressive action the naval staff prepared to risk their submarines. Ruck-Keene and Simpson were ordered to prepare to take their flotilla and six new T-boats into the sea where Horton had been so successful himself, and attack the German iron ore supplies from a base in Finland. Just as Simpson had everything ready, the move was cancelled because an armistice was declared between the Finns and Germany's Russian allies.

Horton's drive for efficiency was soon in evidence. He asked his flotilla leaders to canvass officers on what faults in the design and equipment of the new S, T and U class submarines had been revealed by wartime experience. They made all kinds of practical suggestions for improvements, like providing racks for books and instruments next to the chart table. Ruck-Keene's demands were characteristically forthright. The equipment put inside new boats was often antique – whatever was available and could be spared, given that most ships and aircraft took priority over submarines. For S-boats Ruck-Keene demanded some kind of 'cold cupboard', for they had no fridge in which to store fresh food and that summer some of *Snapper*'s crew succumbed to scurvy. He also wanted 'the most modern W/T [wireless telegraphy, i.e. radio] gear that the service can provide' (instead of the outdated stock they were palmed off with) with special regard to transmissions from periscope depth, because half the time they couldn't make contact. He wanted better hydrophones and much better guns. The ancient three-inch guns on S class submarines were soon notoriously unreliable. U class submarines, originally designed without guns, were being fitted with similarly antique but ineffectively small twelve-pounders. *Una*'s gun, of Boer War vintage, had the letters 'V.R.' cast into the breach.

Then came 'Horton's purge'. Making drastic changes to personnel, he removed the captain of the 2nd Flotilla and replaced him with the brisk and popular 'Colonel' Menzies. Some twenty experienced commanding officers of boats were sent to general service or moved to staff jobs. Simpson noticed that Horton was 'so strongly influenced by first impressions that he seldom, if ever, changed his opinion of a man's character and ability, and this was occasionally unfair'. Horton was convinced that peacetime regulations had made the older officers over-cautious and all the successes so far had been scored by younger men like Bickford.

The principal result was wholesale change in the 2nd Flotilla, where not only the captain but all the commanding officers went. By contrast, in Ruck-Keene's 3rd Flotilla nothing changed. Most of those who relinquished command were, like Willie Banks, pushing forty and afterwards became valuable members of flotilla staff or commanded destroyers. In a few cases aggressive men were retained despite their age. From this time, however, anybody who looked tentative in attack might be dismissed and most people were removed from command as soon as they touched thirty-five.

To fill the gap Horton recalled men in their early thirties who had been sent into general service after their first submarine command because there were not enough boats to go round. At the same time more young officers were recruited. An invitation was sent for two Royal Naval Volunteer Reserve officers to join submarines. After a friend had been chosen and had volunteered, Edward Young, graphic designer and amateur yachtsman, asked to be added as a third volunteer, chiefly because it was a way to learn celestial navigation.

Horton's next initiative was to move his headquarters away from Aberdour in Scotland. Watson had put up with being on the Firth of Forth when his administrative department was in Gosport, but Horton was strong enough to insist on change, even though for him personally the loss of 'the golf course just outside the front door' was a sacrifice. Dudley Pound suggested he move into the Admiralty but Horton wasn't having that either. He took over three floors of Northways, a block of flats in Swiss Cottage sufficiently large for his administrative staff to move up from

Gosport to join him. It was situated midway between the Admiralty and the headquarters of RAF Coastal Command at Northwood, so that it was easy to visit either. Sir Frederick Bowhill, Air Officer Commanding, 'always went to see him or he came to see me as neither of us were very enamoured of correspondence ... We had a very close, and in my opinion perfect co-operation.'

Churchill continued to press for disruption of the supply of iron ore to Germany, but British submarines still had their hands tied. Most iron ore was transported to Germany in Swedish ships. Neutral ships could not be attacked. Nothing could be sunk in the neutral waters off the coasts of Norway and Denmark. German merchant ships could only be sunk after they had been stopped, searched, and had their crews removed. Since submarines carried no boats, searching an enemy vessel was time-consuming and fraught with risk. Often, threatened vessels called in air support before the formalities were completed.

On 21 March *Ursula*, dispatched on a dangerous mission in the shallow and heavily defended Kattegat, carried out the first successful British attack on a merchantman. Just after dark on a clear night George Phillips came across a merchant ship and signalled her to stop and identify herself. The ship claimed to be Estonian but Aston Piper, *Ursula*'s RNR navigator, who had sailed merchantmen in the Baltic before the war, said that was nonsense since there was no Estonian ship that big. Phillips signalled the captain to stop and abandon his ship. Nothing happened, so Phillips put a shot across their bows and they complied. Phillips then fired one torpedo from 500 yards at the SS *Hedernheim*, an iron ore carrier. She sank in five or ten minutes, stern first. Phillips wanted to take a prisoner, so they steered *Ursula* alongside the lifeboat and Piper spoke to its occupants in German, a language he had learned at school and had used in the Baltic. He asked for the captain but was told that he had shot himself. Piper told the chief engineer to come on board. He had a revolver on his belt, so the engineer came readily.

Two days later *Truant* was patrolling off Denmark with a new captain, Christopher Hutchinson. Horton had purged the previous commander, who had not made much of an impression on the crew. But with Hutchinson, said ERA Jack Pook, 'we had three very exciting patrols'. After serving in H-boats since his draft to submarines it was the West Country engineer's first taste of action. Off the Bovberg Light they found a large collier and ordered her to stop. She didn't, so twenty-year-old telegraphist Eddie 'Buster' Brown used the four-inch gun in anger for the first time, scoring hits on the *Edmund Hugo Stinnes IV*. The crew abandoned ship and 'Hutch' sank her with two torpedoes. 'Eventually we picked up the captain and took him as a prisoner of war,' recalled Pook, 'and left the crew to pull for shore.' While Brown blazed away at the bridge because the ship was sending distress signals, Pook, up aft, had little idea whether they were attacking or fighting for their lives. 'One problem with being crew in a submarine is that you don't see anything. The captain is really the only man who sees what's going on and knows what's going on ... inside the boat, you have to judge by remarks passed as to what is happening.'

Pook made friends with the German captain. 'He was a very pleasant chap. He'd been a prisoner of war in the First War and we got on very well with him. He was quite happy to be a prisoner ... and he could speak English.' In his absence the captain was convicted of grave errors and sentenced to six weeks in prison.

Both these operations took place close to and partly in Norwegian waters. Horton had instructed captains to push the rules to the limit. Like Churchill, he was furious at the way the Swedes, Norwegians and Danes, whose ships were sunk by U-boats if found trading with Britain, continued to carry German goods and escort German ships through their waters. In February the War Cabinet authorised preparations for a plan to lay mines in Norwegian territorial waters, violating neutrality, but forcing all traffic into the open where it could be stopped and searched.

But they hesitated to implement the plan, just as they hesitated to seize the Norwegian port of Narvik (from which Swedish iron ore was embarked for Germany in winter), another option under discussion. The politicians agreed that neutral behaviour put Britain at an unfair disadvantage, but Foreign Secretary Lord Halifax and Prime Minister Chamberlain opposed action because of the potentially adverse effect on neutral (chiefly American) opinion if Britain appeared to bully Norway.

The political arguments came to a head on 28 March when Chamberlain finally argued in favour of action. By then Churchill knew that 'a high Swedish source' had warned that the Germans were preparing aircraft and shipping for operations against Norway. The minelay was agreed for 5 April. Horton sent Churchill his summary of the arguments in favour of action, leading to the conclusion that 'England must take control of all those waters which are now being used for such un-neutral purposes', and Churchill incorporated these notes into a radio broadcast he made that day.

Horton called his flotilla captains to a conference at Northways on 1 April. He informed them of the plan to lay mines and told them that this was likely to lead to a German invasion of Norway. Horton wanted every available submarine on patrol, with as many as possible in the Skagerrak and east of the German mine-field by dawn on 5 April. He intended to place submarines off possible landing places and they were allowed to sink transports at sight (although this made no real difference, since distinguishing transports from innocent vessels was difficult). *Triton*, *Trident* and *Swordfish* were already at sea, though unaware that an invasion might be imminent. Five submarines sailed to join them. When the lay was postponed on 4 April until 8 April, five more submarines went to sea while those already out moved further into the Skagerrak and Kattegat. It is likely that these wireless orders to change patrol position revealed the location of submarines to the German B-Dienst radio interception service. On 4 April Horton stressed that transports were an even more important target than warships.

On 7 April around midday Horton received information from Coastal Command that a German cruiser and six destroyers were off Horns Reef heading north. Just afterwards, the Director of Naval Intelligence finally informed operational commanders that:

Recent reports suggest that a German expedition is being prepared. Hitler is reported from Copenhagen to have ordered the unostentatious movement of one division in ten ships by night to land at Narvik with simultaneous occupation of Jutland. Sweden to be left alone. Moderates said to be opposing the plan. Date given for arrival Narvik was 8th April. All these reports are of doubtful value and may well be only a further move in the war of nerves.

Horton sailed six more submarines in anticipation of an invasion of Norway. Three French boats joined them. Horton was the only British leader to draw the correct deduction from the information he was getting. A substantial supply of accurate intelligence had been passed to Whitehall but the Admiralty refused to believe it. The Home Fleet steamed north in anticipation of a breakout into the Atlantic.

Coastal Command had spotted the first German force to sail. *Scharnhorst*, *Gneisenau* and ten destroyers had departed late on 6 April bound for Narvik. At first they steamed in company with *Hipper* and four destroyers bound for Trondheim. During the night they passed well west of *Unity* (possibly knowing her position) without being seen. Bomber Command launched an ineffectual attack on this force, news of which reached the Admiralty in late afternoon.

That morning Ben Bryant drove *Sealion* round the Skaw and through the Kattegat. Sunday 7 April was a lovely spring day. As he crept south, submerged, he passed a procession of fifteen unescorted tankers and heavily laden merchant ships sailing north. Horton had ordered him not to compromise his position by examining merchant ships. 'But were they transports?' Bryant asked himself, because Horton had identified troop transports as the top priority target. 'To me a "transport" conveyed a passenger ship, the familiar Bibby liner, soldiers crowding the upper works.' In fact these merchants' holds were full of troops and equipment. This was a third German group moving north. For understandable reasons, Bryant had blundered.

Around midday one of the leading merchant ships reached the Polish boat *Orzel* off Lillesand. Reckoning the ship just out of territorial waters, her captain Jan Grudzinski surfaced and ordered *Rio de Janeiro* to stop. He gave her a quarter of an hour to abandon ship and then sank her with torpedoes, leaving the many rafts of German soldiers to Norwegian torpedo boats. When questioned, the soldiers claimed that they were on their way to 'protect' Bergen against the British. The German command thought this disaster had robbed them of the crucial element of surprise, but they reckoned without the Norwegian government's obstinate refusal to believe they were in danger of invasion, a delusion shared by the Admiralty.

South of Oslo, Alan Seale and his first lieutenant Arthur 'Baldy' Hezlet were watching the Norwegian coast through *Trident*'s periscope. Seale had arrived in February from HMS *Belfast* to replace one of the victims of Horton's purge. He had only ever commanded a little training submarine. After serving under Menzies in China, Hezlet had replaced *Trident*'s original first lieutenant, who had drowned in *Thetis*. 'We saw these ships going north but we couldn't make them out,' Hezlet recalled. 'We knew they weren't neutral, because neutrals normally had their flag painted beside their names and none of these had. I had quite an argument with my captain, who said there was absolutely nothing we could do. He said, "If we started sinking these things and they proved to be neutral it would be really bad news." But I felt there was something very wrong and a big action was about to happen.'

While Hezlet was on watch a tanker came beyond the three-mile limit and cut a corner across the bay where *Trident* was

lurking. Hezlet called Seale, who 'said he was very uncertain of
what we should do and he hadn't been given any instructions'.
According to the torpedo officer, an animated discussion took
place and it was only after the tanker had passed by that Hezlet
persuaded Seale to act. 'He popped up with the gun and ordered
it to stop. Not only did it stop, but it scuttled, and he then didn't
make a signal to Admiralty which was very unwise.' Like Hezlet,
the torpedo officer found Seale 'not particularly offensively
minded'.

As this was happening Horton was discussing his submarine
dispositions with the Admiralty. Even now they believed they
were dealing with a breakout into the Atlantic by heavy ships
rather than an invasion of Norway, and they instructed Horton
to move submarines away from the Norwegian ports in order to
form a line to intercept the warships as they returned to
Germany. Just in case a landing was planned at Narvik, as they
had been told, or at Larvik, which Naval Intelligence decided
their informant must have meant, *Trident* was ordered to move
from Oslo Fjord to Larvik.

The naval attaché at Copenhagen had seen a battleship, two
cruisers and destroyers heading north at dawn. Near the Skaw,
Bertie Pizey in *Triton* missed them with his torpedoes because
they increased speed after he fired. Tall and handsome but prone
to theatrical rages, Pizey used to throw his cap on the deck and
stamp on it at sights of the Germans speeding up like this. Jacky
Slaughter in *Sunfish* also saw them, growling with frustration as
they were too far away to hit. The sighting reports allowed
Horton to lay a trap for the German vessels in the path anticipated by the Admiralty into the North Sea, but instead they
entered Oslo Fjord, passing the position *Trident* had vacated in
order to follow Admiralty instructions to patrol off Larvik.

On Monday three more German groups moved north: the
cruisers *Köln* and *Königsberg* with escorts and 1500 troops from
Wilhelmshaven for Bergen, *Brummer* and 500 troops for
Stavanger, *Karlsruhe* and escorting destroyers for Kristiansand.

They passed *Unity* and *Spearfish*, possibly knowing where they were. Luck was with them though. The sea was flat calm but it was very foggy. They reached *Truant* off Egersund early in the night. The asdic operator could hear ships' propellers, which seemed to be all around. These were likely to be hostile ships, but 'instruments in those days were not accurate enough to be able to keep me safely on the surface without almost certain collision with ships that were obviously very close and invisible.' Frustrated, Hutchinson 'tried going in various directions on the surface to try to get a clearer picture of what was around. I dived and tried to get some sort of picture by hydrophones.' He couldn't identify a target and the fleeting chance disappeared.

Next morning the newspapers announced that Norway had been invaded, and the Admiralty finally accepted that this must be true. They ordered British submarines to close Norwegian ports. The Germans were using submarines to defend them. By this time there were twenty-two British, French and Polish boats on patrol, thanks to Horton's reading of the intelligence reports. That Tuesday the government decided to allow submarines to sink all enemy vessels at sight in the Kattegat and Skagerrak, and east of the German minefield.

Until that moment captains had simply used merchant vessels for target practice, by wriggling into position to fire and estimating the target's course and speed. In the dangerous Kattegat Jacky Slaughter was doing just that on the afternoon of 9 April. He was a tall, heavily built, unlovely man with an uncanny resemblance to the actor Charles Laughton. Rugged and sometimes terrifying, Slaughter had a fine command of descriptive Anglo-Saxon vocabulary which he used both to endear himself to his men and to reduce those who had offended him to quivering pulp. He was 'the only man I ever knew who could employ the most lurid, Rabelaisian language in one's direction and left one feeling as if bathed in immoderate praise ... ', remembered one subordinate. Chief engineer William Harris was deciphering messages. One of them looked like it bore on rules for engagement, so he sent a

Max Horton, Great War submarine ace and Admiral Submarines 1940–2, played golf every possible afternoon during the war. He played off a nine handicap, which opponents reckoned should have been four, and liked to win, though he was generous with drinks in the bar afterwards *(Getty Images)*.

John Capes, sole survivor of *Perseus* after she hit a mine off Kefalonia in 1941. He swam several miles to the shore and was protected by the islanders until they eventually smuggled him to Turkey *(RNSM)*.

The machinery space aft where Capes was sleeping on an empty torpedo rack (left) before being thrown on to the hydroplane wheel (right) as *Perseus* plunged to the sea bed.

Kostas Thoctarides swims along the hull of *Perseus* where she now lies on the sea bed. His exploration of the interior of the submarine confirmed every detail of Capes's account of his escape. *(Kostas Thoctarides)*.

A post-war view of Fort Blockhouse at Gosport, guarding the entrance to Portsmouth harbour. This was HMS *Dolphin*, the headquarters of the Submarine Service *(IWM HU)*.

A trainee emerges from the hatch in the escape tank at Fort Blockhouse wearing his DSEA set *(IWM)*.

The depot ship *Medway* with the submarines of the 1st Flotilla *(RNSM)*.

First lieutenants enjoying a convivial evening at the Officers' Club at Wei Hai Wei in 1932. On the left, Ginger Harvey, Hugh Dewhurst and Ben Bryant. Nearest on the right, Dickie Gaisford *(RNSM)*.

The rum issue in *Regulus* at Singapore on Christmas Day, 1939 *(RNSM)*.

Philip Ruck-Keene (above) in 1945. Wartime leader of the 3rd then 1st Flotillas, he was 'a huge bull of a man ... hard as nails in resolve, flexible in action and, above all, realistic'. Right, Shrimp Simpson, the tough and resourceful captain of the 10th Flotilla during the seige of Malta *(RNSM)*.

Torpedomen playing cribbage in the fore ends of *Seraph*, crammed full with gear *(RNSM)*.

Britain's first wartime hero: Edward Bickford in *Salmon*, after torpedoing two cruisers and a U-boat in December 1939 *(Getty Images)*

Bill King cheered into harbour in *Snapper* after sinking four ships in April 1940 *(RNSM)*.

Sealion at Harwich, base of the 3rd Flotilla, in January 1940. The winter was so cold that the harbour iced over *(RNSM)*.

Hugh Rufus Mackenzie on board *Medway* in 1942; the mayor of Gosport sitting between Hugh 'Rider' Haggard and his father at the adoption ceremony for *Truant* in 1943 with members of the crew; Jacky Slaughter in *Sunfish* after sinking three ships in April 1940 *(RNSM)*.

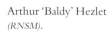

Arthur 'Baldy' Hezlet *(RNSM)*.

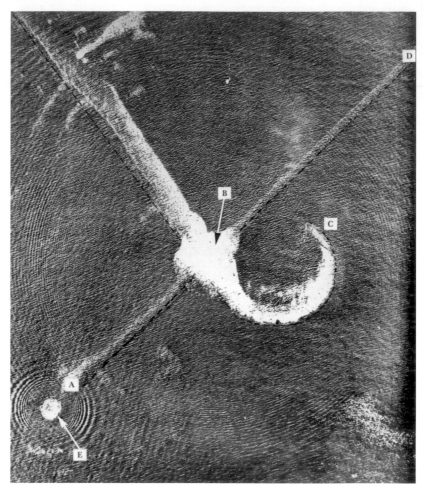

This attack by John Roxburgh in *United* in June 1943 was photographed by a PRU Spitfire from Malta. It took place a mile off Capo del Armi in the Strait of Messina. *United*'s victim was the 5153-ton Norwegian liner *Ringulv*, which had been requisitioned by the Kriegsmarine.

The submerged *United* fired a full salvo of four torpedoes at a range of 900 yards on a perfect ninety-degree track from A. Two hit the *Ringulv* at B. The track of the two that missed continued to D and beyond. The liner, disabled, turned in a circle to C. She sank within five minutes. One of two escorting aeroplanes has dropped a bomb close to *United*'s firing position at E. *United* had already dived to 120 feet and turned off track. The wake of the escorting German torpedo boat can be seen bottom right. In a counter attack she dropped twenty depth charges close enough to break a number of lights in the submarine *(RNSM)*.

messenger to tell the captain. Slaughter asked for the message word by word as it was decoded, ordered the torpedoes to be brought to the ready and continued with his dummy attack. 'Sink ... all ... ships ... at ... sight ...', read the message as the enemy ship approached the firing position, 'in ... the ... Skagerrak ... and ... Kattegat.' 'Fire!' ordered Commander Slaughter. The 7000 ton *Amasis* sank.

At about the same moment *Truant*'s engine room was celebrating the birthday of one of the artificers, short, stocky Bill 'China' King, when they were called to diving stations. After half an hour 'the captain came on the Tannoy and gave everybody a blast for being slow to get to diving stations as he'd missed an attack on a flotilla of destroyers.' As time went by, submarines learned that it was better not to attack destroyers because they were difficult to hit and angry when missed.

Two hours later *Truant*'s asdic operator told the captain he could hear very faint propeller noises to the north. Gradually they became louder and eventually Hutchinson saw a German cruiser approaching with three small destroyers. He manoeuvred inside the screen and thought he was in perfect position, but when he next raised the periscope the Germans had turned away. There was just a chance of a long shot and *Truant* got away a salvo that crippled the *Karlsruhe*. She stayed afloat but she was a lost cause, and eventually one of her own escorts had to deliver a *coup de grâce*. *Truant* was heavily counter-attacked but eventually she escaped, Hutchinson signalling his success and his intention to return to base.

That night *U4* caught *Thistle* on the surface recharging her batteries and destroyed her, along with her fifty-three crew. *Thistle* had previously attacked and missed *U4* and only had two torpedoes left. Next day *Tarpon* attacked *Schiff 40* with two torpedoes, but missed; she and her fifty-three crew were also lost.

The main body of Admiral Forbes's Home Fleet had been attacked from the air. A destroyer sank and a huge bomb landed on his flagship but failed to explode. Forbes announced he was going to operate in northern Norway and was leaving the south to submarines because his ships could not operate there in the face of German air power. Further south, however, his own air power struck an even more significant blow. *Königsberg*, damaged by Norwegian shore batteries, was sunk in Bergen harbour by Fleet Air Arm Skuas. It was the first time that a capital ship had been sunk by air attack. Nevertheless, after so many near misses, Forbes feared that the next capital ship to be sunk by dive-bombers would be one of his own.

That Wednesday British submarines crowded into the Skagerrak. As the morning mist lifted Lieutenant Bill King, looking through *Snapper*'s periscope, found the sky black with streams of German planes flying to and from Norway. On water the Germans were concentrating all their efforts on getting supplies across to Oslo, and were massing their anti-submarine vessels in the shallow seas. Several submarines attacked, but missed by firing too few torpedoes or setting their depth too low. Jacky Slaughter spent much of the day tracking the troop transport *Antares*, missing her once before finally sinking her and killing 500 German soldiers. In the afternoon, Bertie Pizey in *Triton* sighted a convoy of fifteen ships carrying 8500 troops, 1500 vehicles and supplies to Oslo. He fired six torpedoes from about a mile and a half away and sank two troop transports, *Friedenau* and *Wigbert*, and an escort vessel, drowning 900 German infantry.

Jock Forbes in *Spearfish* watched Pizey make this attack. *Triton* herself escaped, but one of the escorting destroyers found *Spearfish*. She took an intense battering from sixty-six depth charges in an hour and was hunted for the next six hours by three German destroyers. Forbes finally lost them by steering underneath other noisy ships, using the wall of sound from their engines to confuse the listening hunters. Forbes had not been long on the surface recharging his batteries on a dark, clear night when just after midnight his first lieutenant spotted the bow wave of a darkened ship two miles away. Thinking it was a destroyer, Forbes started to turn away, then realised it was a battleship approaching at speed. They readied the torpedoes and Forbes fired a salvo of six by eye before making off on the surface. Two of his torpedoes hit the pocket battleship *Lützow* returning from Oslo. She was left drifting and slowly sinking, with both propellers blown off and her rudder jammed. A Danish tug took her in tow but ran her aground on a sandbank. Bryant was told to look for her but couldn't find her, and *Lützow* reached Kiel on 12 April. However, she was so badly damaged that she did not sail again until 1941.

Triad was off Oslo Fjord looking for German warships. *Lützow* had already left but *Triad's* new captain Eric Oddie, a large ginger-haired Irishman with a ruddy face, sank the transport *Ionia*. She was *Triad's* first kill. 'Faces lit up as if illuminated by an interior lamp,' recalled stoker Syd Hart. There was a babble of excited voices, followed by 'a crisp reminder from the Captain: "We haven't won the war yet! Silence!"' But although they heard many depth charges as they retreated, none came close.

Bryant in *Sealion* was having a frustrating time. Most of his patrol had been in the dangerous shallows of the Kattegat, constantly plagued by fishing vessels, many of which were actually anti-submarine trawlers. He had let the *Otterberg* go because she was not on his list of German ships and he had happened to be in the wrong place when warships passed. On Thursday afternoon another ship came by, but its flag was hanging limply. The red and white that were visible might be Danish or Norwegian or German. Then the wind blew and the Swastika streamed out. Bryant fired and waited nervously. After two minutes a huge column of water erupted and the *August Leonhard's* bows rose into the air as she sank stern first. The water was so shallow that her bridge, funnel and masts remained visible as Bryant let the crew, one by one, see their first victim through the periscope. 'Will the crew be all right, sir?' asked a stoker.

For *Snapper's* navigator, 12 April was his first wedding anniversary. John Bromage was thinking of home when they spotted a tanker. Bill King missed it with torpedoes because it was much smaller than he had thought, but chased it for seven miles before ordering it to stop. The tanker kept going, so King ordered gun-layer Myles Lawson to put a shot into the forepeak. There was a massive explosion as Germans dived over the side: the tanker had been carrying aviation fuel. The gunlayer, thereafter known as 'One shot' Lawson, was astonished. They nosed around picking up the crew as King watched anxiously for aircraft. The first bomber appeared as King reluctantly allowed his third officer to drag in the last German.

King now moved from the Skagerrak, which was full of air-craft, to the Kattegat, which was full of trawlers. As he made his way in, harassed by minesweepers and trawlers, Bryant was trying to make his way out with a defective engine, having been ordered home. To avoid an anti-submarine sweep he risked escaping on the surface over the sandbanks on the Danish side. They evaded more trawlers in the Skagerrak and dived just in time to avoid bombs from an Anson, before being met at Harwich by an anx-ious Ruckers, who had brought Marjorie Bryant with him.

Meanwhile, back in the Kattegat King was woken from exhausted slumber by a shout of 'Captain in the control room!' A convoy escorted by destroyers had emerged from the mist. The hydraulics that opened the bow caps had failed and the torpedo-men had to open them by hand as King swung *Snapper* round to a position to attack. A destroyer raced overhead and the first lieu-tenant struggled to keep the boat trimmed. King loosed off five torpedoes on an instant calculation, doubtful of success, and was almost surprised to hear a loud bang as the 6150 ton German merchant *Florida* sank. Not far away Jacky Slaughter sank *Schiff 35*. The next night King was peering into the murky light before dawn when his third officer saw something. King glued his binoculars to the bearing and glimpsed shape after shape in the mist. The bow caps were permanently open now on the surface so he was able to react quickly, firing a salvo on a sportsman's guess. What he took to be a convoy of troop ships turned out to be minesweepers, but he sank two of them.

As the S-boats came home, Ruck-Keane organised enthusiastic receptions for them. The civilian maintenance technicians he had hired to support the boats in the railway workshop were invited on board *Cyclops* to welcome their charges home and other ships at Harwich were alerted. It was great for morale. When *Snapper* returned from her successful patrol, with sailors at ease on the casing and King conning the boat, 'We saw lines of sailors waiting on the deck of every ship in harbour. From their neat blue ranks a hurrah arose. They were giving us a "cheer ship". This was indeed a moving moment . . . The spring grass of the estuary had never looked so green.'

It was vitally important to attack German supply convoys for Norway but each day it was becoming more difficult. The submarines that Horton had amassed at the beginning of April were running out of torpedoes and having to go home. As they brought captured Norwegian and Danish boats into action, the Germans had more and more anti-submarine vessels available. Each night was shorter and brighter than the last, making it harder for submarines to operate in dangerous areas when they had to recharge their batteries to survive. They had to move away from convoy routes and hostile guards for the precious hours of darkness. The anti-submarine vessels did not have to do anything – their presence in itself would force British boats into defensive rather than aggressive mode.

In the evening of 15 April, *Sterlet*'s signalman Harry Thomsett spotted the anti-aircraft training cruiser *Brummer* in the dusk. They were close, and although the Germans saw the torpedo tracks, *Brummer* could not avoid a strike that blew her bows off. *Sterlet* though was probably sunk in the counter-attack by the escorts, for she failed to return from patrol. Harry's brother Jim Thomsett, in *Warspite*, had just been involved in the second battle of Narvik. *Warspite*'s spotter planes had destroyed a U-boat, though another U-boat claimed to have hit the battleship with a torpedo that failed to explode.

On 18 April *Seawolf* sank another German supply ship, but she was one of only five British and four French submarines now on patrol. Horton had repeatedly demanded destroyer sweeps to deal with the troublesome trawlers and minesweepers. After much persuasion Admiral Forbes scheduled one for the night of 17/18 April and then cancelled it at the last moment for fear of losing more of his precious destroyers to air attack. Only the French were brave enough to help. Three of their fast destroyers made a sweep on 23/24 April. They sank two patrol boats and a trawler before withdrawing. On the way home they came under heavy air attack but escaped without damage. 'The refusal of help from the Commander-in-Chief and the final solution of calling on the French to pull our chestnuts out of the fire put Ruck-Keene and me in a highly critical mood,' recalled Shrimp Simpson.

Horton was still not satisfied that his men were holding their nerve and taking enough risks. On 21 April 'Colonel' Menzies noted in his diary, 'I had the very difficult task of telling the boys that they could afford to stay at periscope depth until the hunters were upon them and that they should not retire because they hear H.E. What they dislike are the bangs.' He removed Alan Seale from command of *Trident*, perhaps at Seale's own request, though Hezlet's views on Seale's unaggressive performance would have condemned him in the current climate. Menzies was happy with most of his boys, though: 'In the afternoon I had a good walk and then had a supper with Sladen, "Hutch" and Van der Byl. They with Pizey are a great team and I think that Hitler will know when they return to the fray.'

Shrimp Simpson remembered the Norwegian campaign as a missed opportunity – a story of frustration. The opportunity for him was the moment of invasion. Had the government allowed submarines to attack merchant ships, far more damage could have been done. Horton had twenty submarines with 250 torpedoes in place to thwart Hitler's move against Norway and they were not allowed to act. Even allowing for the likelihood that at key moments the Germans – through their code-breakers – knew where submarines were, it would still have been possible to sink far more ships. Had the Admiralty taken notice of its intelligence, and had Admiral Forbes had the panache to send a large force of destroyers into the Skagerrak on 7/8 April, the whole course of the war might have been different. If Forbes was waiting to refight Jutland, others were learning faster.

From the point of view of the British Admiralty the Norwegian campaign was embarrassing, but from the German point of view it was extremely costly. German naval losses were so great that any further seaborne invasion was difficult to contemplate. *Blücher*, *Lützow*, *Königsberg*, *Karlsruhe* and *Brummer* joined *Leipzig* and *Nürnberg* on the casualty list and twelve out of twenty-two destroyers had been sunk. In June *Scharnhorst* and *Gneisenau* were also put out of action.

Most of the capital ships were victims of submarines. In the Norwegian campaign proper there were on average fifteen Allied submarines on patrol. For the loss of *Thistle*, *Tarpon* and *Sterlet*, they sank *Karlsruhe*, *Brummer* and three minesweepers, and seriously damaged *Lützow*; they also sank thirteen merchant ships and damaged five.

U-boats did far less well. During the campaign there were usually about thirty at sea, concentrated around the invasion ports in the north. They sank a submarine, a minesweeper and four merchant ships, losing two boats sunk and two damaged.

The Germans blamed torpedo failures and claimed they would have created far more carnage had their torpedoes only worked. It wasn't always the torpedoes that were at fault, however, and in several cases the torpedoes did not fail, they missed. Intelligence was also to blame, for the British had evened things up. On 15 April the destroyers *Fearless* and *Brazen* caught *U49* and from her they also captured a chart showing the position of all the U-boats in the North Sea.

When the Germans investigated the alleged torpedo failures they discovered one interesting fact that had caused both sides to miss. High pressure within a submarine during long dives disrupted the torpedo depth setting, causing torpedoes to run deeper than their set depth. This probably contributed to many misses by both sides on shallow targets like submarines and anti-submarine craft. Both sides were still learning how to use their torpedoes, learning about their peculiarities and faults. Off Norway they learned the hard way about hunting and being hunted.

9

HUNTER AND HUNTED

The hunt began when someone detected a target. By day, submerged, this was probably the officer of the watch, who would raise the larger search periscope at least once every five minutes for a maximum of thirty seconds. First a quick all-round look – all the way round the horizon for ships and across the sky for aircraft. Then a slower, more careful scrutiny of each sector. Never for many seconds: the periscope must not be seen. On sighting something suspicious, the officer's first action was to call the captain to the control room: 'Tell the captain there is a long, low object bearing dead ahead.' On the surface at night it would be one of the lookouts. 'Object bearing red five oh.' (Red meant port, green meant starboard.)

To help identify targets, the officers had a small library of guides to ship recognition and to ship performance and armament. The latest edition of *Jane's Fighting Ships* was supplemented by various publications by Eric Talbot-Booth. *What Ship is That?* included profile silhouettes of all merchant ships and warships at sea, grouped by similar types. *Ships of the World's Battlefleets* and *Merchant Ships* were more specialised. An effort was made in a series of wartime editions to keep abreast of sinkings. Distinguishing between *Karlsruhe*, *Nürnberg* and *Leipzig* was a matter of tiny detail in the profile and position of masts and equipment, observations that had to be made when any of the vessels might be doing up to thirty-two knots.

Theoretically, the captain was never on watch, but in practice he might well be there already, sweeping his binoculars on to the bearing. In the case of Christopher Hutchinson and *Karlsruhe* it was the asdic operator who heard faint propeller noises to the north while submerged, so 'Hutch' was at the periscope scouring the horizon in the right direction when the masts of what he identified as a cruiser and three light torpedo destroyers appeared over it coming towards him – as good a situation as possible. The search periscope was bifocal and Hutchinson adjusted it until two images of the enemy vessel appeared above each other. Then he could say, 'My range is . . . ' and the ERA standing behind him would read off the range, as shown by the periscope, to torpedo officer Donald Watson and navigator Bernard Mansfield.

Hutchinson now had to manoeuvre his boat to a position between the protective escorts and the big prize, the cruiser. The escorts were usually two or three thousand yards from their charge, and the ideal firing position for the submarine was about 1200 yards from the target's beam at ninety degrees to its path. He thought the escorts and cruiser were capable of thirty knots, *Truant* of nine submerged (and that only for a very short time). In this case the escorts were the torpedo boats *Greif*, *Seeadler* and *Luchs* and they were rather faster.

The Truants went to action stations with the most proficient crewman on each piece of kit. The captain gave the order to bring all tubes to the ready and the torpedomen, under the truculent Australian torpedo gunner's mate Gus Fisher, let water into the torpedo space from within the submarine so that the weight forward didn't change. The next order was 'Begin the attack.' From now on navigator Mansfield plotted the relative positions of *Truant* and the enemy on paper. First lieutenant Reginald Whiteway-Wilkinson supervised the trim. Torpedo Officer

Watson worked out from the range and bearing of the target the deflection angle and the firing interval for the torpedoes. To help him, in this brand new boat he had a Submarine Torpedo Director or 'fruit machine', a state-of-the-art but still very primitive computer, which worked out the deflection angle and firing interval from figures fed into it. Torpedoes moved at forty-five knots, the target at an estimated twenty-three. The submarine had to aim ahead of the target in order to hit her; the calculation worked out how far ahead. It was, of course, a constantly evolving calculation.

'Hutch' took the boat down to sixty feet and put in a burst of speed to get within the screen – between the nearest escort and the cruiser, and well ahead of both. The second coxswain on the after hydroplanes set them to 'hard-a-dive'. Coxswain Ron Adams on the forward planes directed the boat's nose down and levelled off at sixty feet. They were staring at big, round shallow-depth gauges which gave a very exact reading to a depth of 100 feet. The less detailed deep gauge was calibrated to 500 feet. Ralph Merritt set the motors to full speed both. Then, as Hutch's order rang through on the motor room telegraph, he slowed right down so that the captain could raise the smaller attack periscope without it 'showing a lot of feather' (creating a visible wash). All this took about twenty minutes. Hutch signalled the leading stoker, who worked the hydraulic control to raise the periscope. The huge, heavy brass cylinder rose from its well and Hutch squatted, seized the handles and pressed his eye against it. His knees straightened and a finger movement told the stoker when to stop it rising. An ERA stood behind the skipper to once more read off the bearing and range on the periscope to Watson and Mansfield.

Hutchinson 'found that I was in an ideal position to be able to fire'. He lowered the periscope so as to be invisible and waited for the cruiser to reach the firing position. The torpedomen readied all ten forward firing torpedoes and opened the bow caps. About two minutes later he raised the periscope again, 'hoping that I would be able to give the order to fire fairly quickly'. One look revealed that everything had gone wrong. 'To my disgust I saw that the cruiser and her escorts had altered course about seventy degrees to the eastwards, placing me in a most unfavourable position. She was rapidly running away from me. It was a case of now or never.' The range was now 3500 yards on a 130 degree track (or compass bearing) instead of 1200 yards on a 90 degree track.

At 1856 Hutchinson began to fire a dispersed salvo of ten torpedoes at six-second intervals. The targets were moving, so a second torpedo might hit a target that the first torpedo had missed ahead. The torpedomen could set the depth at which the torpedoes ran. Hutchinson ordered the first two to be set to ten feet as a compromise, the next six to twelve feet for the cruiser and the last two to eight feet for the escort. One of the officers set a stop watch and called 'Fire one! . . . Fire two!' at six-second intervals, finishing after a minute. Torpedomen, listening on headphones, pulled the lever that released each torpedo as the order came. The asdic operator listened to confirm that the torpedoes were running.

As the torpedoes left and water flooded in to balance their weight, the 'submarine became slightly heavy', to quote the patrol report. This phrase conceals drama. It seems that momentarily Whiteway-Wilkinson lost control of the trim: the last torpedoes may have been fired pointing a little downwards, or at any rate *Truant* ended up below periscope depth, unable to see and fighting to regain stability without breaking the surface. A torpedo runs at rather more than 1000 yards a minute, so the Truants expected detonations in about three minutes. A torpedo boat moves a little slower, at about 800 yards a minute, so if one saw the torpedo tracks at an early stage it could be upon them quite quickly.

Two minutes and forty-five seconds after the first torpedo was released the Truants heard a loud explosion. They heard a second a minute later and a third fifteen seconds after that. The asdic operator thought the noises sounded similar to those he had heard from the merchantman they had sunk, a noise like rending metal. That previous occasion was the first time any of them had heard such a sound, so it was difficult to be sure. Half a minute after the third bang, Whiteway-Wilkinson regained periscope depth and Hutchinson took a look. He saw 'nothing but a very enlarged after-part of a destroyer which was right on top of us. In fact, I was staring at a fat cook at the galley door.' They dived as fast as possible and turned ninety degrees away from the firing track. Had Hutchinson appreciated the imminent danger he would ideally have turned away earlier, but at that stage they were fighting to get their depth right.

Immediately the hunter became the hunted: 'retribution was bound to follow, and sure enough, it did.' At this date German submarine hunters normally carried only eighteen depth charges each, although later they carried as many as fifty. There were several types of depth charge with different performances. Potentially the most destructive were the WBD, which weighed 397 lb including an explosive charge of 276 lb and travelled through the water at 11.5 feet per second. They could be set with a time fuse to explode at any of six different depths up to a maximum of 394 feet. If they exploded within twenty-six feet of a submarine they were capable of breaching its pressure hull and destroying it. An explosion at a range of up to fifty feet might cause fatal damage. The other types had smaller charges of 132 lb, which gave them a killing range of eighteen feet. The WBG variety had a similar performance to the WBD. The WBH sank faster at 14.3 feet per second, to a greater maximum depth of 492 feet, while the WBF were the weakest, sinking slowly to a maximum of only 246 feet. The crudest way of releasing charges was to push them down a ramp over the stern, but most German boats also had six depth-charge throwers to project single charges up and over the side.

As they ran in to attack, the enemy would lose any contact they had made with a submarine by listening with the hydrophones or by pinging with sonar (if they had it). For this reason attacks were made at speed and it was useful if charges sank quickly. For the same reason this was a good time for a submarine to move quickly to a different position.

When the charges exploded they damaged the submarine through both primary and secondary shock waves. The initial shock wave from the explosion would cause serious damage if the detonation was sufficiently close, and an explosion underneath a submarine could do much more damage than one above it. Subsequent shock waves, resulting from the expansion and contraction of the gas bubble created by the explosion, would bend the metal of the submarine in and out repeatedly and could cause the hull to burst, especially at any seams. If a second depth charge exploded on the other side of the submarine at roughly the same time as the first, it reinforced the effect of the secondary shock wave, and chiefly for this reason depth charges were usually dropped in pairs or 'patterns'.

For *Truant*, one and a half minutes elapsed between seeing the destroyer and the explosion of the first depth charges. On a word from Whiteway-Wilkinson, the outside ERA flooded Q – the quick diving tank – and *Truant* dived to sixty feet. She could have reached 150 feet or more in the time and the Germans probably set their charges to detonate at too great a depth, expecting her to have dived as quickly as possible. Nevertheless, they exploded below the boat and not far away. The submariners thought they were dead. The forehatch lifted, admitting water, and then closed again with the clips intact. The noises were stupendously loud. 'The first two explosions were very violent indeed. Everything appeared to jump around. Anything that was loose in the control room, such as a logbook, leaped off its table. Various pipes began to hiss compressed air. Leaks began appearing, and the stern began to get heavy and our depth increased.'

It was particularly terrifying because they were now in the unknown. Even Hutchinson had 'only once heard a depth charge in my life until this occasion, and that was at the safe distance of about five miles away'. They were 'facing a weapon that was new to us'. They had no measure of experience by which to judge what was happening to them. No way of knowing how good the enemy were, what knowledge they had, what weapons they had, how determined they would be. 'Hutch' ordered another dive to 150 feet, but neither hydroplane would work and depth control was lost.

Jack Pook was right aft, in charge of the machinery there. He quickly established that the after hydroplane could be controlled locally from where he was. But as the secondary shocks took effect, he 'saw the water coming in through the tanks. The after tank was full up, the bulkheads started to leak and we were very heavy aft, so we were at an angle.' After twenty minutes there was water coming in around the after hydroplanes and from the stern gland. The boat's angle increased. Ahead of Pook in the engine room water was flooding into the circulating system, while in the motor room sparks were flying from the main motor switch gear. He was kept busy at first because the 'stern glands were leaking and I had to tighten those up. We had to hammer up the bulk-head of the trim tank which had been damaged. We were jamming off valves which had blown open with the charges.' The stern glands were inaccessible and had to be tightened evenly while the propeller shaft was rotating, a tortuous and delicate job. Uneven tightening would produce serious overheating, which would cause even more trouble. Hutchinson 'tried to pump water out from a tank aft, but quickly stopped because it would have acted as a certain marker to those on the surface'. The oily water would have given them away. 'Our Sperry compass was going round in circles, as was the magnetic compass, with the explosions shaking up the metal of the ship's hull.' This sort of damage was typical of severe depth-charging that just failed to sink a boat.

Up above them *Greif* had stayed by the slowly sinking *Karlsruhe*. Once it was clear the cruiser was lost, she took her crew of about 830 men on board. *Luchs* and *Seeadler* were hunting. After each attack the destroyers stopped to listen, using echo sounding. The Truants could hear this as an eerie, repeated 'ping'. They also heard a more mysterious sound 'like gravel dropping on the hull' that baffled and frightened everyone in *Truant*.

Then one of the destroyers would race in to where they thought the submarine was and drop their 'ashcans', as depth charges were known from their shape. Hutchinson had taken *Truant* down to 320 feet. He kept moving at three and a half knots because there were too many leaks to remain stopped. All other machinery was switched off, including nearly all the lights. With the Sperry compass stopped and the magnetic compasses still going round in circles, he was using the rudder blind, trying to keep stern on to the enemy in order to present as small a target as possible. They were in 620 fathoms of water, so there was no chance to employ the familiar Great War tactic of lying on the bottom with everything switched off. But as far as possible they conserved energy, oxygen and battery power: 'you didn't move about too much, you made sure you didn't drop anything, you spoke in whispers, you didn't use the Tannoy or anything like that.'

The experience of danger in a submarine varied according to where you were stationed. 'If you're in the control room you know what's going on, but in the engine room you haven't an idea. That's the worst part about it. If you don't know anything, your mind starts working.' It was worst if you were in some compartment alone. 'I was in the forward pump space and you're on your own. All you've got are six valves, an indicator, and you just sit there and you have to either Flood or Pump. You're on your own, you don't know what's happening, and every little noise . . . Whereas if you're with somebody it helps.'

The attacks continued for more than three hours, while *Truant* circled. Some of the depth charges exploded dangerously close but Hutchinson attributed survival to going deep, 'which was a great depth then, and I'm quite sure this saved us and that the depth charges were exploding well above us'. Pook remembered

Truant 'riding at a nasty angle with bow up, stern down, due to the leaks aft' and reckoned that in the stern they were at '420 feet which was way over our diving depth'. The safe depth to which T-class submarines were tested was 300 feet. The pressure at that depth was 9¼ tons per square foot. *Truant* had a riveted hull and at depths below 300 feet the hull began to make a groaning sound as it suffered under the strain. The noise served as a warning, but it must have been constant and alarming for Pook and his mates in the stern.

Pook felt fine while he was busy, but 'if there was nothing to do we laid in bunks and waited' and that was worse: 'It was terrifying, there's no doubt about it. I don't care who it is that's been on these jobs, you must be frightened. It's not the charges that are frightening, it's the waiting for them, particularly in a submarine where you hear the destroyers coming towards you. And you know that the next thing you are going to hear is a depth charge ... You hear the propellers through the water, the thrum-hum of the propellers. Gradually it gets louder and louder, almost like a train going over the top.' Then there was the wait as the charges fell through the water at between seven and fourteen feet per second, depending on the type of charge – most likely at the slower rate this early in the war. So Pook would have waited the best part of half a minute before the explosion.

Syd Hart, the Lancashire stoker, described his first experience of a dangerous attack, which came ten days after Pook's:

> It was possible to hear depth charges speeding down through the water towards us, and even before they exploded, easy to realise they were coming annoyingly close. Then, for the fraction of a second, the whole undersea seemed to burst wide open.
>
> The whole of *Triad*'s interior became nothing but a blurred vision, for all the world like a cinema screen when the film being displayed runs off the rails and goes crazy. Paint tore off the bulkheads, lights tinkled down to the deck as if somebody

had been using them as targets at an Aunt Sally stall. And before the crashing din of the first attack had died down, a second pattern of depth charges was speeding through the water towards us. All eyes turned up towards the deck-head. Whoomph! Tah-whoomph! Whoomph! There was the same fantastic blur inside our narrow ship; she bucked and plunged as if she were a bronco being spurred to madness. A voice grunted: 'By the b—y hell, those were close!'

Hart found himself looking around at his mates, drawing comfort from the thought that they would all go together. He took inspiration from Albert 'Snowy' Whitbread, a blond reservist with a grown-up daughter, who stood by the fuel oil tanks. 'On Snowy's lips was the faint suspicion of a smile. Solid as the Rock of Gibraltar, he looked. "Good old Snowy!" I thought. "I hope my nerve's as good as that when I've turned forty!"'

Pook, too, found that being in a group helped: 'I wouldn't say that people showed their fear. You're all together, you're all on the same boat, and I think it's a matter of disciplining yourself . . . You don't show it. You're probably churning over inside but you don't show it.'

The noise of a depth charge exploding was extremely loud and terrifying. One captain likened it to being 'in a fifteen-inch turret standing between the guns when the guns go off'. People who were capable of silent comedy in these circumstances were invaluable. Hutchinson found himself enormously grateful to the ship's cook, Arthur Renaut: 'As we heard the destroyer coming closer and closer overhead about to chuck another load of ash-cans at us, cookie, who was peeling potatoes, used to flip a potato in the air with his finger and try to make it drop in the pan to coincide with the next *whoompha*. This distracted attention and helped enormously in helping to keep people's nerve.'

After nearly three hours, when it had been quiet for fifteen minutes Hutchinson decided to bring the boat up, but as they reached 150 feet there was a new explosion. It is possible that this wasn't in fact a depth charge but *Greif* giving the *coup de grâce* to *Karlsruhe* with a torpedo. But they went back to 300 feet and waited some more.

By now, after eighteen hours submerged, the battery was low, the air was foul, and there was a pressure of four and a half inches within the boat. The normal limit to the endurance of a submerged boat was about thirty hours, depending on her size, the number of crew, their physical condition and the quality of the atmosphere. By now the atmosphere in *Truant* was deteriorating. 'The air was getting thick,' Pook said. 'You start to pant, your senses start to go a little bit, you don't think so quickly.' After waiting an hour or so longer, 'Hutch' took the boat very slowly to the surface. There was nothing in sight. He opened the hatches carefully to release the pressure and allow in enough oxygen for the stokers to start the twin engines that they had christened 'Adolf' and 'Hermann'. The only problem now was that they were somewhere close to occupied Norway; the sky was overcast and they had no compass. Hutchinson steered downwind, hoping the wind was blowing from the same direction as earlier in the day. Then, to his relief, the stars came out and he set a course south-west.

Truant's ordeal was not unusual, but Hutchinson was probably lucky that he was forced to keep the motors running. At this early stage in the war commanders tried as a rule to remain still and quiet. *Trident*'s first lieutenant Baldy Hezlet explained, 'This was early on in the days of submarine warfare and we weren't very experienced. We were quite certain the enemy had hydrophones and could hear us if we made a noise. We therefore tried hard not to use any machinery, to do everything as silently as we could. Of course, if you don't use any machinery in a submarine it will do as it likes and you begin to lose control.'

Trident had gone back out on patrol in late April with a new commander, Slasher Sladen, in place of the cautious Alan Seale. Sladen and Hezlet found that all the enemy traffic was going up narrow channels within the Norwegian islands while they were patrolling outside and achieving nothing. 'This captain was made of really stern stuff,' recalled Hezlet. Sladen took them right up Kors Fjord just south of Bergen. It was highly dangerous, but they got their reward when they drove the big merchant *Cläre Hugo Stinnes* ashore on 2 May. At that point Sladen said, 'I think we'd better get out of this,' so they cleared off down Kors Fjord at top speed on the surface. They had just reached the entrance when aircraft and anti-submarine vessels appeared and the hunt began. At one point they were very deep, with the stern down like *Truant*, only with no motor. Sladen was still anxious that there should be no sound. 'Eventually we had to do something,' recalled Hezlet, 'because the bilge water was getting near the electric motors and he said, "Well, get some buckets." We bailed the water out of the engine room, passing these buckets through the submarine and poured them into the torpedo compartment, which made less noise than pumping. This decreased the angle and then a stoker in the engine room dropped a bucket which made a huge clatter. Everybody burst out laughing, easing the tension.'

Being responsible for the trim, the precise and intolerant Hezlet was probably not amused by his inability to maintain a fixed depth. They reached a point where *Trident* was still sinking and in danger of going too deep and imploding. Sladen said, 'I think the best thing is to blow a little into the main ballast to stop her going down.' So they did that. 'But of course,' said Hezlet, 'you lose control because, as you come up the air expands and becomes more buoyant and after a very short time we were roaring up out of control and burst right out of the sea.' Fortunately, the enemy had gone.

As April turned to May and June, life became progressively harder for submarines in the Skagerrak and off the Norwegian coast. Once the Germans were able to base planes on Danish and Norwegian airfields, their anti-submarine patrols were extensive and aircraft could quickly be called to assist a ship under attack. At this time of year the water was crystal clear and submarines could be seen from the air while shallowly submerged. Similarly, the acquisition of Danish and Norwegian patrol craft and trawlers meant that there were numerous flotillas of small craft available, capable of hunting and based close to the scene of operations.

These operational inconveniences were compounded by the familiar Scandinavian problem with light: 'too much dark and damn little light in the winter and vice-versa in the summer', in Hutchinson's words. In summer this meant that there was very little safe time available to recharge the batteries. In mid-May there were five and a half hours of darkness in the Skagerrak and just two and a half off Trondheim. By June it simply never got dark off Trondheim or further north and an aeroplane might find you in the middle of the night; further south the slot during which the batteries might be recharged safely was only a little over three hours in the Skagerrak, and anti-submarine vessels interrupting a charge could put a submarine in trouble with little more than their mere presence.

This is what happened to Ronnie Mills on 22 April when he arrived in the Skagerrak in the brand new *Tetrarch* with a crew who had barely had an opportunity to work up – to practise together and get to know their boat until they reached a sufficiently high level of efficiency to engage the enemy with confidence. Mills was forced to dive with his battery charge incomplete and was kept underwater all next day by patrol craft. At six in the evening he sighted an escorted merchant ship, closed at top speed and missed with two torpedoes. The next thing he saw was three destroyers in line abreast following the torpedo tracks towards him. 'I crash-dived to 300 feet which was supposed to be our maximum depth, and two minutes later I heard the hydrophone effect of destroyers coming overhead and a loud series of bangs as they discharged their depth charges. This went on for about half an hour. They dropped thirty depth charges very close to me. Everything rattled and shook. I was glad to think that they were exploding in shallower water than I was.'

For a time it was quiet. Then they heard the destroyers moving away and new vessels coming in. Mills tried to move using one motor but that brought a volley of depth charges. He discussed the situation with the engineer officer, very conscious of a discussion he had had with the doctors called in over the *Thetis* tragedy. They had given him their opinion that, in situations where high pressure from submersion in deep water was combined with foul air, life expectancy was not much more than twenty-four hours. If this was true, they were not going to make it to the following night without releasing the pressure and getting some fresh air.

Mills decided to risk surfacing among the hunting vessels. He came up very gradually, lashed the conning tower hatch before he knocked off the clips, and got the signalman to hold his legs. When he opened the hatch they were both blown into the air, but Mills managed to clutch on to the forward periscope with the signalman still holding his legs. The Tetrarchs manned the gun and started up the engine, sucking in air while they headed for the nearest vessel, blasting away. 'We then got their searchlights on us, and I saw there was another ship fairly close by, so I gave the engines a couple of minutes to clear the atmosphere and then, when the nearest vessel got within 500 yards of me, I crash-dived back to 300 feet. Actually, we went down in a very steep dive to 400 feet before I could check it and then I did a rather spectacular surface,' recalled Mills. 'I was trying to control the ship from diving twenty degrees bow down and I steadied her up at 400 feet, over-corrected and came shooting up to the surface again.' They broke surface before he could regain control and then shot back down to 350 feet. This time he managed to stay there.

'I said the answer was to remain stopped and hope that they will go away. I called trim at 350 feet, and my engineer and I stayed in the control room for the rest of the night and the next day anxiously watching the bubble on the hydroplane unit, and if the bubble started to go forward it meant the bow was coming up and vice versa. I got a man with a couple of buckets of water to come into the control room, and as the bubble tended to go forward so he walked through the submarine to the for'ard end until the bubble came to central and he came back again when the bubble went the other way, and so on. This proved very satisfactory, and we held trim stopped for a period of twelve hours.'

Holding trim stopped was an art form that might be made easier by sitting on a layer of water of a different density. Submariners were always searching for layers; as they came to realise, cooler water was denser than warmer water and the change baffled sonar impulses, so that a submarine could hide under a layer. It was also possible with care to ride on a layer with all machinery switched off. Layers were common where fresh water flowed into seawater. Submariners usually found them by accident, recognising them because they affected the trim so that the submarine suddenly dropped or rose.

After forty-three hours Mills finally decided it was safe to surface, only to discover that he had drifted fifty miles and was now off the brightly lit coast of Sweden. None of the charges had been close enough to do any serious damage, but the ability of the enemy to hunt in relays had made life very difficult. It was a terrifying first patrol.

10

NIGHTMARE SUMMER

The summer of 1940 was a summer of shattered nerves.
Hutchinson had done well. Captain Menzies rated him
highly. 'Everybody had faith in Lieutenant Commander
Hutchinson,' said ERA Pook. But Hutchinson couldn't sleep. He
went to see the doctor, who gave him powerful sedatives, but he
was soon sent on patrol again. It was a dangerous mission, requiring a ninety-mile voyage up Hardanger Fjord near Bergen to land
a party of soldiers before attempting to rendezvous with the
Norwegian submarine *B1*.

The first night out, there was suddenly 'a great red flash, huge
explosions and then this terrific shaking'. Hutchinson dived deep
and began to investigate the damage. Jack Pook was on watch.
The explosions had been underneath the boat and they had split
the batteries. One had several cells broken, water had got in and
it was producing chlorine gas. They reckoned they had probably
been torpedoed by a U-boat whose torpedoes had gone off pre-
maturely. Hutchinson decided that there was no alternative but
to return to base and by the time they arrived back the crew were
wearing gas masks.

Hutchinson was thinking hard. 'It was on the way back to

Rosyth that I realised my nerve had partly gone.' Tortured with guilt and shame, he was trying to decide whether it was irresponsible to keep going or whether in truth his motive was cowardly: to get out and save his own life. Once more, it was the lonely decision of a commander: 'I made the decision that although I could be accused of letting the side down, I did not think it was fair to take on a wartime crew in my condition.' He told his first lieutenant and years later could still remember 'the look of horror on his face. I made a signal that I was returning to base and that the commanding officer needed a relief . . . I could barely face my crew.' Back at Rosyth he was sent to hospital.

At the beginning of May the sun came out and day after day was fine, the sea clear and still, betraying to watching eyes the slightest error with a periscope. Bill King in *Snapper* 'sweated every second the periscope was raised'. With sea and sky blending into a pale haze, distance was difficult to judge. When King in the Skagerrak finally saw a ship, he had to use the periscope as little as possible and 'now the almost psychic accord that existed between me and my leading stoker, whose job it always was to work the periscope control levers, was precious indeed. He responded to my hand and voice with quick delicate brilliance. Our lives depended on his talent.' They got three torpedoes away but King could see their wake clearly as they raced towards the target. The enemy would avoid them.

On 5 May *Seal* laid a minefield in the Kattegat, but herself hit a mine while trying to escape from armed trawlers. She was able to surface, badly damaged, and the captain tried to get her to Sweden, but the engines broke down. Eventually her captain decided to surrender to an enemy seaplane. He was sure the boat would sink, but in fact the Germans managed to bring it into port in triumph.

The capture of *Seal* came as a bad shock at home because nobody knew what information the Germans might have got their hands on as a result. In case their codes were compromised, submarines adopted the Playfair Code, an emergency measure that proved a great setback to the German B–Dienst. In fact, the Germans learned little from *Seal* since her captain had done everything he should have done except succeed in scuttling the boat.

At this time, Ben Bryant and Jacky Slaughter were further into the Skagerrak than King, testing just how bad conditions now were. They found progress difficult, being frequently forced to dive by aeroplanes and patrol boats. In his patrol report to Horton Bryant failed to account for one day. The shrewd admiral noticed and forced Bryant to admit nervously that on that day he had retreated to a quieter area, gone deep and got some sleep. The admiral 'broke into a broad grin: "Quite right too, I always used to do that."' Sleep was a problem. There was discussion at the time as to whether submarine commanders should use a drug like Benzedrine to keep them awake while on patrol. It was a tempting idea, but Horton decided against it. Sooner or later the effect would catch up.

At Harwich the French 10th Flotilla, with their depot ship *Jules Verne*, had reinforced Ruck-Keene's 3rd Flotilla. Each of the French boats was given a British liaison officer, a signalman and a wireless operator, in an attempt to make sure that they understood British signals. John Stevens, who had been in *Triumph* when her bows were blown off by the mine on Boxing Day, reported on board *Cyclops* at Harwich having been appointed to her for 'special service'. His quarters were right aft in *Cyclops*'s overhanging poop, known as the 'Arab Quarter'. He found himself liaison officer to *Circe*, a small, 600-ton submarine with snazzy French design features such as torpedo tubes mounted in turrets outside the pressure hull that could be swivelled to fire at any angle, and a 'kiosk', a small chamber above the pressure hull from which the boat was controlled underwater. The captain, Lieutenant Frossard, chose not to speak English and Stevens's French was limited, but Lieutenant Bellet, who was reading *The Pickwick Papers*, bridged the gap. Leading Signalman Jelly handled visual recognition, while

Leading Telegraphist Hewitt read signals received on the British submarine broadcast.

Stevens found the dining in *Jules Verne* fabulous, and the four-course lunch at sea with copious wine, rounded off with coffee and a liqueur, was barely less acceptable. Between noon and four 'Le Patron', the French equivalent to a naval coxswain, controlled the ship on the periscope. From his red beard Stevens soon became 'Barbe Rouge' or 'Henri Huit', the latter on account of his supposed likeness to Charles Laughton in *The Private Lives of Henry VIII*. Jelly and Hewitt were doubtful about French cooking, and ate their own corned beef and baked beans, occasionally sampling a French dish if it looked safe. While the French sailors drank wine, Stevens administered their customary daily tot of rum.

Circe's first patrol was twice interrupted by returns to base for minor repairs. Captain Ruck-Keene sent for Frossard and Stevens. 'Frossard was subjected to a severe dressing down in English; he probably understood little or nothing, but he must have been in little doubt that the tall and angry British Senior Officer facing him was displeased with a second premature return.' Stevens was then also 'told to do better in no uncertain terms'.

The minelayer *Rubis* under Georges Cabanier did do much better. She appeared at Harwich on 1 May and undertook three successful missions. For the French, however, the situation was becoming complicated. On 10 May Germany invaded Holland, Belgium and Luxembourg and Churchill became Prime Minister. Three days later Panzer divisions crossed the Meuse into France.

All the way through the Norwegian invasion Edward Bickford's boat *Salmon* had been undergoing a refit. He had taken advantage of the time and his engagement to Valerie Courtney, 'one of Britain's most beautiful young yachtswomen', was announced on 8 May. Five days later the couple were married at All Saints Church in Harwich. Most of Bickie's colleagues were on patrol but Bill King was there. He shot up to London afterwards and returned to find that as a result of the capitulation of Holland, *Cyclops* had left for the relative security from German bombers of Scotland, taking all his clothes with her. *Jules Verne* left too, leaving Shrimp Simpson at Harwich to adapt Parkeston Quay into a new home for a flotilla of five H-class anti-invasion scouts.

Several Dutch boats succeeded in escaping from Holland to Britain. Of these only *O13* was in a position to fight immediately, but four brand new boats would be ready to do so after a little work. A new 9th Flotilla base was set up at Dundee under Captain 'George' Roper to look after the various Allied boats now directed by the Royal Navy, with accommodation in an orphanage and workshops in a marmalade factory near the harbour. In early June Admiral Horton paid a special visit to Dundee to congratulate Captain Cabanier and the crew of *Rubis*, whose mines had sunk four ships and whose crew had instantly acquired Scottish girlfriends.

Efforts were now focused on Norway, where an Allied expedition was attempting to seize Narvik. *Narwhal* and *Porpoise* were laying minefields around Norwegian ports. The news from France was worse each day, with the French terrified that Paris was open to attack. On 16 May a conference at the Admiralty decided that there was a real danger of an invasion of Britain and that submarines should be redeployed to give advance warning of any sudden German move. They were to signal first and engage afterwards. Most submarines moved south, contrary to the wishes of Admiral Forbes who wanted them in Norway. *Severn* and *Truant*, however, remained in the perpetual daylight off Narvik, guarding the flanks of an expedition that was bogged down in deep snow, even in mid-May. In France the British Expeditionary Force was in full retreat towards Dunkirk, and while it prepared to leave the French submarines sailed from Dundee for Brest. There was one exception: *Rubis* was asked to stay and continue her highly successful minelaying operations. The French Admiralty agreed.

Things were looking bad when King went on patrol on 24

May, but he did not imagine how bad. When he was diverted southwards from his original position he had no idea that he, Bryant, Jacky Slaughter and another colleague were guarding the north-eastern flank of the Dunkirk evacuation which began on 27 May. Two H-boats kept watch to the south-west. On 28 May Belgium capitulated. The Dunkirk operation ended on 4 June with nearly 340,000 troops lifted but nearly all of their equipment lost.

Narvik was finally captured by the Allies on 28 May, but they decided to pull out again immediately. As the Dunkirk evacuation ended, so the much smaller evacuation of Narvik began. By ill luck, the Germans chose that moment to send *Scharnhorst*, *Gneisenau* and *Hipper* with four destroyers on a sweep to clear a path for German merchant ships and destroy British merchantmen. On 8 June they ran into the aircraft carrier *Glorious* (commanded by Guy D'Oyly-Hughes) and sank her, but *Acasta*, one of her escorts, torpedoed *Scharnhorst*, doing serious damage, though this was not known to the British at the time since *Scharnhorst* then sank *Acasta*. The German battle group retreated to Trondheim, drawing British submarines back to Norway, though even in the south the nights were only half as long as the time required to charge a submarine's battery.

King had become extremely tense. In the beautiful weather he went for 'long introspective walks in the sunlit woods bordering the Firth'. Feeling the weight of responsibility for his crew, he could no longer relax with them, but was instead 'trying to keep my brain taut for the violent battles which occurred on every patrol. I was too alone to talk to anyone. Only the woods or the brief company of women lent a momentary calm.' Joe Blamey in *Porpoise* had been transferred to Blyth, where the crews were accommodated in huts. He asked his wife Clare to come up from Plymouth and rented a couple of rooms for them. Crewmen were now required to be ready for sea at any moment in case of invasion and on several occasions a policeman woke Blamey and his wife to tell him to report to his boat. King calculated that in an emergency he could reach *Snapper* from his Edinburgh hotel in six minutes if he drove his green sports car at over 80 m.p.h. At one false alarm it worked, but unfortunately John Bromage's successor as navigator copied King on the next patrol and got left behind.

At sea the distressing signals requesting missing submarines to report their position became ever more familiar. The Polish submarine *Orzel*, famous for her escape from the Baltic without so much as a map, disappeared in late May or early June, almost certainly mined. The Dutch boat *O13* was lost on her first patrol in mid-June possibly mined, possibly rammed by the Polish boat *Wilk*. Opportunities for attacks meanwhile were few and far between. On 16 June Ronnie Mills in *Tetrarch* sank the large German tanker *Samland*. Minefields laid by *Porpoise*, *Narwhal* and *Rubis* accounted for a number of ships, but the big minelayers were slow to dive and *Porpoise* was twice caught by aircraft. She survived on both occasions, but the polished cynic Philip Quellyn 'P.Q.' Roberts and his crew were badly shaken. Then came one big success. David Ingram, who was well past retirement age but took over the big, fast, river-class *Clyde* in April, managed to get away a long-range salvo at a German battlegroup on 20 June and achieved one hit on the bows of *Gneisenau*, forcing the German battleship to return to port and putting it out of action for six months. The Admiralty thought Ingram might have hit *Scharnhorst*. It was only when both *Scharnhorst* and *Gneisenau* went into dock that the Admiralty realised that neither was fit for battle.

Elsewhere, June 1940 was catastrophic. On 10 June Italy, with a large modern fleet and nearly a hundred submarines, entered the war on the side of Germany. British Mediterranean possessions and trade routes were suddenly vulnerable. Worse followed within a week. On 16 June France asked Britain's permission to conclude a separate peace. The War Cabinet agreed on condition that the French sent their fleet to British ports. But in the confusion of that day, when Reynaud resigned and Pétain took over, the British ambassador gave the French the impression that the stipulation had been dropped, while the British believed that the French had betrayed them and that they had stopped fighting – neither of which was true. The French submarines that were fit for sea left Brest just before the Germans arrived on 18 June. The gigantic ocean raider *Surcouf* and five others sailed to Plymouth. Unfortunately they had no torpedoes, but it was possible to adapt two to fire British ones so they were selected for active service. Other boats were scuttled at Brest to prevent capture.

French efforts to reach Britain were rewarded with an order to remain in British ports or risk bombardment. To be on the safe side Admiral Pound decided that the French vessels should be seized at dead of night. 'Operation Grasp' did not impress the French very much but they surrendered their vessels bloodlessly, except in the case of *Surcouf* at Devonport where two British submarine officers and a rating were mortally wounded. *Rubis* might also have been seized but for the diplomacy of Horton and Roper, who offered her men the chance to join the Free French and fight on. All but a handful of *Rubis*'s crew accepted the offer.

Meanwhile, Britain was braced for invasion. Warned by the Admiralty that such an event was expected that weekend, 6–7 July, Horton sent all his submarines to sea. As he wrote at the time:

> Personally I do not believe it, but perhaps there may be feints or raids from Norwegian ports, and I am covering them all on the W. Coast. I think it more likely they will continue their preparations for a large-scale landing in Kent ... but these things take time, and I now postpone the likelihood of serious attack until the end of July. Meantime they will be ranging their aircraft against us – preparing aerodromes, etc., along northern France and intensity of air raids is bound to increase. They will not start an invasion until their arrangements are perfected.

Horton had to guard against the possibility of invasion but he believed that the threat was probably a diversion, having the benefit of drawing British strength away from convoy protection. 'Again I state', he insisted on 7 July, 'that my opinion is that the Hun's principal weapon to be used against us is blockade and not invasion.' Incensed by the lack of air protection for convoys and worried that there were simply not enough fighters, he hoped that Fighter Command was preoccupied 'by what they realise is in store for the country and therefore do not want to waste any aircraft in supporting us on the sea – but it is all part of the same problem'.

To less well informed observers invasion seemed to be the next logical step. The Luftwaffe looked invincible. The Kriegsmarine was altogether less powerful, even with the resources of the various conquered nations, and the Royal Navy ought to be able to stop it, but the navy hadn't stopped it invading Norway. Should an invasion force succeed in crossing the Channel there seemed to be precious little to halt its progress. It is not surprising that submarines were diverted to anti-invasion activities, although pre-war economies did leave them with certain drawbacks as front-line scouting units.

Simpson's anti-invasion submarines were unable to report enemy movements off Holland because their First World War radios only had a range of sixty miles. This issue was resolved by Simpson's new electrician assistant from the volunteer reserve, Sub-lieutenant Penfold. A chum in the Air Ministry supplied him with six modern Wellington bomber radios to replace the inadequate antique sets in the H-boats. The navy could not find modern radios for its submarines but the RAF had far more radios than bombers. And there was a second problem: having no asdic sets, they had to feel their way into Harwich with a man swinging a lead for soundings – an uncomfortable job, since he was a certain casualty if the submarine had to dive for aeroplanes. There was no room in the naval dockyards to make alterations but the civilian volunteers at Parkeston Quay soon did the job with asdic sets procured from naval stores. In June Simpson got a new engineer, Sam MacGregor, with whom he formed a lasting partnership. His submarines even had the odd success: on 21 June *H44* sank a Danish merchant ship and a month later the studious David Wanklyn in *H31* sank an anti-submarine trawler.

At Gosport the training routines continued with occasional disruption from air raids. Joe Brighton was taking the course to qualify as a TGM. Since joining the navy in the twenties Norfolk boy Brighton had been all over the world. He began in cruisers, qualifying as a leading torpedoman (LTO) in 1930. At that point he joined submarines, going out to China the next year. He came back in 1935 and was rated petty officer. He spent three years in home waters before going out to China again to join *Proteus*. He had returned home in January and was able to enjoy some leave with his wife Phyllis and their young children, Myrtle and Pat, who were living with Phyllis's mother in Cosham.

The first daylight bombing raid on a British city on 12 August hit Portsmouth Harbour railway station. In a surface shelter about a hundred yards away a shower of railway tickets to St Leonards on Sea landed in Brighton's lap. Most of his nights were spent in air raid shelters, either at home or as duty watch in *Vernon*. He was ashore when the duty watch were called in to sail small boats across the Channel to take as many men as they could from the beaches at Dunkirk. He found the TGM course 'very hard going', because 'all the electrical side of the course was to do with every class of warship except submarines', but he was one of the six out of the class of twelve that passed.

Ben Skeates had volunteered for submarines in January but went out to Norway in the cruiser *Enterprise*. She came back at the end of May, carrying the Norwegian government and twenty tons of gold. His draft to *Dolphin* came through on his return. 'I packed my gear, and with shouts of "Sooner you than me sparks" and "Mind you don't fire them bloody torpedoes at us, that's all", departed, tinged with eager anticipation of what lay before.' Since his first days as a boy at *St Vincent* in 1935 he had mostly spent his time in cruisers in the Mediterranean and at home. Having passed his DSEA test in the tank on 30 June, he joined submarines in early July as a member of the spare crew in *Dolphin*. It was often possible to get home to Longwood for weekends, sometimes using rum as currency. On one occasion a German bomber ditched a stick of bombs over the cottages at Old Down, narrowly missing his home. He did the odd patrol in *Ursula* before taking a promotion course in late summer.

Ruck-Keene's S-boats were out on patrol again in late June. The Admiralty signal that invasion from Norway was imminent sent them out there with orders to 'report and then attack' – report any enemy invasion force first and attack it afterwards. As Bill King put it, 'The word "attack" was hardly necessary, so unlikely was it that we could finish a broadcast before being destroyed.' Submarines were, as submariners understood, expendable. The stress of their high-risk existence was showing now in little physical ways. All the commanders had ridges on their fingernails corresponding to their periods on patrol.

The permanent daylight made life off the Norwegian coast extremely unpleasant as well as dangerous. 'Now we were having to keep submerged for about eighteen hours out of the twenty-four and then desperately try to recharge on the surface between enemy air patrols. At the end of these long dives our air was so deficient in oxygen one could not light a match and breathing came in heavy laboured gasps.' Jumped by a plane in the middle of the 'night', King realised that in the twilight of midnight planes could see the submarine's shadow before the lookouts could see the plane. He changed his policy and surfaced in daylight to charge the battery the moment an aeroplane had passed. Finding many hunters and no convoys, he decided to go further out to sea, guessing that ships might have been routed in that direction:

[I] hoped this bet was due to real wisdom and not stemming from an inner desire to escape harassment. I was getting prone to mental self-torture. Was it clever to rely on this surmise that convoys would be further out? Or was I getting in a blue funk? Submarine captains are incessantly forced to make such decisions. Nightly. Daily. Now it seemed hourly. When is the risk to one's ship justified? When is one fighting too carefully from personal weariness?

On this occasion, King's hunch proved correct and on 3 July he sank a ship from a convoy of twelve small merchants escorted by twelve armed trawlers and aircraft. He was hunted for a while but his pursuers were distracted by a new contact. Ben Bryant had attacked the same convoy from long range, but his torpedoes were seen by an escorting Dornier which then attacked *Sealion*. He had already gone deep into the Skagerrak, but found it so dense with aircraft and patrols that 'it was no longer a case of whether we could operate, it was a case of whether we could get out again'. They had succeeded and were diverted to join King off Stavanger, where the invasion fleet was supposedly gathering.

The Dornier dropped depth charges which almost blew *Sealion* out of the water. The first lieutenant stopped the boat just before it surfaced but it hurtled down again, with the motors on full speed to try to regain control. At this point the trawlers found *Sealion* and more depth charges rained down. The lights went out, the asdic and depth gauges failed and paint fell around them. They turned on the emergency depth gauge to find they were already past 300 feet and falling. The coxswains wrestled with the planes in a cacophonous, shuddering blackness pierced only by the pencil light of torches. Eventually the boat stopped porpoising and they realised the hunt had lost them.

That night Bryant surfaced to charge the battery but had to dive for a plane with only half a charge. The next time he came up he was attacked immediately by a Heinkel. With the battery almost flat, he sat it out for the day on a layer of denser water. Mike Crawford, the torpedo officer, reckoned the crew were getting pretty shaky. Every time Bryant came up for a look there were anti-submarine boats in sight. 'The hours dragged by, everyone had headaches, sleep was impossible, one's body felt cold and clammy.' Continually renewing the trays of soda lime that were supposed to soak up carbon dioxide, they held out until midnight when they surfaced with nothing in sight. Bryant and his lookouts were immediately sick. Down below there was not enough oxygen for the diesels to start until the fans had been running for some minutes. In the distance they could see tracer bullets and flashes.

The flashes came from *Shark's* last fight. She had tried to charge her battery in what her captain, Peter Buckley, thought might have been a safe area before patrolling off Stavanger, where the Germans had air bases. In the night she was jumped by a plane; its bomb jammed her hydroplanes and rudder together and caused leaks astern. Finding himself unable to keep control under water, Buckley sent an appeal for help and tried to fight it out on the surface until assistance arrived. The Germans sent in fighter planes, and after two of the crew had been killed and Buckley and eighteen others wounded, *Shark* ran out of ammunition to fight the ten aeroplanes that were attacking. Faint with loss of blood, Buckley deputed his first lieutenant to complete the scuttling before surrendering.

Nobody knows for certain what happened to Bickie's *Salmon*. Having left Rosyth on 4 July to help to guard against the phantom invasion that was supposed to be brewing at Stavanger, she did not answer signals, one of which routed her across a recently laid German minefield of which the Admiralty had no knowledge. Whether she had been bombed, as was thought at the time, or, more likely, mined, the weakness of naval intelligence and operational deployment at this time contributed to Bickford's death and embittered his few surviving colleagues. Churchill, who had met Bickford twice, wrote a letter of sympathy to his mother and generous obituaries appeared in the press, but the wisdom of operating submarines off Norway was once again thrown into question. It was done because the RAF could not fly reconnaissance missions over Norwegian ports and survive, while the territory was judged suicidal for surface vessels. But it was barely less suicidal for submarines; and was it really necessary to maintain a close watch on Norwegian ports? The cost was certainly high.

Thames disappeared on her first patrol, having been under repair since the start of the war. She probably sank the torpedo boat *Luchs*, possibly while attempting to attack *Gneisenau*, and may have been lost in the counter-attack. Or she may simply have hit another mine. *Spearfish*, with her popular commander Jock Forbes, was caught on the surface by *U34* and sunk. *Narwhal* was sunk by a Dornier that hit her with a bomb before she could dive. The minelayers were particularly vulnerable to air attack because they dived so slowly. It took *Porpoise* up to eighty seconds to get under. They found that by cutting extra holes in the mine casing they could do it in sixty, but as Joe Blamey remarked, 'an aircraft could travel a long way in that time'. After *Narwhal's* sinking, operations off Norway by *Porpoise* were suspended until there was more darkness. *Rubis* was already out of action. Having expended her supply of French mines, she was being adapted to take British ones. French mines were not the only item of which there was a shortage. Supplies of modern torpedoes were also running out and boats were using old Mark IVs, which frequently failed to run.

Truant very nearly joined the casualty list. Her new captain was Hugh Haggard, with Bill Jewell joining at the same time as first lieutenant. At six foot five Haggard was a giant, ill-fitted to cramped submarine life. The 32-year-old had joined submarines late without having done particularly well at anything and spent what he described as 'a miserable few years' in the service before the war, 'spurned by his contemporaries who had been there for years'. Having recently passed his perisher, he was in *H44* when war broke out and had spent months as a spare commander at Rosyth before being given *Truant*, just as she was sent into the everlasting daylight of north Norway.

The summer weather was delightful, and it was a strange experience to watch tractors ploughing the land at midnight, with the sun still over the horizon, while charging the battery in a state of constant fear. As it turned out, *Truant*'s closest shave came when David Ingram in *Clyde* caught her on the surface and fired a spread of six torpedoes at very short range. Fortunately he missed. When she returned to port, Horton sent for Haggard and 'treated him roughly, telling him, "If I allowed myself to be seen in that manner he would find someone else".' He told Ingram, similarly, that if he couldn't hit a submarine with six torpedoes at that range he would find someone else who could.

The casualties inevitably began to have an effect. *Narwhal* and *Porpoise* were sister ships and chummy boats. They had sailed down from Blyth to Immingham together to embark mines, but only *Porpoise* came back. 'It wasn't a pleasant task entering our friends' cabins to pack up their personal belongings.' The news a few days later that *Spearfish* was missing hit Blamey even harder. Jock Forbes was an old rugby team-mate, while *Spearfish*'s chief ERA Stan Peel was a very old close friend from *Oswald* days. In Malta, Joe Blamey and Clare had lived in a flat next door to Stan and his wife Joan.

Half the original 3rd Flotilla had gone. Bill King 'grew to notice the special expression which was stamping itself on the faces of wives and families round a submarine base. At the start of the war they had appeared nervously hopeful. Now they wore a hypnotised look, and any conversation stuck almost embarrassingly to platitudes about the weather.' Bryant and King were particularly deeply affected by the loss of their friend Bickie, the light-hearted, optimistic, positive life and soul of their war effort. King drove himself on, desensitised and deliberately emotionless. 'It was August when our eighth patrol ended and I knew the nightmare summer to be drawing to its close. As the nights lengthened and grew into real darkness, those of us who were left would have a fighting chance.' By mid-August there were eight hours of darkness in the Skagerrak and seven off Trondheim. 'As we slid under the Forth Bridge I heard my bridge telegraphs man announce to his mate in a dreamy Yorkshire accent, "Well, I'm going ashore to have a nice invigorating fuck."' King intended to do likewise.

Bryant found this easily the worst experience of his war. Long afterwards he wrote:

> Somehow the horror of that grim summer which claimed half our flotilla lies almost forgotten – the translucent seas, with never a ripple to hide us from our foes above; the cloudless skies, that seldom darkened in those northern latitudes to give us the blessed shield of invisibility for which we craved to charge our batteries; the everlasting anxiety as to when we could venture up to change the foul air in the boat; men panting like dogs in the carbon-dioxide laden stench we breathed; the plaintively repeated signals from our base asking for one or other of our flotilla mates to report their position – the sign that yet another boat was overdue; all these things are but unreal memories.

Bryant saw himself as a professional fighting man and enjoyed most of his war, but 'for the C.O. of a submarine, the summer of 1940 was sheer nagging hell; I think that only two C.O.s of our front-line boats who saw the summer through, went on again. I cannot speak for Bill King, but I fancy that like me, he was never again the C.O. he might have been.' As far as retirements went he was not far wrong. As well as Seale, Dickie Gaisford and Hutchinson, who had pulled out in April or May, Oddie, John Studholme, Slaughter, Roberts, Bertram 'Boogly Woogly' Taylor, and Van der Byl all retired from active command in the summer or autumn. Most were reaching or had passed Horton's cut-off point of thirty-five. Gregory, at thirty-one, took a year out and then returned. Bryant himself was thirty-five in September but kept going.

The Battle of Britain had moved from ports to airfields. Ian

McGeoch had been appointed first lieutenant of *Triumph*, which was still under repair at Chatham after hitting the mine in December. He and his wife Somers watched the dogfights over their picnic on Bluebell Hill. A few weeks later a bomb demolished the house next door to the one where Somers was crouching behind a sofa. She emerged covered in dust but unhurt.

In August Max Horton visited Harwich to inspect Shrimp Simpson's improvised base. As the Battle of Britain developed he had told Simpson to be able to evacuate all torpedoes, stores and staff at the shortest notice. At the end of August Horton suddenly arrived by car. It was the first time Simpson had met him. When Horton asked him for his evacuation arrangements, Simpson made a phone call and within ten minutes a train appeared with technical stores, spare torpedoes, a personnel carriage and a restaurant car. The train was kept with steam up, the driver and fireman living by the phone in a neighbouring signal box. A Wellington bomber radio maintained contact between the train and Horton at Northways. 'I like that,' said Horton. 'It's good because it works.' Shortly afterwards Horton summoned Simpson to Northways. At their meeting on 7 September he appointed Simpson to command the base at Malta, where he intended to establish an increasing force of the new U-class submarines. Afterwards, from a stationary train, Simpson watched the first heavy daylight bombing raid on London.

Massive new recruitment continued. Jack Howard, the diminutive sailor from Sheffield who had joined the navy in 1935 and ended up in the *Hood*, decided to volunteer for submarines and took his course in November before being sent up to *Cyclops* at Rothesay. His brother Leslie was called up on 22 April 'until the end of the period of the present emergency'. He chose the navy, trained at *Ganges* from June to August 1940 to become an ordinary seaman and during further courses in Portsmouth chose to volunteer for submarines, hoping to be with his brother. For a time in spring 1941 the brothers were both based on *Cyclops* at

Rothesay, but whereas seaman Jack remained attached to the training flotilla, the inexperienced Leslie found himself sent to *Dolphin*. From there he was given a 'pierhead leap' into the undermanned submarine *Torbay* when she was suddenly sent to the Mediterranean at a time when half her crew was on leave.

The submarines destined for Malta were mostly still building or training. Ben Skeates received a draft to join *Upright* ready for trials but soon found himself in *Utmost*. David Wanklyn was appointed to command *Upholder*. Norman Drury was drafted from *Sturgeon* to run the telegraphy department in *Unbeaten*. *Utmost* under John Eaden was nearest to being ready and was working up when on 16 September the Germans bombed the Clyde. They hit a merchant ship berthed not far from *Cyclops* and *Utmost*. Afterwards, Eaden went over to help:

> Saw three men amidships sitting on a raft. One man had something on his lap which he was crooning to. Went over to talk to them and discovered the man had a decapitated head on his lap – apparently belonging to his best friend. The men were completely shocked. Removed the head as gently as possible and dropped it overboard. Surprised how heavy it was.

As an advance guard Horton sent out a squadron of four T-boats, led by Ronnie Mills of *Tetrarch* with *Truant*, *Triad* and *Triton*. *Utmost* followed at the end of October. That month Horton turned down the offer to succeed Sir Charles Forbes in charge of the Home Fleet, feeling that with no control of aeroplanes it was a poisoned chalice. He preferred to stay with submarines.

11

NO TEARS!

I hate this finish to everything as much as you do, especially as there has been no chance of seeing you first. It is a little hard after three years to be robbed of the leave I had so much looked forward to. But I do hope you won't be sad – any of you – because really the world is so unsatisfactory just now that one can hardly grumble at being forcibly removed from it. In any case I shall watch with interest your doings on earth from my next port of call and if I can be of any assistance to you there I shall do my best to render it. And in a few years time no doubt we shall all meet again and the things which have seemed so important on this earth, which have made us sad or glad or happy or angry or bored or excited or disappointed will all have been forgotten in the context of that new place. And so good-bye and remember

No Tears!

With all my love to you all

Ian

Ian Anderson addressed the envelope 'Only to be delivered in the event of my decease'. On 19 May 1940, when he wrote this,

he was a year overdue for leave. His submarine, *Odin*, was crewed
by men who had been gathered from every submarine in the
China flotilla and put into *Odin* in order to go home on leave in
August 1939. Then war intervened. Anderson had pasted into his
diary the *Daily Express* headline of 7 August, 'No War This Year',
with the comment 'Ha bloody ha!'

On 3 September he had been ashore at Penang looking forward to 'a bathe at the swimming club and a drink there and then
a monumental meal at the Runnymede Hotel'. *Odin*'s officers
swam, enjoyed 'an icy shower to wash away the sweat of a submarine' and dressed.

> We had just started our first drink in the cool and quiet of the
> evening. Not a breath of wind anywhere and not a ripple dis-
> turbed the surface of the pool in which was reflected the rosy
> tinge of the setting sun. No more peaceful setting could have
> been found and war and strife and guns and gas seemed things of
> a past nightmare. And then I was approached by a boy who said,
>   'Are you Lieutenant I.M. Anderson?'
>   'Yes.'
>   'Telephone, please.'

He realised at once what was coming:

> The 2nd Coxwain at the other end of the phone informed me
> that the telegram to commence hostilities with Germany had
> come, and everyone was recalled. Trying to make it sound as
> if it was the sort of thing which happened every day I told the
> Captain, who was there too, and we all had another drink on
> it before setting off back. On the way we passed the
> Runnymede and ... I thought enviously of the dinner that
> awaited us there and which Hitler had robbed us of.

They were ordered back to Singapore, then to Ceylon where
they were kept at short notice for sea, like the surface ships.

Another naval staff unfamiliar with submarines was imposing rules that were normal for sailors with proper accommodation in their vessels, but totally inappropriate and hideously uncomfortable for submariners. Anderson found it 'maddeningly stupid to confine 50 men to a submarine in this climate after 4½ weeks of the life, and shows a complete lack of understanding of a submarine's capabilities by the C in C and his staff . . . Submarine living in harbour could hardly fail to sour a saint.'

Anderson learned by letter that his girlfriend at home of nearly three years had got engaged to someone else. Everyone was getting engaged – 'even Basher Coombe has done it'. The dedicated, patriotic orphan Desmond Martin had proposed to his sweetheart Joanna Dennistoun and received her reply by telegram in late September. Martin was actually permitted his leave, and arrived in Britain by troopship in December for a wedding in April. Ian himself had 'a red hot romance with Dorothy' but found his leave cancelled and arrived in Malta just before Martin's wedding in London.

Once at Malta, *Odin* went straight into dock with a leaking water pump and compressor. When the first lieutenant, Mervyn Wingfield, left for his perisher, *Odin*'s captain wanted Anderson to replace him but the 1st Flotilla commander, Captain Geoffrey Keble-White, refused. So they waited, playing tennis, idle because patrols were forbidden in case they provoked the Italians, 'until the Ice-cream merchants over the way can make their minds up who's going to win'. Conditions at the largely derelict Fort Manoel were spartan, though their Chinese servant Ah Chee, who had remained with them, did his cheerful best. The 'troops' were housed in a converted stable block, while the officers held a rat hunt in the mess. On 2 June the Italian newspapers were saying, 'Our war machine is ready; the time has come for us to enter in.' The Scottish rugger player's response was 'Well let them come; they'll get that richly deserved heavy hack up the backside they've been asking for for so long.' Two days later Anderson wrote, 'Tonight we sail . . . I don't think I shall take this

diary with me; it would be a pity for it, as well as myself, to be
fish food if the worst occurred.'

The Mediterranean fleet was under the command of Sir
Andrew Cunningham, known from his initials as ABC. To a large
extent he retained the traditional independence of Mediterranean
admirals, acting as a kind of viceroy in his area, so that his organisation was substantially independent of London. *Odin* was one of
six submarines based at Malta under acting captain Sydney
'Sammie' Raw, a kindly forty-two-year-old made obdurate by
responsibility, who had fought at Jutland before joining the
Submarine Branch. The minelayers *Rorqual* and *Grampus* were
there because the store of mines had been left at Malta when in
September 1939 the Admiralty ordered Cunningham to take the
main fleet to Alexandria. *Olympus* and *Otus* were in dock, there
being no dock at Alexandria. *Orpheus* and *Odin* were now ready
to patrol. *Medway*, along with *Parthian*, *Phoenix*, *Proteus*, *Pandora*,
Oswald and *Osiris*, was at Alexandria under Keble-White, a 45-
year-old First World War submariner with a great deal of staff
experience. Cunningham had executive command of Keble-
White's submarines; they were only under Horton's administrative
control.

The naval intelligence organisation in Alexandria started out
even smaller and more primitive than the main centre in London.
It relied on direction-finding, low-grade signals intelligence, traffic analysis and scraps gleaned from insights into the Italian Army,
Air Force and diplomatic codes. The naval codes had been
broken, but the Italians sensibly changed them the moment the
war started. Initially, there was a vast effort to learn and remain
abreast of call signs and other details of enemy organisation to
identify boats, codes for routes, patrol areas, ports and bearings.
There were very few planes available for photo reconnaissance
and there was nobody trained to interpret the resulting photographs, although the situation improved when three Glenn
Martin Marylands arrived at Malta in August 1940. These were
American-built former French planes, relatively fast, with a long

range suiting reconnaissance, and their crews were immediately trained in ship recognition. But even when there was good intelligence, nothing was usually available to deploy in time to act on it.

The Italians were strong precisely in those light forces in which the British were weak. They could deploy 130 destroyers and torpedo boats, 100 submarines and about 100 naval aircraft. Their battle fleet appeared rarely, partly because they had very little oil, but fuel went much further among the submarine hunters and escort vessels. Their other forte was minelaying. Between 6 and 12 June they laid 2900 mines, and that was only the beginning. Their aim was to seal off the Sicilian narrows either side of the island of Pantelleria with minefields stretching to Cap Bon in Tunisia and to Sciacca in Sicily. In most places there were four lines of mines set twelve feet apart to catch ships. One line northeast of Pantelleria was set at thirty feet to catch submarines at periscope depth. There were gaps ten miles wide off the coast of Sicily and six miles wide off Cap Bon. British submariners guessed that the deep water close to Cap Bon would be difficult to mine and used that passage, which did indeed prove safe. A similar mine barrier was supposed to seal off the Strait of Otranto between Otranto and Albania, and Mussolini boasted that no submarine could get into the Adriatic. The British were uncertain about the extent to which this barrier really existed.

Hugh Mackenzie had been in the Mediterranean since the start of the war. His boat *Osiris* went to Malta with *Oswald* and *Otway* in September 1939 having been commissioned from the reserve group, with crews consisting largely of reservists. Over the winter they had done very little except to give elementary lessons to the untrained Hull fishermen whose conscripted trawlers formed Malta's anti-submarine defence force. There were long beery sessions in the Dun Cow, and Mackenzie explored the island on foot, frustrated at his inactivity, especially when others got away. Shy and diligent David Wanklyn went home in *Otway*. The athletic, level-headed and dependable Bill Jewell went off to become a first lieutenant. The only bonus was what Mackenzie was learning from his captain. Richard Sheridan-Patterson's nickname, 'Sherry P', reflected his fondness for the good things in life, but in a submarine he was unhurried, never flustered, and a wizard with a periscope. As a captain and mentor he was wise and sympathetic. He provided constant tuition with a running commentary as he conducted attacks, but in February 1940 he was purged on account of his age.

'Ginger' Harvey, who replaced him, was also over-age and had retired in 1934, so Mackenzie was puzzled by this inexplicable change for the worse. Where Sheridan-Patterson had been cool and calm, Harvey was rash and excitable. But what really alarmed the junior officers was that, as soon became obvious, once 'under water he had only the vaguest idea of what was happening around us on the surface of the sea as revealed through the periscope. If ever the submarine expression of "lost in the box" applied to anyone it certainly applied to him in full and I have never stopped wondering how on earth he got through his "perisher."' When the Italians declared war on 10 June *Osiris* was off Suda Bay in Crete, an anchorage the British were keeping an eye on for their own use. In the Mediterranean, the same prize law that had applied at home still governed submarine conduct. Suspicious merchant ships had to be stopped, searched and sent to Alexandria as a prize. Only military vessels could be attacked and apart from submarines there were few of these about. *Osiris* had two quiet patrols.

Charles Anscomb had joined *Parthian* in China in February 1939 as coxswain. He was now thirty-one, and *Parthian*, known as 'Peanut' from her identity letters PN, was his sixth boat since joining submarines in 1932. Anscomb recalled:

> She was rather odd in having been dockyard built. The Admiralty constructors at Chatham had put pipes, valves and wheels in the most extraordinary places, arrangements which the private firms would never have passed. She had also

become known in the past as 'the lame duck of the flotilla', owing to her gift for usually doing the wrong thing. She was tricky to handle and always in trouble. Controlling *Parthian*'s temperamental, elderly hydroplanes was rather a strenuous job sometimes. I knew that well enough. They were the old, peacetime submarines of The Trade, ample, leisurely, lazy ladies, a little set in their ways from so many sunny years of showing the flag.

Fortunately she had a very fine captain. Michael Rimington won the confidence of his crew when he took them through a typhoon in 1939. At thirty-six, he, too, was over-age, but he was not the sort of man you told to retire if he didn't want to. The lower deck called him Von Rimington because of his Prussian discipline, but forgave him because he was fair, generous and dedicated. One man was anxious because his wife needed an operation that he couldn't afford. As coxswain, Anscomb was intermediary between the crew and the captain. 'Rimington sent for him at once, told him that the necessary money would be deposited in a bank in the man's name and that he was to make the arrangements for his wife to go into hospital at once.'

Anscomb respected that: 'The money came out of the captain's own pocket. Wouldn't you work hard for a man like that? Especially when you knew he drove himself far harder than anyone else?'

Their first patrol billet was off Tobruk in Italian Libya. Nothing was moving except a little boom defence vessel which came through the anti-submarine nets guarding the harbour for a short cruise twice a day. Inside the harbour was the old Italian cruiser *San Giorgio*. After a few days it occurred to Rimington to follow the launch as the boom gate opened to let her back into the harbour and torpedo the cruiser from beneath her. This they did, but unfortunately the cruiser was also protected by an anti-submarine net and the torpedoes exploded harmlessly. A destroyer came out from the harbour to put in a half-hearted counter-attack, but *Parthian* had orders not to attack destroyers and Rimington thought it best to move away a little further down the coast. At midnight, however, they received a signal that an enemy submarine had just been sighted returning to Tobruk.

All next morning they waited submerged in the area through which the enemy submarine ought to pass. Early in the afternoon the officer of the watch raised the periscope to have a quick look round and suddenly grew tense. Everybody in the control room sensed it. 'Tell the captain there is a long, low object bearing dead ahead,' he said. Rimington ordered the tubes flooded and passed the range and bearing to the electrical artificer operating the 'fruit machine'. At the order 'Sixty feet!' Anscomb tilted the submarine's bow down. 'Group down. Slow both motors. Periscope depth – up periscope!' Rimington took another look and made adjustments. He took yet another look. He was only 400 yards away from the Italian submarine. He fired. Four torpedoes left the tubes at three-second intervals.

'An agonizing, breathless pause. Then *Parthian* shook to a tremendous explosion.'

When *Parthian* tied up alongside *Medway* the duty watch started fuelling and taking in stores while the rest of the ship's company were given twenty-four hours' leave. All the officers except the duty officer went aboard *Medway*. Suddenly ship after ship sounded the 'still' on the bugle and Anscomb realised that the commander-in-chief was approaching the *Medway*. He grinned at the confusion on the depot ship as people scurried to the quarterdeck to receive Admiral Cunningham, but stopped when he realised that the C-in-C wasn't going to *Medway* at all. 'The admiral's barge came right round *Medway*'s stern. I thought *My God, he's coming here* . . . In frantic haste I grabbed up a bosun's pipe and rushed along to the casing.' Cunningham jumped on to the saddle tanks and climbed up to the bridge, waving aside Anscomb's attempt to pipe him aboard. He went straight down into the torpedo compartment where 'Roger' Backhouse, the torpedo gunner's mate, was overhauling his beloved torpedoes.

'"So this is where the work is done," Cunningham said as he clambered over the greasy sides of the torpedoes on the deck in the torpedo space. He walked right through the submarine complimenting everybody in a friendly easy manner. Then the captain arrived and I heard the C.-in-C. congratulating him. It was the first time I had ever seen an admiral behave like that.'

Parthian's was an isolated success for the Alexandrian flotilla. In Malta things went disastrously. Sammie Raw sent *Orpheus* to the huge harbour at Syracuse. *Rorqual*, commanded by Hugh Dewhurst, was to lay mines off Brindisi and then go on to Alexandria. *Grampus* was ordered to lay mines off Augusta. *Odin* was to lie in ambush off Taranto, the principal Italian naval port.

Odin was surprised on the surface just before midnight by the destroyer *Strale*. In darkness the submarine's deep blue was more conspicuous than the destroyer's light grey. *Strale* missed with torpedoes, but then blazed away with her guns as she charged *Odin* to ram her. The captain fired a torpedo from a stern tube before diving just in time. *Strale* hurled depth charges over the side but did not hunt for long.

Two hours later and about nine miles away the torpedo boat *Baleno* saw *Odin* surfacing. She also charged in to ram and *Odin* dived again. As she passed overhead, *Baleno* dropped a pair of depth charges, before turning and dropping three more. In the morning reconnaissance aircraft saw oil slicks in both areas and the Italians claimed to have sunk two submarines. What seems more likely is that the first attack badly damaged *Odin* and the second finished her off. We will never know whether Ian Anderson and the crew of *Odin* fought to control an unstoppable dive or died instantly as depth charges breached the pressure hull and great jets of water burst in.

On 13 June *Grampus* reported by radio a successful minelay off Augusta. She attacked but missed a submarine; next day she attacked the chaser *Polluce* and missed her too. *Polluce* was one of a group of anti-submarine torpedo boats that came to be known to British submariners as 'the Italian A-team'. The best of them,

Circe, spotted *Grampus* on 16 June. *Polluce* and *Cleo* joined in and *Grampus* did not survive.

Air raids on Malta started on the first day of the war and *Olympus* was hit by a bomb while in dry dock. Vice-Admiral Sir Wilbraham Ford decided that submarines should pull out of Malta and join the rest of the fleet in Alexandria (a first consequence of the short-sighted decision not to carve blast-proof submarine pens out of the rock before the war). *Orpheus* was on her way to the Egyptian coast when she was depth-charged and sunk by the destroyer *Turbine* north of Tobruk on 19 June. Sammie Raw must have been in shock, though whether there was anything sinister about his losses is difficult to determine. The Italians and Germans had an agreement to share intelligence, but whether the Germans shared their knowledge of the British naval cipher is not clear. For their own part the Italians were highly skilful in the art of DF. The Admiralty's reaction was to order the remaining submarines in the Far East to the Mediterranean.

The collapse of France made the situation in the Mediterranean look desperate. The loss of France's fifty-three Mediterranean submarines and destroyer force was serious but the loss of her ports was much more so. Malta was isolated. It was just under a thousand miles to Alexandria and just over a thousand to Gibraltar, with no friendly harbour in between. On 17 June, when the French were asking permission to make a separate peace, an Admiralty memo recommended 'the withdrawal of the Eastern Mediterranean Fleet to Gibraltar as soon as it is apparent that French control of the Western Mediterranean is about to be lost to us'. Admiral Cunningham was violently opposed to such a defeatist course but Churchill vetoed the idea anyway. The French made an armistice with Italy on 25 June. Thanks to the terrible confusion between British and French authorities over the future of the French navy, with Britain trying to persuade the French to fight on or sail to British ports and the French, for various understandable reasons, reluctant to comply, just one of the fifty-three Mediterranean submarines declared for Free France. François

Drogou in *Narval* left Sousse against orders on 24 June, signalled 'Betrayed all along the line. I am heading for an English port', and appeared at Malta two days later.

Chiefly in order to impress on America the idea that the British Empire would fight on, Churchill decided that French ships must be seized or attacked. Those at Alexandria submitted but, under intense political pressure at Oran, Admiral Somerville eventually opened fire, causing huge loss of life and lasting resentment. Somerville had *Pandora* and *Proteus* under his command. He ordered them to sink French ships on sight and on 4 July Tubby Linton, commanding *Pandora*, sank the sloop *Rigault de Genouilly*, having mistaken her for a light cruiser. The Admiralty had tried to countermand Somerville's order and apologised to the French, though goodness knows what the French made of an apology delivered the day after the massacre at Oran.

On 18 July the politicians finally authorised a 'sink at sight' policy for merchantmen within thirty miles of Italian-held coasts (these including Libya and Albania). Merchant ships were now targets, although attacking oil supplies coming through the Dardanelles remained impossible and Italian ships could sail safely through Vichy French territorial waters.

In any case, there would soon be no submarines left to do any sinking. On 16 July, off Augusta in Sicily, *Phoenix* attacked the tanker *Dora*. She missed and was herself sunk in a counter-attack from the torpedo boat *Albatros*, which had been the first boat to be fitted with Italian sonar. On 30 July *Oswald* unsuccessfully attacked a convoy and reported a sighting of enemy cruisers. The next night she was surprised on the surface by the destroyer *Ugolino Vivaldi*, one of five sent in line abreast to find her on the bearing of her radio transmission. 'Frosty' Fraser had been decoding a signal with Michael Kyrle-Pope and when he reached the bridge the destroyer was on to them before his eyes became used to the darkness. *Vivaldi* rammed them and simultaneously threw depth charges which exploded under the engine room, lifting an engine off its bedplate. A fuel tank was ripped open, water poured into the torpedo space and Fraser ordered the crew to abandon ship. They were taken prisoner.

This was the only occasion when an investigation after the war found fault with the conduct of a British submarine in the face of difficulties. It concluded that *Oswald* had given up too easily. Michael Kyrle-Pope's former girlfriend Suzanne Layton was informed about the loss of *Oswald* some months later and heard at the same time that Michael had been shot trying to escape. Her sister's husband Jimmy Prowse had already left the boat to take his perisher.

By late July, five British submarines out of ten that were fit to fight in the Mediterranean had been lost. Being ignorant of the cause in most cases, the staff officers blamed mines. On Raw's advice, Cunningham ordered his commanders to keep outside the 100-fathom line and advised them to stay beyond the 200-fathom line. This kept them clear of mines but also kept them clear of targets, which tended to hug the coastline. In some areas it took them many miles from land. Since they were still forbidden by the government to attack merchant ships more than thirty miles from hostile coasts, they were left with precious few targets. In July Max Horton offered Cunningham four T-boats, but Cunningham said that what he really wanted were smaller boats that were less visible and quicker to dive. This conversation led to the deployment of the U-class boats, designed merely to train British destroyers in hunting, to active service in the Mediterranean.

At the beginning of August Sammie Raw was promoted to captain and replaced Keble-White in charge of the 1st Flotilla. *Perseus* was the first of the Far Eastern reinforcements to arrive. Peter Bartlett and his 'perfectly groomed' first lieutenant Alastair 'Pansy' Mars learned that five submarines had been lost and that Rimington's U-boat was the only significant success. Their prohibitively defensive routine was to proceed dived at sixty feet by day to avoid being seen from the air, never to go into water shallower than 200 fathoms because it might be mined and never to attack trawlers, minesweepers or small destroyers. Bartlett was told that 'reports of heavy traffic across the Adriatic might be worth investigating'. He noted wryly that 'this is what passed for intelligence'.

The patrol didn't go well. On 26 August he attacked a merchant ship off Durazzo (Durrës) but he underestimated the target's speed and missed. At the worst point in the counterattack, the leaking stern was at 480 feet with the ERA stationed there up to his neck in water. On the way out, the navigator's poor grasp of navigation by the stars sent *Perseus* into a cul-de-sac the wrong side of the island of Sazan and the Karaburun Peninsula, and it did not help that Mars monopolised the heads with dysentery. Mars went to hospital on his return to port and did not emerge until he was ordered to Britain for his perisher.

'What passed for intelligence' turned out to be the first sign of the deployment of Italian troops and supplies to Albania in preparation for an invasion of Greece. The crucial period was 10 to 20 September. Unfortunately, only one submarine at a time was deployed in the Adriatic. It was Ginger Harvey who got a crack at the troopships and storeships. 'The excitement aroused by meeting such a variety and number of potential targets was exhilarating, only to be matched by immense frustration as *Osiris* failed again and again, for one reason or another, to complete a successful attack,' Mackenzie recalled drily. They found the perfect chance on a small convoy of empty steamers, but Harvey was suddenly distracted by a destroyer and it took 'much prompting' from the junior officers to get him to fire. They waited but there was no bang. Then, a minute later, they heard an unexpected explosion. Up went the periscope and Harvey announced excitedly that they had hit a destroyer on the far side of the convoy. At last they had hit something with a torpedo, even if they had watched 40,000 men and 35,000 tons of supplies sail by unscathed.

This token sinking in the supposedly impenetrable Adriatic prompted Sammie Raw to copy Horton's Great War publicity stunt. Just outside Alexandria *Osiris* was told by signal lamp that 'a special recognition signal in a sealed package marked JR to be opened by Commanding Officer only is being sent to you in my motor boat. It will meet you at the boom. *Osiris* is not to come alongside until this identity signal is showing.' The package contained a Jolly Roger. Thereafter, first in the Mediterranean and then elsewhere, it became customary for boats to signal a successful patrol by flying the pirate flag when they returned to base.

It was Mackenzie's last patrol in *Osiris*. A signal came through instructing him to join the January perisher course at Gosport. He was excited but apprehensive. Although he had not yet heard a depth charge, he had learned much about human relationships and something about submarine attacks, both from Sherry P and from Ginger Harvey, whose tremendous courage was sadly undermined by 'his inability to interpret correctly what he saw through the periscope'.

Once Raw realised that the invasion of Greece had begun he ordered the newly arrived *Rainbow* and *Regent* into the Adriatic. On 4 October *Rainbow*'s commander made a classic mistake in allowing a convoy he was attacking to get too close and was run down and sunk by the merchant ship *Antonietta Costa*, which steamed on, blithely unaware of any collision until she reached port. A few days later the Irish hooker Hairy Browne, commanding *Regent*, fatally damaged the same *Antonietta Costa* off Durazzo.

Reinforcements were also arriving from Britain. Hugh Haggard and George Salt in *Truant* and *Triad* led the way, with Ronnie Mills in *Tetrarch* and Jumbo Watkins in *Triton* a few days behind. *Truant* and *Triad* travelled together as far as Land's End, escorted by the *White Bear*. They had orders to get to Gibraltar at top speed, but *Truant* was ahead of schedule when Haggard sighted a merchant ship that he thought was probably making for Bordeaux. As they approached, the ship lowered a lifeboat and began to sink. It turned out that this was the Norwegian *Tropic Sea*, captured north-east of New Zealand by a German raider, with the Norwegian crew and the British crew of another captured ship aboard as prisoners. The German prize crew had almost made it home after thousands of miles when they decided to scuttle. Haggard took in the Norwegians, surrendering his cabin to the captain's wife while he and Bill Jewell, both tall, crammed into the ward room. The British sailors were packed into other messes. With no room for more, they put the Germans in one boat and the Norwegians in another with the Germans' guns, reported the incident, and carried on for Gibraltar.

Haggard was met by the chief of staff, who handed him a letter marked top secret and told him to open and read it in his presence. It was a letter from Raw, warning him of the clarity of Mediterranean water and instructing him not to patrol during the daytime at periscope depth, not to go within the 100 fathom line and not to surface during the day. Having served for years in the Mediterranean, Haggard reckoned he was familiar with the conditions and took the letter to be guidance rather than an order.

With little to do to the boats, the crews of *Triad* and *Truant* spent their days together sunbathing or fishing and their nights in the Universal or Trocadero bars. On the last night most of them stayed aboard. It was a beautiful evening with the water lapping softly against the sides of the submarines. Leading seaman John Jones brought up his guitar and played tender, haunting music that floated across the harbour while the Truants and Triads lazed around, occasionally joining in choruses. Then Frank Johnson, now coxswain of *Triad*, and Ron Adams rounded up their men.

For Coxswain Adams and his Truants the holiday mood continued as their boat cruised in the Bay of Naples en route to Malta. One hot, scented Mediterranean night off the honeymoon island of Ischia, Bill Jewell spotted a large, darkened merchant ship. Haggard stalked it and from close range got three hits from three torpedoes. It had an explosive cargo and went up like nearby Vesuvius. *Triad* had no such luck and once again found herself outmatched by her lucky sister ship. Syd Hart was ill. Sent to hospital in Malta, he hoped to recover in time for the next patrol but the doctor decided he would have to miss it. His stoker messmates Geordie Thompson, Bill Thomas and Taff Evans visited him the afternoon before they sailed and Evans pressed a pound note into his hand.

Meanwhile, *Triton* and *Tetrarch* had arrived. Jumbo Watkins and his Tritons also had tales to tell, having sunk a ship off Genoa and bombarded Vado and Savona with their gun before torpedoing a ship in the harbour. Ronnie Mills found his old friend Peter Bartlett at Malta entertaining girlfriends of Hairy Browne, while *Perseus* was refitting in the dock. Mills and Bartlett rented a flat in St Julian's Bay and Mills decorated the dining room with a cartoon frieze on the theme 'Careless lives cause talk'. Mills devised patrol orders with Haggard, taking dangerous positions themselves and giving what they thought were relatively safe ones to Salt and Watkins.

Salt's billet, however, proved anything but safe. On the night of 15 October Bandino Bandini, commander of the Italian submarine *Enrico Toti*, sighted a British submarine on the surface about 1000 yards away and turned to attack. *Triad* saw the Italians first and fired a single torpedo which Bandini avoided by turning. The submarines raced towards each other, firing all their guns. *Triad* scored hits on *Toti*'s bow and control tower but fire from *Toti*'s four machine guns drove the British gunners below. The boats passed within four feet of each other and *Triad* began to dive. Bandini fired a torpedo, but the range was too close for it to arm itself and it failed to explode. Just as *Triad* was disappearing, his gun's crew scored two direct hits on *Triad*'s hull. Her stern rose vertically in the water and then slid below. There were no survivors.

Syd Hart was still in hospital when he heard that *Triad* was overdue. He sat slumped on the veranda with tears in his eyes, mind numbed but filled with flashbacks of friends. A week later he went to the ship's office to find out what he was supposed to do next. 'Good God man, you're supposed to be dead!' came the reply.

In the Pay Office he saw his own name in the ledger with a red line through it and the letters 'DD' next to it. 'What does DD stand for?' asked Hart. 'Discharged Dead,' he was told. Officially Hart was missing presumed killed. He sent a cablegram to Lancashire to reassure his parents. That evening, as he crossed the little bridge to the Sliema mainland, he met George Spendlove of *Tetrarch*. Spendlove, who had often passed evenings drinking with the Triads, thought he had seen a ghost.

When Hart explained, Spendlove decided they must celebrate. They went into the Great War Bar and Spendlove ordered three drinks. The barmaid looked oddly at him, but it was too early in the evening for him to be drunk. 'Here's to the crew of *Triad*!' toasted Spendlove. They drank and poured the third drink away. Hart ordered three drinks and they drank a toast to Cullingford, pouring the dead man's drink away. 'The barmaid looked hard at us, but made no comment. We were paying "the shot"; it was no affair of hers and it went on that way all night, a toast to Thomas, Evans, Howels and the rest.'

Next morning, 'with a head like the capstan', Hart decided that the best way of avenging his mates was to volunteer to join *Triad*'s successful sister *Truant* at the first opportunity.

Truant had ended her latest patrol in Alexandria, where Haggard reported to Captain Raw. He was puzzled to find his reception 'somewhat icy'. The officers there were downhearted at the casualties they had suffered: so many of the men from the elite China flotilla had been killed without even getting home to Britain. Haggard was ordered to patrol an area twenty-five miles east of Tripoli where there should have been targets because the Italian army had gone on the offensive, invaded Egypt and captured Sidi Barrani. However, Raw thought the area was mined and instructed him to remain fifteen miles off the coast, and as far as possible to stay below periscope depth during the day. Haggard saw nothing but some minesweepers. By plotting their courses he established where the swept channel was and, ignoring his instructions, followed it to within seven miles of Tripoli. But he still didn't find a target (because the Italians were approaching Tripoli from the west) and returned to Malta. There, as luck would have it, a stoker left the boat and Syd Hart volunteered to replace him.

In late October the Italians invaded Greece, providing further opportunity for attacks on sea transport. *Truant's* next patrol billet was fifteen miles off the coast of Italy. Haggard didn't like his orders and, 'thinking things must have changed', approached the Calabrian coast. He damaged the torpedo boat *Alcione*, before in night attacks sinking first the *Sebastiano Bianchi* and then the 8177-ton tanker *Bonzo*. The Italians had very few big tankers and disrupting their supply of oil was of the highest importance, so this was a triumph.

The attacks had proved difficult, however, because modern Mark VIII torpedoes were running out and *Truant* was armed with old and unreliable stock. Two broke surface and one shot off in the wrong direction. The tanker was particularly difficult: 'They don't burst into flames. It's very difficult to get them to burn. If you hit them they have a disconcerting liability to ride higher in the water. Tankers were much safer to serve in than others.' In the end he closed in to 900 yards in order to hit the ship hard enough to sink it. Getting in close was Haggard's preferred method: 'I could very seldom resist having a look through the periscope to see the result – I didn't always do so, but I would if I could. I never regarded myself as being a very good submarine attacker – there were some who were quite brilliant, but I was certainly nothing like that and I therefore always attempted if possible to press home my attack as closely as I could.' After that he 'thought the best thing to do was to continue one's course, and by the time the escort of destroyers had come round to where one had fired the torpedo one was then on the other side of the target and one probably had half an hour or more's start to get lost'. He reckoned other people thought this a bad idea, but 'it usually worked very well indeed'.

Haggard's latest success went down even less well with Raw,

who 'didn't complain to my face but complained in two pages of foolscap to the Commander-in-Chief that I was operating in a dangerous manner and disregarding all the instructions and guidance I was given'. There was no confrontation, but Haggard 'did tell Raw that if he was dissatisfied I would be very pleased if he would relieve me if he could find someone better'. He put Raw's resentment down to the fact that 'his own flotilla didn't sink ships but this new man from home did'.

The Italian invasion of Greece resulted in the small Greek submarine fleet joining in on the British side, but losses continued to mount. In mid-November 'Flick' Currie, a captain Mackenzie held in high regard, left Alexandria driving *Regulus* for a patrol in the Adriatic and was probably mined. Jumbo Watkins took *Triton* from Malta to the southern Adriatic on 28 November. She sank a 6040 ton merchant ship but was herself sunk, probably by the counter-attack from torpedo boats or possibly later by *Clio*. Raw attributed her loss to mines in the Strait of Otranto. The last loss of the year was the Greek *Proteus*, which sank the 11,452 ton passenger liner *Sardegna*, now being used to transport troops, before being herself depth-charged, rammed and sunk by the escort *Antares*.

When the Truants arrived in port from patrol, the first few drinks of ice-cold beer in a small bar in Sister Street tasted like the nectar of the gods. They drank their way from talkative to devil-may-care to, around midnight, the inevitable gloom; 'not exactly maudlin, but, let's say, over-sentimental', Hart rationalised. 'One of the recently lost submarines was *Triton*, with Tom King, Willie Kane and Gilbert Quick aboard – tried and true comrades – and talk revolved around them on this particular night; we spoke feelingly of the sprees we'd shared with them in the past in just such surroundings as these.' Then someone would dump more bottles on the table, with 'Bear up my hearties!'

The period of leave took its course, until they were ready for patrol again with a new first lieutenant. Bill Jewell's back had gone and he was in hospital. 'The last hour before departure would always bring the crews of other submarines, who had arrived from patrol after ourselves, to wish us luck. We knew to a man that the chances of a happy return were exactly like tossing a penny, heads we did, tails we didn't. The unvoiced question in our minds was: Which way would the penny fall for us this time?'

Submariners were affected by the loss of boats close to them, but generally they did not have the big picture of just how bad the losses really were – being rather more than 50 per cent in a year. It was the flotilla staff who saw what was happening, had the depressing task of writing letters to next of kin, and were then faced with the attempt to strike a balance between hitting the enemy and preserving the diminishing stock of submarines and colleagues. Submarines were being built at about same rate as they were being sunk. Men were harder to replace.

12

DRAFTED DOLPHIN

At Suez Alastair Mars and Hugh Mackenzie joined the troop-ship *Britannic*, formerly the pride of the White Star Line, for the voyage home for their perisher course, which was set for January 1941. The passengers were army wives and families being evacuated from Cairo. By the time the ship reached Aden, Mars was engaged to the prettiest girl aboard, 'Ting', governess to an army family. In the cathedral at Mombasa he married her, with Mackenzie as best man.

From Liverpool, Mackenzie caught a train to report to Northways. He was the first submariner of any seniority to return from the Mediterranean since war broke out, and Horton gave him a forty-minute grilling which left Mackenzie immensely 'heartened and impressed by his all pervading depth of knowledge of submarines, their weapons and equipment and by his under-standing of the problems and difficulties faced by those who manned and operated them. It was a totally inspiring experi-ence . . . From then on I would have done anything he asked me.' The officers were allowed three weeks' leave before the course began in January.

Pat Steel, who had inadvertently sunk *Oxley* in 1939, was in

charge of the perisher course. Mars and Mackenzie were joined
by three others. Once they had gone through the theory with the
attack teacher, they moved north to Rothesay to practise in the
venerable *Oberon*, currently commanded by the notoriously
quick-tempered Bertie Pizey. Each day they took it in turns to
give orders, while Pizey stood by, ready to take control if anything was about to go drastically amiss. They all passed the
course – according to Mars, Mackenzie came top – and became
spare officers in the new 7th Training Flotilla. In April Mackenzie
got *H43*; in June Mars took command of *H44*. Young officers
were being pushed through very fast. Desmond Martin had very
little experience as a first lieutenant when he took the course that
winter, but was given *H28* in April with his daughter Jane less
than a month old.

At the end of October 1940 the H class anti-invasion submarines commanded by Shrimp Simpson had moved north to
Rothesay to resume their training duties. Edward Young was the
only Volunteer Reserve recruit to make the grade. His friend
Harold had suffered claustrophobia the moment he entered
Otway and dropped out, while the third was deemed 'temperamentally unsuitable for submarines' during the time they spent
in destroyers before the submarine course began. So Young
became the first RNVR submarine officer. He did six weeks at
Gosport while the Battle of Britain was at its height and then,
with a fellow trainee, joined *H28*, commanded by Mervyn
Wingfield. They carried out one patrol from Parkeston Quay,
during which Wingfield missed a barge escorted by minesweepers. During a brief counter-attack Young heard his first depth
charge, alarmingly loud but harmless. It was a first for Wingfield,
too, since he had left *Odin* at Malta just before the Italians
declared war. Their next patrol was cancelled after their companion boat, *H49*, was sunk by trawlers and they moved north
to join the training flotilla.

Like the perisher practical course, the training flotilla was based
on *Cyclops*. Commissioned before the First World War as a repair

ship for the Home Fleet, she was a boat for which the surface navy had no further use, so she was passed to submarines. Known as 'Cycle-box', the coal-burner was uncomfortable and generally inadequate. The training flotilla had two purposes: to give sea experience to new officers and ratings and to provide practice targets for destroyers and corvettes that were learning to hunt U-boats. The destroyers were based at Campbeltown, Tobermory, Ardrishaig and Londonderry, so the submarines were often dispersed to these outposts.

Wingfield left *H28* to take command of *Umpire* and Leslie Bennington took over. Bennington was the officer who had risen from the lower deck via the mate scheme. Having avoided a friendly torpedo in *Swordfish* and survived a mine in *Triumph*, he had won a DSC in *Tigris* before taking his perisher in the autumn. Young was chiefly struck by Bennington's obsessive dedication: 'He talked endlessly in his deep voice about submarines and the submarine service, which for him was a kind of religion ... He professed to have no interest in women, and liked nothing better, when ashore, than to sit drinking beer and talking submarines by the hour.' But Bennington also had human qualities, being 'a terrible man to wake in the morning; when we were living in the boat he would lie in his bunk smoking cigarettes and drinking cup after cup of tea until two minutes before harbour stations, when he would miraculously appear on the dot of time and give orders with his accustomed precision. He never to my knowledge ate breakfast.' Most of all he was a good man from whom to learn how to command a submarine, 'a wonderful teacher', 'a quiet but strict disciplinarian' with 'an unobtrusive way of showing his appreciation of good work'.

The turnover of men in the training submarines was fast and continuous. Young had left by the time Mackenzie, as spare officer, took over from Bennington while 'Ben' got his medal and went on leave. Mackenzie and Bennington were old friends from peacetime, so Mackenzie was confident his would be a well-run boat.

Around 0400 on passage to the first day of exercises a steamer cut across *H28*'s bows. By throwing the engines full astern Mackenzie slowed the boat sufficiently for him to hit the steamer rather than the steamer hitting *H28*, which would have sunk her. In the forward torpedo compartment, one of the crew heard a cry of 'Hard a port, shut off for collision stations!', then he fell backwards and was hit by a shower of tinned food. He shut the bulkhead door and retreated towards the control room, only to find himself locked out. He heard Mackenzie's voice, 'Go forward and see if we are letting in any water,' and the reply, 'What me?', before announcing, 'It's dry forward and for Christ's sake let me through!' The damage took some explaining to Bennington and Horton, but no one was hurt, and the fault lay with the steamer.

Much worse befell Young, who had joined *Umpire* at Mervyn Wingfield's request. Built in Chatham, she joined an east coast convoy for the Clyde for sea trials. A Heinkel made her dive for real before she had ever conducted a trial dive, but it went well. Then one of the diesels failed and *Umpire* fell behind the convoy. Off Cromer during the night they met a southbound convoy that was on the wrong line. To avoid it they had to steer to port rather than to starboard, as was conventional. Soon afterwards Wingfield, who had been called to the bridge, saw a trawler attacking. In an attempt at evasive action, he steered to port and was rammed. He clung to its side, yelling, 'You bloody bastard, you've sunk a British submarine!' as his boat sank beneath his feet, leaving him and three others in the water.

In the plunging submarine first lieutenant Peter Bannister took charge. With Young's help he shut watertight doors and organised the men. Fortunately, they were in shallow water, and the bows embedded themselves in the bottom with the control room depth gauge reading sixty feet. Many years later Young wrote an account of the horror that followed, involving various small, haunting, technical mistakes of his own, and writing about it caused the nightmares from which he had suffered since 1941 to

stop. A man hammering at a watertight door that Young had had
to shut, moaning 'My pal's in there.' No panic, but a kind of
'mental concussion'. Finding himself alone in the control room
and panicking before locating Bannister, a vomiting ERA and
another seaman above him in the tower. Half the crew survived.
The Chief ERA and the TGM organised the escape of nearly all
of those in the engine room, but Bannister drowned after reaching the surface. Young wondered whether to leave submarines,
but decided that would be worse than staying. After survivor's
leave he was appointed to *Sealion*.

The training establishment at Rothesay remained in place
along roughly the same pattern for the rest of the war. The
Admiralty's other initiative was less successful. Worried by the
battleship *Scheer's* attack on the *Jervis Bay* and her Halifax convoy,
they decided to use submarines to escort Atlantic convoys. It was
actually a compliment to the submariners who had done so well
at sinking capital ships during the Norwegian campaign that, for
once, they were in demand. The idea was that the convoys, like
a honeypot, would attract raiders and then the submarines could
pick them off.

Horton opposed the idea. Apart from the diversion of precious
submarines away from offensive patrols, there were all kinds of
practical problems. The huge convoys covered a vast area of sea
and battle cruisers could attack from miles away. Submarines were
not fast enough to go chasing after the enemy, especially submerged. There were all too obvious dangers that they might be
mistaken for U-boats and attacked by their own side. The Dutch
O14 had recently escorted HX79, a convoy homeward bound
from Halifax, which lost twelve out of forty-nine ships to a pack
of five U-boats. *O14* had insufficient fuel to zigzag with the merchant ships, had fared no better than the surface escorts in
locating the attackers and had herself nearly been hit by torpedoes. Horton flatly refused to allow submarines to operate in the
Western Approaches but conceded one submarine to be based at
Halifax and used for the first leg of the journey, where she might

deter German surface raiders and was less likely to be sunk by her own side.

Porpoise sailed for Canada with a convoy at the beginning of December. Joe Brighton joined her for the voyage, after which he was to be TGM of a spare crew based at Halifax. She had to zigzag on the surface and was not allowed to dive until the escorts turned back for home. After that she escorted homeward-bound convoys to twenty-five degrees west, and then returned to Nova Scotia with an outward-bound convoy which she picked up at sea.

The weather was atrocious for the whole of the winter. The temperature was below zero, and the boat was heavy with ice. The seamen slept in the mining room on beds saturated in condensation, with water swilling over the iron decks. The woollens knitted by charitable ladies soon became so foul with oil and filth that they had to be thrown away. But woollens were invaluable. For the first time Joe Blamey wore the long johns, tight-fitting round the ankles and under the armpits, with which he had been issued on joining submarines. The watch-keepers had to be helped out of garments that were almost frozen solid, their beards and eyelids coated with frost. In late January, with German battle cruisers on the loose, *Porpoise* was sent off after a convoy that had already left. The weather was so bad she never found it.

One particular storm in February was the worst Joe Blamey had ever encountered. They lost touch with their convoy and all they could do was to try to keep *Porpoise*'s head into the seas. It was impossible to dive, water poured into the control room, and when rubbish was thrown out in the evening, that usually poured back into the control room too. Cooking was impossible, so what food they ate came from tins. Eventually Micky Power, the Irish mining ERA, could stand it no more and baked some potatoes, but his relief was short-lived. One of the spare torpedoes broke loose. They managed to secure it again without anyone being mangled, but sadly the bags of potatoes, eggs, carrots and onions stored in the torpedo compartment were now mashed with the oil and seawater.

After two days the captain asked Blamey if he could somehow shore up the bridge structure because it was being stove in by the waves. He fought his way up the ladder to the bridge, to find that where the sky should have been was a sixty-foot foam-capped wave. A lookout, lashed to the railing, warned him to hold tight and he clung on grimly. Blamey kept a number of four-inch pit props for emergencies such as this. He cut some to size and, assisted by a sturdy stoker, heaved them to the bridge along with a sledgehammer and wedges. They lashed themselves to the metalwork and hammered in the supports while waves crashed down, the submarine pitching violently and rolling through an arc of over eighty degrees. When they were in a trough the waves were forty feet above them.

On 14 February 1941 the Admiralty overruled Horton and ordered the whole 2nd Flotilla and the large French *Surcouf* – complete with a disgruntled 'Colonel' Menzies in *Forth* – over to Halifax, where *Porpoise* had already been joined by *Severn*. Some of the boats were too badly damaged by storms to complete the crossing. The submarines did their duty escorting convoys but they never sank anything. When the repaired *Scharnhorst* and *Gneisenau* appeared in the area, they were dissuaded from attacking convoys by the sight of the old battleships that were already escorting them; the submarines ordered to pursue them never got close. Meanwhile, a new 8th Flotilla at Gibraltar was ordered to escort convoys to and from the Rock against the attack of German battle cruisers, a task they continued to carry out until the end of May.

The news that *Scharnhorst* and *Gneisenau* were making for France brought further panic. Every available submarine was sent into the Bay of Biscay to form what the submariners referred to sardonically as an 'Iron Ring' around St Nazaire. Training was suspended and the old submarines of the training flotillas rushed into the fray again. *Torbay* was sent off while her first lieutenant and half her crew were on leave. Tony Miers, her pugnacious captain, who was not getting on well with the first lieutenant,

promoted fourth hand Paul Chapman to first and filled up his
crew from the depot ship before tearing off in a stolen sweater
knitted by Mrs Winston Churchill. Leslie Howard was one of
those bundled into the boat to become torpedoman and lookout.
Some of those left behind were delighted: 'I had missed Torbay,'
remarked Alexander McCulloch, 'Hallelujah!'

In *Unbeaten* Norman Drury, thirty years old, was an experienced man in charge of communications in a very inexperienced
crew. The ruggedly handsome captain, Teddy Woodward, who
was the same age, had carried out invasion patrols in *H28* but this
was his first operational submarine. Drury had joined *Unbeaten*
while she was building at Barrow. Trials off Dunoon had not
gone smoothly. During a gale *Unbeaten* broke adrift and swept
down Holy Loch out of control. She dragged her anchor,
bounced off the cable of a German prize and ran aground. They
got her off three tides later and went back into dock at Barrow.
Since then they had been practising as an asdic target at
Dartmouth. Suddenly they were sent off to Brest. The weather
was so bad that they couldn't have attacked even if they had seen
the battle cruisers.

The weather proved too much for the old H class boats. *H31*
lost her fore planes on the fifth day but stayed out. Skipper Reg
Whiteway-Wilkinson announced that even if they couldn't fire
torpedoes submerged, they could still make a surface attack and
an enemy report, and they could always ram. The other officers
had a nasty feeling he meant what he said. He had also told them
to call him if the boat neared a depth of seventy feet, because
nobody trusted *H31*'s pressure hull. After a while the RAF discovered that the battle cruisers had already reached Brest before
the submarines were in place. The boats stayed, but the ships
showed no sign of coming out. Bill King's former first lieutenant
Bevil Heslop, commanding *H32*, decided to call it a day when
the boat's fore planes broke and two Dutch boats also dropped
out with weather damage. Eventually the Admiralty gave up and
dispersed their 'Iron Ring'. Meanwhile, the Norwegian coast was

left unguarded and *Hipper* and *Scheer* returned to Germany unopposed.

Teddy Woodward took *Unbeaten* back to Gosport, where the crew had a few days' leave. Inevitably, they became chummy with some of the spare crew, one of whom was Jack Casemore. He was drinking with one of *Unbeaten*'s torpedomen, who told him, 'We need an electrician.' Casemore replied, 'I'd love to go on the boat,' so his companion fixed it up. They were sailing for Gibraltar the next day. Casemore went on a last run ashore with some of the crew who took the ferry to Portsmouth. They were in a pub at the top of Queen Street as an air raid began. When bombs started dropping they evacuated the pub and sheltered in the entrance to Woolworths. The bombs came alarmingly close, so they ran over to Aggie Weston's hostel. A moment later a bomb hit Woolworths just where they had been standing. At this point they began to get nervous. 'Someone said they knew where there was an air raid shelter, so we crossed the road again and started to go towards the harbour, when Aggie Weston's was hit. Arriving at the air raid shelter, we found the police there as it had received a direct hit.'

Michael St John had passed his perisher with Mars and Mackenzie. A friend of Ian Anderson in China, he claimed to be able to trace his ancestry back to the Norman Conquest via the longest line of undischarged bankrupts in England. Now St John found himself in charge of the elderly *L26*, undergoing a major refit at Devonport. Progress was slow, partly because of the Blitz, but chiefly because of the dockers. St John was used to them, but his Australian chief engineer was unfamiliar with British industrial practice. When he arrived Gilbert Kerr was already there: '"You the Skipper? I'm Kerr, your new Engineer Officer," he said as he crushed my hand to pulp in one of the largest mitts I had ever seen.' 'Digger' Kerr could not grasp 'the dockyard officers' "we couldn't care less" attitude, the entrenched, obstructive and ridiculous demarcation rules, ruthlessly applied by the dockyard "mateys", were beyond his comprehension. Their self-serving attitude in wartime drove him barking mad.' Kerr's outbursts of rage repeatedly drove them off the job and their union representatives complained to the Admiral Superintendent.

Since Kerr was invariably right, St John found it difficult to explain to him 'the arcane, antediluvian practices that had, for generations, obstructed and debilitated our naval yards. For him, they were simply unbelievable.' The Admiral Superintendent ordered St John to 'stop the rot' and then, over a bottle of Plymouth gin, 'bemoaned the imponderable problem of the dockyard's appalling lack of morale' before asking, 'somewhat desperately I thought, if I had any constructive suggestions'. He hadn't. He summoned Digger, who was twenty-eight years old to his own twenty-four, and told him in future to keep his mouth shut. 'This was happening in the midst of the Nazis' saturation bombing of Plymouth and Devonport', which St John reckoned one of his 'more rugged war experiences'. Day and night, high explosive and incendiary bombs rained down. The dockyard 'mateys' invariably 'took to the hills', leaving the crews and the staff of the naval barracks to act as air raid wardens and fight fires.

St John could see the boat from his office window and was constantly glancing out, on the lookout for trouble with Digger. One day they were replacing the hull plates over the engine room when St John saw Digger in hot dispute with the pompous and obstructive foreman. 'Grabbing my cap I dashed across but was too late. As I drew near I heard him shout, point blank into the foreman's face, "You fucking well make me sick", whereon he opened his large mouth and was copiously sick over the foreman's trousers and boots. It was a stunning performance.' Those of the crew who were present 'fell about in rapturous merriment' while the dockers 'were turned to stone, months agape'. It was total victory. 'We never had another spot of bother completing our refit, for the dockyard could not do enough to satisfy our every whim – anything to hasten our departure.'

When *Porpoise* returned to Scotland for her refit in May she was sent to Greenock, which had suffered a very heavy bombing attack. Scotts shipbuilding yard had no electricity so *Porpoise* served as a generator for a few days. At Troon, a gang of workmen with a foreman in charge came aboard to see about the removal of the main battery with its 336 cells, each weighing half a ton. Normally this was a job that was done by dockyard workmen, but the Troon dockers had never seen a submarine battery and when they realised the enormity of the task they simply walked out. The crew were astonished and disgusted. It was wartime and the dockers earned far more than they did. Some would have been happy to have 'machine-gunned the bastards'.

Porpoise remained at Troon until September, with the crew living ashore on their allowance of 30*s*. a week. Joe Brighton found a single room in a council house near the beach where Dilly – his wife Phyllis – could join him. They shared it with an elderly lady and her very aged mother, who was bedridden and incontinent and usually chose mealtimes to bawl out 'Bertha, I've shit the bed.' There was also an evacuee from Glasgow with her little girl. But Joe and Dilly were delighted to be together, sitting on the beach, taking out a sailing boat, getting the bus to Burns country. The children, Myrtle and Pat, were safe in the country near Romsey and the couple visited them when Joe took a course on submarine mines at Roedean School. After this he became mining torpedo instructor and a permanent member of *Porpoise*'s crew.

Joe Blamey had hoped *Porpoise* might put in to Devonport, but realised this was unlikely given the bombing. As they approached the Clyde the Admiralty announced that Plymouth had been raided heavily but casualties among the families of service personnel were light. The fact that such a signal had been sent, however, was alarming to Blamey, whose wife and daughter were living there. As soon as he could Blamey made the tortuous train journey south, filled with trepidation, not knowing what he would find. He grabbed the only taxi, aghast at the scenes of devastation in St Budeaux. But Clare and Joan were OK. The house had been damaged and Clare had left the shelter to put the fires out. Clare, Joan and Clare's sister Violet had been sleeping in the air raid shelter for weeks on end. He parked Joan with his mother and took Clare back to Troon. After an initial run-in with the dockers, he eventually made friends with the senior foreman and work began to proceed smoothly.

Halfway through the refit a new sub-lieutenant turned up. Immediately he asked Blamey if he would show him over the boat and explain everything to him. Ian McIntosh was a 21-year-old Australian who had completed his course six months ago but was only now with his first submarine. It was some time before Blamey learned why. McIntosh had been one of 550 passengers in the *Britannia*, on his way to Alexandria, when a German raider set the vessel on fire and forced the captain to abandon ship. Because he had some experience of small boats, McIntosh took charge of lifeboat number seven. They were 600 miles west of Freetown, with eighty-two people in a lifeboat designed for fifty-six. They soon lost touch with the other boats, so McIntosh recommended trying to sail to Brazil. His reading had told him that was easier than trying to reach Africa; apparently you needed to head west to avoid the worst of the Doldrums and could then pick up the south-west trade wind. The others agreed. He calculated on twenty-eight days, which meant a daily ration of an eggcup full of water, one ship's biscuit and a share of two tins of condensed milk. 'After about a week or so some of the crew started dying; the deaths then became really fairly frequent. The odd thing was you could see who was going to die two or three days before they did. You could see when they'd given up hope and, once they had, they died.'

McIntosh was determined to live, because he was deeply in love with a girl he had just met. Being the best sailor, he stayed on the helm twenty-four hours a day, keeping the wind behind him. On the twenty-second day he smelled land and the water changed colour. Later on they sighted land, but there was a strong surf running so they followed the coast north. They were thirty-eight by then. Next day they landed and a few of the strongest walked inland, where they made contact with natives and eventually with civilisation.

When he returned to England Horton sent for him. He said, 'Well McIntosh, you've got the one attribute that every submariner needs, you've got luck. Which boat do you want to go to?' McIntosh had worked out which of the boats that could take him would be the first into active service, and answered, '*Porpoise*.'

Meanwhile, *Porpoise* was being adapted. The sub and her torpedoes were painted dark blue for the Mediterranean. Twelve 1000 gallon oil containers appeared, fitted with wheels so they could run on *Porpoise*'s mine rails. Eight 4000 lb bombs were loaded on in containers. Clare stayed till the last day because Blamey thought he might never see her again; Dilly's parting with Joe was sad because losses in the Mediterranean were so high that 'it seemed at the time unlikely that we would survive.' Four of the six minelayers in *Porpoise*'s class had already been sunk. Full of misgiving, their upper casing filled with block-busting bombs and high octane aviation fuel, they set out for Malta. The new captain, Bertie Pizey, had orders to take as few risks as possible en route.

This meant that the only minelayer left in home waters was the French *Rubis* based in Dundee, where the Frenchmen and their adopted dog, Bacchus, had made themselves very much at home. In August a new liaison officer joined *Rubis*. Ruari McLean was a pre-war friend of Edward Young and shared his passion for typography and design. As captain of *Rubis*, Georges Cabanier had been succeeded by a tall Savoyard called Henri Rousselot, formerly the first lieutenant. On McLean's first patrol, a minelaying operation off the Norwegian coast, Rousselot, who did his own navigating, made a perfect landfall. They began to lay their mines in the morning. Rousselot shouted '*Mouillez un!*' from the kiosk, and in the control room a button was pressed and a mine dropped away. After laying a first group of ten mines they moved on to the next position, but before they got there the captain called for torpedo action.

Rubis had never yet fired a torpedo so there was great excitement. But when the captain called '*Feu*!' nothing happened. The torpedo ran hot in its tube. After some furious arguments and a good lunch, they proceeded to lay the next field of mines.

The three Britons – McLean, signalman Tim Casey and telegraphist Jimmy Green – sat in silence in the ward room listening to the hum of the engines, the orders and the 'ting' as each mine left the boat. Suddenly Rousselot called them to torpedo stations again. They had no idea what was going on. After a very short attack Rousselot fired two tubes, and after six seconds there were two terrific explosions. All the lights went out, glass smashed and the bows shot upwards. Everyone was ordered forwards and the bows fell. They hit the bottom and sat on the seabed, a mile from the coast of Norway. Silence was ordered but not kept. They soon learned that *Rubis* had sunk a ship. A succession of Frenchmen shook hands with the captain and then, eyes gleaming, went to tell Green and Casey how pleased they were. 'Two torpedo – *boum*! She sink!'

There was a counter-attack and five depth charges exploded, but they weren't close enough to do any harm. Rousselot told McLean that in the middle of the minelay, two ships that he had been ordered to attack approached with two escorting trawlers. He decided to finish laying and then attack, even though by that time the targets were only 400 yards away. This was potentially suicidal, and *Rubis* had been damaged by the explosion of her own torpedoes hitting the target.

After eighteen hours, with the air foul, Rousselot tried to surface, hoping the trawlers had gone. He succeeded at the fourth attempt. The captain opened the voice pipes first and the crew's ears popped at the change in pressure. Then he opened the hatch, bringing a rush of cold air and a nauseating stench. They had surfaced just beneath a lighthouse which began to signal to them. Casey answered by flashing some choice four-letter words with his Aldis lamp. There was no further reaction.

After a while the engineers managed to get the engines

started. McLean signalled Dundee that *Rubis* was damaged and couldn't dive but had sunk a ship. Three Blenheims, two destroyers and a cruiser were sent to meet them. In the morning they saw the Blenheims; shortly afterwards their engines died. The batteries were on fire, giving out blue flames and smoke. Soon the dog Bacchus and everyone but the radio operators were up on the wooden deck. At nine the Blenheims left. At dusk three Beaufighters appeared, flashed 'Good luck' and went away again.

They managed to restart the engines long enough to send a signal giving a position and reporting that they were stopped. At midnight they received an answer saying that the ships sent to rescue them were searching sixty miles to the south, that being where the Blenheims had said *Rubis* was, and unfortunately the rescue ships had orders not to enter the German minefield in which *Rubis* was now adrift. A later signal announced that three Catalina seaplanes would pick up the crew after they had scuttled the *Rubis*.

Orders to sink their beloved boat spurred the Frenchmen into action. By dawn the fumes had died down enough for the electricians to find that sixty of the 200 battery cells were undamaged, and by coupling them they produced enough power to run the blowers that enabled the diesels to be operated. At ten they managed to start the engines and that night, after a Blenheim pointed them in the right direction, they found their escort. Filthy and exhausted but in relative safety, they enjoyed one of the meals for which French submarines were to become famous: soup with sherry, cold ham with cucumber and salad on silver dishes, anchovies, spring onions, hard-boiled eggs, hot French tinned peas and new potatoes, fruit salad and dried apricots, washed down with the normal ration of red wine plus the last two bottles of white burgundy that they had smuggled from France. Then coffee and cognac. The captain jerked his thumb at the rescuing British cruiser *Curaçao* and said, 'They are jealous – aboard there, mashed potatoes.' Then he lay back and slept for the first time in four days.

Edward Young joined *Sealion* at Portsmouth for patrols in the Bay of Biscay. There were only three of the original twelve S-boats left now. *Swordfish* had been mined in November 1940 near the Isle of Wight. *Snapper* had a refit during the winter and when she was ready to patrol Bill King was ill. He had been suffering from nightmares, waking drenched in sweat, and ended up in hospital. So Jimmy Prowse, Diana Layton's husband, took *Snapper* to patrol off Ushant. King found him charming, but it was his first mission as a spare commander. The weather was terrible and King lay awake thinking about his boat and his people. *Snapper* didn't return. It now appears that she was sunk by minesweepers after a failed attack, although the Germans made no claim at the time. *Sunfish* had been bombed in dry dock and badly damaged. 'Skips' Marriot, *Sealion*'s sardonic chief ERA, who loped around the boat wearing a strange cardboard headpiece stuffed inside a faded balaclava, had noted down a song, 'Ten little S-boats'. It was based on 'Ten green bottles', with spaces left by Marriot for the last three.

Young was reassured by the hardened veterans in *Sealion*, but he still found his first dive since the disaster in *Umpire* difficult and spent his first watch on deck in near panic. The night was pitch black and he constantly imagined ships coming at them fast out of the dark. But apart from a hazardous rendezvous with a French agent in a fishing fleet the patrol was uneventful. Ben Bryant was a calming, arrogantly assured presence and gradually Young regained his nerve.

With so many of Marriot's contemporaries dead and ninety-two submarines building, new men were conscripted into the service. Horton sought permission to have the whole of the Royal Navy's 1941 officer intake drafted into submarines, and got it. Large numbers of ratings were brought in, against their own better judgement. Fred Buckingham found himself with a draft chit to *Dolphin*. 'Submarines were the last thing in the world that I wished to serve on,' he said, but he thought he was safe because he had varicose veins, which before the war had always meant disqualification from submarines. Having failed to impress the Chatham medical officer, he detailed his defects to the medic at Gosport who listened patiently and asked, 'Do you think you can keep going for three months?' Buckingham answered in the affirmative. The doctor said, 'That's alright then. You're fit enough, for that's the average submariner's life expectancy nowadays.' His courses at Gosport and Blyth were followed by an examination which 'needless to say no one failed'.

Jim Thomsett, having served in the battleship *Warspite* for several years, had a very close brush with death off Crete when a bomb hit the spot he had just vacated and killed a friend. *Warspite* needed repair, so Thomsett was sent home in the *Empress of Canada*, and found his mother deeply depressed by the death of his brother Harry in *Sterlet*. Jim started courting his childhood sweetheart Eileen, who lived in the same street. When his leave ended his mother said to him, 'Son, you won't go into submarines, will you?' And he promised, 'No.'

When he reported for duty he found he had a draft to *Dolphin*. 'I vowed then that I would not pass the course,' he said. But it was now hard to fail. In his draft of twenty-eight there were only two volunteers. On their second day at Fort Blockhouse they saw the doctor and took the DSEA test. 'We was taken up to the tank, we was given the drill as to what to do with the equipment and we had to put the equipment on, go into a chamber three at a time where it was flooded up and just open the hatch, go through the thirty foot of water and do the surfacing routine and that was that,' recalled Thomsett. 'Little did I know that once I'd passed that I was a submariner.'

During his training period on *H50* he met a 'towny of mine from Deal' who told his mother where he had seen him. Before he knew it he was bound for the Mediterranean in the new submarine *P36*. 'The only thing I was worried about was that I hadn't told Mother.'

Arthur Dickison was drafted into submarines in July after a shortened course as a telegraphist, during which time he married

Clare, a girl he had met as a teleprinter operator at Chatham. Not knowing naval jargon, the realisation that their draft to *Dolphin* meant a draft to submarines came as a horrible shock to his group of trainees. Two of the class failed the DSEA test, but the rest went north to *Elfin* at Blyth for sea experience and further courses. There, most of the day was filled with classes on how to use the echo sounding, sonar and hydrophone equipment, the radio transmitting and receiving gear, and all the other jobs (except electronics) that were normally carried out by the specialists in each field. The group also gained plenty of practical experience helping to service the incoming operational submarines.

They were trained to do everyone else's job because in an emergency they might have to. 'If you were in the control room, and near the main ballast diving vent panel, you pulled the vent levers,' recalled Ben Skeates. 'You pulled them in the correct order, else the bleeding sub would go down head or tail first, or even sideways. That's how the instructor put it to us. If you were near the main battery exhaust fans you switched them off and closed the sea vents for diving, and so on.' A few more people were weeded out at this stage because 'some people ... who had passed the test in the tank, could not stand the submarine once they got on it, they were claustrophobic, they could not stand the atmosphere of being in this sardine can locked up ... and were immediately sent back to general service. One or two of my quite good friends didn't make it that way.'

Eight of Dickison's draft went on to join the 7th Training Flotilla at Rothesay, where Dickison had spells in *H28*, *H33*, *H50* and *Sealion*. George Colvin was now her captain, but a notice appeared advertising that Ben Bryant was raising a crew for a new boat and if any of the Sealions wanted to volunteer they should put their names down. Bryant's Sealions had talked him up, several volunteered and Dickison decided to add his name to the list. After seven days' leave with Clare, Dickison returned to Gosport to prepare for his exam and wait for his draft chit. One by one the telegraphists were sent off to submarines. Eventually

Dickison received his orders to join a boat that was being built at Birkenhead. There he reported to his boss, petty officer telegraphist Alf Paris, a cheerful redhead, who told him the boat was S-class and the skipper was Ben Bryant.

Sealion was on her way to Polyarnoe near Murmansk. Germany had invaded Russia in late June and the Soviet Union had become an ally rather than an enemy. In August Boggy Bone's *Tigris* and Slasher Sladen's *Trident* had gone to Polyarnoe to help the Russians. Now *Sealion* and *Seawolf* relieved them. Colvin, slight and intelligent, with pale skin and bright red hair and beard, charmed Edward Young, who 'grew to like him more than any other submariner I ever met'.

The voyage was 'a succession of mountainous seas and nights of misery'. Young and the navigator tried to make light of the situation. Each time they relieved each other's watch, they played pompous, humourless U-boat officers, speaking comic German and ending ritually, 'Gott strafe England!' with Nazi salutes. 'The lookouts thought we were quite mad.'

When they arrived, *Tigris* had already departed, and *Trident* soon followed. Both craft went home carrying reindeer presented by the port admiral at Murmansk. The submariners had admired the local sledge transport and Sladen had mentioned that in winter his wife had difficulty pushing a pram with two children up the hill. A sack lowered in by the Russians as *Trident* departed was found to contain a reindeer, and they named her Pollyanna after the port. She quickly became the crew's pet and was fattened up on Carnation milk, to the point where they had difficulty getting her out of the hatch at the end of the voyage. She eventually found a home at Regent's Park Zoo.

The Sealions found the Russians unfriendly and suspicious, although the officers once invited those of a neighbouring submarine to a night's drinking, and somehow within a few hours of arriving their veteran torpedo gunner's mate, who played the accordion with passion, was incorporated into a memorable musical show put on by the Russian fleet.

Sladen had sunk some big ships in August but by now the Germans were taking more care. Targets were scarce and difficult to find in the prevailing darkness. Once *Sealion* shot up a Norwegian vessel, taking the captain prisoner. When he was shipped to England Colvin gave him an introduction to his mother. Colvin was a sensitive soul. He didn't let it affect his fighting judgement, but Young reckoned he could not see a torpedo hit without 'picturing vividly in his imagination the twisted steel, the torn flesh, the inrush of water, the choking lungs'. As he hit a merchant ship just under the bridge, Young heard him say, 'God how I hate doing this.'

Arctic Russia was an unappealing backwater. The focus of the British submarine war had by now shifted to the Mediterranean. Alastair Mars addressed the crew of his first operational boat, *Unbroken*, bound for what Mussolini called 'Mare Nostrum'. He told them they had two jobs – to be successful and to survive. He promised that he would be demanding, that they would have to work, and that they would be rewarded with success. He finished with 'One final thing. What is good enough in other submarines will not be good enough here. Nothing is "good enough" for me. I'm going to have the best, and only the best – and you're going to give it to me.'

A few days later he walked through the boat. Mars bars were part of service rations and the crew had pinned up advertisements for them in every mess: 'Mars are marvellous', a blonde announced, and 'Nothing but the finest ingredients is good enough for Mars.'

13

SINK, BURN AND DESTROY!

During the winter of 1940 the Malta submariners left Fort Manoel and moved to the Lazaretto, the seventeenth-century quarantine building, built with stone quarried from the limestone rock face against which it stood. It was a beautiful, honey-coloured structure, 500 feet long and 100 feet wide, looking out over Marsamxett harbour towards Valletta. The water, forty feet deep, lapped against its southern front. The Lazaretto was two storeys high and on the northern side the roof was at ground level. Corridors ran the length of the southern front at both ground and first floor level, open to the air through huge arches at the east end allowing access to unload from the sea. Accommodation for the officers was located above these arches to the east, with 'cabins' around a central ward room and large sofas around the windows in the airy corridor. Messes and accommodation for ratings were at the west end.

Six U-class submarines reached Malta between December and February and on 8 January 1941 their captain, Shrimp Simpson, arrived in a destroyer with a supply convoy from Alexandria. In Egypt he had been briefed by Andrew Cunningham, his chief of staff, Manley Power (who was a former submariner) and Sammie

Raw. So far, they admitted, the campaign had gone badly – nine merchant ships, a submarine and a torpedo boat sunk, a total of 35,000 tons (more than half sunk by *Truant*). For this modest score, nine submarines and about five hundred highly trained men had been lost.

Cunningham told Simpson that he had a free hand, subject to orders from above. The staff believed the losses were due to mines and Cunningham advised Simpson to keep his boats to deep water, but crucially he didn't order him to do so. Perhaps, in the light of Hugh Haggard's successful insubordination, Cunningham was not sure that Raw's caution with regard to mines was justified. Simpson had some days to study charts, read patrol reports and talk to the officers at Alexandria. He decided to disregard the threat from mines, except in the approaches to ports and in the Sicilian narrows.

The practicalities of administering submarines in the Mediterranean from London are revealed by a surprising exchange between Horton and Cunningham's staff in February 1941. Horton demanded monthly reports on the activities of the Mediterranean submarines and complained that he knew nothing of their war experience, considering information essential so that he could remedy material defects and prepare personnel. Alexandria replied that knowledge of what was happening in home waters was equally meagre there 'and more information is obtained through conversation with officers from U.K. than through official channels'. Detailed reports were too long for telegrams and ordinary mail travelled extremely slowly, if it reached its destination at all.

At the Lazaretto Simpson met Robert Giddings, known as 'Pop' because he was in his fifties. A sales representative for Saccone & Speed, he had returned from naval retirement to run the Lazaretto base. Geoffrey 'Bob' Tanner, staff officer (ops), was an old friend who had left submarines when his eyesight deteriorated. Later in the year Hubert Marsham left his submarine *Rover* to become Simpson's assistant as Commander S10. On 10

January Sam MacGregor arrived with the convoy from Gibraltar as head engineer and began to scrounge whatever was needed to equip a submarine workshop.

The most serious problem was procuring and maintaining torpedoes. There was still a severe shortage, and production was running way behind demand. In 1940, when submarines alone required 1200, just 939 tinfish were made and most of those were destined for aeroplanes, destroyers, cruisers and torpedo boats, which also needed them. No reliable figures exist for torpedo supply, perhaps because the subject is so embarrassing, but at the end of 1940, after 299 had been fired, there were fewer than 100 in reserve. The shortage was most acute in Malta. When the fleet withdrew in 1939 *Maidstone* and *Cyclops* took the stock of submarine torpedoes to Britain. *Medway* brought the Far East reserve to Alexandria so that in January there were sixty spares there, but Malta had only those landed by *Otus* and *Olympus* when they went for refit. Submarines on passage to Alexandria had their torpedoes removed and a number of Mark IV destroyer torpedoes were converted for use in submarines, but torpedoes remained scarce and precious, and usually also old and unreliable.

Simpson's arrival coincided with that of Fliegerkorps X, the Luftwaffe's specialists in sea attack, who had been so successful in Norway. On 10 January, as Simpson went to report to Malta's naval commander Admiral Ford, bombers struck the Maltese aerodromes. Simultaneously, out at sea, thirty Stukas dive-bombed the aircraft carrier *Illustrious*. They scored six hits, but *Illustrious* limped into Valletta. On 16 January the bombers came to finish her off in French Creek, Grand Harbour. From his sofa on the Lazaretto balcony Peter Bartlett had a fine view of the Stukas diving below the Valletta skyline and then pulling out over the submarine base, waving as they passed. Simpson was in Valletta and noticed how effectively clouds of dust from the Maltese stone hid the target, but he was anxious because there were damaged submarines in Grand Harbour. *Upholder* was in dock for degaussing, a scientific technique for reducing the magnetic field of her hull so as not to attract magnetic mines. She was berthed only fifty feet astern of *Illustrious* but, remarkably, she came through unscathed.

The arrival of the Luftwaffe was a response to Italian defeat. The British had counter-attacked in Africa and were advancing through Cyrenaica. In January they captured Tobruk and Derna. Hitler decided the front needed stiffening. By the end of January there were two hundred German fighters and bombers in Sicily and they raided Malta continuously and ferociously. There were 107 raids in February and 105 in March, while in April the weight of bombs increased dramatically and devastating parachute mines were introduced. The one modern facility that Malta did have was radar, so the raids could be detected as they developed. When aircraft appeared on the radar screen a red flag was raised on the flagpole of the Auberge de Castille, the highest point in Valletta, and the air raid siren was sounded when the formations began to move towards Malta. Simpson had Maltese Boy Scouts watching from the roof of the base, and they ran along the roof sounding a horn when and if it became clear that the enemy was aiming for Valletta.

Admiral Layton's daughter Suzanne had moved into a room in the St James Hotel in Valletta and started work for military intelligence in the Auberge de Castille, coding and decoding messages. She joined the Union Club in Strada Reale for lunch. Her soldier husband visited about once a week for a couple of hours. As the bombing grew more intense, she slept in a cave under the hotel until one day a bomb hit it, whereupon she moved to a flat in the Mountbattens' house between Valletta and Sliema. The Sliema Club still held its Saturday evening dances. Her husband tried to arrange his leave to coincide, but when he was on duty Hubert Marsham would often ask her out, collecting her on his motorbike. That way she got to know the Malta submarine officers and when a raid on Valletta threatened, Simpson sent Marsham to fetch her to the safe rock shelter on Manoel Island where she would sit out the raid with the submarine crews.

One day the bombing started as she and Hubert were on their way. He increased speed and raced through the deserted streets. They were strafed on one straight and as they skidded to a halt at the shelter, Hubert told her to jump and run for it. He flung down the bike and followed. That day the sick bay overhead took a direct hit. Forbidden to enter, she swept up glass nearby.

Apart from that one strike, and some stray bombs landing nearby on Manoel Island, the submarine base came through the first German blitz untouched. In fact it was never deliberately targeted. A German map found in a bomber in April had 'U-boothausen' marked in Msida Creek, half a mile away from the Lazaretto. Nevertheless, Simpson employed Maltese quarrymen to dig into the rock behind the Lazaretto, carving out bombproof workshops and sick quarters.

At the end of January *Truant* left Alexandria to patrol off Benghazi in order to ensnare retreating ships. Once again Haggard watched the minesweepers, plotted the swept channels, and then crept in close. There was a plane circling overhead as he tried to fire three torpedoes across the minefield in shallow water. Immediately after firing there was an explosion that put nearly all the lights out and blew *Truant* to the surface. The aeroplane swooped and bombed her. The crew fumbled around in the darkness as Haggard tried to take the boat to deep water. There was an ominous scraping noise along the hull, as if they were dragging a mine cable. When they surfaced at night they were relieved to find it was the jump wire that had broken. Hart and his stoker mates Goldsack and Nuttall reckoned a torpedo must have hit a mine, but it was more likely that a faulty torpedo had hit the bottom and exploded. The radio was a write-off, the asdic wouldn't work and the battery was damaged, but they were still fit to fight.

Angelo Coliolo of the armed merchant cruiser *Attilio Deffenu* was not far from Tripoli escorting a convoy home, when he saw a submarine surface suddenly and open fire. Coliolo's third shot landed within fifty metres of the submarine, which then dived astonishingly fast. Thinking he would be hunted after dark,

Coliolo turned the convoy back towards port. At 1710 their shadowing aircraft opened fire, dived and twice bombed something to the left. Coliolo headed that way and saw the tracks of two torpedoes pass him thirty metres to his right. He raced down the tracks, saw the plane drop another bomb, fired at the spot the bomb dropped and saw a bubble of air. Setting his charges to fifty metres he dropped three as he passed over the air bubble, then saw another air bubble and dropped three over that.

Down below at 150 feet '*Truant* rose and fell with the force of the explosions like a sportive porpoise.' Pook, Hart, Brown, Haggard, Goldsack, Smithy and the other fifty Truants shared that fear again: pounding hearts, then 'the feeling that all the blood had been drained from our bodies, whilst all around us the lamps tinkled down, smashed to smithereens, and the bulkhead corking sprayed everywhere like snow, smothering our bodies'. Fortunately for *Truant*, Coliolo only had six depth charges. He returned to Tripoli.

With no torpedoes left, no radio, no asdic and a damaged battery, Haggard headed for Malta. This was dangerous since they weren't expected. They arrived at midnight, just as David Wanklyn was leaving for patrol in *Upholder*. He saw *Truant* first, stalked her and challenged four times by signal lamp before telling his first lieutenant, 'No, that's a T-Class – leave it alone.' The moon and the lights of Malta made it easier to see from *Upholder* than from *Truant*, but it was not the first time that John Smith and *Truant*'s other lookouts had been caught napping.

Simpson remembers his commanders talking to Hugh Haggard about night attacks. Lieutenant Dudley Norman took the advice to heart. His Uprights walked across the 'cat' – a string of empty oil drums, with gang planks and guide ropes – to the mooring platform on 18 February and they were hardly out of the harbour when the Lewis gun opened up to explode acoustic mines ahead of them by firing into the water. On the second night Norman fired at an unescorted tanker and set it on fire. He let the crew have a look at it through the periscope as it burned.

After checking the anchorage off Sfax, Norman moved on to the shallows around the island of Kerkenah. Night fell. For the second time in the month a big troop convoy was moving from Naples to Tripoli in four liners, *Esperia*, *Conte Rosso*, *Marco Polo* and *Victoria*, covered by two cruisers with destroyers. The senior asdic rating heard them first, reporting high-speed propellers closing rapidly from the north. On the bridge, signaller Arthur Smith and lieutenant David Swanston peered northwards and saw dark objects. Swanston realised *Upright* was fine on the port bow of three ships in line ahead and ordered the right course for attack before calling Norman. Counting the revolutions, the asdic operator got the target's speed and Norman fired on the surface before diving, turning off track. He raised the periscope in time to see the torpedo hit. One big explosion was followed by a second and parts of the ship were blown high into the air. She sank quickly and 464 of her crew were killed. The sinking was confirmed by a Tunisian source, who reported caps washed ashore bearing the name *Armando Diaz*. When the wreck was dived in 2004, the cruiser was found to be 160 metres long with a thirty-metre section entirely pulverised by the torpedo.

Norman's achievement was impressive considering that, apart from their small size and quick diving time of sixteen seconds to periscope depth, the U-class boats were ill-suited to operational use. Intended for training rather than combat, they were very slow, barely reaching twelve knots on the surface, poorly armed, and thoroughly cramped for the crew of thirty-one. *Ursula* had six bow tubes, the others four, and the remarkably old twelve-pounders they were given were useless against most targets. Their maximum diving depth was 250 feet, which was barely adequate, and their trim was extremely sensitive. In rough weather there was little chance of any sort of accuracy and they had a disconcerting tendency to break surface after firing.

At 1141 on 9 March Ben Skeates in *Utmost*'s radio office took down a signal from Hubert Marsham at the Lazaretto and brought it to captain Dick Cayley. It informed them that early that morning 'three enemy merchant ships passed Kelibia roads Southward 14 knots'.

Angelo Coliolo was on his next run to Tripoli in *Attilio Deffenu* with the 2584 ton *Fenicia* and the 5683 ton troop transport *Capo Vita*. They had left Trapani, made Cap Bon and were crossing the Gulf of Hammamet when at midday *Capo Vita* whistled and turned right. Coliolo made out a torpedo track and sped along it toward the submarine. *Capo Vita* exploded and instantly sank:

> An enormous, fantastical ball of fire, accompanied by dense, reddish smoke, rose for thousands of metres, and spread outwards for over 1000 metres, engulfing the S.S. *Fenicia* as well. The sea all round was literally full of columns of water, thrown up by debris of every sort falling from a great height. I narrowly managed to avoid it by heading into the wind. When the wind cleared the smoke away there was no sign of the S.S. *Capo Vita*.

Coliolo could find no trace of the submarine either. He dropped five charges set for fifty metres and then went to the site of the explosion to look for survivors. He could find none, only bits of wood and barrels.

That night Cayley replied to Hubert Marsham: 'One got torpedoed and then there were two.'

Coliolo led *Fenicia* towards Sousse, zigzagging furiously. Later, they were ordered to resume course for Tripoli. At 2230 he reached the first buoy marking the Kerkenah shallows. A convoy passed them heading for Italy. At 0655 a torpedo hit *Fenicia*, setting her on fire. 'Great flames rose from the ship and spread across the sea for hundreds of metres.' Coliolo rushed towards the position of the attacking submarine dropping charges but could find no trace of it. '*Fenicia*, on fire and with her stern almost underwater, still had her engines running and was heading away towards the South, followed by a trail of fire.' He hunted for half an hour then, with only one charge left, and *Fenicia* sinking, went to rescue survivors and take them to Tripoli.

Dick Cayley of *Utmost* and Tony Collett of *Unique* had each sunk their first ship. Cayley soon added to his tally. On 28 March he sank the *Heraklea*. She was carrying troops and the escorts merely searched for survivors. Cayley gave his men a look through the periscope. One of them said 'it took me years to get over the sight of that stricken ship and the men struggling in the sea.'

The damage done to Italian convoys by submarines, even now they had discovered the convoy route, nevertheless remained small. The key convoys carrying the Deutsche Afrika Korps out to Libya made it through unmolested. Similarly, the Italian luxury liners got the armoured Ariete and motorised Trento divisions across without loss. In February 79,000 tons of Axis supplies reached Africa with just a 1.5 per cent loss. In March it was 95,000 tons, though with a significantly improved 9 per cent lost. In April nearly 60,000 tons of supplies and 20,000 tons of fuel reached Rommel with 8 per cent lost. The losses were not great enough to do more than irritate him. That month he chased the small British force left in Africa back to the Halfaya pass on the Egyptian border. The main British army, despatched to Greece, was soon in rapid and desperate retreat as the Germans invaded Greece and Yugoslavia. Admiral Cunningham came under immense political pressure to stop supplies reaching the Axis forces.

The only bonus was that the arrival of the Luftwaffe brought with it the first good intelligence through the interception of enemy messages. The German air force codes had been broken in 1940. On 7 April the Admiralty informed Cunningham that 'advanced elements of German 15th Armoured Division were embarking at Palermo on or after 9 April probably for Tripoli'. David Wanklyn, lurking off Cap Bon, knew about a 'troop convoy' leaving Palermo to pass him on 11 April, which made it particularly galling to Sammie Raw that Wanklyn had fired all his torpedoes at lesser targets – and missed – before the convoy appeared. Irritated that Wanklyn had wasted one torpedo at a range of 6500 yards when Raw had issued orders not to fire at more than 2500 unless the target was extremely valuable, Captain S1 summed up Wanklyn's performance as 'extremely disappointing'. Raw was under pressure – from Churchill ultimately – because things were going so badly. This was the third patrol on the trot where Wanklyn had expended all his torpedoes without success, and they had very few torpedoes. Simpson defended his former first lieutenant against Raw's wrath but he could see the writing on the wall.

But Wanklyn's luck changed. On 24 April he sank the 5428 ton *Antonietta Laura*, then blew up a grounded destroyer and a supply ship that had been carrying a Panzer division headquarters unit. He then attacked a convoy, sinking one German merchant and damaging a bigger one. The crew had taken the opportunity for rapid looting of the supply ship, which had contained 'a good few German soldiers and a good stink coming from them', and entered Lazaretto Creek, as one Upholder recalled, 'with a guard of honour on the far casing wearing German tin hats, carrying German tommy guns and flying the German ensign'.

Hugh Haggard, now known to his crew as 'Rider', was perfecting the surprise gun attack, which Buster Brown, the telegraphist gunner, enjoyed very much. Off Apollonia they surfaced suddenly and sank a little submarine chaser. Next they had an important and dangerous mission – to slip right up to the boom protecting Tripoli harbour, surface just before dawn and shine a beacon light for Cunningham's fleet to bombard the Libyan port. Churchill had wanted him to block it with a battleship but settled for a distant bombardment, while Admiral Pound insisted to Cunningham that 'every possible step must be taken by the Navy to prevent supplies reaching Libya from Italy'.

As the submarine crept in they talked in whispers and Hart

watched the chief electrician rig up a beacon light. Woken later from sleep, Hart went to his watch-diving post on the forward ballast pump. Two large ships, escorted by destroyers, had just passed overhead to enter Tripoli harbour. Everyone felt sorry for Haggard, whose mission prevented him from sinking them. Eventually, they rose to the surface and crept towards the boom using the silent motors while the electricians positioned their beacon on the bridge. At 0400 they switched on the light, shells whistled overhead and Tripoli burst into flame. Five hundred tons of explosive was aimed at the docks with very little military effect. The port was back in action next day.

However, these loud noises made good publicity and they were having the desired effect on Churchill's American cousins. On 1 May *Truant* left for a refit, which everyone assumed meant they were going home. Haggard begged for a short patrol on his way to Gibraltar and on 6 May sank the troop transport *Bengasi* off Sardinia. At Gibraltar the troops bought silk stockings for their loved ones, but instead of heading for Britain *Truant* crossed the Atlantic. America was allowing docking facilities to British ships.

Hart found the Americans incredibly generous and hospitable. At New London, Connecticut, a clerical mistake meant the Truants could not be paid, so the Americans declared that everything was free. At Portsmouth, New Hampshire, Joe Rice of the US submarine *Trout* drove Hart, Goldsack and Nuttall around in his car. *Truant*'s proud record as top sinker was frequently boasted but cut no ice with one marine who claimed his uncle's boat had sunk four times the tonnage. When Frank Nuttall questioned this, the marine explained that his uncle was captain of a German U-boat. Telegraphist Buster Brown, who had arrived suffering from crabs and scabies, fell deeply in love with a girl called Dorothy Parker and promised to go to America after the war. She gave him a Parker pen when he left. Haggard found himself reunited with some Norwegians he had helped to escape from Norway in order to stage a propaganda re-enactment for Louis de Rochemont's *March of Time*. He found it 'a tremendous change to feel that one was in an absolutely safe land'.

As *Truant* left Malta, Casemore's *Unbeaten* and three other U-class boats arrived. *Usk* was overdue. Never heard from after reporting intense anti-submarine activity off Cap Bon, she may have been mined. The new arrivals were soon out on patrol, the inexperienced crew of *Unbeaten* receiving a fiery baptism. They left Malta on 11 May and close inshore Teddy Woodward attacked a group of schooners with three torpedoes from long range, though he missed. The next day he followed a laden schooner into the anchorage at Al Khums. They crept along the bottom to within 1000 metres and then surfaced with the hatch open and the crew swarming to the gun. Jack Casemore saw the Italian crewmen diving off the bowsprit.

The following evening Woodward was manoeuvring inside a destroyer to get at two merchants. Jack Casemore was at his diving station on the helm, steering the boat. Suddenly, *Unbeaten* hit bottom at a spot where their chart showed deep water, bouncing up to twenty feet. The destroyer was so close that Woodward was certain they must have been seen. When he reached periscope level the escort was 600 yards away and approaching at high speed. It was probably too late to dive to avoid collision, even if there was now more than eight feet under the keel. He muttered, 'Oh my God!', then yelled, 'Stand by to be rammed,' and 'Shut watertight doors,' ordered a swing to port to take a glancing blow and bolted for the control tower hatch. 'Tosh' Harding, the raw-boned southern Irish coxswain, grabbed him by the legs, said 'I wouldn't do that, sir!' and pulled him down while the first lieutenant dived the boat.

They waited for the crash. Nothing happened. *Unbeaten* reached the bottom here at sixty feet. They waited twelve minutes, then took a look. Their target was now 4000 yards away. The destroyer must never have seen them at all and had just turned away at the end of her zigzag.

After two days of poor visibility, Woodward found a destroyer escorting a transport, and fired a spread of three torpedoes from 3500 yards. They were in eighty-four feet of water with the boat in level trim. The first torpedo was faulty, hit the bottom eight seconds after firing and exploded, throwing *Unbeaten* up to eighteen feet. The second torpedo was fired with the bow pointing downwards as the first lieutenant struggled to recover the trim. After that the bow went down heavily with the stern in the air. Woodward tried to stop the third torpedo, but it was too late. It went straight to the bottom and exploded. *Unbeaten* was going at full speed, 90 off track and had just struck bottom at seventy feet when the first four depth charges fell.

They stopped the motors and slid silently down to the bottom at 140 feet, using the motors to slip northwards when the noise was covered by explosions. The first two patterns fell short, the third straddled them. Water burst in through a stern gland. Between each attack the destroyer paused to listen, then raced in dead at them. At that point they shifted position. The very young and inexperienced assistant asdic operator Maidment was sobbing. Drury went over and put the spare headphones on, taking over the work of locating the enemy. The destroyer seemed to be transmitting sonic at a high-pitched frequency. It dropped a total of twenty-two bombs over three-quarters of an hour, then sat still on their starboard quarter.

After waiting another three-quarters of an hour they started the hydraulic pump. Immediately, the destroyer moved in, stopping again much closer to them. Risking the possibility of reinforcements arriving, Woodward decided to lie still until dark. He hoped the destroyer might drift and lose them, since its hydrophones seemed much more effective than its sonar. Four hours of silent tension. Then the destroyer got under way and moved. Two and a half hours later asdic operator Peter Birnie again heard 'HE' – hydrophone effect or engine noise – at 130 revs. It sounded like a destroyer but it might have been another vessel passing. The officers held a conference. Woodward asked Drury to come to the ward room and give his opinion. He said he thought the destroyer had gone. Woodward decided not to move until midnight, at which time *Unbeaten* surfaced. There was nothing there. Jack Laurance started the engines and they set course for Malta. When they reached Valletta, Woodward cleared the lower deck and apologised, assuring the crew 'that that incident will never happen again'.

After this patrol they got a new first lieutenant. Aston 'Peter' Piper of *Ursula* had complained to Simpson that another RNR officer, junior to him, had been promoted earlier than he had, so Simpson offered him *Unbeaten*, whose first lieutenant was going home to take the command course.

Upholder was on patrol near the Strait of Messina. David Wanklyn had made two attacks, damaging a French ship. Trying to attack in a U-class submarine was frustrating, though, because you could never chase a convoy with any chance of success. The first despairing attack at 7000 yards had been a waste of torpedoes and in the counter-attack the asdic set was damaged beyond immediate repair. They were returning towards Malta with two torpedoes left. Mike 'Tubby' Crawford was on watch about twelve miles off Augusta in fading light on 24 May when he made out a dark shape approaching them. By the time Wanklyn closed in, the target had become four beautiful passenger liners, silhouetted against the afterglow of sunset, moving fast at eighteen knots, guarded by four torpedo boats.

The four liners were *Conte Rosso*, *Marco Polo*, *Victoria* and *Esperia*, carrying troops to Libya. Sweeping a few miles head, well out of sight, was the 3rd Cruiser Squadron. The Italians' air escort had just left and the convoy had stopped zigzagging temporarily to make it easier for their new air escorts to find them. The Glasgow-built *Conte Rosso*, a 17,879 ton luxury liner, was on her seventeenth crossing to Tripoli by the route to the east of Sicily, which was short and difficult to mine. She had begun life carrying passengers from Italy to New York and had latterly plied between Trieste and Shanghai, taking many Austrian Jews to safety. This evening the sea was choppy and many of the 2482 soldiers on board were seasick. As the largest and nearest of the four, Wanklyn chose her as his target.

Upholder closed to 1600 yards submerged, unable to hear the escorts, while the swell made it difficult to see them. Wanklyn only just avoided the *Freccia*, but steadied on his director angle and fired his last two tinfish. *Freccia*, only 400 yards ahead, saw the tracks and sent up a green flare. Wanklyn dived to 150 feet as *Freccia* closed in. If *Conte Rosso*'s lookouts saw the light they saw it too late. Both torpedoes hit and water flooded into *Conte Rosso*'s bows. At first the soldiers mustered on the poop according to drill, but as the stern rose into the air the order 'Si salvi chi può' saw them jumping into the water and frantically swimming away from the ship. She sank bow first after fifteen minutes, the whirlpool she caused dragging about a thousand people under with her. Only 239 bodies were recovered. The escorts and some trawlers from Augusta rescued 1432 soldiers and crew.

Meanwhile *Freccia* hunted *Upholder*. With no asdic, Wanklyn could only hear the roar of the hunter as she passed overhead. He stood in a corner stroking his beard, giving quiet orders to the helmsman and explaining to the crew the strange sounds they could hear. Once there was something that sounded like a wire dragging down the hull. Eyes turned to Wanklyn, who announced confidently that it was the sound of the ship breaking up. *Freccia* dropped thirty-seven charges over two hours and some were close. It was the worst depth-charging they had yet experienced. The signaller couldn't take it and made a dash for the hatch, although they were 150 feet down. He was wrestled away. Only when they reached Malta did they learn the magnitude of their success – a huge liner and the best part of two battalions destroyed at a stroke.

On 20 May the Germans launched an airborne invasion of Crete. It should have been Malta: that spring the Oberkommando der Wehrmacht had been asked whether it would be better to invade Malta or Crete, and all services had agreed that the key target was Malta, to secure the sea route to Africa. Hitler overruled them.

Crete fell, but casualties to German paratroops were so severe that, although the British didn't know it, there was little chance of a second airborne assault. Cunningham's fleet also took a terrible mauling from the air as they evacuated the army, losing three cruisers and six destroyers sunk and many other vessels including the flagship *Warspite* damaged. After Crete, Cunningham was hard pressed to do more than supply the beleaguered garrison of Tobruk. Submarines were now his only means of satisfying Churchill's repeated demands to slash at the Axis supply lines.

Fortunately, a number of factors had shifted in their favour. First, Fliegerkorps X left Sicily and moved to Greece, as the Luftwaffe units there moved on to support Hitler's attack on Russia. Air raids on Malta decreased to a point where life almost returned to normal. By August they averaged one every twenty-four hours and many came at night. Big convoys got through to resupply the island, bringing precious torpedoes.

Second, the capture of an Enigma machine in May had led to breakthroughs with the German naval cipher. Meanwhile, the Germans had persuaded the Italians to use an Enigma-based cipher known as C38m for messages about naval transport and supply convoys. Bletchley Park broke into this in summer 1941 and had it mastered within months. Although it took time to learn how to use the information, from July Raw and Simpson received 'advance notice of virtually every convoy and important independent ship that sailed with troops or supplies across the Mediterranean', usually identifying the ships and escorts, and often with sufficient detail and sufficient warning for them to have submarines lying in wait for the enemy in the right place at the right time. They had similar information in smaller quantity about the Aegean and the western Mediterranean.

Air reconnaissance was needed to verify these reports – which along with the rest of the information obtained from the decoding of enemy messages were collectively given the code name 'Ultra' – and get precise locations. The two sources of intelligence worked well together, with Ultra targeting the limited resources of air reconnaissance and air sightings providing the alibi for the use of Ultra. On the front line of decryption were the Y-service listening stations. The principal field stations for the navy in the Mediterranean were at Ras-el-tin and later Mustapha near Alexandria, and in Malta. They listened both to uncoded conversation and to coded messages. Much useful information was also passed from the RAF Y station at Heliopolis near Cairo. Coded messages were sent to Bletchley Park for decryption and then returned to the Operational Intelligence Centre at Alexandria, which communicated with Cunningham's staff. From the OIC instructions were passed to the captain of the 1st Submarine Flotilla, a telephone line having been laid across the harbour to HMS *Medway*. Captain S1 issued orders or sent signals to his boats.

The pressure to sink, burn and destroy continued to grow. In June Tony Miers appeared in the Aegean with all *Torbay*'s guns blazing. His first victim was a sailing boat flying the swastika which blew up when the second round of four-inch hit it. 'The occupants did not appear to be soldiers,' Miers reported, so he left them clinging to wreckage. When the occupants were soldiers he sought to annihilate them, 'using both Lewis guns to destroy the boats and personnel'. On 5 July he sank the submarine *Jantina*, but most of his victims, in the immediate aftermath of the bitter battle of Crete, were caiques carrying soldiers and stores.

One of these episodes, which may have involved shooting German soldiers who had sought to surrender, was raised many years later as a potential war crime. The details are murky, variously recounted, and possibly not palatable, but the practicalities of submarine warfare need to be considered. Taking numerous soldiers prisoner was impractical and potentially suicidal. Miers certainly did mow down soldiers in rubber boats. This troubled some of his men, but not his superiors. Raw reported to Cunningham that 'The operation against the caiques was a model of efficient destruction', while Cunningham reported to the Admiralty that 'This was a brilliantly conducted offensive patrol', admiring the 'offensive spirit' that made Miers 'an outstanding submarine commander'.

The first Ultra decrypt received in time for action came through on 23 June, revealing that four fast liners full of troops were about to leave Naples for Tripoli by the eastern route through the Strait of Messina. *Urge* was south of the Strait and Wanklyn and Woodward sailed to join her, but an air strike caused the convoy to turn back. When the convoy sailed again, the ships passed *Urge* while her commander, Edward Tomkinson, was busy launching a commando attack against the railway at Taormina. Submarines were used to attack trains on coastal railways with their gun and to send commandos ashore to blow up railway lines in order to disrupt rail transport, since there was then no other means of doing so. This was fine, but it removed them from their primary task of sinking ships. The convoy reached Tripoli safely.

Two more convoys, announced at short notice by Bletchley Park, went by unscathed. But on 11 July a message to Shrimp Simpson gave three days' warning of a convoy of about six 5000 ton vessels leaving Tripoli at 1600 on 14 July, passing Lampedusa at 0500 on 15 July and west of Pantelleria at 1400 the same afternoon. Reg Whiteway-Wilkinson, once *Truant*'s first lieutenant, arrived at the Lazaretto with *P33*. She had sailed on 11 July for Lampedusa and was therefore in the right area to intervene. Simpson had time to have the convoy observed from the air to provide an alibi for the secret intelligence on which his mission was really based. When the convoy approached the gap in the minefield off Cap Bon less than an hour behind schedule, Whiteway-Wilkinson crept within the screen of six escorts and sank the *Barbarigo* with two torpedo hits. Fifty depth charges put his steering gear and hydroplanes out of action and he stopped a dive at 330 feet, just as rivets were popping and leaks spurting into the distorted pressure hull, but he survived to return to Malta. The Italians attributed the loss to the air sighting and the bottleneck at the minefield, but in reality this was the first sub-marine success for Ultra in the Mediterranean.

Simpson was ordered to provide cover to the north of the convoy codenamed Operation Substance from Gibraltar to Malta. To do this he decided to find a new route under the Sicilian minefield known as QBB 65. The idea was to arrive south of Sciacca at dawn and then run submerged at 150 feet, steering 300 blind for fifty-five miles to surface south-west of Marettimo after dark. The mines were set to catch vessels on the surface, with a proportion set to catch submarines at periscope depth, but it was always possible to snag one of the wires by which the mines were tethered. Dick Cayley volunteered to go first and make the shore fixes – take bearings on landmarks on shore – to secure the route. *Utmost* left on 17 July, with Ben Skeates, as assistant asdic operator, helping to plot the route. She came through successfully, signalling 'Utmost to S10. Next please.' As usual Cayley had passengers: this time the commando team of 'Tug' Wilson and marine Hughes, who were becoming an institution at Malta. Cayley was always the most willing of Simpson's captains to take risks. He watched in amusement as Wilson blew up a train and a naked bathing party of Italians was arrested on the beach.

Things were not all one way. On 20 July one boat was lost to depth charges and a few days later, after making a series of mistakes, another had to be scuttled and her crew was captured. Then the Italians tried a daring attack on Malta.

Before midnight on 25 July Simpson was summoned to naval HQ because something odd had appeared out to sea on the surface warning radar. Wakened at dawn by gunfire, he raced to Fort Manoel to get a clear seaward view out to sea. What he saw were fast motor boats, zigzagging towards the harbour entrance at forty knots. When they came within effective range the multiple Hotchkiss guns at Fort St Elmo opened up and mowed them down. As they sank they exploded. The idea had been for midget submarines to create gaps in the harbour boom for the motor boats to race in and sink the supply ships of Operation Substance. But the midgets failed in their task and the motor boats never got near. Nothing escaped from the attack but the depot ship. The radar had proved its worth: without it the guns would not have been manned and ready.

Parthian was due for a refit. Michael Rimington sank his second submarine off Beirut in June, and in July he slipped into Mitylene harbour to do some damage to ships supporting the invasion of Crete. He tried to fire a 'parthian' shot (Anscomb's pun) from the stern tubes, but these held antique Mark II torpedoes from Malta. Although one ran straight and true, the other surfaced, porpoised into the air, then landed in the water and went round in circles, causing pandemonium in the harbour. It was Charles Anscomb's last taste of action in *Parthian* except for a brief attack from British coastal defence vessels off Gibraltar. When they reached Gosport and the crew split up, Anscomb stayed to kick into some sort of shape the new crew who were to take the boat to America. Then he left to stand by the brand new *Tempest*, feeling he had lost a part of himself.

In mid-August, decrypts revealed another trip by the luxury liners with troops for Tripoli, this time taking the western route round Sicily and down the Tunisian coast. *P32* and *P33* were already off Tripoli and on 18 August *Unique* under Baldy Hezlet was sent to join them. When Hezlet arrived he contacted *P32* using Morse code sent by asdic pulse, but could not get in touch with Whiteway-Wilkinson's *P33*. In *P32* they heard what they thought was a depth-charge attack in *P33*'s area and they too failed to contact Whiteway-Wilkinson's boat. *P33* never reappeared, sunk either by depth charges or by a mine.

That day *P32*'s asdic operator heard a convoy approaching through a swept channel the other side of the minefield. The commander, David Abdy, decided to dive under the minefield and attack. As he came up there was a terrific explosion and the boat plunged to the seabed at 210 feet. One of the escorting planes saw the explosion, but five merchants and six escorts swept by without noticing. This left Hezlet alone outside Tripoli.

Ahead of him on the route of the liners, which were carrying the Trieste division, Tomkinson's *Urge* and Teddy Woodward's

Unbeaten lurked south of Pantelleria. The following evening the sea was rough and the little subs couldn't keep a steady trim. Escorting aircraft saw *Urge* below the water. She was forced deep and hunted by the lead destroyer. Woodward launched four torpedoes from 6500 yards: one misfired, while the others were seen and avoided by the liners turning sharply.

Hezlet spent the day watching minesweepers keeping the channel clear. On the morning of 20 August the vessels offered the first sign of the approach of the convoy as they swept ahead of it. *Oceania, Neptunia, Marco Polo* and *Esperia* were escorted by five destroyers, two torpedo boats and two MAS boats – small torpedo armed motor boats – with two seaplanes and two fighters overhead. Hezlet crept to within 650 yards of the rear ship in the port column and fired four torpedoes. A MAS boat passed overhead just as he was about to fire and the first lieutenant almost lost the trim as the torpedoes left, but three of them hit the 11,400 ton *Esperia* near the bridge, in the boiler room and aft. She sank ten minutes later, but in water so shallow that she did not drag the swimmers with her. Hezlet sped away at sixty feet. The planes dropped bombs and two of the boats hunted but failed to get close, while the other escorts rescued 1139 of the 1170 men on board. Later in the day a seaplane saw *Unique* while she was at periscope depth and made an accurate attack which ruptured a fuel tank. Hezlet left at once for Malta, trailing oil fuel.

In mid-September the cryptographers predicted that a convoy would be leaving Naples by the eastern route via Messina to Ras el Hanra on 19 September and so to Tripoli, travelling at seventeen knots. Air reconnaissance confirmed the convoy's departure and Simpson set up an ambush north-east of the landfall. It was all arranged at short notice and Tomkinson, just in from patrol, refused to go, so the forward patrol line consisted of Woodward, David Wanklyn and Johnny Wraith (a term mate and friend of Hugh Mackenzie at Dartmouth, who had taken over *Upright*), placed to make a night attack, with Hezlet, now in *Ursula*, covering behind them to mop up submerged by day. They reached their positions by midnight and checked them using asdic.

At 0307 on a clear night Woodward sighted the enemy eight miles north. Drury tried to warn the others with asdic and when that failed sent a wireless message. Wanklyn received it at 0340 and sighted the enemy six miles away ten minutes later, closing at top speed on the surface, while Woodward followed the convoy. Although his gyrocompass had failed and the ship was yawing in rough water, Wanklyn fired at 0408 as two ships overlapped. The range was 5000 yards but it was dark. Two tinfish hit, sinking *Neptunia* and stopping *Oceania*. *Vulcania* sped up from seventeen knots to her maximum twenty-one knots, while the destroyers rescued the passengers.

Wanklyn dived and closed in while his crew reloaded torpedoes, a long process. Wraith tried but failed to cut off *Vulcania*, while *Unbeaten* and *Upholder* both closed in on *Oceania*. Woodward raised his periscope and exclaimed, 'My god, everything is lit up, search lights everywhere,' and began an attack on the damaged ship. Wanklyn was forced down by a destroyer, ran underneath the target and fired two torpedoes from the other side. *Oceania* sank as Woodward was about to pull the trigger. According to Casemore,

> one minute later our asdic rating Jock Birnie reported fast running HE sounds, like a torpedo. We immediately flooded Q and went to 90 feet and she passed right over the top of us. Some short while after, we heard the strangest noise as though there were nets being pulled over us. It was only later, when our captain said all trace of the troopship had vanished but the destroyers were still picking up survivors, that I realised the noise we heard was the troopship breaking up as she went down.

None of the subs had been able to sink the destroyers, because they had all set their Mark IV torpedoes deep for the liners and the torpedoes' depth settings couldn't be altered once they were in the tubes.

At first light Hezlet saw the pilot boat sent out from Tripoli to guide the convoy in. His asdic rating heard *Vulcania* rather ahead of schedule. Hezlet fired four torpedoes from 3500 yards, setting them for the convoy speed of seventeen knots that Ultra had reported. Unfortunately, *Vulcania* had increased her speed and the torpedoes missed astern.

After this disaster the Italians abandoned big troop convoys using liners, four of which had now been sunk. In September 29 per cent of cargo and 24 per cent of fuel sent across to Africa was lost on the way. Rommel was demanding shorter supply lines and safer supplies before he would contemplate an attack. He wanted Benghazi and even Derna used to land supplies rather than Tripoli. The Italians were thoroughly alarmed by what seemed to be brilliant British collaboration between aircraft and submarines, each guiding the other towards victims. Bletchley Park lapped up their complaints that submarines infested their routes and had sunk their best troopships.

At this grim moment in the war submarines gave the British something to cheer about. Cunningham told the Admiralty that 'every submarine that can be spared is worth its weight in gold'. The German navy's man in Rome, Admiral Weichold, reported that 'the most dangerous British weapon is the submarine, especially those operating from Malta ... A very severe supply crisis must occur relatively soon. This is because Italian freight space which is sunk cannot be adequately replaced and also because air transport can never be a complete substitute for sea transport.' The naval staff agreed and Hitler's headquarters agonised that 'enemy submarines definitely have the upper hand.'

14

BAND OF BROTHERS

'Rum-issue time! This for a new-joining rating is the time when he sizes up and is sized up by his new shipmates. Quite a lot can depend on those first, quick impressions.' Syd Hart was shifting from *Truant* into *Thrasher*, from a band of tried and trusted brothers to the unknown. His new colleagues looked promising at first sight: 'Digger' Berwick from New Zealand, always laughing, happy-go-lucky Harry Rampton, 'Nippy' Remplance, ridiculously good-looking twenty-year-old Fox and the instinctively dependable old Dan Conroy, hair of ropeyarn and blood of Stockholm tar. 'Each man – commissioned or not – has a definite and ultra-responsible job to do, whether dived or surfaced, and all hands carry themselves as skilled specialists should, proudly but without swagger, showing respect to companions and expecting it in return.'

Thrasher's career had begun badly – her first captain was sacked – and the men were still a little insecure, only beginning to gain confidence as the new skipper, Hugh Mackenzie, began to sink ships. It was easy for Hart to fit in. His new shipmates were in awe of him from the moment he revealed his old boat was *Truant*, one of the top scoring subs. As they awarded him sippers from their tots they too became 'a band of brothers, all for one and one for all'.

Jack Casemore, the pugnacious torpedoman from *Unbeaten*, judged people by how they behaved under depth-charging. A tough youngster who had boxed at school and never shirked a fight, in his first armed merchant cruiser he had won respect by beating up the bully of the mess. He didn't think much of 'Acker' Varley, *Unbeaten*'s third hand, because, he said, with depth charges 'he had one finger up his nose and the other up his bottom, and as the charges came he would jump in the air and change hands'. Varley once asked why they called him Acker – a nickname was usually a compliment – and they replied 'Because there's ninety-eight Ackers to the pound, sir.'

Casemore felt sorry for cases like *Unbeaten*'s young telegraphist, who sobbed his heart out during the first attack, but people like that had to be removed, both because they had a bad effect on the others and because they couldn't do their job properly while sobbing. The signalman from *Upholder* who had panicked during the counter-attack after sinking the *Conte Rosso* also returned to general service, despite his pleas to stay. Simpson tried to reassure him that he had nothing to be ashamed of. These breakdowns really seem to have been remarkably rare – they draw comment in memoirs rather than being suppressed. Bill King described two in *Trusty* – one man ripping up the ward-room pin-up girls and another running madly up and down the boat. In both cases the stress arose from being bombed in harbour and King commented, 'Thank heaven no one was ever taken this way when submerged.'

On the other hand there were people like Peter 'Jock' Birnie who, having survived the sinking of *Unity*, had come to *Unbeaten* from *Upright*. 'He was short, scruffy and had hair and a beard which was grey to fair and his beard stuck out at right angles to his face; but on his asdic set he was faultless.' Birnie would give a running commentary on what the destroyers were doing, telling those in the control room when the depth charges had hit the water, interspersing this with lots of funny comments that helped to ease the tension in the boat. Tosh Harding, the Irish coxswain who stopped Woodward surrendering, was very highly rated by his crew. 'Generally,' Casemore reckoned, 'if they were good under attack they were all right. The majority of people were good.'

Stoker Philip Le Gros, known as 'Froggy' though he was a New Zealander, remembered the scrutiny of his shipmates during depth-charging. 'Secretly they kept an eye on you, some blokes particularly when it was a bit tense. They kept an eye on people and probably made a note on how you behaved.' He remembered 'one leading stoker, Mick, his eyes always used to bulge and he would say, "Oh, if they want to kill me for God's sake kill me, don't frighten me to death".' George Curnall of *Upholder* admitted of the *Conte Rosso* counter-attack that 'I was pretty shaky, could not stop my legs from shaking, but did not let anybody notice it.' After hitting another ship 'we received 42 charges very near. Indeed, once when we were expecting to hear the next one explode we heard one of the destroyers pass right overhead and, boy, we had our hearts in our mouths. I could literally hear my knees knocking.'

There was a certain amount of bravado. Casemore remembered coming off watch with Frank Haddon, newly joined to replace the young telegraphist. They were 'standing in the galley drinking a cup of cocoa when there was a scraping noise on the outside of the pressure hull. Haddon said to me in a rather strained voice, "What is that?" I replied rather nonchalantly, "Oh, I expect we are running through a minefield. Don't worry, we are below them".' The idea that you took enemy fire silently without showing fear was an aspect of naval pride that went back at least as far as the mid-eighteenth century.

It was easier if you had absolute trust in your shipmates, but rubbing along in conditions of such close intimacy and privation for three weeks or so was hardly straightforward. Leslie Howard, the wartime conscript from Sheffield, said of *Torbay*, 'It was claustrophobic and a lot of chaps had to come out of submarines because of it. We used to get on each other's nerves sometimes as well – there'd be rows from time to time. But it was never anything serious. Most of the time we were really close.'

That was in retrospect. Arthur Dickison's journal was more immediate: 'it was bad enough on patrols but to have "moaners" around made it worse!' Submariners were intolerant of laziness or incompetence for reasons of self-preservation, though. When the asdic rating was caught sleeping on watch in Peter Forbes's boat he had no sympathy, 'the asdic rating is the ears of the boat and I for one want to see my wife again'.

Every boat had its share of characters. Casemore had joined *Unbeaten* after drinking with Roy Dunbar, a very clever twenty-year-old no-badge petty officer leading torpedoman who was in charge of the boat's electrics. To be a petty officer at that age was quite an achievement and quite a responsibility. Eventually, according to Casemore, whose patrol station was in the motor room with Dunbar, he cracked under the pressure and left the boat before the commission finished. Patrick 'Micky' Stanley, the outside ERA's mate, had been training to be a doctor but 'got mixed up with women', emigrated from Eire to England and joined the navy. (Every Irishman in the navy was 'Micky', just as all Millers were 'Dusty', all Turners 'Topsy' and all Scotsmen 'Jock'.)

Comical asdic ratings were always highly regarded and Peter Birnie was also a skilful caricaturist. 'If something out of the ordinary happened in the course of a day, that night a cartoon would go up on the notice board.' One day in the summer of 1941 the captain was suddenly called to the control room. Teddy Woodward jumped from his bunk naked but for a towel, which he wrapped round him as he started the attack. 'Half way into the attack the towel fell from him, but he carried on stark naked. That evening Jock's cartoon went up on the notice board with the caricature of Teddy dancing round the periscope with the biggest genitals imaginable. We all thought that Jock had gone too far and that he would get a telling off by the skipper, but no, Teddy loved it and I believe he kept all the cartoons that Jock did.'

Petty officers tended not to mix freely with junior ratings because it was difficult to be over-familiar with people you gave orders to. The characters Charles Anscomb remembered from *Parthian* chiefly belonged to the petty officers' mess – senior figures such as torpedo gunner's mate Robert Backhouse, always known as 'Roger' after the admiral. Backhouse was about thirty and 'a torpedo fanatic, a man of superlative skill at his trade'. He slept with his torpedoes, never in his bunk in the POs' mess, and only left the fore-end space for meals or the heads. He played a mandolin and spent his idle time learning new songs.

Backhouse's apprentice was 'Scratch' Nicholas from Fowey, subsequently rated petty officer and second coxswain. He was a fine if fiery-tempered seaman and an excellent cook, expert in fish, who came into his own when a shoal of bream was washed on to the bridge and trapped there. Victor Bartlett, the outside ERA, kept 'Peanut' – *Parthian* – afloat. His diving station was the main blowing panel in the control room, from which all the main ballast tanks were flooded and blown, but he was answerable to the engineer officer for all machinery outside the engine room and did more than anyone else to 'keep *Parthian*'s innards from seizing up with senile decay'. He was a keen photographer, but 'an untidy old devil' who used a small nut and bolt instead of a collar stud. LTO Apperly, on the other hand, was always immaculate. He was the youngest petty officer and being newly married, always volunteered to go and collect the mail when *Parthian* returned to harbour.

The ERAs, similarly, kept themselves to themselves. Casemore felt they 'always thought they were better than the seaman ratings' and slightly resented the fact that 'seamen had the executive power'. They were frequently better educated than seamen, often being grammar school scientists. On depot ships ERAs had their own messes and Joe Blamey was familiar with his colleagues in most other boats. When Blamey went 'ashore with the lads' in Malta, the 'lads' were *Porpoise*'s ERAs, Yorkshireman Tommy Hargreaves, Micky Power from Eire, Jock West from Edinburgh,

Jock Forrest from Kilmarnock and Taff Hughes from Swansea. After a few drinks Forrest and Hughes invariably started thumping one another and had to be pulled apart and sent home in separate horse-drawn carriages.

Early in 1942 they found the ERAs' club in Malta still functioning. The Maltese stewards, Tony and Manuel, were still there, but there was nothing to eat and not much to drink. Eventually, this was the only service club left. The Officers' Club, the Writers' Club, the White Ensign at Valletta and the Canteen at Corradina had all been wrecked by air raids.

Patrol routine had not changed very much from early days. The weather in the Mediterranean was generally pleasant. For Hart, 'the first night out always meant loneliness; an impression that we were something the rest of the world did not want.' He remembered watching Hugh Haggard bent over the chart table, studying his patrol areas and the courses to steer, and looking 'indescribably lonely'. Food remained good. A big boat like *Porpoise* had the 'refrigerator well stocked' and 'there was bags of spuds, oranges and any kind of fruit was stacked in the fore ends'. Even the little Malta-based boats ate well on patrol, their sea stores being immune from Maltese rationing. It wasn't the same on land in Malta, where even the submariners were relatively rationed. The bread allowance was three slices a day and at one time Shrimp Simpson had to quell a near riot when the troops discovered that the officers were eating potatoes when they couldn't get any.

Rules on smoking varied from captain to captain. Leslie Bennington, who took over *Porpoise* in May 1942, himself a chain smoker by inclination, 'always allowed a smoke around about noon, and again just before surfacing at dusk. Word would be passed by tannoy, "One each apiece all round." Now the air would be quickly blue but very soon was filtered by our lungs. Such a break was a Godsend and we blessed old Bennington for his consideration. The highlight of the day was of course when we surfaced at dusk with an empty sea. We could breathe the cool air as it was dragged down the conning tower by the engines. Then we could light up and smoke at will.'

There was one addition to the leisure facilities. From May 1943 the *Daily Mirror* produced a newspaper especially for submarines. *Good Morning* ran for 924 days, seven days a week. Six copies of each issue were printed for every submarine. The papers were sent to the Admiralty, who allocated the right number to each base, and then to the GPO to be flown out to the bases. There they were distributed to each submarine and each day's issue was handed out by the coxswain. They were numbered so that the cartoon stories – 'Jane' and 'Buck Ryan' from the *Mirror*, as well as specially invented series such as the 'Ship's Cat' – could be read in sequence, but they contained no hot news and no dates. Instead, they were packed with news from home addressed to individuals. More than 1000 families of submariners were visited by one of two reporters employed by the *Mirror*. *Good Morning* No. 36 carried a story about the birth of Bryant's son with a photograph of Marjorie and baby and another 'of his daughter Patricia, with her doggie'. They also contained full-page and smaller pin-ups. The *Daily Mail* could only respond by establishing the Good Evening Club at Dunoon to provide much-needed leisure facilities for the training flotilla.

At Malta Bob Tanner produced a monthly 'Lazaretto magazine' to dispense local information and amusement, and some individual submarines created their own journals like the 'Safari Indicator' edited by Dickison. News sheets like this could be used to keep the crew informed. Crews very much preferred captains like Cayley and Woodward, who kept them in the picture as far as possible. Haggard 'liked to keep my crew well informed on what's going on' and reckoned he was only caught out once or twice not telling the truth. 'There was an occasion when we were having a bad time and I told the crew all was well and almost as soon as the words got out there was a ghastly explosion very close to us. I thought that the crew needed a little bit of calming and I didn't get it right but they forgave me for it.'

Of course, even the officers puzzled about the peculiar accuracy of their intelligence. One of Tubby Linton's couldn't believe how you would be 'given a rendezvous to be at a certain position for no reason and you'd find a convoy turned up'. Norman Drury said, 'I don't know where the British got their information from, but there was a very busy fifth column somewhere in Italy passing information to the Allies about the movements of convoys.'

In Alexandria and Gibraltar, shore life was based on the self-sufficient 'mother ships' *Medway* and *Maidstone*. Both of these purpose-built submarine support vessels had stores of torpedoes and shells, fuel, water and stores, together with medical facilities, sophisticated workshops manned by experienced personnel, communication and command units, and accommodation for the submariners attached to them and for spare crew. There were messes for each of the various ratings and bars to match. On *Medway* in Alexandria harbour gin was 2*d*. a tot, whisky 3*d*. and fifty Players cigarettes 1*s*. 3*d*., all of which prices were cheap. Air raids were infrequent in Gibraltar – although there was an ever-present threat from Italian frogmen surreptitiously based at Algeciras.

In Alexandria the threat of raids on the harbour and air bases increased in 1942 as the enemy got closer, but essentially life continued as normal. The first thought of submariners reaching Alexandria was mail. Runners from the communications department fetched the post as soon as they reached the ship. Telegraphists were debarred from the usual sweepstakes on when the first lieutenant would give the last order, 'finished main motors and steering', having already made an estimated time of arrival signal. 'Getting the mail kept you sane and content and not getting any we got so depressed,' wrote Dickison, who arrived in *Safari* in 1942. A few people never received any mail, but generally the runners for both officers and men produced something. Officers had pigeonholes in their ward room in the depot ship; the removal of the names of officers who had been killed was always an uncomfortable moment.

The first harbour job was to clean the boat, which many did en route. The next thought was the bathroom. Filthy, smelly men revelled in fresh water on the depot ship, having been starved of it for sweaty, nervous weeks.

Then they dressed up 'tiddly' smart in shore rig and went ashore. A crumbling lane called Sister Street, the red light district in the old town around the harbour, was where most of the men started and finished. Joel Blamey disliked the people and found the place filthy and smelly, but others were less squeamish. The Fleet Club, where Hart played the tombola with Goldsack and Nuttall, was the standard safe rendezvous for sailors ashore, away from the native bars. There was a lavishly comfortable cinema. Mary's House was a famously civilised brothel for officers, with a large lounge bar on the ground floor in which the girls gathered when not otherwise engaged upstairs. They were said to take on thirty-five men a night each. Mary also had establishments in Port Said and Cairo. When, in 1941, the bar of the Alexandria House was hit by a bomb that caused numerous casualties, filling the wards of the military hospitals, Mary switched her shocked Alex girls to Cairo and her Cairo girls to Alex.

Officers were given generous hospitality by local residents. Cyril and Gabriella Barker, from an old established cotton-broking dynasty, who organised a concert party called the Desert Angels, also entertained naval officers. Peter Bartlett was one of those invited to spend his leave with them, with swimming and croquet parties in the afternoon, followed by cocktails, dinner and bridge. At their house submariners mixed with drivers of the Long Range Desert Group, mostly from New Zealand.

In very occasional rotation submariners based at Alex were able to take short rest breaks in the luxurious houseboat *Puritan*, moored on the Nile at Gezira. Egyptian stewards in long flowing robes and red fezzes showed them to their cabins, telling them to ring if they needed anything. This was heaven. The committee of the Cairo Sporting Club gave them free use of its swimming pool, tennis courts, bowling greens and horse riding facilities. On the opposite bank was a houseboat used by nurses, and for five fabulous days Syd Hart listened to the music drifting across the river in perfect night air. Anscomb shared the bridal suite with *Parthian*'s chief ERA. *Parthian* was having her after planes repaired at Port Said and Anscomb returned to another houseboat, this one old and filthy, where he ran a beer bar selling beer at half the price charged on shore, until Rimington, dissatisfied with their accommodation, had them moved to the Semiramis Hotel. At Port Said some of the men got into trouble with the security police and others 'wrecked the bar at the Seamen's Institute in the course of a terrible battle with a bunch of Australians in which no holds were barred and every man fought until he passed out'.

Before Greece was overrun submarines were occasionally allowed leave in the Piraeus, the port of Athens. Anscomb recalled how, just after Michael Rimington received a medal, they went ashore, trying to improvise decent clothes. 'When Victor Bartlett got to the iron he somehow managed to get the electric lead underneath his trousers when he was pressing them. It made an astonishing wriggly pattern, but he didn't care. He just pulled them on, shrugged into an old shirt, firmly bolted his collar fore and aft as usual, and ambled ashore with a huge grin to paint the Piraeus red.'

Malta, having no depot ship, was always different, and as life there became harder, it became increasingly informal. When a submarine came in to Malta everyone spent the first few hours clearing and cleaning the boat, then if it was a 'make and mend' (unless something urgent was pending) the duty watch stayed on board and those off duty went ashore. They went in pairs with an 'oppo', or in small groups. Casemore's constant companion was Norman 'Dickie' Dowdell, who came from Nottingham. Seamen usually paired up with seamen and stokers with stokers, and although the two groups might mix, the difference between them might also provide an excuse for a fight. Casemore recalled that 'there was an Irish stoker on our boat who, if I met him ashore and he was drunk, he'd want to fight me and I always won largely because he was drunk.' Fighting was common and became even more prevalent and violent where sailors could meet groups of Australians or Americans, as they sometimes did in Alexandria and later in Beirut and Algiers.

Sometimes submariners caught a dghajsa – a Maltese water taxi, resembling a Venetian gondola – over to Valletta and went down the Strada Stretta, 'The Gut'. 'It's got a terrible reputation, but all the sherry queens I met did no more than talk and drink with you. Buy them a sherry and they'd talk to you – to stay the night cost a quid, a fair bit of money in those days,' said Casemore. ' The sherry queens knew all the news and would tell you a boat had gone down way before you knew it. They'd got it over the radio from Italy – a lot of Maltese spoke Italian and those that didn't could understand.'

According to Ben Skeates, one of *Utmost*'s radio operators, John Meyerhuber (known to the crew as Schickelgruber, British radio propaganda's name for Hitler) fell in love with a sherry queen called Janie:

> Everybody knew her, or knew of her, she was a good looking woman. Like many other young ladies in many other ports, they usually just stand, or sit around, waiting for some lonely matelot to offer them a drink. It was useless trying to make Meyerhuber understand that she was to be seen any night before the bar closed, standing on a table, offering the key to her flat to the highest bidder. In fact I swear it made him more decided than ever that he would marry her and save her from a life of disgrace.

Fred Buckingham frequented the Lucky Wheel, where he knew a Maltese girl from when he had been in Malta in 1935. Helen was 'a nice girl, a bit too strict morally', with whom he repeatedly tried his luck and failed. Tubby the obese Maltese waiter served him real White Horse whisky. Once, another

waiter gave Buckingham the ersatz stuff that everyone else was
drinking and got a proper telling off from Tubby: 'Sparks is a special customer. He must have White Horse always. This stuff is for
other people.'

More often submariners still went to one of the many gaudily
curtained bars along the nearby Sliema front. The Dun Cow was
a traditional favourite with submariners, and crewmen of *Osiris*,
Truant and *Umbra* all remember drinking there. The proprietress,
Anne, was a generous soul, ready to lend money just before a
patrol or extend credit with a 'Pay me any time', perfectly well
aware that submariners frequently never came back. Dickison of
Safari preferred Tony's Bar, Casemore liked Charlie's Bar and
there were many others, until they ran out of beer. Then people
drank what they could. The fake whisky served at the Lucky
Wheel was made and supplied by Greek traders from Alexandria.
Ambeet, a local 'wine', accounted for many a hangover. For officers, the Sliema Club with its Saturday night dance was the
principal attraction ashore.

After the German attacks intensified in January 1942 runs ashore
became perilous. Buckingham and coxswain Harold Lindsay 'had
drunk our tots when the sirens sounded. As neither of us were on
duty we decided to beat it to the shelter as quickly as possible. We
had just cleared the pontoon when the planes came over, so we hit
the ground. Harold suddenly let out a yell, "I've been hit in the
arse!"' Doctors removed the shrapnel and he only missed one patrol.

On another occasion *Umbra* was due to go on patrol one
evening and Buckingham stayed in the Lucky Wheel until the
last minute. As he left a raid started. 'I was late already so I
couldn't hang around just because of an air raid. Going full speed
ahead carrying a fair cargo of White Horse, with bombs falling
and guns firing, I was suddenly halted in my tracks. Something
hit the road just in front of me and bounced up and hit me on
the knee. I bent down and picked up a jagged piece of brass ...
I hurried back just time to change into my disreputable steaming kit and get aboard.'

There was a rest camp at Ghain Tuffheia on the coast on the opposite side of the island, where submariners were occasionally able to enjoy seven days of swimming and sunbathing. Even this might be rudely interrupted, as Buckingham recalled. 'A number of us were sitting outside a hut watching a dogfight going on over the harbours when suddenly one fighter plane broke away and turned in our direction.'

They dived for cover when 'little puffs of sand squirted from the ground and rapidly approached us'. One such attack was blamed on Buckingham's skipper, Lynch Maydon, who took pot shots through his window at German fighters until one of them replied with cannon fire. 'I was woken by shells coming into my room and was lucky to survive,' recalled a colleague. 'Others didn't.'

By spring 1942 large parts of Sliema had been reduced to rubble and very few bars were open. Now the non-duty watches went ashore to escape from the bombing. Casemore used to catch a bus to Mosta, a town near the centre of Malta, and walk up to Mdina or St Paul's Bay. 'On the outskirts of St Paul's, I used a cafe to have a drink and if they had any food, have something to eat, generally a bit of bread and cheese and would chat to a girl that served in the bar.' One day, the owner asked him if he would marry the girl. She was pregnant. Her boyfriend was an RAF pilot who had been killed, and her uncle, the owner, offered Casemore £100 and a flat to live in if he would give the child a father. 'I was very tempted as I had a premonition that I was not going to survive much longer, I even wrote to my sister Joan, telling her what I might do.' But in the end he decided not to.

Such thwarted romance was made that much harder to bear by the sight of Teddy Woodward, Casemore's captain, walking arm in arm with 'this truly gorgeous blonde. We were really envious because she was really lovely.' It was difficult to dislike Woodward, though. 'He was a very nice man and extremely good as a commander.' Officers rarely socialised with the men, but 'when Ted got his DSO the non-duty watches and the officers went ashore

for a big booze-up in one of the bars near the bridge going to
Sliema from Lazaretto. One of the crew could do forty verses of
Eskimo Nell and another did *A fair Chinese maiden by the name of
Hu Flung Dung*. Ted said "I've been awarded the DSO on your
behalf". He didn't say that for the next one.'

Dick Cayley began each period of leave by taking *Utmost*'s
crew for a drinking session. As Ben Skeates recalled:

We (that is the whole crew), took over an entire bar in Sliema,
and settled down to a couple of days' celebration. The Captain
had the floor first; he would climb up onto a table and play a
short ditty on his harmonica. He would then address the company, I quote: 'Ladies and Gentlemen, I can't dance and I can't
sing but to show my appreciation of your company, here is my
dirty big arse.' He then did a short pirouette type jig on the
table; turned his back to the audience and dropped his pants,
and there it was. It never failed to get a rousing reception.

When submariners felt they had a good captain, they often
became devoted to him as the crews of *Unbeaten* and *Utmost* were
devoted to Woodward and Cayley. While any crewman could
make a fatal mistake, they all handed over the principal responsibility for their fate to the captain the moment they sailed in his
boat. In some ways this was comforting and one of the attractions
of submarines, as one submariner argued:

For those who don't fancy being wounded or maimed, it is the
surest way, provided one has confidence in the Captain. He
alone can size up the opposition through the periscope. For all
the others on board there is no difference between a real attack
and an exercise off Campbeltown . . . until after our torpedoes
hit. Once submerged there is no individual act of bravery or
cowardice expected of anyone except the man on the
periscope. The crew simply hope that the Captain will get
them out of any trouble he gets them in.

Teddy Woodward was a blond, athletic, good looking thirty-year-old in 1941, a champion middle distance swimmer. Off duty he lived to party. Hugh Mackenzie reckoned he was 'a mathematical genius' and Aston Piper was 'pleased to be serving under Woodward who was an extremely brilliant submarine officer [and] had the knack of imparting his submarine knowledge to the crew'. Woodward followed the eighteenth-century custom of handing over his boat to Piper, his first lieutenant, as soon as they reached harbour and disappearing in search of recreation. Simpson wrote:

> The pace he set himself during rest periods in Malta would have put most men in hospital. He would arrive at Lazaretto from the rigours of holiday in Malta's 'watering resorts', which never seemed closed to Woodward, looking pale and in need of a complete rest. He would climb to the conning tower and say, 'Let go everything. Slow ahead port,' and would escape from the dangers of a social sea lion amongst the mermaids of Malta's coastline into the refuge of a wartime submarine patrol.

By the time Piper had taken the boat to the patrol area Woodward was fresh as a daisy and ready for anything.

If Woodward charmed Simpson to the point that he would put up with this sort of behaviour, Dick Cayley was probably Simpson's favourite – 'My best C.O.' Married to Nancy Coutts since 1933, he was 'roly poly', slightly chubby, but a good-looking man with swept-back black hair and grey eyes. Born in India, he was the son of a colonel who had fought in the Boer War and the Great War. In harbour he always appeared light-hearted, even flippant. He carried the mouth organ that won him the nickname 'Harmonica Dick' in his uniform pocket and was 'a great asset to the mess'. Behind this mask he was 'a shrewd, tough, brave man who volunteered for special duties and undertook them with a balance of caution and determination'. At sea he slept at night in the conning tower, in a hammock slung under the chart table. During the day he read or, like George Colvin, did gros point needlework. He was 'entirely unselfish and for the flotilla'.

Cayley had fine junior officers. First lieutenant Charles Oxborrow was, in Jim Murdoch's words, 'one hell of a gent', a former Fleet Air Arm pilot. Murdoch remembered an occasion when 'he won a bet . . . that he could load a tin fish on his own – the stakes a glass of gin against a tot of rum. Oxborrow won.' Robert Boyd took over from him as 'Jimmy' (first lieutenant), having been navigator, and was with *Utmost* throughout her commission. He was an Ulsterman, thin, gauntish with sticking out ears and ice-blue eyes, 'a cool customer' according to one of the officers in *Untiring*, the boat in which Boyd scored a string of successes as captain after he left *Utmost* and passed his perisher.

Simpson's other favourite and personal protégé was David Wanklyn. After Wanklyn's first sinkings, Simpson put him at the centre of the patrol line for all the most important jobs. While this favouritism contributed to Wanklyn's mammoth total of tonnage sunk, Wanklyn rarely let Simpson down. The retiring and modest Wanklyn was widely liked, and people were pleased at his success. He remained friends with his Dartmouth contemporary, the black-bearded Tony Collett. Collett bought a horse and trap and together they drove around the countryside of Malta. Solid rather than brilliant – Simpson dismissed him as a plodder – Collett's agricultural knowhow came in useful when Simpson decided that it would be a good idea for the submariners to keep pigs. Simpson anticipated the danger of starvation given a likely Axis blockade and persuaded the canteen committee that this was a good opportunity to vary their diet, feeding the pigs on leftovers. The first pigs were slaughtered in June 1941.

The dominant characters in Alexandria were Tony Miers and Tubby Linton. Miers was extraordinary. He narrowly avoided losing his boat after a series of collisions and near misses during working up, his knowledge of engineering was poor, he was not a great shot with a torpedo, and he had a terribly short and violent temper. His first lieutenant occasionally had a black eye, he hit teenage midshipman Ronald Drake for assuming an aircraft was friendly and Tono Kidd the engineer was heard more than once saying 'Do not hit me, Sir'. On the other hand he was extremely dedicated (he also slept on the bridge), quite fearlessly zealous and fiercely loyal to those who could stand working with him (quite a few officers and men couldn't).

Miers obtained an astonishing number of medals for himself and his crew, although post-war analysis shows that *Torbay* did better under his successor Robert Clutterbuck. Leslie Howard remembered once that 'some of the lads went on shore leave and got in a fight with some general service chaps. When they came back, Commander Miers had them in to see him and gave them all punishments, cancelled leave, that sort of thing. Then when he'd finished he said to the lads: "Did we win?"' With the crew Miers retrospectively got the benefit of the doubt; as stoker Le Gros put it, 'Whatever he had wrong with him, he always got us home.'

Some officers were not so forgiving. Tony Troup, who was Linton's third hand, then first lieutenant, remembered being punched by Miers for no obvious reason on *Maidstone*: 'Perhaps it was because I was too young and he was the almighty Crap. He was a bloody shit and carried on being one.'

Tubby Linton shared Miers' strength of personality, but not his more obvious weaknesses. Linton was self-contained and a much more accurate shot. Usually taciturn and slightly unapproachable, Simpson sometimes found him blunt and abrasive and he could be intimidating. He had sunk some big ships in *Pandora* before building *Turbulent*, which arrived in March 1942 and immediately spread terror in the Aegean with her gun. Like Miers (and Bone, Roberts and various other officers), Linton was credited with more sinkings than post-war analysis justified, but he still sank the third highest tonnage of any commander (Hezlet placed him behind Wanklyn and Haggard). His young officers (Tony Troup's twenty-first birthday was 18 July 1942) were utterly devoted to him.

The strain on officers was tremendous. Antony Cleminson

joined *Turbulent* as navigator in 1942, having been drafted into submarines. He had a difficult time and couldn't cope with keeping trim and simultaneously using the periscope, with the duty watch looking on critically while ostensibly scrubbing round his feet. This made him 'claustrophobic', and in the end Linton told him, 'If you do suffer from this it is quite obvious you must come out of submarines.' So, after three patrols, he did.

Many captains fell ill. Ian McGeoch got a stomach ulcer and then pneumonia. Desmond Martin also contracted pneumonia. Alastair Mars and Michael St John suffered bouts of dysentery. Bill King was repeatedly ill. Dudley Norman had to go home from Malta, as did Tom Barlow. Then there were those who needed a break: Mars went home early with 'frayed nerves'. Simpson relieved quite a number of commanders, either because their nerve had gone, or because they were not performing well enough. Sometimes they told him they felt they couldn't continue, sometimes he made the call. Sometimes he wished he had made the call sooner. This was the flotilla captain's agonising job. 'Hearing my story of the patrol,' Hugh Mackenzie wrote, '"Ruckers" promptly told me that I had had enough, I was worn out.'

Good people did gradually become worn out. The more thoughtful tried to analyse their own reaction. McGeoch wrote, 'For the first time in five patrols I was conscious of being over-tired. I believe that my officers noticed it, although I do not recall any of them making a comment to that effect. No doubt all of us had had enough of being keyed up to concert pitch.' In retrospect he felt that 'my total capacity to master events was a finite quantity; and although some of it was restored during each spell in harbour between patrols there was an overall and cumulative loss – like a steel spring that when fully compressed and released fails, by an increasing amount over time, to return to its original shape.'

King was tortured by self-doubt in 1941: 'To sink one ship only out of the crowd we had seen preyed on my mind. So many chances lost, so much bad luck – or was there no such thing as

luck? Was it only me?' His confidence was so low that 'It crept
into my mind that the time might have come to go to the
Captain Submarines and ask for relief', but then, 'two older married members of my crew confessed their nerves were cracking,
and I heard myself pressing them to go on.' Like McGeoch, he
found strain cumulative. By late 1941, 'I was tired to the bone.
I knew that I hated killing. I hated sinking, burning and drowning, and after two years of almost incessant under-sea action I
thought I'd been depth-charged enough. I desperately wanted to
cease hunting ships. I also wanted to cease being hunted myself.'
Halfway through the war 'none of the old clichés about honour,
duty or country rang any sort of bell. I had not much emotion
left in me, but suddenly I discovered what I did care about – the
simple seamen who'd stood two years of war and were going on
to the bitter end, sweating, grease-covered . . . '

As they themselves became veterans like King, the simple
seamen took refuge in what one officer called 'the pride of the
submariners'. He defined it as 'a pent-up feeling, a consciousness
of being one of a tightly-knit band of men cut off from most of
the normal naval experience and living pent-up lives in incredibly cramped quarters, embarked on missions that are dangerous
in themselves before ever a glimpse is had of an enemy'. In
wartime the submariner was in constant danger. If anything went
wrong, there was only the escape hatch. 'With such inescapable
facts tucked away subconsciously, the submariner sets about for-
getting all about them: but they are there, hovering about below
the surface of the mind as the submariners' own craft moves
about below the surface of the seas. Among men who find themselves in such circumstances, it would be unnatural not to find a
special kind of bond being forged.'

15

NO MARGIN FOR MISTAKES

The worst thing about travelling from Scotland to Malta with eight 4000 lb bombs and 12,000 gallons of high-octane aviation fuel strapped to the top of the boat was that *Porpoise* was so slow to dive out of sight. Indeed, the heavily laden submarine was given so little chance of escaping aircraft that she was ordered to travel submerged by day. This made progress very slow, but relatively safe, until they were crossing the Bay of Biscay when the weather cut up rough.

Porpoise was never good at keeping at periscope depth with a following sea and she kept breaking surface. Suddenly the officer of the watch saw a plane diving on them and ordered Q tank flooded for a crash dive. Being only just above the surface, *Porpoise* slipped out of sight quickly enough, but with the extra weight the submarine then dived steeply. The officer was so relieved at escaping the plane that he forgot to order air into Q to halt the dive. Skipper Bertie Pizey rushed in to take control as the submarine plummeted. Joe Brighton was on the hydroplanes but couldn't stop her and watched in horror as she went off the shallow depth gauge. By blowing every tank Pizey halted her as she went off the deep water gauge. She was now below 350 feet when her safe depth was 250 feet, and the hull was making horrible creaking noises. They recovered control just in time. An ashen-faced Joe Blamey reported that the struts supporting the hull had bent and when they reached Malta they found the hull had contracted by half an inch all round, the first stage of fatal implosion.

Lesser mistakes had Bertie Pizey jumping on his hat. To put them on their mettle he teased his inexperienced officers mercilessly, to the point where the young Australian Ian McIntosh once lost his own temper and called Pizey a 'Pommie bastard' to his face. McIntosh thought he would be thrown out of the boat when he reported for punishment, but 'there was Bertie beaming all over his face and saying "Hello Pommie, come in ... " He always called me Pommie from then.'

Porpoise landed her cargo at Malta and quickly moved on to Alexandria. She didn't pause for long there. 'We soon learned we were on a quick return to Malta, carrying essential dried foods, ammunition, kerosene, 18" torpedoes for the aircraft, mail and anything that could be stuck inside a submarine. This was the first of many runs.'

At about the same time that *Porpoise* reached Malta in September 1941 there were other new arrivals. Bill King appeared at Malta in a new submarine, *Trusty*, and a Polish boat also arrived in September. *Sokol* was a British U class submarine given to the Polish crew of *Wilk* when their own boat was damaged beyond repair. On being deployed to the Mediterranean, the captain, Boris Karnicki, found himself in a dilemma because although his government was at war with Germany, it had not yet declared war on Italy. The two Catholic countries were traditional friends. Karnicki resolved the situation at Gibraltar by gathering his crew and announcing 'I, Boris Karnicki commanding O.R.P. *Sokol* declare war on you, Benito Mussolini!'

The officers rented a top-floor flat on the Sliema front with a grand piano in it. 'They were a wild and utterly charming bunch,' recalled Suzanne Layton. 'Boris was devastatingly sexy and attractive, and had a beautiful speaking voice with a delicious accent;

he was also a superb dancer.' He often took his 'little English rose' out to dinner but she resisted his persistent attempts to get her into bed; she 'had a shrewd suspicion that others succumbed'.

Late in September *Truant* returned from the USA, receiving the signal from Cunningham, 'Welcome back to the Mediterranean. We're expecting great things from you.' But the US refit had been unsatisfactory because all the parts were different, and Jack Pook was not happy with the engines, Adolf and Hermann. The engineer officer had just appointed Syd Hart acting stoker petty officer, which gave him the frightening responsibility of keeping the stokers in order in port and keeping watch on the diving panel when at sea. 'Instead of being snugged up in the warmth of the engine room, here I was clad in several sweaters and a heavy duffle coat in the chilly, damp control room, with the air rushing down the conning tower at gale force, as the hungry inlet valves on the engines sucked greedily at it.' Occasionally a sea would come pouring through the hatch, half flooding the compartment.

Hugh Haggard, *Truant*'s commander, had been thinking of asking to be relieved, but ABC's greeting changed his mind. Haggard was offered any patrol position he liked. He asked for the whole of the Adriatic. This came as a shock to the crew: 'the much-dreaded Adriatic, well-known to all submariners as the worst patrol area of them all'. They had passengers: the dapper little commando Tug Wilson and his equally slightly-built accomplice. Haggard found Wilson 'a splendid man, very brave and very competent and in many ways the most frightful nuisance because he always wanted to do something'.

Haggard told the crew that he didn't believe the Adriatic mine barrage existed, but he would take no chances. Approaching the Strait of Otranto by night he would dive at dawn to 150 feet and run submerged all day. In the event the asdic rating heard ships above them. They surfaced in the middle of the supposed minefield and torpedoed a fat German merchant ship. The escorting armed merchant cruiser tried to ram them, but Haggard ducked underneath and tried to torpedo it from the other side. The next day he missed an unescorted ship in ballast but shot it up and set it on fire. The *Padema* burned for seven hours before the charred hull was towed in.

Finally, Haggard surrendered to Wilson's badgering. He landed the pair of commandos, who were determined to blow up an electric train on the main line to Milan, ran the bow aground so as not to drift, and promised to give him until 0100. The submariners waited nervously as several steam trains passed, before Tug returned an hour and forty minutes late. An electric train went up in a great explosion nine minutes later.

Soon after, in fog in shallows off Venice, Haggard stalked a ship that turned out to be a lighthouse, and abruptly the engines broke down. 'We got back thanks to the engineering staff who were very experienced and quite magnificent,' Haggard recalled. They turned for home having received their recall signal, but Haggard continued to be aggressive to the point of rashness. In shallow water off Ortona roads he attacked a convoy of tankers. He fired four torpedoes and dived, whereupon *Truant*'s nose drove into a mud bank. The navigator had warned Haggard it might happen, so he didn't feel terribly clever. Repeated attempts to reverse out failed. A small destroyer chugged up and stopped over their stern, which was only sixteen feet under water. Haggard and Pook both worked out that the destroyer could not drop charges without blowing herself up, but she might fix a grapnel on them or she might call up planes with bombs. Watertight doors were sealed and the navigator took the confidential books to the engine room. This was the last move before surrender.

It was Hart's job to destroy the papers; lifting the plate to the bilges, where they would perish if necessary, he was startled to come face to face with a terrified rat. Normally he would have killed the trapped animal, but in these circumstances he couldn't help sympathising with its plight. As he climbed out, little Ernie Goldsack was giving a pantomime performance of himself and his giant skipper pulling a plough in captivity.

They waited, filling the time with further repairs to Adolf and Hermann, the two engines. It was Halloween and the evening promised its share of terrors. Incredibly, nothing happened. At nightfall they tried the motors again and this time the bows came unstuck. Haggard had forced the crew to practise going astern while dived with the after hydroplanes controlling depth and the forward ones the angle of dive (the reverse of their normal roles). Now, the drill they had often cursed as a waste of time was the means of their escape.

When *Truant* surfaced, the smell of oil everywhere revealed why the enemy had been reluctant to act. Haggard had sunk a tanker: any explosion would have set the whole roads alight. The ice-cold beer in the Fleet Club at Alex had never tasted so good.

Hugh 'Rufus' Mackenzie had been in the Mediterranean since July. At first he worked as assistant to Hairy Browne, who had passed Horton's retirement age of thirty-five and become Staff Officer (Operations) to the first flotilla. In *Medway*'s palatial operations room, the COs of submarines that were not on patrol gathered daily to exchange views and gossip. There Mackenzie was exposed to 'fleet operation orders and directives, intelligence reports of every description, individual submarines' patrol orders and their subsequent detailed patrol reports, a constant flow of signals'. He revelled in the opportunity to learn how things were done. Daily intelligence reports on the Italian convoy situation, based chiefly on information gleaned from Ultra, started to appear on 5 October 1941. Then came a signal from Simpson requiring a CO to take command of *Thrasher*. Browne told Mackenzie to take Simpson's signal to Sammie Raw, the senior submarine officer in the Mediterranean, and to make sure that the last bottle of champagne in the ship arrived while he was there. The bottle appeared and Raw appointed Mackenzie to *Thrasher*. Mackenzie kept the cork.

Mackenzie found that Simpson had sacked Joe Cowell, *Thrasher*'s captain. Cowell had only been in the Mediterranean since July, had fired and missed with twelve torpedoes in three attacks, and felt he hadn't been given a fair chance. But *Thrasher's* crew was restless and unhappy. On a first patrol off Benghazi the only target Mackenzie found was a large schooner. He had orders to be economical with torpedoes but he risked one and missed. The enemy crew must have seen the torpedo because they abandoned ship. Mackenzie closed in, and after nine rounds from the gun the schooner exploded. This first small victory cheered his disgruntled crew.

When he returned, he found Max Horton was in Malta, making a tour of Mediterranean bases. He reminded a parade of all the officers and men in harbour to keep their standards high: 'There is no margin for mistakes in submarines, you are either alive or dead.' Horton had long talks with many COs, trying to identify problems, and gave them a morale-boosting speech. 'Think of yourselves as Derby winners – top-notchers in your class,' he urged. It was a phrase they liked. A weary Bill King, nodding at the table, registered the words 'a million pounds' and jerked awake. But Horton was not offering them a million pounds, just saying they were worth it. Nevertheless, the visit was a tonic for tired men and the publicity Horton promised was welcome.

Mackenzie got a pleasant personal surprise. At the time of his perisher course he had scoured Fort Blockhouse for the motor car that he had left there before war broke out. His Bentley had last been seen dumped on the playing fields, but had disappeared. At the Lazaretto Sam MacGregor sought him out to tell him he had recognised it and parked it safely in a shed in the garden of an old lady on the outskirts of Fareham.

On 18 November the British launched Operation Crusader to relieve Tobruk and capture advanced airfields. Submarines were deployed to watch the Italian fleet. Dick Cayley received a signal telling him that Italian cruisers were expected to move and ordering him to intercept them in the Strait of Messina. A second signal told him they were coming and gave him their expected route. He remained on the surface during the night stopped, without charging the battery, with Ben Skeates and his boss Tom Cockburn listening on the asdic. It paid off. Around midnight Cockburn heard engine noise five miles distant. Closing in on the bearing, Cayley saw three destroyers escorting three cruisers in line astern. He fired a salvo of four torpedoes at the last cruiser and Skeates confirmed that they were running. The first hit *Trieste* amidships and there was a huge explosion. Cayley allowed Skeates a look through the periscope and he saw huge flames lighting up the sea. *Trieste* reached Messina with difficulty and was out of commission for six months.

The three destroyers put in a sustained counter-attack, during which Cockburn on the asdic tried to guide Cayley's attempts to avoid the depth charges. After a while Skeates relieved his exhausted boss. They suffered some damage, 'a number of bulk-head fittings, such as large electrical distribution and fuse boxes, "HP" and "LP" (high and low pressure) airlines, and overhead light-fittings that were welded to the bulkhead broke loose and blew a few fuses', but Cayley slunk off through the gaps between escorts. As the hours went by the air grew fouler. Skeates 'sat beside the electrical artificer. He was wheezing like an old bellows, and when I mentioned it, he replied that I was no better.' Eventually they surfaced. 'The diesels roared out, until the vacuum produced by the engine air intakes was almost high enough to burst our eardrums. Then he called up to the seaman, waiting on the ladder up to the conning tower, to open the hatch. In rushed a vast quantity of fresh air and salt water, it really stunk, like nothing I have ever smelt before or since.'

The Italians continued to try to push through supplies. Angelo Coliolo was on his thirty-third escort mission in the armed merchant cruiser *Attilio Deffenu*, accompanying two merchant ships from Patras to Brindisi. He was almost home when a torpedo hit his own ship and she began to list to starboard, down at the bows. Coliolo scattered the convoy, sent out an SOS, and ordered his crew to the boats, a task they carried out in an orderly manner. Satisfied that he had sunk the leading ship,

Mackenzie was peering through his periscope, trying to make the others out in the pouring rain. The second ship changed direction, spoiling his shot. Then she seemed to stop, so he fired a torpedo, but she began to move again. Another look round revealed a cloud of smoke approaching fast from the direction of Brindisi, so he dived and made off. Captain Palmas of *Strale* had left his own convoy to hunt the attacker. As Mackenzie made off, reloading torpedoes, he heard intermittent depth charging for an hour and a half, but nothing close.

November was disastrous for Axis logistics. They had tried to send 79,208 tons of supplies and fuel to Libya, but only 29,843 tons had arrived. Thirteen cargo ships and three destroyers were sunk, and two cruisers badly damaged. The greatest carnage was caused by the surface ships of 'Force K'. This group of cruisers, based at Malta, had the speed to intercept any enemy force that Ultra and air reconnaissance identified and generally beat the submarines to it.

In September 1941 Bletchley Park had for the first time decrypted signals in the German army Enigma. These revealed that Rommel was rationing water, food and fuel. In October he was also short of 88mm ammunition for his best tank and anti-tank guns. In October C38m, the cracked code used for Italian convoys, told them that the Italians were transporting troops by air and in destroyers and sending fuel to Bardia and Derna in submarines, travelling submerged. The loss of the liners, combined with Rommel's demand for a shorter land supply line, meant that smaller convoys of fast military ships brought supplies to Benghazi and Derna rather than Tripoli. When the war began the Italians had 548 ships of over 500 tons, to which they could add 56 German ships that had been in their ports, totalling just under a million tons. By the end of 1941, 201 ships of 779,409 tons had been sunk. A large number more were confined to port under repair, and new ships were not being built anything like fast enough to replace losses.

However, the balance of power in intelligence had changed

again. In September Italian agents broke into the American embassy in Rome, stole a code book, copied it and returned it. The Italians were now reading all messages in the American diplomatic code and the German B-Dienst was reading it too. They also gained insights into the British naval ciphers, but the American diplomatic code was the big coup. Unfortunately, it was being used by Colonel Bonner F. Fellers, the intelligent and energetic American military observer in Cairo, to report to his superiors exactly what was going on in the Mediterranean theatre. He had almost unlimited access to British information, but fortunately he was not a party to Ultra. Thus he only betrayed the cover story when he revealed repeatedly to the listening Italians and Germans that 'Malta air forces report two merchantmen ... '

Nevertheless, his reports allowed the Axis to take evasive action. Convoys began to do the unexpected, changing their route or timing and frustrating submarines in ambush.

The military balance of power also changed with Hitler's reaction to the pessimistic forecasts of his Mediterranean staff. He ordered six U-boats to the Mediterranean in October and ten more in November, although 'Jantje' van Dulm in *O21* sank one of them. The arrival of the U-boats paid immediate dividends. On 14 November they sank the Gibraltar-based aircraft carrier *Ark Royal* and on 25 November the battleship *Barham*. That month German technicians arrived to fit the *S-Gerät* (German sonar) to Italian anti-submarine vessels. In early December Fliegerkorps II began to deploy in Sicily. They caused fifty deaths in Malta in December and eighty in January. In February they dropped nearly 1000 tons of bombs and killed 200 people.

Suddenly, there was a new threat – and a new ally. On 7 December the Japanese attacked the US fleet at Pearl Harbor. The following day Roosevelt announced that the USA was at war with Japan. On 10 December Japanese air attacks sank the battleships *Prince of Wales* and *Repulse* off Malaya, north of Singapore. On 11 December Germany and Italy declared war on the USA.

With no prospect of supplies, Rommel decided to lift the siege of Tobruk and pull back. Off Taranto, Johnny Wraith's *Upright* sank two ships approaching the port and was severely counter-attacked. The Italians decided to move the battleships *Littorio* and *Vittorio Veneto* to Taranto from Naples. Tomkinson in *Urge* and Collett in *Unique* were guarding the Strait of Messina and Tommo hit *Vittorio Veneto*, putting her out of action for three months.

On 16 December the Italians left Taranto in force to get a convoy to Africa. Jack Casemore was on deck as *Unbeaten* charged her battery when Jock Birnie heard very faint HE. As the Italian battle fleet neared the noise became terrifying. *Unbeaten* dived under some E-boats – German motor torpedo boats, rather larger than the Italian MAS, with a crew of up to thirty – and after she had surfaced again they heard and saw the bow waves of destroyers. 'All four torpedoes were ready to fire as this large battle fleet came into our line of fire, when suddenly they altered course and I can still see their massive bow waves coming straight for us.' Woodward crash dived to ninety feet and Casemore 'heard the roar as they went straight over us; everyone was so disappointed but also relieved'.

Cayley in *Utmost* saw the fleet in the distance and fired a despairing long shot, but the Italians got through. A radio warning from *Utmost* put surface forces protecting a Malta convoy on their guard and next day the warships met in the First Battle of Sirte. Both sides succeeded in protecting their convoys, but Force K raced from Malta to cut off the Italian supply ships. It ran into a minefield. Two cruisers sank and two were damaged. Next day, 19 December, came a further disaster. The battleships *Queen Elizabeth* and *Valiant* were both sunk in harbour at Alexandria in a brilliant and daring attack by Italian frogmen with miniature submarines. For Cunningham this was the lowest ebb.

Nearly all the Malta boats were in port for Christmas Day, the day Hong Kong surrendered to the Japanese. Jack Casemore got into a fight over Christmas dinner and had two bottom teeth knocked out. Tomkinson wrote home:

The little boat is working very well and all the sailors are in great heart. We gave them all a bottle of beer on Christmas Day and had a few minutes talking with them. They are so good and have to work very hard ... I spend a lot of the day in a deep rock shelter, which I reckon to be the safest place to be found.

I'd give a lot to be able to go home to see Myrtle and Bridget ...

Late on Christmas evening Simpson wandered into the ward room and found the duty officer alone. He bought him a drink then told him to go ashore and enjoy himself. He would take over. Everyone was tired, and torpedoes were running short again. Submarines refitting at Malta were now allowed to take away only two torpedoes each, and those were old and unreliable.

Utmost was going home. The remaining few days were to be spent clearing up, paying bills, servicing the equipment for the run back to England. Ben Skeates retired to his flat in Sliema to sort out his gear and get ready to go. He turned in for the night, but at about 11.30 the sirens woke him. He lay listening to the screamers on the bombers as they dived. The all clear sounded and he dozed off again. He didn't hear the second raid start, but he remembered dreaming that the bedroom wall was splitting wide open.

When he regained consciousness he was pinned down on his back with his arms spreadeagled and an immense weight on his chest. He lost consciousness again. He drifted in and out, hearing the screamers, and 'each time the vibration sent a stream of fine sandstone dust into my mouth, nostrils and eyes'. Then he woke up in a clean white bed in the Blue Sisters Hospital in Sliema. 'A nurse was busy with scissors, trying to cut away the hair from my head. There were some deep gashes in the scalp, and she thought my skull had been fractured in several places.' Rescuers had spent twenty-seven hours digging him out of the rubble caused by a 500 lb bomb that had gone straight through his bedroom and exploded on the ground. His skull was fractured where it had hit a sharp stone and his right leg was broken, but an unbroken sandstone block had fallen over his chest, protecting him from further rubble and allowing him to breathe.

His head was throbbing but the nurse cutting his hair hurt more. Hair, blood and sand were all dried into a mat so hard that it made the operation very painful. The nurse was sympathetic, and told him they would stitch his head when she had cleaned it up. There was no anaesthetic available, so he downed a tumbler of coarse South African Cape brandy to dull the pain. Cayley and most of the crew visited him in hospital, and when *Utmost* was due to sail for Gibraltar Cayley sent a stretcher party and put Skeates in a hammock on board, for the trip west. But despite the coxswain's best efforts, the wounds in Skeates's scalp turned septic and they had to leave him in a hospital ship in Gibraltar when they went.

As the old submarines began to leave, new ones replaced them. Five of them arrived in January. Jim Thomsett found himself a torpedoman in the fore ends of *P36* under Noel Edmonds, who landed two Special Operations Executive (SOE) agents near Monte Carlo before going on to Malta. There they found *P38*, and *Una* under Desmond Martin, who was much disconcertingly inexperienced. Since coming back from China he had carried out a few war patrols as first lieutenant from Harwich, where Simpson had got to know him (and thought him 'sound'), but most of his time had been spent training or in a boat that was being built or doing trials. He must have been nervous. The last two boats were *P39* and Lynch Maydon's *P35*, later known as *Umbra*. Maydon, tall, dark and dedicated, had been first lieutenant of *Porpoise* under Simpson and the truculent Fred Buckingham was his petty officer telegraphist.

Early in the New Year Teddy Woodward sank a U-boat. Aston Piper was on watch at the periscope of *Unbeaten* in rough weather south of the Strait of Messina at 1013 on 12 January when Peter Birnie in the asdic office heard HE. Piper swept on to the bearing; when, two minutes later, he saw something on the horizon, he called Woodward, who was resting. The commander leapt out of his bunk, put up the periscope and identified a German U-boat. Woodward closed very fast and fired four torpedoes, hitting it with two, ten minutes after the boat was first heard. Piper was full of admiration for his speed and precision. After going deep in case one of the torpedoes circled – they expected one gyro failure in four – Woodward looked in vain for proof of his success. He said, 'First Lieutenant, see if you can see something . . . I can't see a thing.'

Just as Piper put his eye to the eyepiece he saw a hand coming out of the water and said 'There's a German up there just behind us.' Woodward surfaced and Casemore pulled the German through the hatch, whereupon he spewed up copious quantities of pasta. 'One or two of the sailors rather spoilt him by giving him tots of rum at night,' Piper said. He made the German, whose name was Hans Ploch, clean out the boat.

Early in January 1942 *Trusty* and *Truant* were given orders to sail for the Far East, both carrying extra men as advance elements of a new submarine base. Syd Hart was not going with them, having almost completed his stint of time abroad. He saw off his chums in pouring rain, feeling like he had lost a leg and waving sadly as *Truant* disappeared into the murk.

After three weeks with *Medway*'s spare crew Hart was drafted to *Thrasher*. She sailed on Friday the 13th, to the horror of her crew, but three days later superstition had brought no ill effect. Loud snores were all that troubled the damp, muggy, darkened stokers' mess until the tannoy came up with a sharp 'Diving stations!' Men tumbled out of bunks until only Syd Hart and the forty-year-old salt Dan Conroy were left, since this was their diving station with the after hydroplane and steering gear. The depth gauge showed thirty-two feet and the movement of the gear suggested an attack. A rush of air pressure announced the departure of three torpedoes and almost simultaneously came a screaming whine overhead, followed by terrific explosions.

Tannoy orders for going deep. As they watched the depth gauge settle, Hart told Conroy those were bombs and since the plane would have marked them they could expect depth charges.

They heard the charges swishing down, then the explosions as 'inside, strained and anxious, we glanced upwards, expecting to see the whole fabric split wide open.' Then silence, the motors stopped, the men tense as the enemy listened for them, until 'as the escorts came in again, the beat of their propellers plainly audible, the telegraphs rang to "Half ahead" as we tried to creep away from the danger-zone.' Another pattern of depth charges and another nerve-racking silence. The roar of the enemy and *Thrasher*'s stealthy response. 'Strained faces and bulging eyes.' Explosions, a shower of cork and the tinkling glass of smashed lights. '*Thrasher* plunged up as if a volcano had erupted under her, she bucked savagely and plunged down again ... trembling like a whipped dog.' But after that attack the escorts appeared to lose contact and the noise of them receded.

Well after dark *Thrasher* surfaced with her habitual alarming list to port. She charged her engines and set off toward Taranto. As Hugh Mackenzie tried to sleep he heard something rolling around above him. He told the officer of the watch to send someone to investigate. There was a 100 lb bomb on the casing, while another had made a hole and was rolling around between the casing and the pressure hull.

The way to get rid of the bombs was to drop them over the bows with the submarine going full astern, but to reach the second bomb someone had to crawl under the casing and push it through its hole, before carrying it to the bows. First lieutenant Peter Roberts and second coxswain Thomas Gould volunteered, being theoretically responsible for the casing.

Thrasher lay stopped, lookouts with eyes peeled. If they had to dive while Roberts and Gould were under the casing they were dead. Two hours passed slowly. The second bomb was hard to shift and emitted an unpleasant twanging noise when it was moved. There was an eerie, tense silence inside the ship. They heard with relief the order, 'Full astern!' and the bombs were gone. Mackenzie gave a brief commendation of the two in his patrol report and was then woken by Sammie Raw, with an order from ABC to write the incident up more fully with a recommendation for awards. Roberts and Gould were awarded the VC in June.

Charles Anscomb could never like his new boat, the slim, streamlined *Tempest*. 'Her steering was light and accurate, and ... her hydroplanes ... were a dream of precision and dependability after *Parthian's* temperamental old flippers. She was a faster diver than *Parthian*, and far more easily controlled. But my old love died hard.' *Tempest* was merely a lethal weapon. The crew comfort and space for stores of 'dear old spacious *Parthian*' gave way to better machinery and 'a smoother, deadlier performance. *Tempest* was a tiger shark of a thing, a killer.' Approaching Malta, steering on the bridge, Anscomb 'could see the war as a red glow ahead on the horizon'. The bombing was so intense that they lay off, watching, 'waiting for the blitz to subside. As we stared at the awful, burning horizon we realised that we should be there ourselves the next time the bombers came.'

Next day they saw what was left of the Valletta the old regulars had loved.

The houses and high-piled palaces around Grand Harbour were in many places piles of rubble now, and a film of honey-coloured dust lay upon the sparkling blue of the harbour. The docks were smashed and sunken ships blocked the creeks and the main harbour, waterlogged merchantmen sitting on the bottom, destroyers with their whole bows amputated or sunk in mid-stream with their empty crows' nests watching a forlorn graveyard of fine vessels. It looked as if Malta was crumbling into the sea.

It was a brief visit. The Malta submarines were sent out to guard a convoy that was trying to reach the island from the west without any air support and with only cruisers and destroyers as escorts. *P36*, *Urge* and *Unique* patrolled the Strait of Messina and *Una*, *Tempest* and *Upright* covered Taranto to sink or at least report Italian heavy ships.

In *Tempest* a raw rating had left his oilskin to dry over an electric fire. The ship rolled, the oilskin fell, and before the fire was discovered and controlled it burned out the asdic motor. The chief electrician worked on it for three days but could do nothing. Now, if *Tempest* was hunted, its crew would no longer know where the enemy was. On 12 February Lieutenant Commander Bill Cavaye was called to the periscope and saw a big tanker, but he identified the target as an 'untouchable', a ship that must not be attacked.

A couple of hours later *Una's* watchkeeper spotted the same ship. Desmond Martin was in his bunk with a high fever that turned into pneumonia. He dragged himself to the periscope, fired three torpedoes from 2600 yards and sank the *Lucania*. It was a good shot at a valuable target but unfortunately he too had been told not to attack this particular ship.

In *Tempest* Anscomb heard a huge explosion. They closed up at action stations again and went to have a look. Through the periscope Cavaye saw his 'untouchable' settling down in the water. The *Lucania* had been given safe conduct from the British government for its humanitarian mission to fuel a ship evacuating refugees from Africa. 'That piece of clumsiness brought the anti-submarine boats out. We went down deep again and listened to them thrashing angrily about over our heads.'

Among those who responded to the SOS from the *Lucania* was Captain Palmas, commanding the torpedo boat *Circe*, freshly fitted with German S-Gerät sonar and German depth charges. *Circe* was a proven hunter, having already sunk *Grampus* and *Union*. Palmas had orders to hunt out the submarine that had sunk the *Lucania* and his crew was not in a mood to be merciful. At first he could find nothing but he lurked around, expecting his quarry to surface in the dark.

Anscomb 'had the first watch on duty as bridge lookout. The sea was moderate now, and it was pleasant after being dived all day to smell the clean air and look at the cool blackness of the night.' He turned in after a blank watch. It was 0300 when he was woken by the klaxon. Cavaye had seen a destroyer and thought he could get an attack in, but as he manoeuvred he saw her bow wave turn to 'a furious boiling of white foam' indicating ramming speed, so *Tempest* dived. 'We went down steeply and heard the thumping of his engines. He was on us. My stomach went cold. Then I almost gasped with sudden intense relief as I heard the noise dying away again. He had missed us on the first pass.'

Anscomb got the sick feeling and the thumping heart he always had. Most of the crew didn't know what was coming. 'Being depth-charged is something which cannot be imagined. It is a terror which has to be experienced.' He heard the destroyer approach again, watching the depth gauge at the after hydroplanes, whirling the wheel as Cavaye ordered 150 feet, imagining the depth charges sinking with them.

I had my eyes on the pointer. It was passing fifty feet. We'd never do it ... The dial shook and the pointer danced before my eyes. There was a tremendous, gathering surge of clanging thunder ... seat, wheel, hands, brain, dials, deck, bulkhead, deckhead, everything *shook* like an earthquake shock as if every atom in the ship's company were splitting. Then it was dark, nearly all the lights gave out. Instruments were shattered, wheels locked, glass tinkled over the deck. We were still going down. I watched the pointer ... 150 ... 155 ... 160 ... 165 ... *We were out of control.*'

Anscomb and second coxswain Burns fought the boat and checked her at 350 feet, bringing her back to 150. 'Swiftly the damage reports came in. Nearly all the instruments and lights throughout the boat had been put out of action. The fore-hydroplanes and hydrophones were damaged beyond repair.

Worst of all, one of the propeller shafts had shifted in its housing. That accounted for the loud continuous knocking sound we could hear.'

They stayed stopped at 150 feet. Anscomb got that strange feeling he always experienced at times of extreme stress, a sense of utter detachment from what was taking place around him. They waited. Above them they heard the destroyer when it passed overhead, but there were no more charges. The cook made some tea and cocoa and passed it round with biscuits. Hours passed. At 0700 they thought the enemy might have gone away; then they heard engines very close overhead and a pattern went off right alongside. 'Dazed and shaken and scared we hung on and hoped against hope.' The master gyroscope was smashed and they were relying on 'faithful Freddie', the magnetic compass. Chief stoker George Spowart came charging into the control room to stop a spout of oil fuel that was flooding in. Electrical artificer John Winrow laboured with the gyro but he couldn't make it work. Anscomb was holding depth with the after planes.

They could hear the destroyer's sonar pinging them. For a time they kept *Tempest* under control.

Then the ring main shorted onto the pressure hull, blowing the main fuses. This put the ballast pumps out of action. This meant that the compensating tanks and auxiliary tanks had to be trimmed by using our compressed-air supply, when air was priceless to us. The boat was forced down willy-nilly to five hundred feet completely out of control. I was helpless on the planes. There wasn't a thing I could do to stop her.

To arrest the dive they had blown the main ballast tanks with precious compressed air. Then, to stop the boat shooting to the surface, they had to flood the tanks again, making noise and sending up huge air bubbles. Deadly 'eggs' 'burst all round us as we sat and shook in the semi-darkness, with only the secondary lighting flickering palely like candles guttering in a dank tomb and the ship lurching and wallowing between a hundred and five hundred feet and things breaking loose and crashing about us'.

The strain was telling on both machinery and people. 'Bulkhead fixtures and spare parts were torn from their housings, and hurled across the narrow spaces.' The boat was continually either bow up or bow down, and the angle was so acute at times that the bubble in the fore-and-aft spirit level would disappear completely. 'In the engine room heavy spares like the big breech ends from the diesels, each weighing half a ton, were sliding dangerously up and down the steel deck at each plunge and lurch.' They were carrying spares for the submarines at Alexandria as well as sacks of mail for the fleet. These all broke loose and smashed about.

The emergency lights dimmed to a faint glow. With the main electric cable earthed against the hull, Anscomb was dreading fire and electrocution. Then, after three hours, it stopped. They looked about them. 'John Winrow, creeping through the submarine on the track of some electrical repair, accidentally kicked a bucket which clattered with a deafening noise along the deck. "I'll have that man shot!" shouted the Captain.'

Up above, Palmas had decided that the air bubbles meant that the submarine was badly damaged, but he had very few patterns of depth charges left. He was signalling to Taranto for reinforcements. Then he ran in again.

Salt water had seeped into broken containers of sulphuric acid in the battery compartment and the boat began to fill with chlorine gas. Being trapped in a boat full of poison gas was, Anscomb said, 'the ultimate horror of all submariners'. There was no escape now. 'The boat was just a pitch-dark, gas-filled shambles, flooding at the after-end.' Cavaye decided to try to surface. He told the crew to put on their Davis escape gear, gave the order to abandon ship and told Anscomb to take her up. 'The after-planes were still working. I turned the wheel and gave the boat tip-helm. Slowly she responded and started on her way up.' The senior officers were to clear the compartments and muster the men in the control room to escape. Torpedo Gunner's Mate Campbell was to light the fuse of the demolition charge before leaving.

As soon as *Tempest* broke surface Cavaye opened the hatch with the signalman hanging on to his legs. The men began to leave the ship and *Circe*, half a mile away and closing, opened fire with machine guns. The first men to leave were hit and several killed outright. More were killed in the water. Anscomb stayed in the control room until the boat was clear, then Chief Engineer Blatchford told him to go. He followed the TGM up the ladder.

When I got up on the bridge I saw that the submarine was well down by now. Visibility was good, but the sea had got up since I had last seen it the previous night. It was February and the sea looked cold, but I took one look at the gun flashes from the destroyer, climbed out of the bridge over the blind side, and slid into the water. It was cold all right. Using my escape set as a life-jacket I swam away from the boat and tried to herd those of the survivors that I could see together.

The sea was running too high to see more than the top masts of the destroyer. Then they disappeared. Anscomb thought it was the end. He was utterly cold and chilled. 'I had my old feeling that the whole thing was completely unreal, that it did not involve me at all, that I was dreaming it.'

After two hours in the water he was hauled semi-conscious over the propeller guard into the destroyer. Twenty-three survivors out of a crew of sixty-two had been picked up. The rest were shot or drowned.

Two days later Noel Edmonds of *P36* sighted two cruisers and four destroyers heading south through the night. He fired a full salvo but they were four miles away and he missed. He reported them and a Fleet Air Arm attack also missed them. Jim Thomsett in the fore ends helped reload the tubes. Next day Edmonds saw

the same ships again, came closer, missed the fast-moving cruisers but damaged a destroyer. Most of the seven other destroyers
closed in to hunt and dropped 216 depth charges while
Carabinieri was towed into harbour. Fortunately for Thomsett and
his mates, none had *Circe*'s S-Gerät. The noise was terrifying but
the damage was limited to cork and light bulbs. Of course,
nobody knew that the ships would not find them, and the crew
remained under water and under stress for twenty hours.

Captain Palmas was on the hunt again. Four new arrivals at
Malta, *P38*, *P34*, *Una* and *P39* had been sent to form a patrol
line across Tripoli to intercept two fast and heavily escorted convoys whose arrival was predicted by Ultra. At 1014 on 23
February his sonar operator reported an echo 1800 yards away.
Palmas signalled convoy K7 to turn 90° to port while he turned
to starboard and increased speed along the bearing. His lookouts
spotted the periscope 1000 yards away and they raced towards it
at twenty knots, slowing to fifteen as Palmas aimed at the air bubbles left by the diving submarine. He dropped all the charges he
had ready at once, six from the rails and four from his German
throwers, set to explode at seventy metres.

In a flurry of bubbles from compressed air, *P38* came to the
surface to be met by randomly thrown depth charges and a hail
of machine-gun fire from aeroplanes and escorts that killed one
of *Circe*'s ratings. *P38* disappeared again. Palmas called off the
other escorts and waited, finding the echo of the submerged submarine. Suddenly it shot to the surface like a dolphin and then,
with its screws in the air, plunged down again. Palmas waited,
with the echo once again showing on his S-Gerät. His device
could not measure the depth of the submarine but the seabed at
this point was 350 metres, at least twice the depth at which the
submarine would implode.

Palmas did not have to wait long. A mass of bubbles and oil
rose to the surface and among them the excited Italians spotted
evidence of their kill: a polished cupboard door, a table top, a bag
of flags, a human lung.

16

COUNT THE DAYS

The Germans had learned that the Lazaretto was a submarine base, and on 13 February 1942 they went for it. In the morning a few Stukas dropped bombs near enough to make the building shake. Usually, raids on Malta came at ten in the morning and three in the afternoon, so Jack Casemore decided to make his way ashore before the afternoon visit. His oppo, Dickie Dowdell, had been going too, but changed his mind at the last moment, so Casemore set out on his own.

There was some waste ground between the base and the little bridge on the Sliema front. The air raid sirens had already gone but I thought I could get ashore before they arrived. Well I was halfway across this waste ground when the bombs started to fall. I believe they were dive bombers and they were targeting our base and submarines and as they were pulling out of their dive, they were machine gunning; first the bullets were in front of me and then they were just behind me. I was so petrified, I was running backwards and forwards and eventually hid under a huge oil tank.

When he crawled out he found the base wrecked. Buckingham had been inside, in the toilet. 'While standing there doing what comes naturally, and blissfully thinking of another couple of hours head down, there was a God-almighty explosion. Cutting it off short, I returned to the mess and found it still intact, but through the archway the next mess was an absolute shambles. Four people had been killed, one being from our boat, and several injured.' Two parachute mines had hit the west end and brought down the ceilings of the mess decks.

Four anti-aircraft guns were set up around the building. On 17 February bombs hit the officers' quarters. The captain and three officers of the Greek *Glaucos* were killed. The officers moved what could be salvaged from their possessions into the empty underground oil tank and there also Simpson established his office.

In March over 2000 tons of bombs were dropped on Malta, but in April the attacks were most intense. A total of 6700 tons of bombs were dropped – every day for more than a month, the island was subjected to a raid the size of the famous attack that destroyed Coventry. At the end of March the Admiralty sent Cunningham to America.

The submarine base was a priority target. Half the crew of *Umbra* were in the Dun Cow one day when 'wave after wave of JU88s came over and dropped their loads in the creeks. They did no damage, and did us a favour if we had chosen to take advantage of it. José, the landlord, dived for the shelter at the first bleep of the siren, leaving us to help ourselves. Believe it or not and strange as it may seem, we paid for what we took.' On 6 March Jim Thomsett's *P36* needed patches after a near miss and bombs sank the fuelling lighter forty feet from *P39*. Half her battery cells smashed and she had to be towed to the dockyard. Gordon Selby had just left *Upholder* with a promotion to coxswain in *P39*. The only injuries he had to deal with came from broken glass. The old lighter *Talbot*, nominally Simpson's flagship, was sunk.

Simpson ordered his submarines to remain submerged in the

harbour by day. On 8 March *Umbra* was holed by the clump block of a buoy as she dived to the bottom of the harbour, flooding the torpedo space. Buckingham and the other nine men of the duty watch got her up with difficulty. A bomb hit the farmyard, killing a sow, her litter, many rabbits and the turkey. Formal rules were abandoned: 'we were going ashore in seaboots and our working clothes almost. We were expecting to be invaded anytime and were told, when ashore, if we heard there had been a landing, to get back to the boat as fast as possible because our orders, if this happened, were to get to sea as quickly as we could.'

On 17 March the Polish *Sokol* returned from patrol. While she was moored by the Lazaretto to unload, five bombs fell within thirty yards, causing cracked batteries and damage to her air and water lines and telemotor system. She had to go into dock. Next day the crew unloaded the torpedoes under air attack. Between Lazaretto and Grand Harbour a pair of fighters attacked the boat. The dockyard workers refused to work during raids, but Boris Karnicki ordered his crew to continue removing the batteries as the bombs fell. He wanted *Sokol* out of Grand Harbour fast because a convoy was expected and this was likely to attract intense air attacks.

Two ships reached Grand Harbour but the dockers unloaded very little of their cargo. The heaviest attacks came on 26 March. One of the merchant ships, still loaded with ammunition, torpedoes and bombs, was set ablaze, so the dockers took cover. In Dockyard Creek a bomb exploded underneath *P39* and broke her back. The crew were in the shelters. Another 1000 lb bomb landed close to *Sokol* but failed to explode.

By 31 March *Sokol* was in French Creek with the Greek *Glaucos* and the cruiser *Penelope* for degaussing, repaired and ready for patrol, when she was seriously damaged again. The boat filled with chlorine. The engineers generated power from the main engines, got the fans working and pumped out the acid and salt water. Seven volunteers worked all night in gas masks disconnecting the damaged cells. *Pandora* arrived that night and unloaded the petrol she had brought. Next day, some of the crew took her round to Hamilton Wharf in Grand Harbour while others went by boat to prepare to unload her cargo of stores and torpedoes quickly so as to get away that night.

There were raids all day, but the earlier ones were merely a reconnaissance for the afternoon attack on all visible submarines. In early afternoon *Pandora* took two direct hits, one bomb going down the engine room hatch so that a flame like a blowtorch came out of the hatches. She sank in four minutes. Most of the crew had gone below and twenty-seven were killed, including Drury's friend Arthur Vernon who had been TI (Torpedo Instructor) in *Sturgeon*. The stoker petty officer had just decided to man the anti-aircraft gun and woke up in hospital twelve hours later.

P36 was alongside the Lazaretto when a bomb fell between the building and her trot. The lights went out and the few officers and ratings on board were driven out by chlorine. Thomsett was up in the Lazaretto mess and he with the rest of the crew came out to try to keep the sub afloat. They passed a wire round the conning tower and attached it to an arch, but the wire snapped and *P36* rolled over and sank. At the same time two bombs narrowly missed *Unbeaten*, lying submerged in Sliema Creek with a skeleton crew of six commanded by the new first lieutenant, Godfrey Place (Piper having returned in March to take the perisher course). Casemore was asleep in the fore ends when 'suddenly, red, white, yellow, blue and green lights flashed through the boat, the next I remember is finding myself in the corner of the after port bulkhead, with my two boatmates. We could hear water pouring into the tubespace but the bulkhead doors were closed and we had water leaking from the forehatch. All the lights had gone out, so we were in complete darkness.' At first they went into escape routine, then Casemore shouted through the voice pipe to see if there was anyone further aft. Place answered and let them into the control room. They reported the problem. Eventually Simpson arrived in a rowing boat and told them to surface. After several attempts to expel enough water with pressurised air they succeeded.

On 3 April commandos volunteered to help the crews remove cracked battery cells from submarines. The next day the Greek *Glaucos* was sunk. Simpson ordered his submarines to lie on the bottom in deep water outside the harbour. This policy was problematic, both because of mines and because it did not allow the submarines to react to the expected sudden attack on Malta by surface forces. Miraculously, *Umbra* was repaired and back on patrol and even *Sokol* was made fit to reach Gibraltar, having been hidden in Marsa Creek by army camouflage experts.

Throughout this time the submarines continued to attack shipping. On 1 April itself Tomkinson in *Urge* sank the cruiser *Bande Nere*. *Upholder* sailed on 6 April with Tug Wilson to land two Arab spies near Carthage. Five days later *Upholder* met *Unbeaten* so that Teddy Woodward could take Wilson to Gibraltar. Wilson paddled from one boat to the other and was greeted by Godfrey Place with the cheerful advice, 'Piss off, Tug – we've got two feet of water in the fore-ends and the batteries are gassing. You'll never make it to Gib.'

Wilson carried away a letter from David Wanklyn to his wife Betty: 'count the days, they are not so many. Only 59.' He had been telling her it would not be long before he got home since at least the previous November.

In December the *London Gazette* published the announcement that Wanklyn had been awarded the Victoria Cross for sinking the *Conte Rosso*. Betty Wanklyn had been congratulated by Max Horton and the press had taken photos of her son, Ian, clutching the medal. *Upholder* was then out on a frustratingly blank patrol from which Wanklyn returned exhausted on 23 December. While he was asleep Simpson had someone remove Wanklyn's shirt from his cabin, sew on the VC ribbon, and put it back. It wasn't until lunchtime that he looked in the mirror, saw the ribbon and stormed into the mess to ask whose idea of a practical joke it was. Simpson showed him the *Gazette*.

Now it was Wanklyn and *Upholder*'s last patrol and the boat would be home in less than two months. Simpson signalled *Upholder* with orders to ambush a convoy to Tripoli along with *Urge* and *Thrasher*.

But on 14 April 1942 air escorts spotted a submarine stalking a convoy near Tripoli. The four planes, two Me 110s and two Dornier 17s, swooped in to attack the submerged boat and very quickly saw a dark patch rise to the surface, which they took to be leaking oil indicating a sinking. They dropped smoke floats to mark the position, but no further sonar echoes were heard. This is thought to be the way that *Upholder*, Wanklyn and his thirty-one shipmates were lost. For Betty, the counting stopped at fifty-six days.

Simpson wanted to keep his submarines at Malta, both in order to oppose enemy ships that might bombard or invade the island and because leaving would be so bad for morale. But he was wavering. With minelaying E-boats based at Licata as a new threat, he was promised improving fighter defence. When the forty-eight Spitfires flown in during April were shot to pieces before they could do anything, Simpson's patience snapped and he ordered the submarines to leave. His fury with the RAF and the government's refusal to release more of the 2000 Spitfires defending Britain in 1941 to protect Malta was undiminished many years later: 'the British government's policy to use Malta as an air strike base, rather than a secure naval offensive base from early 1941 was a gross error, only over-ridden in its stupidity by the Axis failure and procrastination in not capturing the island.' For, after all Kesselring's good work, Hitler had again postponed Operation Hercules. During April the British decrypted a number of German intelligence reports based on information gained via the American diplomatic code they had stolen, the so-called 'good source', and became aware that they had a major security problem. However, the Germans' information suggested that an invasion of Malta might be unnecessary since it was at the point of collapse.

Between 26 April and 4 May the remaining boats of the 10th Flotilla left Malta. Simpson arrived at Alexandria by plane on 4 May where he met Philip Ruck-Keene, who had just replaced Sammie Raw as Captain S1. Raw took over responsibility for operations at Northways under Horton. All Simpson's boats arrived in Egypt except Tomkinson's *Urge*, which engaged a sailing vessel with gunfire on 29 April and while shooting it up was dive-bombed and sunk by an Italian biplane. On 8 May *Olympus* called at Malta and embarked the crew of *P39* and a number of other passengers for Gibraltar. She hit a mine off Malta and sank.

Unbeaten reached Gibraltar safely, despite Place's pessimism. Casemore remembered tying up to *Maidstone* and shouting up to an old shipmate on the deck of the mother ship above, 'when suddenly a flight of aircraft came diving over the harbour and as one man we all dived into the fore ends. Suddenly realising that they were friendly, as there were no explosions, we crawled out of the fore-hatch giggling like a lot of school girls and the men on *Maidstone* looked at us in amusement; we were quite obviously bomb happy.' *Unbeaten* went into dry dock, where they took out more cracked batteries and patched her up for the journey home.

She was joined at Gibraltar by *Torbay*, who had been active to the last. In late February, lookout Leslie Howard had spotted a destroyer in the dark and roused Miers, who slept on the bridge. They bolted below and dived, but Miers's pillow jammed in the hatch so he couldn't close it. He slammed the lower hatch shut and the conning tower filled with water as depth charges rained down. They escaped, but it had been close. In March Miers rashly attacked a destroyer and almost paid the price when it hunted him. Undeterred, he followed a convoy into Corfu harbour and torpedoed three ships, fatally damaging one. It was another dangerous exploit. When he returned to *Medway*, Sammie Raw judged that 'It is evident that Commander Miers is in need of a rest.' Cunningham recommended Miers for the VC, ostensibly for the Corfu harbour raid.

Miers refused Raw's invitation to leave his boat and made aggressive attacks to the end, although on the last patrol even his loyal first lieutenant Paul Chapman thought the captain's nerves were fraying. After making a rash and unsuccessful attack, they were hunted mercilessly. Miers told Chapman, 'We are in the most desperate danger you know.' Miers had never said that sort of thing before and Chapman felt that the captain 'was oppressed by the thought that he had taken the pitcher to the well once too often'.

Torbay and *Unbeaten* arrived at Portsmouth together. The band was playing on the jetty and 'Pusser' Darke and other senior officers met them. 'After *Torbay* had tied up,' Casemore recalled, 'we followed suit with all the pomp and glory of returning heroes.' The two non-duty watches were given weekend leave, so Casemore went up to Bromley, pleased to see his family again and tell them of his adventures. Getting off the bus at Bromley Common, the first person he met was old Mr Dumwell, a neighbour. Casemore said hello and 'expected him to say, I haven't seen you for a long time, where have you been. Instead he said, "What, you home again young Jack?" I could have hit him.'

After the weekend they took *Unbeaten* to Chatham for a major refit in dry dock and most of the troops were drafted elsewhere. Teddy Woodward took over as teacher of the perisher course. Norman Drury left to become an instructor in asdics and spent the rest of the war teaching. 'I didn't want to go to Malta again,' he said. 'Once is enough in anyone's lifetime.'

Leslie Howard, meanwhile, went to a party at Fareham where he met a girl called Margaret, whose aunt was the hostess. It was a rowdy affair, but Margaret and Leslie managed to find a quiet corner. They wrote to each other after Leslie went with *Torbay* for a refit at Devonport. *Torbay* was to have a new captain, Robert 'Rumble' Clutterbuck, but since Tony Miers was taking a desk job many of the crew remained with the boat. Miers took Clutterbuck to his club, booked him a first class sleeper for the journey to Devonport and met him at the station. After a hectic round of parties, 'Crap was escorted by his ship's company to the midnight train, while maudlin songs were sung until it pulled out.'

On 26 May Rommel attacked the Gazala line just west of Tobruk. From the 'good source' he had an exact knowledge of British strengths and dispositions. There was very fierce fighting, but by the third week in June the British were in full retreat. Tobruk surrendered on 21 June. In the middle of the battle, however, a deciphered enemy report in which the 'good source' compared British methods unfavourably with American ones finally gave the head of military intelligence the clue he needed. He wrote 'Prime Minister, I am satisfied that the American ciphers in Cairo are compromised. I am taking action.' The Americans dithered, but accepted on 16 June that their military attaché's cipher was being read and by 23 June had introduced a new one. Rommel's 'good source' suddenly dried up.

It was too late for the commando attacks on aircraft in Libya and in Crete that were designed to help the convoys Harpoon and Vigorous get through to Malta. These were betrayed and the Italians were waiting for the attacks – those on Maleme airfield having been launched from the Greek submarines *Triton* and *Papanikolis*. The convoys were heavily attacked from the air and most ships were sunk or turned back. Practically no supplies got through – although, crucially, minesweepers reached the island.

Syd Hart left *Thrasher* at the end of May with a draft to go home after two years in the Mediterranean. Stokers Remblance and Berwick tried to persuade him to stay, but he felt it was time to see England again. He saw the boat off for patrol on 9 June, and a few days afterwards everybody in the *Medway* began to work frantically to get all base gear on to the ship before Rommel arrived. He was now storming into Egypt and it seemed nothing could stop him reaching Alexandria.

On 25 June Auchinleck took personal command in the desert and decided to make a stand on the line of the station of El Alamein, where there was a strip thirty-five miles wide, very rough inland, between the impassable Qattara Depression and the sea. It was the one place Rommel couldn't outflank a defending army, but it was only sixty miles from Alexandria. This put the fleet within striking distance of German bombers.

The decision to evacuate Alexandria was taken on 27 June. All personnel were recalled and heads of department had to make sure that anything being repaired ashore was back on board. There were heavy air raids on 29 June. *Medway*, the Greek depot ship and all submarines except *Porpoise* left at dusk. Joe Blamey worked through the night to get the starboard engine ready and continued working the next day, alone in the harbour with the immobile *Valiant*. Joe Brighton had a favourite Greek shop whose owner had become a friend. He 'went ashore just before we sailed to say good-bye to the Greek, and buy a few bits. Now, walking through the streets I wondered what the hell had happened. In place of the Union Flags etc., the shops were festooned with German and Italian flags, all ready to greet the Conquering Heroes. This Greek friend of mine, he remained in his shop. I could see that he was terrified that he should be seen talking to me, so seeing how things were I just gave him a miss.'

In *Medway* Hart went for a breath of serene night air before turning in. Next morning, before going down to the workshops, he took another look at the screening destroyers with the sun dancing on their bow waves. He had just finished the first job of tidying up when three bumps were heard. The submariners recognised the sound and a distant shout of 'Abandon ship!' confirmed their thought. Very quickly they were up the ladders from the orlop deck just below the waterline to find the ship already listing to starboard so heavily that no boat could be lowered. Hart knew he should go to the port side to avoid being sucked down when she sank but could not face the awesome dive. Instead he risked sliding into the water on the starboard side and swimming round the stern, making distance from the sinking vessel. Eventually he headed for the scrambling nets of a destroyer and, when safely within distance of rescue, turned on his back and floated, just in time to see *Medway*'s bows rise into the air and disappear with a final sucking swish. Hart couldn't help but admire the attack made by *U372*.

The submarines moved temporarily to Haifa while Ruck-Keene began to develop the French base at Beirut for British submarines. Destroyers recovered about half the stock of torpedoes carried in *Medway*, while others had been moved by land.

There was panic in Cairo. Wednesday 1 July became known as Ash Wednesday thanks to the burning of official files. That day Rommel attacked at El Alamein but the line held. On 4 July, after three days of attacks, he was beaten. For the British Empire that day was the turning point of the war, though it was not so clear at the time. Syd Hart met *Thrasher* when she came in from her patrol and with other survivors of *Medway* went home in *Otus*. Hart's return to England was as much of an anti-climax as it had been for Casemore, but without Casemore's hero's welcome to the submarine base.

Casemore found himself drafted to *Sealion* as second coxswain under Bobby Lambert, who had been a spare commander in Malta. The coxswain drank too much rum and Casemore, already respected as a seasoned veteran because of *Unbeaten*'s reputation, soon found himself running the boat. Jim Thomsett was awarded a period of compassionate leave because his father had just died. During this period he grew closer to his old sweetheart Eileen. He received a draft to stand by *Sea Nymph* while she was building but a muddle over an X-ray brought him back to Gosport.

Tony Miers found that he was to receive his VC from the King, while his crew were to get their medals at a minor ceremony later. This was not acceptable. Miers fought both the naval and the palace staff; finally he forced them to consult the King, who agreed to a joint ceremony. Consequently, on 28 July 1942 the crew of *Torbay* was invited to a party in London, although only those receiving medals were allowed beyond the palace grounds. Leslie Howard invited his parents, Edward and Eva, but they didn't want to go so far so he invited Margaret, who lived in London. She bought a special hat for the day. Following the presentation Miers threw a party at a hotel, and after that Margaret guided Leslie and various boatmates around a number of hostelries. Locals bought them drinks and even gave them money on seeing their submariners' hats. As Leslie staggered back to Battersea on her arm he said, 'I think we ought to get married.'

On the night of 21 July Simpson, MacGregor and Tanner returned to Malta and between 20 July and 15 August a new 10th Flotilla reassembled there. *Una*, *Uproar*, *Ultimatum* and *Umbra* were joined from Gibraltar by *Unbroken*, *United* and *Unison*. With *Medway* sunk and Lazaretto still rebuilding, submarines achieved little in July, but in that month, under Keith Park, the RAF won the air battle over Malta. More and better planes, commanded by one of the principal protagonists of the Battle of Britain, made it look easy and with Malta defensively strong, the Luftwaffe could never threaten the island again. There was much bitter fighting to come in the air, but it took place over Sicily.

The problem on the island now was food, of which there was very little left. All depended on a huge convoy from Britain, code-named Pedestal. Simpson and Ruck-Keene deployed six submarines south of Pantelleria where Italian cruisers had attacked the June convoy, while Ben Bryant in *Safari* was off Palermo. Alastair Mars with his tall first lieutenant Haig Haddow was guarding the Strait of Messina in *Unbroken*. Tremendous damage was done to the convoy by German and Italian submarines, motor torpedo boats and aircraft. A force of cruisers and destroyers headed straight for the ambush south of Pantelleria but the Italians decided they could not provide sufficient air cover and turned the force back. They passed *Safari* at a distance in the night, heading for the Strait of Messina.

Alastair Mars was eating bacon and eggs when he heard the asdic operator, Jan Cryer, report to the officer of the watch, 'H.E. ahead, sir.' Mars ordered diving stations, and Cryer soon identified the noise as heavy units moving fast. They were still too far away to see with the periscope. Finally Mars saw masts in the heat haze. Haddow told the crew the target was four cruisers. There were two Cant seaplanes above. Putting speeds and courses into the fruit machine, the torpedo officer gave Mars a course for a ninety-degree track. Joe Sizer, the forty-year-old northern coxswain, reported the depth correct. Haddow kept his eye on the depth gauge, Paul Thirsk the navigator bent over the chart. Cryer now wore a fiendish grin. Outside ERA Howard Lewis, a small dark-haired Welshman, watched the blowing panel. The chief ERA stood behind the captain, reading the figures off the periscope. Mars told Haddow there were eight destroyers escorting and Haddow ordered the crew to shut off for depth charging.

At the next look the cruisers had changed course, putting them further away, but they now overlapped. Archdale put in the bearing and asked for a speed. Thirsk worked it out as twenty-two knots from his plot, Cryer as twenty-five for an eight-inch cruiser at 200 revs. Deciding to go for twenty-five, Mars got a director angle of green three-six-and-a-half. The torpedoes were ready, set for a depth of fourteen and sixteen feet. The nearest destroyer was heading straight for *Unbroken*; Mars decided to risk it hitting the conning tower. As the last destroyer passed close by, he fired a salvo of four, dived to eighty feet and hurried south-west at nine knots. After two minutes and fifteen seconds of tense waiting they heard an explosion, and fifteen seconds later another. Their exultant back-slapping was halted by Cryer's report of asdic transmissions. But although they waited silently for an hour as three destroyers dropped 105 ashcans, none were close enough to do more than bring down cork. They moved away under water, still nervous that there might be a destroyer hunting, an aircraft overhead. Next day Simpson sent a signal telling them they had badly damaged two cruisers.

On 18 August *Unbroken* arrived back at Malta to cheering, happy Maltese, and Mars was welcomed warmly by all the base staff. Enough of the convoy had got through to remove the immediate threat of starvation.

While Mars was ambushing the cruisers, *Porpoise* had made a supply run to Malta and was sent to lay mines off Ras el Tin, a headland between Derna and Tobruk on the route taken by ships bringing supplies to Rommel's army. Ultra had tracked the *Ogaden* from her arrival at Benghazi. She was to be off Derna at 0430 on passage to Tobruk following the coast at nine knots, so *Porpoise* was waiting for her. Bennington hit her with one torpedo, and when that didn't sink her he fired another which did. Simpson sent him to meet another supply ship, *Lerici*. On 15 August Bletchley Park learned that Rommel was planning an attack on the line at El Alamein to start on 26 August and also that he was seriously short of supplies. In the evening Bennington made sure *Lerici* didn't reach him. Simpson then sent *Porpoise* to Derna to ambush a third, smaller ship.

This time they may have been picked up by shore radar. It was nearly dawn when the lookout spotted a destroyer. Bennington avoided the attempt to ram, then dived in record time (and according to Blamey they had halved their diving time since the start of the war). The first pattern of depth charges was very close and broke the depth gauges and hydrophones. The port main motor blew its fuses, and the torpedo hatch in the fore ends was taking in water. Brighton reckoned he could feel structural strain caused by the charges, which 'transmits itself to the human body almost as an electric shock causing the same kind of vibration'.

With each run from the destroyer Bennington put in a spurt of speed and changed direction. For two hours the charges continued to drop. Stanley Hawkey, sitting at the telephone switchboard, painted a mark for each one on a piece of wood. Torpedo officer Johnny Pope called Blamey to the fore ends to help deal with the high-pressure airline and telemotor leaks, and he arrived to find the fore-endmen had the place decked out to celebrate Pope's birthday. Blamey wondered sardonically whether he would get another birthday, but 'one joker asked us to imagine the amazement on the face of the enemy sound detector operator when he heard the strains of "Happy birthday to you ..." coming up from the depths.'

Blamey was glad he and his team were busy with their huge spanners. The others waited silently, listening to the eerie pinging of the enemy sonar, the sudden roar of engines, the charges coming through the water ... A second destroyer joined in. Brighton was grateful when the forward hydroplanes had to be operated locally, giving him something to do. Hawkey marked off eighty-seven depth charges. Then, quite suddenly, they stopped. They found later that a lifebuoy and Bennington's sheepskin coat were both missing from the bridge; it appears the Italians took them for evidence of a kill.

'We were in a hell of a mess,' said Brighton. He was in charge of the batteries and 'had the job of assessing the damage and advising what to do for the best'. They carried alkali to neutralise leaking battery acid, but they ran out of that and tried to dilute it with precious fresh water before the seawater got in and created chlorine gas. The high-pressure air leaks had caused a pressure of 5 psi in the boat and the atmosphere quickly became murky. After more than two hours of silence Bennington came to periscope depth, only to find the periscopes were not working. The only thing to do was to get the gun crew ready and surface. As the whistle went for the crew to man the gun, Blamey got the engines started and waited nervously for the shooting to begin. After three minutes the telegraphs clanged to 'Half ahead both' and he sent a stoker to the control room; the man came back with the glad tidings that there was nothing in sight.

They continued to make repairs 'and pumped out as best we could. We were in no condition to submerge if attacked and we were in very unfriendly waters.' Bennington, as he always did after depth charging, asked 'Ginger' Ridley, 'What's the state of the rum jars, Cox'n?' Ridley, as usual, reported, 'Two jars cracked, Sir, and will have to be written off.' Which, of course, meant an unofficial splicing of the mainbrace. They sent a message to base and set off toward Beirut, nursing the engines as they ran on the surface in daylight, dreading an attack and making repairs all the while. They ran through the night, and then in the morning the horrified lookout sighted aircraft coming straight for them. It turned out to be a pair of Beaufighters. They were safe, and they were escorted home.

In August the Axis lost 4000 tons of fuel and 420 vehicles sunk at sea by submarines or the RAF. Rommel's attack at Alam Halfa was short-lived; delayed by minefields, ceaselessly harried by the RAF and desperately short of petrol, he heard of the sinking of two more ships and went back on the defensive. All through September pressure on the supply lines continued as the British poured in fresh men and equipment for an offensive of their own. In October the Axis lost to aircraft and submarines, usually guided by Ultra, 44 per cent of the supplies it tried to transport by sea. Submarines sank thirty-two big ships between June and October, with more than half of the attacks definitely guided by Ultra.

The most dramatic was a trap laid by Simpson with Ultra guidance in mid-October. He began by sending Tom Barlow's *United* off Lampedusa and Basher Coombe's *Utmost* south of Pantelleria. At 0258 and 0505 on 17 October Bletchley announced the departure of a major convoy from Naples to Tripoli: 'Estimated Time of Departure Naples 1400/17/10. 8 knots; to rendezvous with another convoy at 1030/18/10. Combined convoy due Tripoli 1100/20/10.' And it provided their route. That day Simpson diverted *Unbroken* from Al Khums and *Unbending* from Tunisia to join them.

Mars in *Unbroken* had just failed to destroy the *Amsterdam*, a large merchantman beached on mud, with three torpedoes. 'P.O. Willey came in. "Excuse me, sir. Immediate from S.10." With his customary impassiveness he handed me the pink signal slip.' Mars decoded the signal and set off for Lampedusa.

Edward Stanley had been first lieutenant of *Regent* under Hairy Browne, and this was his first working-up patrol in *Unbending*. They had been sent to a quiet area to gain experience, but 'At 1700 on the 17th we were moved to a position south of Pantelleria, as centre submarine of a line of five boats ... We were

Unbeaten moored against the Lazaretto, the 10th Flotilla's base at Malta *(IWM)*.

Manoel Island seen from the air. The seventeenth-century Lazaretto runs along the top of the island with Fort Manoel below it. A bridge linked the island to the Sliema sea front and the submariners' favourite bars *(RNSM)*.

Officers relaxing in the airy corridor outside their cabins in the Lazaretto at Malta *(RNSM)*.

Four of *Truant's* stalwart key ratings: Stoker Petty Officer Syd Hart, Chief ERA Jack Pook, ERA Bill 'China' King and Torpedo Gunner's Mate Gus Fisher on leave at Cairo *(RNSM)*.

Two of *Porpoise's*: Chief ERA Joe Blamey and Torpedo Gunner's Mate Joe Brighton enjoying the Mediterranean sun *(RNSM archive)*.

Jim Thomsett and the photo of Eileen that he took to the Far East *(Jim Thomsett)*; Leslie Howard with the pin-up of herself that Margaret drew for him *(Margaret Howard)*; Jack Casemore *(Jack Casemore)*; Stanley Hawkey with his wife after receiving his DSM: they made the cover of *Defence* magazine *(RNSM archive)*.

The control room of *Utmost* with Dick Cayley at the periscope, Charles Oxborrow, right, supervising the trim, and Robert Boyd operating the fruit machine above the wheel *(RNSM)*.

The Italian light cruiser *Muzio Attendolo* showing the effect of a torpedo hit from Mars's *Unbroken* on 13 August 1942. *Attendolo* merely lost her bows but the heavy cruiser *Bolzano*, hit by Mars in the same attack, was so badly damaged that she had to be beached with flooded magazines. *Bolzano* was salvaged but never repaired *(IWM)*.

A 'perishot' – taken through the periscope – of one of John Stevens's victims in *Unruffled*. This may be the supply ship *Una* sinking off Capri on 11 October 1942. The crew of *Unruffled* would never go to sea without their cat Timoshenko *(RNSM)*.

Half of the crew of *Upholder* with Lieutenant-Commander David Wanklyn (centre) at the Lazaretto. Fred Frame (second left) was chief engineer, John Swainston (right) was coxswain. Everyone in this highly-decorated group died when *Upholder* was sunk except the famously lucky tall second coxswain Gordon Selby (back row centre left in cap) who had just left the boat *(RNSM)*.

Right: Leslie Bennington aboard *Medway*, the day he took over *Porpoise* *(RNSM archive)*; *Far right:* Teddy Woodward at Malta *(RNSM)*.

An Italian sailor watches the submarine *Tempest* surfacing from the deck of the ace Italian torpedo boat *Circe* after a successful hunt on 12 February 1942 *(RNSM)*.

Coxswain Charles Anscomb (right) with two shipmates as prisoners on board *Circe* after scuttling *Tempest* and being rescued from the water *(RNSM)*.

A human torpedo or chariot proceeding on the surface, as they normally did. The chariot could dive to get under anti-submarine or anti-torpedo nets and when close to the quarry in order to release the warhead from the bow and secure it underneath the target *(RNSM)*.

Lieutenants Godfrey Place and Donald Cameron, commanders of *X7* and *X6*, were each awarded the Victoria Cross for their part in severely damaging the German battleship *Tirpitz* in Altenfjord during operation 'Source', the midget submarine attack on 22 September 1943 *(RNSM)*.

PO Tel George 'Guts' Harmer and his assistant Ken Wade attempting to plug a shell hole in the pressure hull of *Shakespeare*, while under fire from a Japanese submarine-chaser. Although unable to dive, *Shakespeare* fought her way out of trouble and escaped with help from *Stygian (RNSM)*.

in position by 0600 on the 18th.' The line was not spread across the line of the convoy, as was usual, but along the route that Bletchley Park had given, so that, if things went well, they might all attack in sequence.

Bletchley Park's signals, with the initial timings corrected, were incorporated in the Operational Intelligence Centre report dated that morning: 'The tanker *Saturno* left Cagliari at 1600 on the 17th and will rendezvous at 1230 on 18th with *Capo Orso*, *Beppe* and the *Titania*, all having left Naples at 1600 on the 17th. The convoy will proceed to the west of Malta for Tripoli, arriving at 1300 on the 20th, speed 8 knots.'

It didn't mention the eight destroyers and two seaplane escorts. Ben Bryant's *Safari*, just in from a successful patrol, was rushed out again, as Arthur Dickison noted in his diary: '18 October. We spent most of the day storing up before leaving harbour at 1600. John Devlin [the navigator] told me we were heading for a place called Pantelleria. We arrived on our station about two hours later but sighted nothing.' Aircraft brought further news. 'That night there was a constant hustle between the wireless office and the ward-room as signals from Malta detailed the convoy's strength and course,' wrote Mars. 'Shrimp's final signal pointed out that the destruction of the convoy could make "all the difference" to the war in north Africa.' Montgomery's Alamein offensive was due to be launched on 23 October. The British submarines raced for stations on the projected track.

Utmost was first to sight the convoy. At 0820 her lookouts spotted the Cant seaplanes flying overhead, but even at top speed the blond-bearded former Porpoise, Basher Coombe, could only fire torpedoes at very long range which missed or never reached the convoy. Coombe did the proper but highly dangerous thing and surfaced to send a sighting report.

In *Safari* Dickison noted that 'Next day being Sunday, we were at prayers in the control room when Alf Parris handed the captain a signal. Prayers were abandoned, he went into the wardroom and came back later with the news that the convoy

had been sighted. We had its position and were going to intercept. We surfaced shortly afterwards and sped off on the engines,
400 revolutions together which gave a speed of 16 knots.' In
Unbroken, similarly, Mars 'sat in the ward-room impatient for
some sign of the convoy. But all was quiet until 2pm [*sic*, actually earlier] when *Utmost*, taking a suicidal risk, surfaced to signal
that the convoy was just beyond our horizon . . . I hurried to the
control-room, took over the periscope and had the boat shut-off
for depth charging.'

As *Safari* and *Unbroken* closed in, Edward Stanley, skipper of
Unbending, began an attack. 'At 1153 the mastheads and smoke
haze of the convoy were sighted due north. As they approached,
I could distinguish four merchant vessels in two columns.' An
hour later, from very close range, he fired a full salvo of four torpedoes in a spread, hoping that torpedoes missing the first
column would hit the second. Torpedoman Douglas recalled,

> Our torpedoes were set at a depth of 12 feet although I
> remember the depth mechanism on one tube would not
> engage and the setting had to remain at eight feet. We scored
> hits on a merchant ship of 5,000 tons and one of the escort-
> ing destroyers, both later confirmed as sunk. The remaining
> destroyers counter-attacked and about 60 depth-charges were
> dropped, but Lieut. Stanley cleverly dived under the convoy
> and the charges were not close enough to do any damage.

When he got back from this first eventful patrol they nicknamed
Stanley 'Otto' after the German ace Kretschmer.

Pansy Mars in *Unbroken* made his attack just over an hour later.
He had trouble penetrating the screen of three destroyers in the
choppy sea and fired a salvo at the tanker on the turn. A seaplane
saw him and marked his position and two destroyers attacked as
a team. The crew thought they heard two explosions from torpedoes before 'the familiar noise of an express train tearing from
a tunnel' as a third destroyer made its attack. They waited, 'silent

apprehension, then a great clang on the casing'. A depth charge had scored a direct hit but, by a miracle, had failed to explode on contact. A moment later it went off below the ward room, together with three others in the salvo. If Mars was right, they must have come very close to destruction.

An inferno of ear-splitting, bone rattling chaos was let loose: a lunatic confusion of crashing glass and cursing men as the submarine was turned into a monstrous cocktail-shaker. In the middle of it all, darkness, as every electric light-bulb in the boat was smashed in its socket. A shower of cork from the deckhead rained down. The shock would have thrown me from my feet had I not grabbed at the control-room ladder. The luminous depth gauge needles jumped from their frames and hung drunkenly useless. Gauges throughout the boat were shattered. I started to lose balance and was temporarily paralysed with fear as I realised the bows were dipping. We're sinking. This time we've had it. My God, Ting, I've let you down . . .

But Ting, Mars's wife, was not a widow yet. Phlegmatic submariners calmly repaired all the damage they could. At the darkest moment, Cryer's assistant joker John Jones went across from the asdic to the captain and silently handed him a slip of paper. Mars screwed up his eyes to read it in the dim light: 'Jones, John. Able Seaman. D/JX 254129. Request to go back to General Service.'

The destroyers probably thought they had made a kill but had to return to guard the convoy. Eventually the Unbrokens crept back to Malta, arriving in gas masks against the poisonous fumes of chlorine.

Safari passed *Unbroken* and caught up with the ship that *Unbroken* had damaged and stopped. Dickison noted, 'We started the attack and fired two torpedoes, which must have struck because we heard two explosions. She was later identified as the

SS *Titania* of 5,000 tons. After the attack we dived to 340 feet to wait: another explosion was heard and Ben said that was her boiler blowing up. We went to silent routine.'

It was 0100 the next morning when Tom Barlow closed in, still in rough sea conditions. John Wingate was officer of the watch as *United* 'plunged into a swirling bank of black, acrid smoke . . . and emerged to see the convoy dead ahead of us. The tanker was at 5,000 yards on a 140 track, with a destroyer in between, at about a mile.' It was a surface attack. 'The generators were stopped; the tubes were brought to the ready; Tom Barlow was crouching over his torpedo sight. Three torpedoes were fired and two explosions were heard.' They hit the tanker *Petrarca* (not *Saturno* as Bletchley Park had thought) but tankers were notoriously difficult to sink. She limped on toward Tripoli, leaking oil from gaping holes.

So, with the best possible information, five submarines had succeeded in sinking two merchantmen and damaging a tanker. However, making attacks in rough weather against five ships defended by eight destroyers and three seaplanes was not easy, even when they were moving at only eight knots. This was about the maximum speed for a British convoy in the Atlantic, but half or a third of the speed of most Italian convoys. Life was a lot easier for the German U-boats in the early days, their task to attack twenty slow ships with an improvised escort of one or two antique vessels and no planes.

Nevertheless, in the second half of 1942 the Italian convoys admitted to a heavy defeat brought about by submarines and air guided by good information from Ultra. They were past the turning point. The vast resources of the USA were gradually being mobilised.

Ian McGeoch arrived back at Gibraltar in *Splendid* on 16 October to the happy news of the birth of his son. After a working-up patrol, he returned on 6 November to the news that Montgomery had broken through the Axis lines at El Alamein. He also knew another big operation was brewing, but didn't get a sense of it until that afternoon when he 'walked up the Rock by the steepening path above Europa Point as far as the wartime defences permitted, and stood gazing seaward'.

He had often enjoyed this view both for its scenic beauty and out of a sense of its historic significance for Britain and its navy. He looked first east towards the war in the desert, and then west towards the U-boat war. In that direction he

suddenly noticed that beneath the red ball of the sun as it set in the autumnal haze the horizon was dotted with ships. As I strained my eyes I realised that a vast convoy was approaching, with that deceptive lack of obvious motion characteristic of distant vessels. It was indeed the leading assault convoy of Operation 'Torch' that would land at Algiers and Oran at day-break two days later. Soon the Straits appeared to be completely filled with shipping – the assorted transports, nearly fifty of them, in their columns on a broad front and their escorts stationed all around.

17

SELBY'S LUCK

Gordon Selby, born in 1919, was the son of a Wiltshire far-rier. He started the war with the reserve group and but for a last-minute change of personnel would have been in the instantly torpedoed *Oxley*. Having won several medals with David Wanklyn in *Upholder* and been promoted to coxswain, he was drafted away from her just before the patrol on which she was sunk in 1942. He was in the air raid shelter when a bomb sank his new boat *P39*.

He was only once on the wrong boat at the wrong time. After their boat was bombed, the crew of *P39* boarded *Olympus* with a few men from *P36* for a passage home from Malta. The over-crowded boat sailed at four in the morning with ninety-eight men aboard, and just over an hour later she hit a mine. Selby was in the petty officers' mess, about to have breakfast, when there was a big thump. Almost immediately they were told to abandon ship and he climbed out on to the casing.

P39's bomb-happy chief ERA, 'Shiner' Wright, assumed a plane had surprised them and dashed to the control room to dive the boat. Geordie Talbot, outside ERA of *Olympus*, got there at the same moment, so Wright returned to the engine room. The port engine telegraph went to 'Stop', so one of the stokers stopped it and they decided to shut it down for diving. A group of stokers came from aft and one of them said, 'It's abandon ship.' Then the starboard telegraph went to 'Stop'.

Wright went to the control room to find out what was going on. The compartment was ankle deep in water, there were flashes from electric circuits and the lights were going on and off with the roll of the boat. He rushed back and shouted to the engineers 'Abandon ship!' *Olympus*'s chief engineer was controlling the flow of about fifteen people queuing to climb the ladder to the bridge. The water was coming in through the galley and the first yellow fumes of chlorine were rising. Wright went forward to the gun tower ladder and found no queue. Lieutenant Geoff Bulmer of *P39* was in charge and said cheerfully, 'Come on chief, up you go.'

Emerging from the hatch he could see about ninety people were out and mostly standing on the forecasing. Malta was a shadow on the horizon six miles away with the tiny yellow light of a plane flying above it. Norman Marriott, skipper of *P39*, was trying to signal towards the island with a hand torch because the distress flares fitted on the periscopes wouldn't ignite and the Aldis lamp wasn't working either. People were trying to fire the four-inch gun, but a shell jammed in the breech and broke apart. Wright suggested tipping the cordite out of the cartridge and burning it, which would mean clearing a good space and laying a fuse. Lieutenant Commander Herbert Dymott of *Olympus* shouted back, 'Do what you like,' but it was already too late. The bows were slipping under. When the water reached the foot of the gun tower Wright jumped in and swam away.

At first there was shouting, as people looked for friends or put DSEA sets on those who couldn't swim. Soon the noise died away as they set off in a group in the direction of Malta. The water was cool – an hour earlier Wright had logged the sea temperature as 51° F – but not rough. He passed a floating mine 'with what appeared to be a whip aerial with a wire hanging from it'. One idiot stoker started to swim towards it until they shouted at him. As it became light, Malta was clearly visible a very long way away. The crowd thinned out as people began to give up. Most drowned silently, though one man close to Wright said, 'I'm through' and 'put his arms up in the air and went down'. Wright had stripped to his shorts and navy belt.

At seven o'clock they watched the breakfast raid on Malta and worried that the fighters might shoot them up. He 'had the morbid thought of my daughter as she grew up asking my wife, "Why haven't I got a daddy like other little girls?"' This thought drove him on. When he felt really weary he turned on to his back and floated while he took twelve very deep breaths. Then he swam on. The group had strung out and thinned out further. Gordon Selby and Sid Seymour the PO LTO, both strong swimmers, were up ahead. Selby was a lugubrious lad who didn't look particularly athletic, the son of a blacksmith from Swindon, but he was strong and calm. Norman Marriott drowned close to Selby within a few hundred yards of the beach.

After five hours Wright could clearly see an ambulance on the bank above the beach and two soldiers watching him. He felt very cold. Ten yards from the beach he tried to stand and shout 'Help' but he was still out of his depth. He swam till his knees hit sand. Then the soldiers pulled him out. Geordie Talbot reached the beach, stood up, and fell down dead. There were only nine survivors, three from *Olympus* and six from *P39*, out of ninety-eight.

It took luck to survive in subs, and submariners became even more superstitious than the average sailor. Ben Bryant always went to sea with his lucky cap, his mother's prayer book and a toy dog, while wearing his wife's confirmation chain with a Church of England St Christopher and a Catholic Sacred Heart attached. He was a formal man – some later thought him bombastic – and not everyone liked his enforcement of compulsory prayers every Sunday. Once, someone hid the prayer book. The resulting cancellation of prayers was followed by a 45-hour hunt by destroyers.

The book reappeared and the crew never missed prayers again. When he left, the crew asked Bryant to leave his prayer book and his lucky cap behind in the boat.

Ginger Hiscock, a stoker from *P39* who swam to safety, blamed Wright for the *Olympus* disaster on the grounds that Wright had been mining engineer in *Rorqual*, responsible for sowing mines. 'As ye sow, so shall ye reap,' he repeated mysteriously. More disconcerting was coxswain Shorty Randell's warning to the crew of *Phoenix* that the Lord was calling them and this was their last patrol. A spare crew gunlayer had been instructed to come aboard and was ready to patrol when *Phoenix*'s own gunlayer hobbled back from hospital and sent him back to the *Medway*. Randell took the spare crewman aside and said, 'It's just as well you're leaving the boat because we shall not return from this patrol. The Lord is calling us. Here, take this Bible and when you read it think of me.' The gunlayer thought he had been at the rum bottle, but it turned out that Randell was right.

Some people were just unlucky. Shrimp Simpson remembered seeing an old shipmate, Able Seaman George Harrison of *Triumph*, whose wife had had triplets while they were serving together in the thirties. Simpson cheerily asked after Harrison's wife and sons, and Harrison replied that they had all been killed during the night blitz on Devonport. Harrison himself died in *Triumph* five months later.

On Christmas Eve 1939 a bunch of petty officers from *Seahorse* and chummy boats of the Blyth flotilla went for a drink to the nearest pub, the Astley Arms, two miles down the coast road at Seaton Sluice. They took part in the pub's Christmas raffle. ERA Len 'Tug' Wilson of *Seahorse* won a bottle of Johnnie Walker Red Label. Since they were sailing on Boxing Day, the 23-year-old asked the landlady, Lydia Jackson, to hold on to it until he came back from patrol. By the time John Coote frequented the pub in 1944, beer was short and when it was available Lydia used to hoist a Jolly Roger above the pub so that the submariners knew when to make the trek. Tug Wilson's bottle of Johnnie Walker was still waiting for him on the shelf. Since the submariners knew that *Seahorse* had disappeared, it was rumoured that Lydia was in love with Wilson. The bottle was still there when Coote visited the pub again twenty years after the war. Finally the landlady gave it to the Submarine Museum.

The most level-headed people registered supernatural occurrences. North of Sciathos in February 1944 Aston Piper attacked and damaged a German tanker. Like other tankers it was resilient and refused to sink, and the counter-attack was, Piper said, 'the worst I ever experienced'. His boat was pushed down to 400 feet – 150 feet below its safe diving depth – and they lost all the lights and the compass. 'Naturally,' he recalled, 'one's thoughts go to wondering whether one's not going to come out of it. My wife was in Troon and a photograph of me fell off the wall and she woke up in shock and said "Aston is in trouble", and was upset until she got a letter from me saying all was well.'

Most people, Max Horton excluded, dreaded the number thirteen. Leaving port on Friday the 13th was done, but not done willingly, and people were glad to return from a thirteenth patrol. A superstition grew up about last patrols, largely because the very famous David Wanklyn and John Linton were lost on theirs. Obviously, crews were tired and nervous by that stage. Flotilla captains often deliberately sought to make the last patrol a safe one by sending boats to a quiet area, but this didn't suit aggressive captains. One commanding officer reckoned that 'People cut corners – they became desperately concerned with ever having made a blank patrol. They would go out, some of them, for eight or nine patrols and come back with something in the bag each time, and then on the last patrol they were sent to what was supposedly a safe area – and that wouldn't be good enough. They cheated, they took risks in order not to come back empty-handed.' John Roxburgh, CO of *United*, was tempted to cross a minefield to sink a grounded ship but decided not to.

In fact it was much more common for boats or captains to be sunk on their first patrol. Victims included William Dunkerley of

Thames, Jimmy Prowse with *Snapper*, Johnnie Huddart of *Triumph*, James Livesay of *Undaunted*, David Verschoyle-Campbell of *Stonehenge*, and Hugh Turner who took over the aged, leaky *Porpoise* in the Far East. This is not exactly surprising, because at that stage the captain and sometimes also the crew were inexperienced and more likely to make a misjudgement. The boat might be a relatively unknown quantity. Faults in its equipment might not yet have been detected or the captain might simply be unaware of its quirks of behaviour.

Submarines frequently adopted pets and they soon became a kind of fetish, so that crews refused to leave port until their animal was aboard. The dog Bacchus was idolised by the crew of *Rubis*. *Unruffled* would not sail without Timoshenko, presented to the petty officer telegraphist as a homeless kitten by a Wren at Gibraltar. *Utmost* was also said to have a cat that could not be left behind. The cat Snoopy, brought aboard *Tally Ho* by a stoker returning from shore leave, had to be locked in the captain's cabin forty-eight hours before sailing because they wouldn't sail without it. Snoopy survived to be brought from Ceylon to England and found a home after the war with Leslie Bennington's mother.

The loss of close friends was a blow that was difficult to take. Surviving captains found David Wanklyn's death particularly upsetting, more because they liked him so much than because he was their leading hero. Casemore reckoned that 'one of the most emotional things that happened to me' was clearing the lockers of dead friends. In summer 1941 at the Lazaretto he was detailed to clear out the possessions of the seamen and stokers of *Union* so that a new boat coming from England could use their lockers. 'About four of us from *Unbeaten* were given the job, and on cutting the locks off, started to put their belongings into their kitbags. On opening the lockers we were confronted with photographs and letters from their wives, girlfriends and mothers as well as their personal clothing and mementos.' The tear-jerking emotion brought his own suppressed fears to the surface. 'One could not help reading some of the letters and wondered how this poor bastard had died. Would we on the *Unbeaten* very soon face the same fate and would some other submariner then be stowing my personal things in my kitbag?'

It was difficult to get dead friends out of your head. Every time Ben Bryant carried out patrols between Malta and North Africa in 1942 and 1943 he found himself remembering the charming and dynamic Edward Bickford and their walks on Dingli cliffs before the war: 'we used to make our landfall on those Dingli cliffs; I never sighted them without seeming to see the figure of Bickie.'

The worst and most wasteful way to die was in an accident, and it is a common experience of war that accidents claim quite as many lives as the enemy. Submarines generally simply failed to return from patrol, their loss unexplained. Sometimes, sadly, it could be matched with some instance of 'friendly fire': three submarines were rammed and one depth-charged by 'friendly' ships, one definitely sunk by a bomber and one by another submarine. Sometimes the enemy made a verifiable or accurate claim of a sinking; quite often the loss remained unexplained. Of approximately eighty British submarines lost, the cause of loss of about twenty-three remains uncertain. In these cases the loss was usually attributed to mines and most remain 'presumed mined', but while this was hardly implausible some losses were probably down to accident, perhaps compounded by damage or ongoing structural defect.

Two boats sank during their trial work-up in 1943. It is probably fair to say, given the speed of the emergency building programme, that it is remarkable that there were only two such losses, but it is no consolation to the relatives of those who died.

In both cases it was the design of the log that was at fault, compounded by human error and the placing of a switch. The log mechanism was in a watertight container called the log tank, located beneath the forward auxiliary machinery space under the seamen's mess. Water flowing past the transducer drove the impeller, which provided an electrical signal, proportional to the speed of the boat, to the control room, so that speed could be measured. To check the machinery the transducer had to be raised.

In *Untamed* the transducer got stuck when it was raised for inspection. The navigating officer and TI checking it thought it had retracted fully (though an indicator showed it wasn't) and tried to close the sluice. Instead of closing, the sluice jammed against the transducer, which was still sticking through the bottom of the boat. When they opened the log tank, seawater rushed into the boat at a rate of about two tons per minute. They shut the watertight door to the machine space, but they couldn't shut the air vents – according to the indicators, one of the vents was shut when in fact it was wide open – because the switch operating them had been placed inaccessibly behind reload torpedoes, so they couldn't stop the compartment flooding. With water coming in through the vents they tried to shut the watertight bulkhead door to the accommodation compartment, but there was something wrong with it. They died trying.

There was now too much water in the forward part of the submarine for it to get off the bottom. The remaining thirty-two members of the crew went into the engine room to escape from that hatch in case the control room bulkhead gave way and water got into the batteries. In the engine room they became comatose through breathing too high a concentration of carbon dioxide. The chief ERA managed to open the hatch only to have it slam back on him, and when the four people behind him all tried to get out together they jammed the escape trunking.

Untamed was found soon after the accident and was salvaged, with Arthur Pitt in charge of identifying the bloated bodies. John Coote went into the control room, which remained airtight, and he and others worked out what had happened. The official report effectively pinned the blame on Coote's close friend Peter Acworth, *Untamed*'s navigating officer, but Coote's book later pointed out the design faults and shoddy workmanship concealed by the report. Moreover, in his own submarine (next off the production line) and others of the series the problems were immediately addressed.

Vandal had sunk three months earlier, but she was not found until 2003. She lay in pitch darkness on a muddy slope, so investigation was not easy, but the divers of the 2003 expedition, finding the forward escape hatch open and the others closed, concluded that she had probably sunk for the same reason, although she had been on the surface at the time her log was inspected.

Vandal left the depot ship in the morning for a third day of routine exercises. The boat's position suggests that she was conducting log calibration over a measured mile at the time she sank. An inspection of the log caused the forward space to flood and some crewmen became trapped there. Since they were on the surface, someone opened the hatch to get out, causing water to flood in at such a rate that the boat dived perpendicularly down and hit the bottom hard. Another possibility was that the crew, like that of *Untamed*, couldn't close the bulkhead door. With the hatch open it was impossible to expel the water using compressed air, so there was nothing for it but to swim to the surface.

Attempting an immediate escape from 330 feet of freezing water in February a mile and a half from the shore was not an attractive prospect, so the crew waited to be rescued, quietly conserving oxygen. They were due back at 1900 and could expect a search an hour or two after that. With a boat waiting for them on the surface they would stand a chance. Unfortunately, the depot ship didn't notice their disappearance for fourteen hours. Around the time that the first plane was sent to look for them the following morning they seem to have sent some oil to the surface to signal their position prior to making an escape, but presumably when they crowded into a compartment to get out they all passed out in the same way as in *Untamed*.

For those who survived, these disasters were harrowing experiences. Francis Brooks was commanding *Unity* when she was rammed by a Norwegian ship that had taken her for a U-boat. The staff at Blyth had neglected to tell him about the Norwegian's southbound convoy, which he met in thick fog.

Brooks gave the order to abandon ship immediately and only two people drowned in the boat. Most of the crew survived because the Norwegian captain saw the white ensign at the last moment and came back to rescue them. But it was difficult to keep your nerve after something like this had happened to you. Edward Young and Mervyn Wingfield stayed with submarines after Wingfield's boat was rammed by a friendly ship, but both Francis Brooks and John Eaden (rammed by a destroyer when in *Utmost*) found the experience too much for them.

If a boat was torpedoed on the surface, those on the bridge sometimes survived. Ironically, the survivor might be the look-out who failed to spot the danger. Very few came away alive from submarines that had been sunk by depth charges. A group escaped from the torpedo compartment of *Stratagem* on the sea bed in 150 feet of water off Malacca, and one man, George Oliver, survived the depth-charging of *H49* in the North Sea. He was blown to the surface when the submarine broke up and was found floating by the Germans, but his story remained untold for years because the Navy thought he had died in a car crash, when in fact he was living in Hartlepool.

In the Mediterranean the water was usually too deep for survival, so that only crews that managed to bring the boat to the surface to surrender stood any chance of getting out alive. At some point, as it plunged out of control in deep water, the submarine collapsed. After the war, Tiny Fell took part in an experiment to discover at what depth the S-class *Stoic* would implode. It happenened very suddenly at just over 600 feet, 200 feet below her official safe diving depth. Recovering the wreck, they found a mass of distorted frames and plates. The torpedo hatch had been the weak point. It had given way and been driven by force of water to the very back of the boat. Fell concluded that 'men in a submarine which collapsed under pressure would know nothing. Death would be instantaneous.'

There were only four attempted escapes from sunken submarines. Edward Young escaped from the sunken *Umpire* on the bed of the North Sea twelve miles off north Norfolk. It was only sixty feet down, but even at that shallow depth only half the crew got out and survived the ascent and the cold water. Sixteen died. Two out of thirty-two escaped from *P32*, one out of sixty-one from *Perseus* and eight out of fifty-three from *Stratagem*. In all cases some who escaped from the submarine failed to survive the ascent.

P32 sank in the deepest water. In July 1941 she had her bow blown off by a mine and the eight men forward of the control room were killed instantly or drowned. The boat plunged bow first to the bottom and David Abdy failed to raise it from the seabed where it lay at 210 feet, being in mined shallows close to Tripoli. With the jammed control room bulkhead door holding back the water, and a strong risk of chlorine gas, the crew retreated to the engine room to make their escape. Realising that there would be precious little air and time for twenty-four of them to get out once the compartment was flooded, Abdy asked for volunteers to go back to the control room. Apparently, only the coxswain and the outside ERA chose to go with him. All three of them reached the surface but the ERA died during the ascent. They waited for the engine room party to surface, but when nobody appeared they started to swim towards Tripoli, which was about five miles away. A Cant seaplane saw the two of them swimming, as well as two corpses in the water, and signalled a boat to come out from Tripoli to pick them up. The second corpse suggested that someone had made the ascent from the engine room, but died in the process.

The wreck has been dived and is, as Abdy described it, listing to port with the bow blown off. Both conning tower and engine room hatches are open, so it would seem that the escape attempt from the engine room was begun and – if the Italian pilot was right – somebody reached the surface dead. But overcrowding, panic, insufficient air or some accident apparently caused the others to die trapped in the submarine. Probably the level of carbon dioxide from so many men breathing in a small space caused them all to lose consciousness.

The element of chance played such a part in life in submarines that it is hardly surprising that their leader looked for one quality above all others in his men; as he told the young Australian survivor Ian McIntosh, 'you've got the one attribute that every submariner needs, you've got luck.' One wonders whether Max Horton discerned the lucky aura hanging over Gordon Selby.

Horton met Selby at the inquiry into the sinking of *Olympus*, while Selby was on survivor's leave in 1942. After a spell in a training submarine, Selby went back to the Mediterranean in *Sickle*. *Sickle* was sunk with all hands in June 1944, but Selby had just left to join *Storm*. In 1950 he was drafted away from *Truculent* a few weeks before she collided with a merchant ship in the Medway with the loss of sixty-four lives. He became coxswain to the officers' course, and it was in this capacity in 1951 that he was about to board *Affray* half an hour before she sailed when he collapsed on the jetty and was rushed to hospital. She sank in the Channel that night with the loss of all hands. 'Selby's luck' became proverbial. A grim joke went round that 'should you ever find yourself in a submarine that Selby had just left, it would be safest instantly to desert and accept the consequent court-martial'. Gordon Selby died in 2007 at the age of eighty-seven.

18

THE MOST IMPORTANT TARGET IN THE WAR AT SEA

William 'Tiny' Fell had served under Max Horton many times and had always survived, but he was still nervous as he was ushered into the admiral's office at Northways in March 1942. Horton said 'Hello Fell! What mischief have you been up to? Would you like to come back to submarines?'

Fell was dumbstruck with surprised delight but stammered out, 'Yes please, sir.'

'Well go away and build me a human torpedo ... I'm busy, but get on with the job right away, and report as soon as you've got something. Goodbye and good luck.'

Fortunately, George Roper, chief of staff, was able to explain to Fell what Horton meant by a human torpedo. He told Fell about the successful Italian attack on the British battleships in Alexandria harbour and explained that two of their miniature submersibles had been recovered and would be sent to *Dolphin*. Meanwhile there were photographs. Horton wanted a model as soon as possible. Fell arrived at *Dolphin* that night, his old friend the chief steward found him a plate of sandwiches, a beer and a cabin. Next day he learned that Slasher Sladen was inventing a diving suit and, as soon as he had designed and made two prototypes, would arrive to try them out.

Sladen had just returned in triumph from Norway. Ever since the start of the war the dangerous German capital ships had been the all-important principal target for the submarines attached to the Home Fleet. Of these German ships Churchill pronounced the *Tirpitz*, sister ship of the *Bismarck*, 'the most important target in the war at sea'. In January 1942 *Tirpitz*, *Scheer*, *Hipper* and *Prinz Eugen* were working up in the Baltic, while there were indications that *Scharnhorst* and *Gneisenau* were ready to leave Brest. The 'iron ring' of training submarines deployed off Brest in December had been so battered by the sea that most were now in dock. The Germans escaped through the channel, evading Colvin's *Sealion* and *H34*, the only boats that remained.

The move by *Prinz Eugen* and *Scheer* to Norway was not so successful. They ran through an ambush of four submarines and Sladen's *Trident* spotted them on the surface in the dark. Sladen meant to fire seven torpedoes but only four left the tubes. Nevertheless, he succeeded in hitting *Prinz Eugen*, disabling her steering gear and virtually blowing off her stern.

Hitler had ordered all of the German big ships to defend Norway against a feared attack, either from the Russians on land or the British by sea. Demoralised by the loss of *Bismarck* after a determined hunt by the Royal Navy in 1941, he was averse to raids into the Atlantic and would only allow attacks on Arctic convoys to Russia in favourable circumstances. The British were terrified of attacks by German capital ships on their convoys, but the only way to get at the German ships when they were hiding in port was with new and unexpected weapons.

Horton had always been an enthusiast for the concept of miniature submarines. When Cromwell Varley, a retired submariner, designed a thirty-ton, fifty-foot midget submarine at his yacht-building yard on the Hamble, Horton gave his project Admiralty support. Already, in 1940, he and 'Bertie' Herbert, another Great War submariner and midget enthusiast, were investigating ways of attacking German capital ships in Norwegian ports. The idea was that a minute submarine might be able to penetrate defences designed to defeat conventional submarines. The miniature submarines were designated X class craft. *X3* was launched from Varley's yard in March 1942. It was designed for three men and carried two huge mines, each containing two tons of amatol high explosive with a timer, that might be dropped on the seabed or attached to a target by a diver. Work began at once on *X4*.

Meanwhile, Tiny Fell and Slasher Sladen were at work in the Admiralty experimental tank at Haslar with gear attached to a wooden log and prototype rubberised suits. By early summer they had recruited thirty volunteers and were on their way to Scotland. Fell arrived at Euston to find his men having a party under the train. They had pulled the stationmaster in to join them when Horton arrived with a VIP. There was a sudden silence, and the VIP boarded the train looking furious. Some time later Horton joined in the game of rugby that the recruits were playing in their carriage in order to fight his way through to Fell. He said, 'You seem to have picked the right sort of types but I wish you would not let them attack the First Lord of the Admiralty when I am taking him to inspect the Submarine Flotillas in Scotland.'

Dick Cayley had been appointed to a new submarine, *P311*, one of the latest 'super-Ts', building at Barrow. He got as many of his old Utmosts as possible assigned to the new boat and Ben Skeates found himself with a draft to join her as petty officer telegraphist. After a short tour of the Barrow yard he was taken to the boat to meet the electricians and fitters installing the radio, asdic, radar and associated cupboards. Then he was given an address in Ayr Street, Barrow Island for lodgings. The house number wasn't clear so he knocked on the first door he came to. 'A young lady answered the door. She had obviously been cleaning the grate, or some such chore, as there was a large black smudge on her cheek. When she opened the door, looked up, and our eyes met, it felt as if I had been subjected to an electric shock.' The young lady, whose name was Muriel, called her mother, who told Skeates that one of her naval lodgers was leaving that night and Skeates could have the room. Muriel's father, a chief ERA, had died of pneumonia a few months earlier. She was seventeen and worked in a shoe shop.

That evening Skeates told her mother that he had fallen in love with Muriel. Muriel's mother said that he couldn't possibly know and that she had promised her husband that she wouldn't let Muriel marry until she was twenty-one. Skeates offered to move out but she wouldn't hear of that either. He tried and failed to talk to Muriel until 'on the Friday of the second weekend there, she completely surprised me by suggesting that I might like to accompany her to the Cinema.' They took a bus to the town, and after the film, walked back over the High Level Bridge to the Island. 'During our stroll I told her that I was sure that I loved her deeply, and would wait until she was ready to give me her answer about getting married. I was so relieved that she did not turn me down flat that I completely failed to notice that she was obviously not surprised to hear my proposal.' Over the next few weeks Skeates and Muriel went out frequently and in August she agreed to marry him the following April, after her eighteenth birthday. He was overjoyed, and wrote home to tell his family the good news. When the boat left for the Clyde to carry out her trials, they wrote by return; when it returned to Barrow, Skeates bade Muriel a fond farewell and sailed for Devonport.

To the Admiralty's surprise, the Arctic convoys remained unmolested by German heavy ships until the thirty-six ships of PQ17 sailed in July. The destroyer escort was commanded by Jackie Broome, who had been Tony Miers' captain in *Rainbow* in China. Judged too old to command a submarine, he had been given the destroyer HMS *Veteran* and had, characteristically, applied to join the Company of Veteran Motorists who made the ship a life member. During the Norwegian campaign in 1940 he adorned her bridge with a huge stuffed hippopotamus's head, acquired from Formby Golf Club during a spree ashore. With the destroyers were submarines; once in the Barents Sea, German domination of the air was such that the Admiralty would not risk the cruisers that covered the early part of the journey to Murmansk. Protection in the danger area was delegated to eleven British and eleven Russian submarines, despite the fact that in the constant daylight of July submarines were practically immobile and in permanent danger. There was a hope, though, that they might ambush the big game as it closed in for the kill.

The convoy fought its way through until news that the German capital ships were under way caused the Admiralty to intervene in something close to panic. Showing no faith in the submarine screen, they scattered the convoy, which was then massacred by U-boats and aircraft. Once dispersed, there was nothing the destroyers or submarines could do to protect it. Charles Oxborrow (who had been Cayley's first in *Utmost*) commanding *Unshaken* saw and reported the German heavy ships, but *Tirpitz*, *Scheer* and *Hipper* turned for home just out of sight of Baldy Hezlet's waiting *Trident* because the convoy had already scattered so they were no longer needed. Thus, the Admiralty order served both to destroy the convoy and to remove any chance the submarines might have had of destroying the *Tirpitz*.

It was a bad time at the Admiralty. Dudley Pound's wife died in July and his own health was collapsing. He resigned as First Sea Lord at the beginning of October 1942 and died later in the month.

The catastrophe only hardened the desire for a strike on the *Tirpitz* but it looked as if it would have to be a clandestine strike in harbour. The midget submarines were progressing slowly, but the first raw recruits for them reported to Blockhouse in late May, before taking conventional submarine courses at Blyth and Rothesay where more recruits joined them. In September Baldy Hezlet took charge of training. The charioteers, as the riders of human torpedoes were now known, were well in advance of the X-craft crews. They trained through the year, first in Loch Erisart

where the weather was dreadful, then in much better circumstances in Loch Corrie. There, the first real, live chariots were
delivered.

Each was about the same size as a standard torpedo and painted
green, but was fitted with two slots containing motorcycle-type
saddles on which the charioteers sat. The driver was positioned
behind a big windscreen, operating a joystick and controls. In
front of him was a detachable warhead containing 600 lb of
explosive. The second charioteer was responsible for cutting nets
and fixing the charge. The chariot had tanks and hydroplanes to
take it underwater and was powered by an electric battery which
propelled it, submerged, at about a knot and a half. Getting and
keeping a trim was a nightmare, even after practice.

The first operational plan was devised. A fishing boat commanded by Norwegian Leif Larsen was to deliver two chariots to
Trondheimfjord close to the Asenfjord anti-submarine net that
guarded *Tirpitz*'s anchorage. A trial attack took place in October
and late in the month the attempt was made. It was frustrated by
a violent storm which struck ten miles short of *Tirpitz*. During
the storm the chariots broke adrift from the hawsers securing
them to the boat. All but one of the attacking party escaped on
foot to Sweden.

Quickly, a new plan was substituted to use the chariots in the
Mediterranean, delivered to their target by submarine. One of
the three designated submarines was *P311*, so when Skeates
arrived at Devonport a special steel cylinder was fitted on the fore
casing. It looked like an extra large, external torpedo tube. *P311*'s
first trial dive with chariots attached failed miserably. She sank to
the bottom and Cayley couldn't get her back up no matter how
many tanks he blew. Fortunately they were in the dock with a
telephone line attached and after an emergency phone call a diver
from the surface attached an airline to save the crew from a
watery grave.

Skeates had been suffering from occasional severe headaches,
which affected his temper although he tried to ignore them. One

day, he had just completed a complicated service routine on the asdic oscillator. The goniometer contained some very delicate brass electrical slip-ring contacts. When one of the crew came in utterly soaked and slung his greatcoat over the asdic gear to drain, Skeates blew his top, creating quite a disturbance as he ejected both rating and coat. The following morning Dick Cayley asked what the trouble had been. He suggested that Skeates should get a specialist opinion on his headaches. The base doctor sent Skeates to Barrow Gurney Hospital, a purpose-built mental hospital taken over as a Royal Naval Hospital. Its psychiatric division was headed by the navy's consultant psychiatrist, who subsequently became a professor and author of the standard psychiatry textbook.

Skeates found himself locked in a ward and had all items that might enable him to commit suicide removed. The other inmates were severely traumatised servicemen. He was put through a long series of tests. One

involved a very primitive Encephalograph. The patient was laid out on a marble slab face up. Patches of hair were shaved away in small areas, and electrodes were attached to the cranium, via flexible cables. These in turn were connected to a frightening looking contraption, comprising electric generators, valves and various other gadgets. The whole caboodle finally terminated in three fine ink pens, travelling over a rotating drum, carrying a strip of paper from a roll. The pens produced different patterns when the patient was told to think of various events.

After each test, Skeates was asked to reveal as many of his thoughts as possible, and these were kept with the printout. He was asked about going home on leave, the railway station noises, the guard, the engine, what you saw from the window ... A favourite subject was, 'Think of the most frightening experience you have had during the war.'

He spent three months there, 'kept reasonably patient by the letters I received from Muriel', but it began to look as if he would never get out. Finally, in desperation, he wrote to Cayley. One afternoon, out of the blue, he was taken to see the surgeon captain. He assumed that it was the usual fortnightly interview to tell him that he still needed medical attention, but as he entered the office, he saw Commander Cayley standing there with his back to the window. Cayley told the senior medical officer that he would be responsible for Skeates's discharge, which the Barrow Gurney staff accepted in silence. The hospital held him for a further three weeks, however. By the time he reached HMS *Dolphin*, *P311* had left for the Mediterranean with chariots strapped to her back.

On 9 November Horton hauled down his flag as Admiral Submarines, having been appointed to succeed the gracious and courteous Sir Percy Noble in command of the Western Approaches and the war against Dönitz's U-boats. Horton was neither gracious nor courteous, and his staff soon became used to his being away all afternoon playing golf but requiring them to spend all night awake with him answering questions that began 'Where is . . . x?' followed by 'Why the hell not?' Claud Barry succeeded him at Northways, where the staff relaxed a little.

A strike on the *Tirpitz* now depended on X-craft, and crews for these were being recruited. *Unbeaten*'s first lieutenant, Godfrey Place, was approached by David Ingram, then captain of what was to become the 12th (midget) Flotilla, while the boat was being repaired. He asked Place, 'How would you like to join us and sink the *Tirpitz*?' Place said yes, and immediately took command of the second boat, *X4*, which had just been delivered.

When, in *Cyclops*, volunteers had been sought for 'Special Underwater Services', a bored Vernon Coles had put himself forward. 'Again, it was on a Sunday, just after tot time,' he recalled, 'so I volunteered.' That night he was on the train back to *Dolphin* in Gosport, and he was one of nine ERA submariners to appear before a selection committee under Arthur Hezlet. They spent five days in the tank getting used to being underwater. 'We used

to play ludo on the bottom of the tank on a big steel board and
the dice were about four or five inches square. We used to toss
them in a bucket and then go swimming after them to see what
score we had. On the last day's diving they put wooden blanks in
our goggles so we couldn't see anything.' They wore Sladen
diving suits. 'They are very loose and you get in through the
apron in the stomach. Then you bring the top down like a
jumper and seal the hole with a jubilee clip. The helmet was a
soft-top built into the suit. There were eye-pieces like those in
a gas mask. The oxygen supply came through a mouthpiece
which was strapped on to a harness on the back.'

After her refit, *Unbeaten* went on patrol in the Bay of Biscay
with Jack Casemore's new boat, *Sealion*. She was sunk by a radar-
fitted RAF Wellington while returning at night in her 'safe box' –
the area of sea which friendly aeroplanes were not supposed to
bomb. Most of *Unbeaten*'s crew had joined her recently, but a few
of Casemore's former shipmates were among those killed, including Micky Stanley the outside ERA's mate, young telegraphist
Frank Haddon and Chief ERA Laurance. Casemore almost suffered the same fate. *Sealion* was attacked by night off La Rochelle:

We were on the surface on a very dark and cloudy night, our
asdic rating had picked up H.E., which we were pretty sure
were U-Boats coming to go on patrol in the Atlantic. We had
six different targets and had started an attack on our nearest
one, although we were as yet unable to see her, when suddenly
a huge black object flew very low directly over us. We immediately grouped up and dived but the aircraft returned and
dropped depth charges on us. It lifted our transmission hatch
and flooded our transmission set but our receiver was OK. The
next morning, on receiving our messages from Rugby, one
was, '*Sealion* report your position'.

It was evidence that the RAF had claimed a sinking in *Sealion*'s
area.

In early December *Tuna* dropped ten marines for a raid in folbot canoes against merchant shipping in the Gironde. After damaging four ships, two marine commandos escaped to Spain. The other eight were shot. One of *Tuna*'s engineers was Dick Hodgson, who, having been called up, joined the navy because it offered better pay than the army. He was drafted to submarines, at which he was 'not very thrilled', and then to *Tuna*. The Gironde run was a pleasant break from dull and uncomfortable patrols in the North Atlantic, which Casemore in *Sealion* also hated. That winter 'about twelve of the crew who had newly joined us and had never been to sea before, were seasick. The whole of the patrol was about thirty-six days, it was terribly cold, and we were doing extra watches because of the seasick men. We were getting very wet on look out and the only way you could dry yourself and your underwear was to dry out in your hammock.'

At the end of December, *Sealion*'s captain Bobby Lambert was given a new boat being built in Birkenhead and he asked Casemore and a number of others to join him. Casemore and Harold Gill, his new run-ashore oppo, found digs near the Cammell Laird shipyard. They would visit *Surf* soon after nine in the morning, see how things were progressing and then go off to enjoy the delights of Liverpool. 'We were billeted ashore with an old couple. He was a milkman of about 45 and his wife was about 40. They were a lovely couple. She would worry about Gilly and I and all the terrible girls that were trying to seduce us and he would sometimes take us round the pubs to introduce us to all the dead certs.' Every morning they ate bacon, egg, fried bread and black pudding, 'lived like fighting cocks' and at night went 'out on the town in Liverpool or New Brighton. This wonderful life lasted until mid-February when *Surf* left to work up.'

After his escape from hospital Ben Skeates also found himself with a draft to a new S-class building at Birkenhead. The crew would not be needed for a few weeks, so he applied for leave and

married Muriel on 10 April. After a week's honeymoon in
Barrow, he sent her down to stay with his mother in Longwood
and returned to Gosport before travelling north to Birkenhead,
where he found digs for them both. In a quieter manner they also
enjoyed Liverpool.

Meanwhile the crews of the X-craft trained. It was clear that
no attack could be made at Trondheim during the summer
months of perpetual daylight. The winter months of perpetual
darkness and savage weather were out too, because the midget
submarines were unlikely to arrive at the target intact. The attack
had therefore been scheduled for spring 1943, but it became clear
that the boats would not be built in time for the crews to work
them up to operational readiness. Nor had they worked out how
to tow them to the target. Early in spring Barry had to tell
the Admiralty that the attack would have to be postponed until
the autumn. By April all six operational midgets had arrived. The
experimental chariots and X-craft formally became the 12th
Flotilla and Willie Banks was appointed captain, with P. Q.
Roberts as commander of the depot ship *Bonaventure*. The only
question now was whether somebody else might sink the *Tirpitz*
before the operation took place.

In March 1942 *Tuna*'s captain, Dick Raikes, had sighted the
German ship but she was too far away for an attack. His enemy
report enabled an air strike to be launched, but the *Tirpitz* escaped.
In February 1943 *Tuna* had accompanied the Norwegian *Uredd* on
an SOE operation. *Uredd* entered the fjord and then struck a mine.
'Raikes turned round, and went a distance from land, and sent a
signal I believe to the effect that he had lost his nerve.' Raikes
returned to general service and Desmond Martin took over *Tuna*.
Being sent home in disgrace by Shrimp Simpson had not ended
Martin's career; he came to *Tuna* from *Seadog*. Whatever the state
of Raikes's nerves, *Tuna* was efficient and 'happy' (Raikes himself
considered *Tuna* the happiest boat he ever served in), and Dick
Hodgson found Martin 'a wonderful replacement although obviously very highly strung'. Martin was conscientious to a fault.

In summer in northern waters and possibly in winter, all the time that we were surfaced on the billet for topping up batteries and high pressure air, our captain sat in the control room in semi-darkness. As most of my work was at the same time, I could only wonder what he was thinking about. We would surface in the summer for three to four hours, but surfacing as late as possible and diving as soon as possible. About quarter of an hour before surfacing, Lt. Martin would leave to put on warm and fairly water-proof clothing.

They were about to surface on 7 April when the asdic operator reported blowing noises ahead. The first lieutenant ordered a seaman to ring the fore ends to enquire whether the torpedo instructor was causing the air noises, but he wasn't. 'At this point, the Captain arrived in the control room, got onto the periscope and said, "It's the largest submarine I have ever seen".'

Dick Hodgson heard an engine start on the U-boat so clearly it could have been tied alongside. Martin was still talking, 'Estimated range 600 yards. I want to fire 5 torpedoes at one and a half second intervals.' It was routine to have the torpedoes at the ready when surfacing so there was no delay. Martin got a deflection angle from the fruit machine and fired. 'From the listening gear operator, "Torpedoes running", then two explosions after the right interval for the range, next from the listening gear, "Breaking up noises". After some minutes, we surfaced,' recalled Hodgson. 'I was told there were a pair of overalls hanging on the four-inch gun and then that there was a man swimming round in the water. Much effort was made to try and rescue him with a life-belt ... No luck, he went down after about 8 minutes. We charged our batteries, topped up our air, and carried on with the patrol, probably thinking "but for the grace of God ..."' This was the end of *U644*.

The X-craft crews trained near Port Bannatyne on the island of Bute. A hydropathic hotel there was christened Varbel, after Cromwell Varley and T.I.S. 'Tizzy' Bell, the original training

officer for X-craft, and a shooting lodge at the top of Loch
Striven called Ardtarig, which had belonged to Lord Geddes,
became the forward station, Varbel II. 'The beauty of this', said
Vernon Coles, 'was that in 1922, at the time of the "Geddes
Axe", Commander Varley and Commander Bell were among the
officers who were kicked out of the Royal Navy, so they had the
greatest delight in kicking out Lord Geddes in order to take over
his shooting lodge for the midget submarine base.'

The ERAs kept diving in cold water, overcoming fear. 'When
we went out in *X4* for the first time, it was just like sitting in an
aeroplane.' Coles resented the better treatment given to officers.
'Commander Bell did give us the privilege of having a bucket of
beer a night. We used to take a cup to our room and quaff it.
When we heard the list of ERAs who had been chosen to go, we
knew damn well in our mess that some of them wouldn't make
it. If you spoke with an Oxford accent or your father was an officer you were in, never mind whether you could use a spanner or
not.'

The officers were young, wild and well aware that they might
have a very short future. Godfrey Place married Althea, a second
officer in the WRNS, a few weeks before the *Tirpitz* raid. His
best man was Henty Henty-Creer, who was to command *X5*.
Henty-Creer had been a film cameraman until 1941, working on
The Thief of Baghdad and *49th Parallel*. Paddy Kearon, short,
cheerful, Irish, was in love with a French third officer WRNS at
Dundee called 'Touche'. When he went to see her on the last
leave he took a letter from the Australian Max Shean to his girlfriend Mary, who was also a Wren there. Bill Whittam was
deeply in love with a ravishing girl called Ruth.

The original plan was for the X-craft to attack the *Tirpitz*, the
Scharnhorst and the *Lützow*. All three ships were lying in inlets off
Altenfjord. Spitfires based in Russia took good reconnaissance
pictures. On the last practice run all six midgets 'escaped' undetected and confidence was high.

The six midgets, manned by 'passage crews' who would sail

them up to the operational area, were to be towed to Norway by six conventional submarines and released close to Altenfjord. Henty-Creer in *X5* was towed by *Thrasher*, while Cameron in *X6* was with *Truculent*; *Stubborn* towed Place's *X7*, *Seanymph* towed *X8*, *Syrtis* had *X9* and Ian McIntosh's *Sceptre* had *X10*. Coles was chosen for the passage crew on the *X10* until 'one chap chucked his hand in, and I got a job with an operational crew. Everybody was entitled to throw their hand in right up to the last minute. Three of them did that, so a few of us had to jump in immediately and take over ... ' Coles became ERA for *X9* and Max Shean joined the crew as diver. *X5*, *X6* and *X7* were to attack *Tirpitz*, *X8*'s target was *Lützow* and *X9* and *X10* were to sink *Scharnhorst*.

Thrasher and *Truculent* had five-inch nylon tow wires, but the rest had to make do with four-inch manilla rope. The weather became rough and *X8* broke away from *Seanymph* without the submarine noticing. She was found by *Stubborn*, while *Stubborn* was recovering *X7* whose tow had also parted. *X9* disappeared completely and Paddy Kearon was lost without trace, leaving Coles and Shean without a job. *X8* was badly damaged and had to be scuttled. Place switched with his passage crew early and spent the next day resting.

In the evening the weather cleared and they surfaced to charge their batteries. 'During supper we heard an alarming noise from up forward,' wrote Place. 'I went up on deck and saw a green and black German mine caught in our tow wire and bumping against the bow. One of the mine's horns had already broken so I quickly pushed it off with my foot while I freed its mooring wire from our tow. I breathed a sigh of relief as I watched the mine floating astern.'

The other boats switched crews that evening in better weather. Buster Brown, formerly in *Truant*, was now serving in *Truculent*, Donald Cameron's temporary home:

I was the sparker on duty in the wireless office, just before him and his crew of their X-craft went up *Truculent*'s conning tower

in order to board the X-craft by a rubber dingy ... Lt
Cameron came to check our record of GMT, that we kept in
the w/t office. I had a tiny, tiny bottle of rum I'd naughtily had
bottled from tot, which I offered him to have gulpers when he
was underneath the pocket battleship *Tirpitz*. He laughed and
gave me a wink and slipped it into his Ursula suit pocket
saying, 'Thanks, I will,' and off he went.

On the evening of 20 September the four remaining craft set
out just after dark. 'I wasn't particularly aware of the other three,'
recalled Place in *X7*, 'but I assumed they would be somewhere
nearby. The going was easy and all the warnings we'd had about
tides and the difficulty of finding where you were didn't seem to
apply at all.' Early next day the internal exhaust pipe split and the
fumes had to be extracted with the air compressor. They entered
Altenfjord and saw *Scharnhorst* at anchor. That evening he, first
lieutenant Bill Whittam and the diver, Lieutenant Bob Aitken,
cleaned the boat while the ERA, Bill Whitley, made rough
repairs to the exhaust and charged the batteries.

At 0100 they dived and headed for Kaafjord, where the *Tirpitz*
was lying. 'We found a gap in the anti-submarine nets at the
entrance and entered at a depth of forty feet. Just as we were
coming up to periscope depth to check our position, I caught
sight of a motor-boat and we were forced to dive again, still
uncertain where we were. After a reasonable pause I brought *X7*
up again, but we hit a torpedo net at thirty feet and stopped
dead.' Place could see that the net was a double thickness of six-
inch square mesh, 'nothing like the nets we used in England'.
They tried going slow astern but failed. It took an hour to break
through and they were now behind schedule.

At 0640 they saw the *Tirpitz* about a mile away. Place intended
to dive deep about five hundred yards from the target, pass under
the torpedo nets at seventy feet and lay the charges, then escape
under the nets. At 0705 he took *X7* down to seventy feet for the
attack, but hit a net. He tried again at ninety feet, but got really

stuck. 'When we finally came clear and rose up to the surface I saw that, somehow, we had got under the net and were now about thirty yards from the *Tirpitz*'s port beam. We actually broke surface at that point but no one spotted us, even when we gave the target's side a glancing blow.' So he slipped underneath the *Tirpitz* and dropped one charge forward and one aft. As they released the second mine at 0720 they heard the sound of fighting.

Don Cameron and John Lorimer in *X6* had had trouble with their periscope. Twice in Kaafjord they almost collided with other ships, and only a piece of sharp steering from Eddie Goddard saved them from hitting a buoy, but at 0705 they had followed a German boat through the gap in the submarine net. Then things began to go wrong. They ran aground and broke surface. German lookouts spotted 'a long, black submarine-like object' but thought it might be a porpoise. *X6* hit a rock and broke surface again. This time they were identified. Again they hit something and came up right underneath *Tirpitz*, into a hail of small arms fire and hand grenades. Cameron went down again, ordering the crew to destroy anything sensitive, and at 0715 released both charges under B turret. Then they swam to the surface and were picked up by a boat.

On the German battleship there was such panic that for once they didn't do the right thing. Immediately, action stations was sounded and the watertight doors closed, but it was not until twenty minutes after the captured submariners had been embarked that the order was issued to raise steam. The Englishmen sat in a wet huddle, plied generously with hot coffee and schnapps. Divers went over the side and an effort was made to winch the *Tirpitz* away from *X6*. The interrogation had just begun when the charges went off at 0812. They were all thrown off their feet by the force of the explosion. The Germans opened fire at random, killing many of their own men, and 'everybody seemed to be waving pistols and threatening us to find out the number of midgets on the job'.

Place knew that the timers on the charges had proved unreliable, so he was desperate to get back through the nets as quickly as possible. He spent three-quarters of an hour nosing around the bottom, but whereas it was possible to go underneath British protective nets, the German ones went right down to the seabed. He followed the bottom of the nets but couldn't find a way out. Finally, in desperation, he went over the top, then bottomed again. 'But at sixty feet we hit yet another net and while we were struggling to get free the explosion went up, a continuous roar that seemed to last whole minutes.' The explosion shook them free of the net but damaged X7, so Place took her down to the bottom again. 'The situation was not promising. Water was coming in through the hull glands, but none of the pumps worked and our HP bottles were empty. When we surfaced to check our position our night periscope was hit by enemy fire, and at this point I decided to abandon ship.'

The Germans were dropping depth charges so they decided to try a surface surrender. Bob Aitken heard him say 'Here goes the last of the Places' and open the fore-hatch. Place put his arm out and waved a white sweater. 'The firing stopped immediately so I climbed out on to the casing,' recalled Place, 'still waving the sweater. We had surfaced close to a battle practice target so I thought, "That's fine. I'll hold on to the practice target and bring the crew out."' Just then, X7 bumped into the target and its curved side forced the bows down, 'letting water into the hatch before I had time to close it. Unfortunately the boat hadn't got enough buoyancy to stay on the surface and she went down, leaving me standing on the practice target.'

Place was taken aboard the *Tirpitz*, very disappointed to find the ship still afloat, wearing a vest, armpit-length submarine long johns, and an enormous pair of magnificent leather seaboots he had borrowed from X7's passage captain. At 0843, just after Place went aboard, another X-craft was seen making off five hundred yards away outside the nets. *Tirpitz* opened fire and reckoned to have sunk it, and depth charges were dropped where it disappeared.

This was Henty-Creer's *X5*. Searches in Kaafjord failed to find the wreck but Henty-Creer and his crew didn't escape and were not captured. The damage to *Tirpitz* was so substantial that *X5* may also have dropped her charges under the ship.

The remaining three crewmen of *X7* found themselves on the bottom, calmly got out the DSEA equipment and started to flood the submarine. It took ages, then something fused and fumes filled the flooding compartments so they had to breathe their oxygen. By the time the pressure was right to leave, the oxygen had run out. Bob Aitken couldn't open the forward hatch. He pushed past Bill Whitley, realising he was dead, felt about in the darkness in an effort to find Whittam, then tried the hatch again. He passed out and came to on the surface, having opened the hatch and spread his apron out to slow his ascent. It was 1115.

Hudspeth's *X10* had suffered a series of breakdowns – they had no compass and the periscope motor had burned out – so he decided not to attack. In fact *Scharnhorst* was not where he expected her to be, so an attack would probably have failed in any case. On 27 October they made a rendezvous with *Stubborn*. On the way back a signal from Northways warned of an impending gale and ordered them to scuttle *X10* and return in the submarine.

After the attack all three of *Tirpitz*'s engines were out of action, together with the generator room, all lighting, all electrics and wireless telegraphy, the hydrophones, A and C turrets, the anti-aircraft control position, the range-finding gear and the port rudder. She limped away from the anchorage seven months later and was eventually sunk by air attack.

19

MARE NOSTRUM

Things had changed in the Mediterranean. In early November 1942 the Allies were able to deploy forty-three submarines, thirty-two of which were British and five American, in support of Operation Torch, the 'liberation' of French North Africa.

Submarines were positioned to protect the landings from enemy ships, but the Italians had no fuel and the French no desire to interfere. As it turned out, the most important role submarines played was in enabling the clandestine diplomacy that yielded bloodless victory. Bill Jewell in *Seraph* first landed the American general Mark Clark and his team for talks with the French, then picked up the French general Giraud from a fishing boat off Miramar after waiting for the Frenchman to evade his German tail. The landings on 8 November at Casablanca, Oran and Algiers were practically unopposed. Overwhelming force was something new. The skies were dominated by the Allies, with American planes arriving in huge numbers, and intelligence put them one jump ahead.

For submarines, advance warning of Axis movements derived from decoded radio messages was a crucial advantage. It enabled the flotilla captains to lay traps or to divert the nearest submarine to intercept convoys. This secret information was so valuable that it became an overriding imperative to prevent the enemy from learning that his messages were being read. A heartbreaking issue arose when Bletchley Park learned that certain ships returning from Libya were carrying British prisoners of war. The problem was that there was no plausible reason not to sink these ships. How were you supposed to know that a particular ship contained prisoners so that you could tell your submarines not to sink it? If POW ships consistently escaped and others didn't, the enemy might soon smell a rat. A decision was taken at War Cabinet level not to reveal to submarine commanders which ships were carrying prisoners of war in order to protect the Ultra secret.

An investigation in 1942 established two early cases in which ships carrying prisoners of war had been torpedoed: *Sebastiano Venier*, wrecked in December 1941 after a strike by Bertie Pizey's *Porpoise*, had 2000 POWs on board, of whom 1691 were rescued; and *Tembien*, sunk by David Wanklyn in February 1942 with 390 POWs drowned. Between June and mid-August ten ships carrying prisoners of war were sunk. In all these cases the 'Mediterranean authorities' had been told that the ships were transporting prisoners, but it appears that in accordance with instructions they gave no sign that they knew anything. The report continues with a list of nineteen voyages between August and November where the Mediterranean authorities were informed that prisoners of war were being carried. Despite far greater submarine aggression during that period, only two of the ships were sunk. This suggests a shift in policy.

The sinking of *Scillin* was, for a number of reasons, the worst single catastrophe of the kind. In that case, Shrimp Simpson had issued an order not to sink vessels returning from North Africa: 'Orders to submarines in their original dispositions stated that torpedoes were only to be fired at Africa bound merchant traffic but on this occasion Lieutenant Bromage quite rightly considered that this vessel, which appeared to be coming from Tripoli, might very well be bound for Tunis or Bizerta and decided to attack.' The submarine captain, desperately searching empty seas for targets, was always tempted.

John Bromage had sailed on 3 November in *Sahib*, along with Ben Bryant's *Safari* and Mike Lumby's *Saracen*, to form a patrol line to stop the enemy main fleet interfering with Operation Torch. After the landings Simpson was ordered to disperse and redeploy his submarines to prevent enemy supplies reaching Tunisian ports. He ordered Lumby to patrol between Kuriat and Kerkenah. On 13 November 'the Mediterranean authorities' were told *Scillin* carried prisoners, though it is not clear whether Simpson was told. On 14 November he ordered Bromage to move towards Al Khums and during the moonlit night the look-outs saw a darkened ship.

Built at Port Glasgow in 1903, *Scillin* was normally used for carrying coal and had capacity for 300 people at most. The Italians had packed 814 prisoners of war into her with 30 guards, plus naval gun crews. They had tried to get a thousand prisoners on, but the senior British medical officer protested and some 197 were turned back. The prisoners, captured at Knightsbridge, during the May retreat, or at Tobruk, had already been kept in poor conditions and 50 per cent of the men had dysentery. They were crammed into the hold, which was pitch dark and full of coal dust, with the hatches shut. Many were seasick. The ship wore no sign and displayed no flag. Off Cap Bon, *Sahib* put a shot across *Scillin*'s bows to instruct her to stop. She kept going, and signalled an SOS. Bromage hit the ship with nine shells but she still refused to stop. His patrol report continues:

1950 One torpedo was fired at a range of 750 yards which hit the engine room and the ship sank by the stern in under a minute.

The ship having sunk, P.212 proceeded to the scene of the sinking to see if there were any survivors. By the number of men in the water, it was obvious that she had well over her steaming complement onboard and as we came closer, men were heard shouting 'British Prisoners of War!' Steps were immediately taken to pick up the maximum number of survivors.

The first lieutenant, the engineer and five able seamen got sixty-one survivors on board, three with broken legs and two unconscious. Then they heard approaching engines and left. Bromage remarked that in response to a call from the casing, 'Are there any Englishmen in the water?' the reply from the last man came back, 'No, but there's a Scotsman.' They rescued twenty-six Britons and one South African and took them straight to Malta. The other survivors were Italian. Seven hundred and eighty-seven prisoners of war drowned and their fate was kept secret until 1996.

The best intelligence did not always produce results. One ship in particular, the German *Ankara*, led a charmed life. *Ankara* became the only merchant ship capable of embarking the huge Tiger tanks that were Rommel's most potent weapon in the later stages of the desert war. She was missed for the first time by Tony Collett in February 1941. In August she was one of the missed targets that caused Simpson to sack Joe Cowell from *Thrasher*. In December *Unbeaten* was lying in ambush for her thanks to information from Ultra, but the aircraft that gave him his excuse to attack caused the Italians to change the convoy's route. In July 1942 Tubby Linton missed her. In August Hugh Mackenzie was about to fire when an escort forced him deep.

Ankara now began to make regular runs with tanks for Rommel and became a prime target. In December she was one of several ships missed by Jack Howard's captain, Michael Faber, in *P48*. By now she was known as the 'ghost ship'. On 18 December Simpson directed Ian McGeoch into her path. She was escorted by four aircraft and two destroyers. When he fired six torpedoes McGeoch had the merchant and a destroyer in a continuous line and was quite certain that he had hit both. He sank the *Aviere* but *Ankara* saw his torpedoes and avoided them, capping this by avoiding Mike Lumby's shortly afterwards. Finally, warned by Ultra that she was approaching Cani Rocks, Simpson sent Lennox Napier in *Rorqual* to lay mines in her path. Next day *Ankara* hit one and finally sank, together with her load of tanks.

It was never easy to hit ships when weather and escorts and all kinds of unexpected mechanical problems might intervene. The danger from enemy aircraft decreased in 1943, but the danger from the vastly increased and inexperienced RAF and USAF presence was not inconsiderable. *Thrasher* had been damaged by a Swordfish dive-bomber in October 1942 close to Port Said. In January *Safari* was attacked by an American bomber off Algiers and another American very nearly sank *Sportsman*.

Italian and German escorts were now usually equipped with sonar and with better German depth charges. The short Palermo–Tunis route was exceptionally dangerous, constantly patrolled and protected by new minefields. Simpson found himself drained by 'the gnawing anxiety every hour of every day and night over how my men were standing up to the strain of operating within a narrow channel with barely sea room to manoeuvre, ceaseless enemy patrols overhead and convoys to attack which contained invariably twice the escorts than there were targets'. On 25 November the charming Basher Coombe was killed when the veteran *Utmost* was sunk by *Groppo*. On 12 December Alexander 'Black' Mackenzie's *P222* was sunk by *Fortunale* and on Christmas Day near Zembra Island Jack Howard's *P48* was sunk while attacking a Tunis-bound convoy by *Ardente* and *Ardito*.

Leslie Howard married Margaret on 13 January 1943. After a short honeymoon on leave Leslie took the train back to Scotland to rejoin *Torbay* and was there given the news that his brother Jack was missing, presumed dead. The shock had made his mother ill, so Leslie asked for permission to go back to Sheffield. *Torbay* was due to leave for the Mediterranean, so Lieutenant Clutterbuck refused. Nevertheless, the coxswain who had taken Leslie to see the captain offered to lend him the money to get to

Sheffield. The police visited his mother's house but left before he got there, so he was able to check that she was all right before returning to Scotland. To his horror, *Torbay* had left, but she had engine trouble and had to return to port, so Leslie went aboard. Clutterbuck fined him and took away his leave entitlement, but that hardly mattered where they were going. Margaret drew him a pin-up of herself to take with him.

Meanwhile the chariots and their three carrier submarines had arrived at Malta and were training together under Slasher Sladen's direction. Simpson was delighted to see his old stagers, John Wraith and 'the effervescent, roly-poly figure of Cayley', the latter of whom took out his mouth organ, played a few bars and said, 'Gosh, it's good to be back, sir.' But Simpson was troubled by their assignment, the dangerous nature of which soon became plain to all. In December Peter Forbes of *Trooper*, Wraith's boat, wrote in his diary, 'Our sister ship, *Traveller*, went on a trial for us in Taranto harbour to see if she could stay on the surface there for an hour as we have to do. It couldn't have been possible as she hasn't returned, given up for lost. This sort of thing dampens our spirits.'

Ironically, the big Italian ships then left Taranto after an American air raid on Naples and retired to La Spezia, with two cruisers at Maddalena. Simpson wanted to use the chariots as quickly as possible in order to free the submarines and their commanders for their proper duty. He decided La Spezia was too dangerous, and he and Sladen opted for attacks on the cruisers at Maddalena and merchant shipping at Palermo and Cagliari. Cagliari turned out to be empty, so *Thunderbolt* was redirected to join *Trooper* at Palermo.

Nobody liked the idea of using submarines to launch chariots, because it was extremely hazardous. The submarine had to surface in order to open the containers to release the chariots; these could then be floated off with the divers in control. Having to lie stopped with hatches open and half the crew on deck in dangerous waters was not an attractive prospect, but that was only the worst part. All the time it served as chariot transport, the risk to the submarine was massively increased. The chariot containers made its silhouette much bigger, made the submarine difficult to handle submerged and greatly reduced its seaworthiness on the surface. Dick Cayley took the toughest job and what Simpson considered the best two chariot crews. It was typical of Cayley to have volunteered but Simpson was anxious, though he thought the attack would succeed if Cayley got through the minefields.

Just before Christmas Ben Bryant came in to Malta to drop off some prisoners and spent an afternoon with Tubby Linton, his old friend from cadet days, who had managed to acquire some whisky and soda. Simpson saw Linton about this time and thought 'that he had reached that stage when he preferred the hazards of constant patrol to the fleshpots, or just the comforts of a harbour break, followed by the increasing wrench of that first day at sea. He needed rest but he didn't think so.'

Simpson did all he could to protect Dick Cayley, Johnny Wraith, Cecil Crouch and their crews. Tubby Linton reconnoitred Maddalena for Cayley and Tony Daniell was to pick up the charioteers in a different boat. The chariots would be abandoned. The same arrangements were made for the Palermo attack. Cayley reported safely through the minefield on 31 December, but was never heard from again. He is thought to have hit a mine approaching Maddalena. With him went ten charioteers and many of Skeates's mates, including John Meyerhuber. Muriel received a telegram telling her that Ben was missing. Fortunately she knew that he was not on board. 'Baldy' Hezlet, writing his history of the British submarine war years later, considered the loss of the 'exceptional' Cayley a 'disaster'.

The remaining five chariots were released outside Palermo. Lieutenant Dicky Greenland and Alex Ferrier from Crouch's *Thunderbolt* attached their charge to the new cruiser *Ulpio Traiano* and sank it. They placed limpet mines on various destroyers but unfortunately these were discovered and removed. Then they tried to escape, lost their way, realised they had missed the 0430 deadline when *Thunderbolt* was to leave, and eventually surrendered. Another crew attached their charge to the transport *Viminale* and then gave themselves up. One chariot failed to find the harbour and was rescued. The battery of another exploded and killed one crewman, while the other was captured. One diver drowned when his suit ripped, and his companion couldn't manage alone and was captured. An account written by charioteers concludes, 'It had been worth it,' but submariners were rather more subdued in their assessment. On 18 January 'Lucky' Crouch delivered a pair of chariots to Tripoli to prevent the sinking of a blockship across the harbour mouth by causing it to sink in a different position. The unfortunate charioteer watched the blockship go down before his eyes as he approached. He did succeed in causing the premature sinking of his secondary target, a smaller blockship, and the harbour mouth was sufficiently clear for small coasters to enter as soon as General Montgomery arrived on 23 January.

The death of Dick Cayley, his most adventurous, dependable and lovable commander, was the final straw for Simpson and he left Malta at the end of the month, admitting, 'in retrospect it is obvious that I was getting tired'. He left in the minelayer *Welshman*, which was torpedoed and sunk off Tobruk, though Simpson was among those rescued. He went on to command the convoy escort forces at Londonderry under Max Horton. George Phillips replaced him at the Lazaretto. Submarines were promptly withdrawn from the Palermo–Tunis route, leaving it to bombers.

After returning ill from the Far East, Bill King was posted to Malta to replace Bob Tanner in charge of operations. Conditions in Malta did not help King's health and Simpson sent him on to Beirut, where Philip Ruck-Keene determined to restore him to fitness with a regime of skiing and mountain-climbing. From January to May 1943 King directed operations at Beirut, but nearly all their boats had been sent to Algiers to support the campaign in Tunisia, so the working day was short and stress free. As soon as they could get away they were off into the mountains, taking with them Anita Leslie, tall, thin and willowy, who was running a newspaper for troops from an office in central Beirut. Ruck-Keene had a private villa nearer the mountains to which he invited King. From there they drove to the snowline and, armed with maps and compasses, struck out for the high valleys.

As spring advanced they got up at midnight so as to reach the snowline by 3 a.m. Anita would leave her hotel in ski boots, just as revelling officers came in from a night out. King never forgot seeing the dawn from the summit of Jebel Sanin. Up in the high mountains they skied and then walked down to where snow melted into carpets of wild flowers; having met their Arab drivers in a mountain village, they descended another 2000 feet through the scent of orange blossom that filled the rocky valleys of the foothills. When the snow melted they walked and camped. Before King, his health restored, left to command a new boat, Ruckers took him on a last expedition along the Adonis river. He had fallen in love.

While King and Ruck-Keene were mountaineering, their boats had joined Barney Fawkes's 8th Flotilla in Gibraltar. *Maidstone* moved to Algiers in December with a flotilla of S-boats. She retained her role as a depot where submarines destined for duty further east worked up, but now that the south of France had been taken over by the Germans and the fighting in Africa had moved west the focus of the Mediterranean war had shifted.

Algiers was not an easy place for British sailors, hated as they were by the French for the unprovoked attack in July 1940. Arthur Dickison found a very beautiful front with a squalid Arab town behind and attractive Arab villas climbing the hill behind that. The Safaris were shocked by the pestering persistence of Arabs, particularly the children. There was a curfew at 2200 because the French were hostile and the Arabs little friendlier and more deadly. The Germans had already cleared the shops of desirable goods, and the 8th Army and Americans fought constant running battles in the bars. John Gibson, arriving in June as navigator of *Taurus*, found the Aletti hotel was the key venue, where the women cost 5000 francs a night; there was a cabaret in a shabby café, and one could eat at the Oasis, but Algiers was a poor place for night life. Others, who were based at Algiers later, remembered the Sphinx, the Half-moon and the Black Cat as excellent venues. Crucial supplies of items like beer probably improved as the war receded.

The fighting in Tunisia was coming to a climax. In February Rommel made a fierce counter-attack which routed the inexperienced and over-confident Americans, driving them back to the Kasserine pass. But thanks to attacks by submarines and aircraft, Rommel was so seriously short of supplies that he couldn't follow up further, and had to return to the defensive. The 8th Army's advance was halted at the Mareth line south of Gabes until 28 March when the defences were outflanked.

February and March were highly successful months for the submarines, but bitter losses were sustained. On 27 February the lovable George Colvin was killed in *Tigris* off Capri by Germany's 'ace' submarine hunter Otto Pollmann in *UJ2210*. Colvin had sunk an Italian submarine in December and a big merchant in January and his death was mourned by his many friends. Pollmann was awarded the Iron Cross in May for sinking five boats, though *Tigris* was the only one he actually sank; the others all escaped. Then came the terrible news that Tubby Linton was missing. It was *Turbulent*'s last patrol before returning home. Tony Troup had left *Turbulent* in February for his perisher and there was a new first lieutenant. The day before Linton left Algiers he and Bryant had discussed their age – thirty-seven and feeling ancient. Linton was thought to have sunk 81,000 tons and wanted to reach 100,000. He told Barney Fawkes that he intended to use all his torpedoes on this last patrol.

At the time it was said that he died trying to attack the cruisers in Maddalena harbour. The truth was probably more prosaic, though what happened remains mysterious. On 1 March he sank *San Vincenzo* off Paola and then headed down to Milazzo, where on 3 March he sank two small sailing vessels with gunfire. Then he went north to fulfil Fawkes's instruction to patrol off the Bocca Piccola by Capri on 6 March. Fawkes probably knew from Ultra that a convoy of three merchant ships with five escorts was due to leave Naples for Tunis that day. At 0745 on 6 March *Ardito* saw a Ju 88 bomber dropping a depth charge 3000 metres ahead of her position. The Italian torpedo boat charged to the attack while instructing the convoy to alter course to port. At 1300 metres *Ardito* made contact with her S-Gerät and dropped depth charges. She lost contact at 0935. If *Turbulent* survived this attack she probably hit a mine off Corsica or Sardinia.

The third boat lost was Cecil Crouch's *Thunderbolt*. At 2210 on Friday 12 March he sank the 3100 ton merchant *Esterel* two miles north of Capo San Vito, north-west Sicily. The torpedo boat *Libra* hunted *Thunderbolt* and made sonar contact that night, carrying out seven depth-charge attacks. On Sunday morning the Italian corvette *Cicogna* obtained a contact and at 0734 spotted a periscope 2000 yards away. Just over an hour later the periscope appeared ten feet away. This indicates that Crouch was running blind without hydrophones. *Cicogna* threw depth charges at once, sped away and was turning for another attack when the explosion threw *Thunderbolt*'s stern out of the sea at an angle of ninety degrees, before she sank through a bubbling mass of air and oil. The Italians dropped two more depth charges, producing more air bubbles, oil and smoke. They waited for another hour and then left.

The loss of Linton, then Britain's leading ace, had a depressing effect throughout the Submarine Service. Claud Barry, Horton's successor as Admiral Submarines, flew over for a conference on the suitability of T-boats for Mediterranean service, but they stayed. Afterwards, he addressed the submariners – 'the usual tale of how proud he is of us, how the country is proud of us', wrote ERA Peter Forbes in his diary. 'But those three boats were with us at Malta and we used to know each other very well. Meeting at the ERAs' club ashore and having good times together and it makes you very morbid to think they will never return, our buddies.' Linton was awarded a posthumous VC. Captain Fawkes decided to order Bryant to go home to a staff job after he returned from his next patrol because he was the sole operational survivor of the old, fêted COs. Barklie Lakin took over *Safari*.

Preparations were under way for the invasion of Sicily. One of Bryant's last tasks was a beach reconnaissance of Castellammare in northern Sicily. Edward Stanley's *Unbending* and John Roxburgh's *United* landed combined operations pilotage parties (COPPs) who made surveys of the beaches that were actually used. One folbot of COPP1 that lost contact with *United* off Gela paddled seventy-five miles back to Malta, taking thirty-seven hours. Several fake recce missions were undertaken to confuse the enemy. *Safari* landed SBS men for one such deception in Sardinia, while Bill Jewell in *Seraph* launched 'the man who never was' with fake plans to confuse the enemy in 'Operation Mincemeat'.

At home it was the turn of the Porpoises to visit Buckingham Palace to collect awards. They had arrived at Portsmouth just before Christmas to be pestered by customs officers and the press, and in the evening the petty officers were invited to a huge and emotional party in the ward room. Joe Blamey, Joe Brighton, 'Ginger' Facer the signalman, George Backman the asdic operator and Stanley Hawkey were all awarded the DSM. Hawkey and his wife made the cover of *Defence*, the services' magazine.

Ian McGeoch's return to the Mediterranean in *Splendid* had started badly and he began to doubt himself again. On his first patrol he attacked two U-boats. The first was difficult, but as he stalked the second success seemed inevitable. 'If I miss this, I'm a Dutchman,' he said. From then on his crew referred to him as 'Jan'. But his aim improved. He quickly sank five substantial ships.

On 21 April McGeoch was lurking around the Bocca Piccola waiting for a target to appear when he first heard and then saw a destroyer. Unfortunately, the destroyer saw *Splendid*'s periscope. The German *Hermes* dropped fifteen '*Wabos*' or *Wasserbomben* in the first attack, five minutes after first sighting the periscope, damaging *Splendid*'s asdic set but without causing serious hurt. McGeoch took *Splendid* from 90 to 300 feet and tried to slip away. A second attack twelve minutes later was less accurate than the first. After another twenty minutes *Hermes* started a further attack but broke off because they detected *Splendid* changing course.

The fourth attack, just under an hour after the first detection, was fatal. The submarine's stern went down, the after hydroplanes jammed, water was coming in through the engine-room escape hatch and one of the motors caught fire. McGeoch watched the needle on the depth gauge go off the scale. They had just one chance before they were crushed to death. 'Blow all main ballast,' he ordered and Vic Davis opened the valves with lightning speed. McGeoch felt icy fear. The needle on the depth gauge flickered and began to move. 'Stand by to abandon ship.' The submarine rose faster and faster, leaped out of the water and levelled off with a thump. 'Abandon ship,' McGeoch ordered. The crew scrambled out of the hatches, those who couldn't swim clutching lifebelts, into a hail of machine-gun fire. The hydraulic power had failed so McGeoch and the first lieutenant opened the vents by hand to scuttle the boat. Then he slid over the side and struck out for Capri, an island he had always wanted to visit. The Germans rescued thirty of the forty-eight crew, hauling McGeoch out some time before he reached the shore. Three days later John Bromage and the crew of *Sahib* were captured in a similar manner.

On 7 May Tunis fell to the Allies and six days later the remaining Axis forces in North Africa surrendered. The T-class boats moved back to Beirut, where they found Philip Ruck-Keene's base delightful. There was a large suburban villa for officers and a beautiful barracks for the troops, with long, airy dormitories, mosquito-netted beds, and a huge restaurant staffed by French and Lebanese girls. The Greek base ship housed the crews of a varying number of operational submarines and there was one Yugoslavian boat.

Officers spent mornings on the boat, and after a John Collins or two in the mess, they enjoyed a siesta or swam from the Bain Militaire, a natural bay between rocks with bathing huts and diving boards. They found the French girls inspiring, tanned and lithe, but well chaperoned. The Wrens, white and well-covered, were more accessible. The mess was airy and the bar opened at six. Suitably primed, they then went on to one of various venues. At the Hotel Normandy over gin fizzes they might meet senior army officers and respectable French families. At the Hotel St George there was beer and dancing under the stars overlooking the sea with fellow officers and the glamour girls. Wrens liked the Carlton, where there was good food and wine and an orchestra playing for those who liked to dance.

John Gibson and his fellow officers from *Taurus* usually went to a little bar called the Dugout, where a Czech played the accordion and Russian girls on the bar stools displayed their legs. Getting home after the midnight curfew was always a problem. They would have a last swim and then go to the Café Mimosa, where bacon and eggs were served until dawn. 'The girls were trained in modesty and decorum. It was quite possible to go there several times before realising that sex was lifting a neat head from among the little tables.' Leave might be spent in a hotel in the mountains, walking and mountain climbing, drinking wine made by the monks at the monastery, eating goat steak and fruit.

In June Philip Ruck-Keene dragged himself away from the delights of Beirut to command HMS *Formidable*, Admiral Vian's flagship, and Hugo 'Tinsides' Ionides took over the 1st Flotilla.

Right up to the invasion of Sicily on 9/10 July submarines carried out beach reconnaissance, and seven boats acted as beacons to guide the troops to their beaches. First they laid buoys to mark the landing zones, then they dropped parties on the beaches, then they withdrew to the position where the landing craft should be released from the larger ships. Thirteen submarines screened the landings from attack by Italian ships, but the Italian battleships couldn't sail because they had no fuel. The Germans retreated to the corner of the island near the Strait of Messina and evacuated their troops in mid-August.

Unbroken came home at that time and Alastair Mars stood among wives, sweethearts and parents to greet her as she docked. He had returned in April with 'frayed nerves' and Bevis Andrew took over the boat. Mars joined his wife Ting at Aldeburgh in Suffolk for a long rest, followed by a staff job at Northways.

The tall Haig Haddow had also come home early to do his perisher course, after which he had a period in command of the lend-lease *P556* based at Gosport. He struck up a close friendship there with one of the Wren cipher officers named Jean Smithells, who scored for the *Dolphin* cricket team, captained by Hubert Marsham. Marsham was now commanding *Porpoise* during her refit in dock. Another friend was the 'extremely nice' Sam Porter, who was signals officer at *Dolphin* after bringing home *Tribune* and before taking over *Tudor*, building at Devonport. Mars came down to visit Haddow. Smithells found him 'a bit conceited'. On 7 September they all turned out to welcome home *Safari*. Ben Bryant came down to *Dolphin* to wave her in. Next day, laden with bananas, oranges, lemons and muscatel wine, Arthur Dickison caught the train to Gillingham, and was finally in the arms of his wife Clare.

Although Dickison had his mind on more pressing matters, 8 September 1943 was the day that Italy left the war, a few days after the Allies landed on the mainland. Ian McGeoch, in a POW hospital in the far north, took the opportunity to walk out of the building and, with a lot of help from various Italians, make his way on foot to the Swiss border. Soon afterwards, Charles Anscomb escaped from Maseratta Camp near Ancona. John Gibson of *Taurus* was in a monastery near his hotel in the Lebanese mountains when he was told that Italy had asked for an armistice. The priest who told him habitually avoided political comment, but he did open another bottle of wine.

In the last month of fighting two submarines were lost, Mike Lumby's *Saracen*, depth-charged and forced to surrender by Italian corvettes, and *Parthian*, the venerable 'Peanut', who disappeared in the Adriatic. She was probably mined, though an accident is not out of the question, especially with such an old and battered boat.

The Germans tried to hold on to Corsica, so S and U class boats congregated there. It became clear that holding the island would be too costly and they evacuated with significant losses inflicted by submarines. The process was completed by 3 October, the day that *Usurper* was sunk by *UJ2208*.

Some of the U class boats, including Aston Piper's *Unsparing* and the Polish *Sokol*, were sent to Beirut to replace six T class boats that had left for the Far East. *Sokol* sank two large ships during the last submarine patrol to be carried out in the Adriatic. That sea was taken over by destroyers and motor torpedo boats.

In the autumn the focus shifted to the Aegean, where British troops who had tried to seize various islands were in grave danger of losing them again. On 10 October Johnny Wraith's *Trooper* was lost, presumably to a mine, while trying to defend Leros. As one of the best of the veteran commanders, Wraith was another serious and depressing loss to the service. *Torbay* took *Trooper's* place off Leros, which was under heavy air attack, the Germans enjoying local air superiority. Robert Clutterbuck in *Torbay* sank an Ultra target on 16 October and survived a heavy counter-attack. More submarines attempted to defend Leros in late October and November but the Germans invaded in numerous, scattered tiny craft with air cover. The island surrendered on 15 November and the British army evacuated the Aegean, leaving submarines to hunt.

Sokol especially enjoyed hunting German soldiers in caiques. The Poles hated Germans to a degree that rather shocked their British colleagues. One section of *Sokol's* November patrol report is headed 'massacre of 200 Huns off Mirabella Bay', and it was a cold-blooded massacre. She blew up a schooner heavily laden with German troops using torpedoes because her gun had jammed, as it did almost every time it was fired (Bryant referred to his as an anti-Zeppelin gun). Then she torpedoed a second schooner full of troops, an E-boat and three caiques. On another occasion, surprisingly, she took two ragged and undernourished Germans prisoner. 'They were subjected to re-educational propaganda, i.e., listening to BBC German broadcast, shown illustrated magazines with the situation in Russia and bombing of Germany vividly portrayed. They were surprised by good treatment on board; when captured they could not believe their lives would be spared . . . '

The Malta flotilla resumed attacks in the Gulf of Genoa and the south of France, moving to the Italian base at Maddalena in December. The submarines were commanded by the fine first lieutenants of the earlier aces. The Ulsterman Robert Boyd of *Untiring* had served in *Utmost* under Dick Cayley. Mike 'Tubby' Crawford of *Unseen* had been first lieutenant of David Wanklyn's *Upholder*. Paul Chapman of *Upstart* was Tony Miers's lieutenant in *Torbay*. 'Flash' Gordon of *Universal* had served with Bill King. George Hunt in *Ultor* had been first lieutenant of Philip Francis's *Proteus*. He was the most successful of them all, scoring the most hits per torpedo of any commander and quickly amassing an impressive tonnage of sinkings.

In November 1943 David Ingram took over the 1st Flotilla from Ionides, who went out to command the 4th Flotilla at Trincomalee in Ceylon. At the Tehran conference of Allied leaders Churchill promised Stalin to send six submarines to the Black Sea. Fortunately for those who might have been concerned, it was diplomatically impossible to get the submarines through the Dardanelles and the Bosphorus. The Black Sea was very shallow, allowing submarines little opportunity to hide from hunters, and the many freshwater streams, producing water of varying density, made keeping trim and depth a nightmare there.

Torbay was still roaming the Aegean that November when Roderick Wilmot heard Robert Clutterbuck muttering, 'Well, I don't know . . . What the hell . . . I'll be buggered if I can make this out . . . ' Eventually, he said, 'Number one, come and see what you make of this.'

Wilmot looked through the periscope. He could see three masts and funnels, one belching black smoke, and a thin black rectangle. After a great deal of thought he tentatively suggested, 'You don't think it could be a floating dock, do you, sir, being towed?' Two hours later, from an attack position, it was clear that Wilmot was right. Clutterbuck crept in among the escorts, showing as little periscope as possible. There was a long debate about how deep the dock would be. He set six torpedoes to run at eight feet and fired. They dived off track and at 150 feet stopped to listen. Nothing. No explosion and no counter-attack. Clutterbuck rose to periscope depth and, to his astonishment, 'the entire cavalcade was bumbling along just as before'. It was only doing two knots, so the submarine was able to catch up submerged while Tim Williamson-Napier reloaded two torpedoes set to run at two feet in twenty minutes of hard sweat. This time when they fired and took evasive action there were two deafening explosions. When they looked, the tugs and escorts were all in full retreat and the dock had sunk – the first and only floating dock to be sunk at sea.

Two months later, and before they expected it *Torbay* was sent home for a refit at Chatham. Leslie Howard went to London to see Margaret and she found that he was thoroughly alarmed by the rockets that were being launched at the city. Jack Casemore also returned home in January 1944. He had grown very fed up with the lack of action in *Surf* and had reached the conclusion that the captain wasn't all that determined to get stuck in. Casemore insisted on going home to do a coxswain's course. Having passed, he was appointed to *P556* at *Dolphin*, which enabled him to go to Bromley each weekend to see his girlfriend Joan Surridge.

Attacks from Maddalena were directed at the route from Marseilles and Toulon to Livorno, which was used to supply the German armies in Italy. These finally began to fall back. On 4 June Rome was captured. Two days later the Allies invaded Normandy. At the end of June, after the Allies had pushed up to the Trasimeno line, Charles Anscomb, who had been on the run for some months, slipped through the German lines and escaped by boat across Lake Trasimene.

The base at Maddalena finally closed after the landings in southern France of August 1944 and at the same time the Germans began to pull out of the Aegean. The Mediterranean belonged to the Allies.

20

H FOR HELL

When the Japanese finally entered the war during the early hours (local time) of 8 December 1941, there was not a single British submarine in the Far East to perform the role for which the pre-war submariners had trained so hard. *Rover* was actually present at Singapore, but only fit to be towed to Batavia and then to Colombo as the bases fell behind her. There were eleven serviceable Dutch submarines at Surabaya in Java, seven of which came under British control, but sinkings very quickly reduced this number to three. On 17 December Sir Geoffrey Layton, commander-in-chief of the Eastern Fleet, told the Admiralty that his 'urgent need is submarines and yet more submarines'. So they sent off Bill King in *Trusty* and Hugh Haggard in *Truant*, carrying men and machines to form the nucleus of a new submarine base.

From Colombo in Ceylon, Layton sent King to Singapore because the garrison was begging for naval help. As King reached the Malacca Strait between Malaya and Sumatra a radio message told him that they were now in enemy hands. Singapore was a huge column of black smoke on the horizon. A cloud of Japanese aircraft flew by, ignoring *Trusty*, and they pushed on past feathery casurina trees to the naval base, where bombs were falling through the warm rain. King put on his last white uniform and went ashore to find the staff burning their intelligence records. *Trusty*'s allotted accommodation had just been bombed. The men sat waiting in pools of sweat, with the hatches shut so that bomb splashes could not flood them. In the ruins of the officers' club King found six bottles of Roederer 1929 with the chit book beside them. He and his officers drank the warm champagne, signed for it and dropped the book back in the rubble. King was about to explain to his men that there was nowhere to sleep when Admiral Jackie Spooner climbed down the hatch.

Spooner invited King to stay at his house, and to take whatever he wanted in Singapore for his men. The ERAs repaired an apparently irreparable lorry to carry the crew to the best remaining hotels and King dined in the Admiral's garden, after which Megan Spooner sang for them (the Admiral's wife was a celebrated soprano). For a fortnight they tried to refit and revictual in the disintegrating shambles that was Singapore. Finally, King set out with no orders and no information to try to find the enemy. He headed north and burned one ship carrying vehicles and petrol, using shells to save torpedoes. On 15 February the radio announced the surrender of Singapore. King found no target for torpedoes and eventually made for Surabaya to revictual. Haggard had just left on patrol, having been bombed in harbour and seen an American submarine sunk nearby. King lay in his air-conditioned bungalow fretting about what he could have done better.

At Surabaya in Dutch Java, *Trusty* herself was bombed and suffered damage to a fuel tank. King was about to get the boat repaired in dock when the news came that the Japanese were in Bali. He decided to race for Colombo on the surface. *Truant* followed a day later with a defective engine clutch. Chief engineer Jack Pook found that joints were corroding and he was getting leaks. At one time he had to take a liner and jacket out, put new joints between the liner and jacket, and then put it all back again. *Truant* was hunted by destroyers as she passed through the Strait but survived. King's heart leapt when his old friend Hugh Haggard arrived and assumed responsibility, being senior to him. On 1 April Haggard sank two large Japanese troop transports returning empty from the Andaman Islands. *Trusty* went into dock for repairs. On Easter Sunday she had come out and was loading torpedoes from the depot ship *Lucia* when the Japanese attacked Colombo harbour. The British had Ultra warning of the attack and the fleet was at sea, but *Trusty* had not made it out in time. A merchant ship near *Lucia* was hit repeatedly and sank. A bomb went straight through the mess deck of *Lucia* where *Trusty*'s off-duty crew were breakfasting. It flooded, and as the hatches were shut on the submariners inside they swam out through portholes and scuppers. Only one was killed. Signalman Gates blazed away at aircraft with *Trusty*'s Bren gun. It was the furthest west the Japanese got. They failed to repeat Pearl Harbor because the British had advanced warning of the attack, and they lost a significant number of planes.

The ancient Chinese river steamer *Wu Chang* arrived at Colombo. Although she was flat-bottomed and her pitched roof was rotting, she was built for the tropics and provided comfortable accommodation for the submariners in harbour. But on patrol, conditions were appalling. The heat and humidity were intense. The boats had a primitive cooling plant but it was appallingly noisy, used huge amounts of battery power and in the mess where it was situated it heated rather than cooled. Both boats switched it off. The crews lay on their bunks with sweat pouring off their near naked bodies.

Whenever possible, Haggard stopped for a swim, with a machine gunner on the bridge looking out for sharks, but the crews still suffered terribly from septic prickly heat sores. Haggard foresaw the time when he would be unable to take *Truant* to sea because the crew would be too sick. He reported this and was asked to forward readings of temperature and humidity in the boat. According to the reply he received, 'the figures you supply do not support life'. Then King went down with dengue fever and the spare officer took over *Trusty*. The doctors eventually insisted King should go home.

On the evening of 3 July Haggard chased a 3000 ton ship, missing her underneath with two torpedoes. Haggard engaged with the gun and hit her five times but discovered that the enemy was better armed than he had supposed. Smithy the 'bunting tosser' (as signalmen were known) had his backside peppered with shrapnel and other members of the crew were hurt. Haggard dived and was depth-charged but the enemy ship was sinking. That night *Truant* was repeatedly forced to dive by hunters. Haggard tried to surface the following afternoon to recharge the batteries but the boat was attacked by a plane.

In the evening, with the principal lookout wounded, *Truant* was surprised by a destroyer who switched on a searchlight and tried to ram her. She crash dived to 200 feet and received eleven depth charges dangerously close, shaking the boat and terrifying the crew. 'One charge forced open the battery in board ventilation flap and caused some flooding and not a little panic,' wrote Buster Brown afterwards.

Later in the night they were forced to dive by an aircraft which dropped a flare on them. After a few minutes at sixty feet *Truant* began to lose trim down at the bows. With both motors grouped up and full ahead, the hydroplanes hard-a-rise and two main ballast tanks blown, she still kept going down and hit the sandy bottom at 465 feet. It turned out that a vent had jammed open and let 2200 gallons of water into the tube space. This sort of accident was fatal in deeper water, but 465 feet was perilously close to the limit. 'The sandy nature of the sea bed held the boat fast and some difficulty was found in freeing her.' They tried everything. First 'main ballast, auxiliary and all trimming tanks', then the suicidal things – 'fresh water and oil fuel were discharged.' These were desperate measures in the middle of the Malacca Strait, but miraculously the boat finally rose and there was nobody around to see the oil.

They turned for home, but on the morning of Saturday 11

July the port main diesel failed. The starboard engine had broken down some days earlier, so now the boat was brought to a halt some 1200 miles from base. 'The port engine crankshaft bearing had overheated and "run out", the crankshaft had dropped out of line and bent No. 8 con rod.' The weather had cut up rough, so in order to keep the boat steady Pook and his mates had to work on the engine eighty feet below the surface. After twenty-one hours dived in intense heat and decreasing air quality, Pook succeeded in making the engine work. They went into dock at Colombo four days later.

Pook and his shipmates lived in 'native straw huts with mos-quito net around our rough wooden bed, terrible living conditions'. They suffered one casualty. Leading stoker Ginger Ellis 'had his birthday and through having too many tots of rum, went up to the casing of the boat in dry dock to sleep it off and rolled off the boat in his sleep and fell to the bottom of the dock onto some steel and was killed through the fall.' He was buried in his overalls in a plain wooden box. At the beginning of September, after repair, *Truant* headed for Britain, finally arriv-ing at Dunoon in late evening on 29 November 1943. No heroes' welcome home had been laid on. 'The sentry on the next boat shouted, "Did you get anything?"' said Pook. 'And that after two and a quarter years and 80,000 miles was just about the end.'

Trusty remained on patrol until April 1943 with three Dutch boats, although by October, when five T class boats arrived as reinforcements, only *O24* was operational. This flotilla, based on *Adamant* at Colombo, was to patrol the Malacca Strait in order to disrupt Japanese supplies to their army in Burma and their gar-risons of the Andaman and Nicobar islands. The Japanese had started the war with six million tons of merchant shipping; by September 1943 a hundred Pacific-based US submarines had sunk nearly 2¼ million tons. The Americans didn't really want British submarines interfering in the Pacific, which they con-sidered their domain, but very little Japanese shipping came through the Malacca Strait so they allowed the British to patrol there. It was a dreary thousand miles from Ceylon to the patrol area and there often wasn't much to be found during their brief patrol time before they had to turn back. However, the Japanese had a submarine base at Penang, and Ultra sometimes revealed the time of arrival of enemy submarines so that British ones could be placed in ambush.

Tally Ho was commanded by Leslie Bennington, about half of whose crew had followed him from *Porpoise*. 'Steady' Steadman was first lieutenant and 'Snoopy' Thurlow third officer, both former Porpoises in their early twenties and originally RNR. Steadman was a native of Alexandria and a Muslim. Thurlow had fallen in love with a white Russian aristocrat named Ludmilla in Alexandria, had courted her between patrols and married her in 1942. Ginger Ridley was coxswain, Ginger Facer signalman, George Backman was on the asdic, Joe Brighton was in charge of torpedoes, Taff Hughes was an ERA and Stanley Hawkey was on the gun. Many of the rest came from *Proteus*, and this highly experienced team made *Tally Ho* a crack boat. Bennington struck quickly, sinking a tanker on 10 November.

Mervyn Wingfield had brought *Taurus* from the Mediterranean with John Gibson as one of his officers. Wingfield also scored an early success, sinking the Japanese submarine *I34* off Penang in a snap attack on 11 November, despite running a temperature of 102 degrees. The following night *Taurus* was hunted by a chaser from Penang and in the early morning the enemy nearly got them with depth charges, breaking the Sperry compass and depth gauges. They were in trouble. Wingfield had always loved the surprise gun attack and had won the flotilla gunnery cup as first lieutenant of *Odin* in China. He had his gun crew practising so frequently that they nicknamed him Dillinger after the Chicago gangster. Now he decided to surface and stake everything on a shoot-out. With the four-inch trained on an asdic bearing they surfaced and opened fire. Immediately, Starbuck the gunlayer scored a lucky hit close to the enemy gun. Its crew scattered and the boat veered away. A second shot hit the stern and the chaser caught fire. It turned back and charged straight at them but Starbuck got a third hit on the bridge, killing the officers, then hit amidships, hit the gun, hit the engine room. The chaser was dead in the water, but a seaplane was approaching. *Taurus* hid underwater while the engineers made repairs, listening to the sound of distant depth charges. Then they slipped away in the darkness.

On 3 December 1943 the flotilla moved to Trincomalee. *Taurus* was first to arrive, followed by *Tactician*. Iain Nethercott remembered *Tactician's* captain, Tony Collett, as 'a big black hairy man', a cribbage addict who organised great knockout crib tournaments and might be found anywhere in the boat playing cards. Nethercott himself had a DSM for staying on the anti-aircraft gun while his destroyer sank under him at Dunkirk. Posted to a lend-lease destroyer, he grew bored with convoy duty and volunteered for submarines. He was still a baby-faced boy, but had seen more fighting than most pensioners. The Tacticians had enjoyed some success in the Mediterranean before the move to the Far East and already considered themselves veterans.

They had a rough first patrol in the monsoon season, ill with heat, electrics fusing in the wet, and came in bedraggled. Approaching the brand new *Adamant* was 'like seeing a bit of the old navy', recalled Nethercott. *Tactician* was painted deep green but 'covered in rust with bits hanging off'. When they went aboard *Adamant* the men were stripped to the waist, sweaty, oily and grimy, Nethercott wearing only a pair of 'Afrika Korps shorts pinched in Algiers'. Their bare feet and dirty sandals left a trail of greasy footprints across the perfect white deck. Collett himself, who later took to wearing a sarong on patrol, had merely borrowed a khaki shirt and a sub-lieutenant stopped him to give him a 'full broadside about their state'. Collett put his cap on 'with the old scrambled egg round it' and tore the callow youth to shreds. From then on submariners 'deliberately paddled in muck before they went inboard'.

The Tacticians went off to rest camp. When they came back the whole flotilla was there and the well deck was completely covered with oily engine parts. 'We absolutely wrecked this ship,' recalled Nethercott with relish. Hard-bitten veteran submariners had nothing but disdain for the pre-war niceties that some naval regulars, usually those who had seen little fighting, still sought to preserve.

Trincomalee was a natural harbour, surrounded by steamy jungle. It was merely an anchorage, though, with practically no facilities. To the south was a native village, to the north a newly built concrete naval base that amounted to very little beyond a canteen with severely rationed beer and an officers' club. Trinco soon had a reputation as a tropical version of the grimly desolate Scapa Flow.

But for those who could be happy without bright lights or beer it was not too bad, and for a few months the submariners had it almost to themselves. Gibson of *Taurus* swam and fished, using depth charges to obtain quick results when a meal was needed. The flotilla lieutenants went off in their sailing dinghy to pick up the Wren cipher officers, who had a small house there. In the afternoons they swam and in the evenings they partied at a bungalow owned by a friend from the Cochin Labour Corps, dancing and swimming through the hot nights. After every patrol half the crew went to a rest camp for ten days, high in the hills at Diyatelawa. It was a twelve-hour trip zigzagging upwards in a lorry. There were wooden bungalows with a breathtakingly cold shower and a swimming pool. The walking was pleasant, and you could admire the elephants, but there was little else to do.

In two outstanding patrols early in 1944 *Tally Ho* sank a light cruiser, an army cargo ship and an ex-Italian U-boat. With all the major targets Ultra provided a destination, arrival time and speed that gave British captains in ambush a significant advantage. Problems came with the unexpected. Area H was the patrol area furthest down the Malacca Strait and nearest to Singapore, where there was likely to be most trouble and from where it was hardest to get out. At that point, off Port Swettenham, a shallow sandbank called the One Fathom Bank divided the Strait and forced traffic to pass down a narrow channel. The One Fathom Bank was marked by a pagoda-shaped lighthouse manned by a lookout. Aircraft patrolled frequently; moreover, it was extremely hot, with little depth and little room for manoeuvre. For that reason it was known as 'H for Hell'.

On 24 February Bennington was sleeping on the bridge and heading south in the shallow water near the One Fathom Bank when a torpedo boat emerged out of fog. She was too close to ram, though she tried, simultaneously blazing away with her guns which were too close to train and dropping depth charges wildly. On the second pass, Bennington just avoided being rammed but the Japanese boat's propeller caught *Tally Ho*, ripping jagged gashes through the light plating of the port main ballast tanks, while *Tally Ho*'s own propeller cut a hole in the Japanese boat's hull. Bennington dived to escape, only to discover to his immense relief that the depth charges dropped by the Japanese had so damaged their own steering that they couldn't pursue. *Tally Ho* struggled home, with Joe Brighton emptying torpedo tubes to keep the leaking bows up.

Early in 1944 the Eastern Fleet was reconstituted and based at Trincomalee, which became much more crowded. The depth charges that were now dropped at the harbour entrance to discourage the enemy made swimming in the bay unpleasant, and officers like Edward Young, whose boat *Storm* was one of six newly arrived submarines, went swimming and surfing from beaches further up the coast.

Many submarines now had very young officers and very inexperienced crews, usually stiffened by a few old hands in key jobs. Young was lucky to have a very good engineer officer, an experienced outside ERA in Dick Hodgson from *Tuna*, and a very good coxswain in Gordon Selby from *Upholder*. Other submarines were not so lucky. Hodgson found that *Stonehenge*'s outside ERA had little idea of what his job entailed and when Hodgson visited the boat he noted that the high-pressure gauge didn't work. He predicted in the mess that *Stonehenge* wouldn't last many patrols, and in fact she was the first British boat to be lost in the Far East. Lost with no explanation, she probably hit a mine, but an accident could not be discounted.

Back in Britain, Bill King was given a new submarine. *Telemachus* had a chief ERA who had only ever worked on railway engines. Fortunately, King's engineer officer was an expert, able to train his subordinates in how submarines worked. Ben Bryant was in charge of the training flotilla now, and King found his exacting standards helpful. Bryant believed in preparing for combat conditions. It was now standard practice to drop at least one depth charge within two hundred yards of a training submarine so that the crew was not surprised and stupefied by the 'nerve-shattering noise' when they heard it in actual combat. King himself found 'a curious feeling of restfulness filled me, the restfulness of being sure you can play a game fairly well. Hardly anyone else granted my amount of practice had survived.' In March 1944 *Telemachus* set off for Ceylon. At Suez King tried to contact Anita Leslie but discovered she had left for Italy with the Red Cross. When he reached Trincomalee he found two flotillas there, the 4th of T class under the kindly, grey-haired Hugo Ionides in *Adamant*, and the 8th of S class based on *Maidstone* and now under Captain Lancelot Shadwell, assisted first by Bertie Pizey and then by Tony Miers.

With a diminishing number of targets and an increasing number of submarines, many were employed dropping agents, observers and commandos in the jungle, supplying them and picking them up again. These were always extremely risky operations, chiefly for the landing party, but a submarine was very vulnerable in shallow water and it did not take much accurate shooting to damage the pressure hull. When *Tactician* went on one operation to recover spies, her crew found themselves in a trap. The spies had been caught, the men *Tactician* launched in rubber boats were shot up and they tortured the survivor. From his place on the gun Nethercott could hear him screaming. This was a more menacing type of war, and you never knew whether a rendezvous might have been compromised.

In April the Allies mounted their first big attack in the area, an air strike from the carriers *Illustrious* and *Saratoga* on oil installations at Sabang. *Tactician* was diverted from patrol to act as an air sea rescue boat. When one American plane was shot down, the lookouts took a fix and *Tactician* raced to the spot. Coxswain Henry McNally jumped in with a rope round him to pull the American aboard. It turned out that the man they had rescued, Lieutenant Dale Klahn, was the son of the aircraft carrier's second-in-command and they were richly rewarded with Lucky Strikes and American hospitality.

Young took *Storm* on an operation to land a Sumatran Cambridge student called Monsenor on the island of Pulo Weh before a second air attack on Sabang. They dropped him off without incident, but during the day when they were due to pick him up Young, watching through the periscope, saw what he thought might be the smoke signal arranged to indicate that Monsenor was in trouble. That night they received the right signal, but from the wrong place, and the major in charge of the operation decided not to make the pick-up. The second night they got the wrong signal from the right place. The major was suspicious and frightened but decided this time to go in.

Young watched him until he lost sight of the boat against the land. Suddenly four machine guns and a larger gun opened up from the shore. Young could see the dinghy four hundred yards away and one of the machine guns had switched its aim on to it. Young himself was now extremely frightened. How long should he wait? Would submarine chasers be part of the ambush they had run into? Against his better judgement he waited for the major, got him aboard and raced for safety.

Shortly afterwards Ruari McLean called on his old friend to ask him to drop him off for a beach reconnaissance. Young refused. He had had enough of special operations.

In March and May stories broke about atrocities committed by Tetsunosuke Ariizumi 'the Butcher', commander of the submarine *I8*, who tortured, humiliated and mutilated the crews of a

Dutch and then an American ship. When submariners got word of a U-boat as a potential target from now on, they hoped it was his.

Around June Hugh Mackenzie arrived in *Tantalus*, with Tono Kidd, formerly of *Torbay*, as his engineer officer. He reached Ceylon at about the same time as Bill King and in one of their earlier patrols they elected to take area H together, the area which had become known colloquially as H for Hell. The two commanders spun a coin for who should take One Fathom Bank and King won. On 17 July a submarine passed Mackenzie too far away for a shot and then, heading fast for home down the channel, approached King. He fired from within a mile as the submarine drew level, but *Telemachus* lost trim as the torpedoes left and surfaced like a whale just at the moment that one of them hit. Nobody at base had told the first lieutenant that her latest torpedoes had heavier heads than normal. It wasn't until he got back to base that King received confirmation (from Ultra) that he had sunk the submarine. To his disappointment, she wasn't the Butcher's *I8*.

Five more boats had arrived in June. In August Tony Troup's *Strongbow* appeared, with Joe Blamey as warrant engineer. Troup was a mere twenty-two (though he had learned his trade as number one of *Turbulent* under Tubby Linton) and the other officers were even younger. Blamey was almost twice their age. They found themselves attached to a new depot ship, *Wolfe*, a converted Canadian liner, as part of Jacky Slaughter's new 2nd Flotilla. Huge, ugly and uncompromisingly blunt, Slaughter terrified many young officers, being expressively intolerant of inefficiency, but Blamey reckoned that 'behind that rugged exterior ... lay if not a heart of gold, at least a kindly streak.' As youngsters the two had served together in 1925 in the battleship *Valiant* before joining submarines simultaneously the following year. Slaughter's characteristic greeting, 'Hello Joe you old bastard,' raised young Troup's eyebrows.

The new boats had modern kit. There was better air conditioning, although it was still so noisy and power hungry that it had to be switched off during a hunt. The boats were fitted with surface radar to detect enemy ships and planes. Though primitive and somewhat unreliable, usually having to be turned by hand, it was sometimes very useful. Alastair Mars, who brought *Thule* to the Far East, distrusted his radar and was unwilling to use it; there was also a fear, justified as it turned out, that the Japanese were able to detect radar transmissions.

A more universally welcome device was the bathythermograph, which measured sea temperature and could detect layers of cool water beneath layers of warm water. Layers had been utilised throughout the war as a way of baffling sonar impulses, enabling submarines to hide from potential attackers, but they were common in these waters and the new machine helped to detect them.

For some time the British had been hoping to operate in the China Sea, where the Americans had been locating many more targets than were to be found in the Malacca Strait. The Americans had now agreed to let them operate in the shallows, for which their own boats were unsuitable. In the open ocean the American boats were larger, faster and better equipped. To the irritation of Admiral Claud Barry, Tony Miers (who was American liaison officer before he joined *Maidstone*) had pointed this out publicly.

In August 1944 the 8th Flotilla with *Maidstone* was ordered to Australia, arriving at Fremantle on 4 September. *Telemachus*, *Storm* and *Sturdy* were among the boats that went with her. Ben Skeates, who had gone down with pleurisy and left *Stratagem*'s crew, travelled as a convalescent in *Maidstone*. On the way he undertook the traditional ordeal of crossing the line. A large canvas bath full of seawater appeared on the well deck of the *Maidstone*, and one by one the uninitiated, including Skeates, were seated above it. King Neptune, wearing a crown and carrying a trident, questioned them closely about squid, shrimps and seahorses and read out, from an elaborate scroll, the rules of his kingdom. Skeates was 'shaved with a mass of soap suds and a large wooden razor, given a large flour dough pill to swallow, and unceremoniously dumped in the water backwards'.

He quite enjoyed that, but arrival at Fremantle was not so good. 'The Yanks were already there, with their inane jokes about our toy submarines. Theirs were like battleships, with deep freezers full of chicken and ice cream. Little else except a band that could only play Old Glory, and did so incessantly each time one of their submarines came in, flying a big Japanese Flag for every Kayak they had seen.'

Baldy Hezlet had arrived in Ceylon in July in *Trenchant*, another new boat. In September he was sent to land commandos to blow up a bridge in Sumatra, a task in which they succeeded at the second attempt. He then had to lay magnetic mines in Aru Bay before patrolling off the Aroa Islands, a billet that rarely yielded decent targets. Hezlet was getting bored when he received an exciting signal from Ionides to be in position off the north entrance to Penang by dawn on 23 September. Everyone knew Penang was a U-boat base.

Getting there took all day. After dark they picked up the island by radar and confirmed their correct position by radar and soundings. It was very dark, pouring with rain, and there was a heavy swell. In the morning the watchkeeper was still struggling with the swell and Hezlet went in to take the periscope while his officer dealt with the trim. He saw the U-boat the moment he raised the periscope.

U859, laden with mercury, had travelled several thousand miles from Europe and the only problem on the way had been a slight brush with an aeroplane. She had arrived bang on schedule to rendezvous with her escort into Penang. The escort was late.

In an attack that lasted only ten minutes and in which he impressed his crew with his speedy and effective decisions, Hezlet fired a stern salvo as he turned at a range of only 650 yards. Then he picked up prisoners who had escaped from the torpedo compartment after the submarine hit the bottom. One of them was a very lucky engineering officer with diarrhoea who had been visiting the heads when the torpedo exploded under the ward room. Afterwards, Hezlet made a short trip to Colombo because the commander-in-chief wanted to see him after the success with *U859*. There he 'met a Wren Second Officer from Ireland, who, I now realise, had been involved in the very secret side of the operation against *U859*. She had, in fact, been instrumental in putting us on to the target. She used her Irish connections to meet me and, so tight was the security, that no word of the real reason was even suggested.' The reason was that the Irish Wren wanted to meet the man who had executed the operation that she, laboriously and secretly, had set up.

Next month, in pouring rain through which nothing could be seen from the periscope, George Backman on *Tally Ho*'s asdic announced that he was getting echoes from mines 500 yards on the starboard bow. The tide was pulling them towards what Bennington suddenly realised must be *Trenchant*'s minefield in the shallows off Aru Bay. In the distance Ben could see a submarine chaser, and before long the Japanese boat had made sonar contact and was coming in to attack. The water was so shallow and constricted that Bennington decided to fight it out on the surface. The gun crew were readied and the bearing and range set; then they shot up, firing on the right line but long. The new gunnery officer, Dennis Adams, yelled corrections. Behind Bennington, the Oerlikon gun chattered and promptly jammed. A machine gun on the chaser opened up accurately, punching holes through the bridge breastwork. Adams suddenly spun away and fell. The gun crew paused. Bennington yelled at them. They found the target. A low-flying seaplane appeared, and Ginger Facer brought up a Lewis gun just in time to blaze away at it. The plane was banking low over the sub chaser just as the gunners hit its depth charges. Bennington gave the order to dive but Facer, grinning, saw the plane crash before he left the bridge. Coxswain Ginger Ridley did his best for Adams and for an injured gunner, but Adams died. Soon after, *Tally Ho* was ordered home.

Stratagem, commanded by 'Pat' Pelly, Tony Troup's cousin, and with Fred Raynor, an old mate of Joe Blamey's, as chief engineer, sailed from Trincomalee on 10 November 1944 to patrol off Malacca, further toward Singapore than any submarine had yet patrolled, beyond even H for Hell. They saw nothing at all for six days until they were quite close to Malacca, when they saw many junks of different sizes and a Japanese seaplane on patrol. After two days off Malacca they went further south and saw smoke, which turned out to come from five Japanese ships, escorted by three small destroyers. Pelly fired three torpedoes with 'impact only' pistols and hit *Nichinan Maru*, a 2000 ton cargo ship, in the bows. The destroyers made a wild and ineffective counter-attack, while Pelly retreated to watch. As the ship was still afloat he fired his stern tube at 1000 yards and it split the target in two. In the dark they went north and then returned to Malacca.

Don Douglas, the 21-year-old torpedo officer, woke suddenly to the order 'Diving stations' over the Tannoy. He rushed to his station forward and immediately heard 'Shut off for depth-charging'. The torpedomen sealed the compartment, reported it shut off and waited in nervous silence for four minutes until 'the thrash of the Japanese destroyer could be heard very loud as she passed overhead'. Almost immediately a depth charge exploded extremely close and underneath, lifting the stern and smacking the bow hard against the bottom. All but a couple of emergency lights went out, and five seconds later a second charge exploded right amidships and plunged them into darkness. Douglas flashed his torch at water flooding through the door at the after end of the torpedo stowage compartment. He ordered the watertight doors shut, making sure the three ratings in the tube space were out before the door was sealed. The water was flooding in fast now. It was above the deck boards in the stowage compartment and over their knees. The ratings couldn't shut the after door because there were stores where they needed to stand in order to push the water back.

Arthur Westwood came forward from the control room and said that the captain had tried to blow main ballast but couldn't shift the boat. With incredible speed, Douglas was keeping above water by clinging to a hammock slung from the deckhead. The cook, Bob Weatherhead, talked cheerily about a cake he had made, keeping some of the men from panic. Then he got them singing, but Douglas ordered them to stop and put on DSEA sets. The first he found had a defective valve on the oxygen bottle. The second was working, so he put it over the head of 'one of the older ratings who was panicking and in tears due to the pressure effect on his eyes'. The pressure in the boat was immense and the air full of chlorine. They were all drenched with fuel oil. They could hear air escaping through the hull forward and the water was still rising fast.

Sid Gibbs was in the escape hatch trying to pull back the clips. He shouted to Douglas that he could not move the third clip. Speech was nearly impossible due to the pressure. Douglas swung up into the trunk alongside Gibbs and finally hammered the hatch open with his fist. As he took off the clip the hatch blew open and Gibbs shot out. The hatch slammed shut again, hitting Douglas on the head, but then blew open and shot him out in a bubble of air. There were fourteen in the compartment, of whom at least ten made the surface alive and eight were picked up. Weatherhead didn't survive the ascent and was seen floating face down.

The destroyer circled for about three-quarters of an hour, dropping a lifebelt and some timber. The survivors, all suffering from the bends, were terrified. Douglas tried to calm himself by swimming around to see to the ratings. Westwood's eyes were full of oil and he could hardly keep himself afloat. Douglas fixed him into the lifebelt and then went to help Phillips, who was in a similar plight. A puff of air into his DSEA set kept his head above water but he was almost delirious with shock.

The Japanese eventually lowered a cutter and picked them up, clubbing them as they hauled them into the boat. They tried to make them pull an oar, but most were incapable. Another destroyer arrived. The Japanese were certain there was a second submarine and became furious when the men from *Stratagem* denied it. They were taken on board the destroyer, bound, blind-folded and beaten. They spent a very cold night on top of a hatch, all bound together, still wet. The pain from decompression was at its worst but every time someone moaned the guards hit them over the head with their clubs.

They were taken to Singapore where they arrived the following night, having had no food, and were locked in separate cells, still bound and blindfolded. Then the interrogation began.

Ben Skeates's wife Muriel received a second telegram telling her that he was missing presumed dead, the first time in Cayley's *P311*, this time in *Stratagem*. Soon after came his reply from Australia 'to her most welcome air-mail letter containing a photograph of our first child, a girl. We named her June Ann, and both Muriel and June Ann were doing fine.'

21

ONE JUMP AHEAD OF DEATH

Jim Thomsett married his childhood sweetheart Eileen early in 1943. After his wedding he was drafted to Australia to train Australian submariners. Nine men and three officers travelled from the Clyde to Halifax, Nova Scotia in *Queen Elizabeth*, then to Newark and by train across the USA to San Francisco, by liberty boat to Cairns, and finally to Sydney Harbour. The Australians had been given the Dutch boat *K9*, but it was never fit for service and finally its battery blew. After qualifying as a leading torpedoman in Melbourne, Thomsett joined *Adamant* at Trincomalee. He carried out a patrol in *Clyde* and then one in *Trenchant*, before joining *Thule* when she arrived in Ceylon in November 1944. Key members of *Unbroken*'s crew had followed Pansy Mars into *Thule*: Jan Cryer on the asdic, Johnny Crutch as petty officer telegraphist, gunlayer Pedro 'Nigger' Fenton, Percy Scutt now in charge of electrics.

The main meal was dinner at midnight with a tot of rum. Once they reached the dangerous area it was eaten in red light. Food for submarines remained good. They went out with fresh limes, bananas, oranges and pineapples, potatoes, marrow, cabbage, onions, a wide variety of tinned food, 73 lb of bacon and

70 lb of chicken. At the beginning of the patrol the torpedo space was always full of food, but items like potatoes rotted as the days went by and bread quickly became damp and green. There was a big fridge for the boat but no small ones for the messes, so items like butter were always liquid.

On the first patrol nearly all the crew suffered from heat rash and prickly heat, and many developed septic sores and boils. The sea temperature was 85° F. The boat was never below 100° F and the humidity was tremendous. The battery temperatures were 135° F and the messes above the batteries were 120–130° F. The fresh air temperature of 85° F at night felt freezing. Water was scarce, since some freshwater tanks had to be sacrificed to carry extra diesel for the long distances. Washing was more or less impossible, although Jim Thomsett, now stationed in the boiling motor room, used to drain the water out of the circulating motor, have a wash and put it back again. Stoker Tom Acton was in agony with what seemed severe heat exhaustion. Chief stoker Mount followed suit. When Acton died, Mars became worried he had an outbreak of cholera on his hands. He was ordered to abandon the patrol and rendezvous with doctors on a destroyer. To Mars's embarrassment it was indeed just heat exhaustion.

The war was ending. Victory was only a matter of time, but the Japanese fought on obstinately. It was essential to deny supplies to their army operating in Burma. They transported supplies along the coast in shallow water in a multiplicity of junks, wooden schooners and other small craft, usually crewed by non-Japanese and not necessarily flying the Japanese flag. The job made Mars uneasy: 'There seemed to be nothing for it, we had to gun the junks. Messy but effective. Perhaps the crews could be rescued . . . '

This was usually wishful thinking. It wasn't possible in a submarine to entertain many prisoners for a very long time. Space was obviously a problem but there usually wasn't enough water, given the very long journey home, and it was distinctly dangerous to have suicidal fanatics around delicate machinery. The best that could usually be done, even for neutrals, was to leave them clinging to wreckage some miles from shore. Hugh Mackenzie said, 'It was a policy I did not like and I am glad that *Tantalus* never included "junks" in her tally of victims.'

One of the more energetic and ruthless destroyers of coastal traffic was *Sturdy*, commanded by William 'Singey' Anderson, aged twenty-five. He had been in the merchant navy, volunteered for submarines in May 1940 and won a DSC when *Regent* under Hairy Browne went into Kotor to try to rescue the British envoy to Yugoslavia. Anderson's first lieutenant was a very young and naïve 20-year-old and his torpedo officer, named Hardman, was regarded by the crew as useless, but he had a good navigator and a very competent warrant engineer. The crew, like others of the time, had a core of experienced regulars and a lot of very inexperienced ratings. Roy Watters was a telegraphist, loader on the gun and a member of the boarding party. He reckoned that young officers like Anderson now had an eye on carving a career for themselves in the navy after the war and were anxious to be seen to be zealous.

When Anderson called for gun action stations, the gunners surfaced and quickly opened fire with the usual practised drill. This involved the five-man gun crew: Anderson and Hardman the torpedo officer, the signalman with a twin Vickers, the Oerlikon gunner and Watters the loader. On one occasion they sank two or three barges towed by a tug. As far as Watters could see the barges were full of Japanese troops, and were at any rate firing rifles and machine guns at *Sturdy*. The tug slipped the tow and tried to get away, but the three-inch gunner soon sank it. Then they shelled and machine-gunned the barges, leaving any survivors in the water eight or ten miles from shore.

Sometimes ships were sunk by gunfire alone, sometimes they were stopped, boarded and sunk with demolition charges. On these occasions Hardman led a boarding party of four ratings, one with a tommy gun, the rest with bayonets and pistols, who jumped from the bows, searched the enemy vessel, placed charges and jumped back to the sub. *Sturdy* had to come close without colliding, back off to provide covering fire, return to retrieve the boarding party and get away before the twenty-minute fuse went off.

At first they took a few survivors for interrogation, although Watters reckoned they were there partly to display as trophies when returning to harbour. The coxswain inspected prisoners for venereal disease, he said, and any found to be diseased were put back over the side that night and pointed towards the nearest land. 'Some of the things we did were savage indeed, and since we did any shooting from a very close range, seeing scuppers running with blood was no mere figure of speech, and any prisoners taken were not for any humane reasons.'

Watters drew the line during a patrol in December 1944. The circumstances were exacerbated by an earlier incident in which Hardman, on watch on the surface when an aeroplane appeared, had shut the hatch, leaving behind a lookout who drowned or was bombed before they noticed he was missing. It irritated the short-tempered captain that some of his officers were not very reliable.

One evening they shelled and then boarded a small coastal wooden vessel flying the Siamese flag. It was Watters' job to check the cargo, which proved to be bagged rice. Some people had jumped into the water but there were still about twenty on board, many of them women and young children. Hardman shouted this information to the captain and was told to get on with it. Hardman argued and was 'told, very forcibly to obey orders or face the consequence'. They placed charges and lit the fuse. While Watters waited by the gunwale to jump back, he was approached by a very young mother with a baby in her arms. Tears running down her face, she tried to give him her baby. She was apparently resigned to her own death but tried to save the baby. 'To my everlasting shame, I did not take her child,' he later wrote.

Back in the control room he told the first lieutenant, in front of the control room crew, that he 'refused to take part in any further boarding parties, since I considered I had been party to a war crime. I did this quite calmly, without raising my voice, in a very deliberate manner.' He didn't think it was necessary to have blown up the ship, which was already badly damaged. He thought the survivors could have been left to try to make rafts to get themselves ashore. Expecting to be charged, or at least punished in some way, in fact he heard nothing further about it. After that patrol Anderson returned by air to Britain and was replaced by a much less able captain, 'who missed a very fine target with six torpedoes and got us a hiding in return'.

Most captains were troubled by the order to sink junks. Mars and Hezlet worked out that they could ram them, cutting them in half without having to blow up or shell the crew. Mars tried to take all the crews aboard as prisoners, keeping a few for interrogation and periodically unloading the rest on to captured boats.

Lives were cheap in the Far East. The accidental sinking of boats carrying prisoners of war, which attracted so much comment in the Mediterranean, seems to have been noted less in the Far East, where, apparently, more than 20,000 men were drowned through friendly fire from, in almost all cases, American submarines. The worst single disaster, however, came when on 17 September 1944 Lynch Maydon's submarine *Tradewind* sank the *Junyo Maru* which was carrying, unbeknown to Maydon, 4200 Javanese slave labourers and 2300 Allied prisoners of war, on their way to build one of Japan's infamous railways. In all 5620 of them died, making this the costliest sinking of the war. The sheer scale of cruelty in the Far East dulled sensibilities.

Having escaped from the sunken *Stratagem*, Don Douglas was captured by the Japanese on 22 November 1944. Two evenings later he was given his first meal, a small rice ball, after six hours of interrogation. The previous night he had been interrogated without food. He refused to give the Japanese any information except what international law dictated. The interpreter told him he 'had better give some sort of answer otherwise I would be

shot'. Daily interrogation of two to six hours' duration continued for Douglas and, in a less intense way, for the ratings captured
with him. The interpreter proved to be an ally. He had been
born, educated and brought up in England until his father took
him to Japan in 1940, against his English mother's wishes. He had
then been conscripted. 'Being employed on short wave radio, he
was able to bring me the BBC news each night and in this
manner I was able to keep up with world affairs. He also took
messages to my shipmates, brought me cigarettes and sweets etc
and kept me well informed as to how the others were being
interrogated. Later on I always knew what to expect before I
went in front of my questioners and also if they had any idea of
the answers to their questions.'

After the first week Douglas was only interrogated every third
day. The Japanese were especially interested in codes and radar.
To his amazement, he got away with his story that as torpedo
officer he didn't know about such things. He found that so long
as he gave them some sort of answer they were satisfied. After a
month in the cells at Singapore being fed a starvation diet,
Douglas and two shipmates, Gibbs and Robinson, were flown to
Japan via Saigon and Shanghai. He was then taken to the special
naval interrogation camp at Ofuna outside Tokyo.

At Christmas 1944 *Shakespeare* was on a working-up patrol to
the Andaman Islands. Her captain was David 'Shaver' Swanston,
who had learned his trade as third hand and then first lieutenant
of *Upright*. He had good young officers and his petty officer
telegraphist, George Harmer, was 'a robust, overweight, pot-
bellied and scruffy wireless genius', known as 'Guts' from his
habit of wearing his shorts below his waistline. Ken Wade was
Harmer's principal assistant. On New Year's Day Swanston sank
a sizeable merchant ship and they were able to sew the first white
bar on their Jolly Roger. Early on the morning of 3 January
Swanston sighted another merchantman. He fired torpedoes at
3500 yards and missed. Seeing no escort, he surfaced to chase and
attack with the gun. The Japanese ship pulled away before

Shakespeare's gunlayer got the range, then turned towards them blazing away with her own twelve-pounder. As she turned she revealed a sub chaser, also coming at them fast.

Swanston ordered the bridge cleared for diving, but just as he was about to go, the bridge was riddled with holes and *Shakespeare* rocked violently as a twelve-pounder shell ripped a hole ten inches long and five wide in the pressure hull, just above the water line. The sea poured through it, flooding the auxiliary machinery space and putting the compasses out of action. The ballast pump flooded and broke down, and water poured over the wireless transmitter, giving Ken Wade an electric shock as it died. The ventilating trunking to the battery was shattered and they couldn't shut off the battery compartment before the sea forced its way in, cutting off that supply of power. Swanston went back to the bridge. They were under fire but the chaser hadn't found their range yet.

With the radio useless, Wade and Guts Harmer grabbed blankets, hammocks and cushions and lowered themselves over the side to try to bung the hole with a temporary repair. Then the sub chaser started hitting, and one ricochet blew off Harmer's boots and Wade's shirt and shorts. Another shot scattered the gun's crew, injuring the gunlayer and trainer. The first lieutenant, John Lutley, and a telegraphist took their places.

Swanston fired the stern torpedo but it missed. After an hour the gun crew scored a direct hit on the merchant and the sub chaser withdrew to look after it. Twenty buckets appeared, 'won' by an able seaman before they sailed, and they formed a chain to bale out water. They steered by Faithful Freddie, the standby magnetic compass, supported on the TGM's knees. Trying to attain maximum speed, chief engineer 'Shorty' Hodge seized the piston in the port engine, but he managed to get seven knots out of the starboard engine alone.

At 0930 a seaplane dive-bombed them in a low glide from astern. The second coxswain shot it down with the Vickers gun. Half an hour later two Jakes seaplanes attacked, dropping 50 lb bombs. One flooded the bridge and burst a high-pressure airline in the bilges. For a moment they thought they had been holed again.

Relays of Jakes continued to attack until the early afternoon. Then a bomber appeared, accompanied by two fighter-bombers. From three thousand feet the bomber just missed them with two 1000 lb bombs, mortally wounding two of the crew. Every half-hour groups of four aircraft made single attacks. The Oerlikon finally jammed but the three-inch kept going all day, using all the time-fused ammunition. At sunset a bomber, two fighter-bombers and a seaplane made a last attack out of the sun, before darkness fell and the attacks ceased.

During the night they made various running repairs but had to give up on the port engine and the Oerlikon. At dawn a heavy rainstorm left them in precious obscurity, but when it finally cleared no aeroplanes appeared. Nobody could believe their luck. Wade reminded Lieutenant Lutley that during the night before the fight they had received a signal saying *Stygian* was leaving for patrol. They deciphered it again and set course to place *Shakespeare* on *Stygian*'s route. At nine that night they decided to fire recognition grenades every hour and Very lights every half-hour so as not to be missed. At one the next morning they saw a light and exchanged numbers with *Stygian*.

Her captain, Guy Clarabut, suspected a trap. Being an old friend of Swanston, he asked for the Christian name of Swanston's wife. *Shakespeare* replied, 'Sheila, and your wife's name is Stella.' This satisfied Clarabut and the two submarines set course for Trincomalee. Next afternoon HMS *Raider* took off the fifteen wounded. Eventually HMS *Whelp* (whose first lieutenant was Prince Philip) towed them to Trincomalee.

Strongbow sailed for a patrol in H for Hell on 30 December 1944. On 8 January 1945, in stormy weather, Tony Troup chased and sank a tug and an oil lighter with gunfire. At dusk the following day they spotted a largish merchant ship with two chasers as escorts. Troup plotted its course using radar and caught sight of it in a lightning flash, but couldn't get a shot in. Next day they sank a junk and were briefly hunted by a destroyer before it lost contact. That night was very dark, so Troup used his radar to search for targets. It proved to be his downfall.

In Penang, the Japanese commander Tetsunoke Moriama's submarine hunters based in Port Swettenham got bearings on Troup's radar emissions. For once, Moriama had escorts available to send hunting. At about 0600 on Friday 13 January Troup saw two frigates and two anti-submarine trawlers approaching. *Strongbow* went into silent routine, moving slowly on one motor at eighty feet with Len Ridge listening on asdic in barely two hundred feet of water. Ridge warned that one of the enemy boats was attacking. It dropped three charges fairly close, then another came in with three more charges. First Lieutenant Peter Minchenor got up from his bunk where he was sweating out a bout of malaria and took over the trim. At 0800 it was quiet. Troup came to periscope depth and saw the enemy some distance away to starboard. He crept off in the opposite direction, but half an hour later they made contact again. The captain took *Strongbow* deeper but the first four charges were unpleasantly close: fuses blew, lights shattered and cork came down. But Joe Blamey's team soon had the few leaks of air and hydraulic oil under control and the LTOs got most of the lighting back on.

It became very hot and humid because the fans had been switched off, as had the cooling water to the engines and motors. The surrounding seawater was at 88° F, while the pressure was rising thanks to air leaks. Another attack with a pattern of five put the asdic out and Ridge could no longer tell where attacks were coming from. Blamey, the only person the captain would allow to move, went round the boat to look for damage, distributing tiny amounts of water to those who appeared to be in the worst condition until the ready-use freshwater tanks were empty. To fill them again meant noise. The main motor radiators were close to boiling point and the engines had had no chance to cool, so between them they were cooking the engine room staff. They waited, boiling hot, drenched in sweat, desperately thirsty, tense, full of dread.

Soon after 1400 they thought the end had come. The whole boat seemed to jump. The asdic set blew up with a tremendous flash. A cup on the ward room table leapt up, the saucer disintegrated under it and the cup landed intact. The lights went out again. A jet of air was escaping under the chart table. The boat was suddenly steeply bow down, hit the bottom at 170 feet and stayed there. In deeper water they would still have hit the bottom, only the hull would have been crushed first. Blamey used the noise to pump some water into the ready-use tank.

Troup sent Blamey to inspect. In the engine room the hatch had lifted, even though it was clamped shut from the outside, and water had poured in before it had miraculously sealed itself again. There were several severe air and telemotor leaks to deal with. The stern glands were leaking badly. Soon ERAs and stokers, already dispersed about the boat at their diving stations, were working away as quietly as possible. The electricians conjured up some dim light and by it Blamey worked out that the after hydroplanes had been thrown out of phase with their indicator, so the coxswain had inadvertently taken them down, not some sudden intake of water. That fault was soon repaired, but the steering mechanism was more badly damaged. The engines had lifted and Blamey worried about the alignment of various parts when he tried to start them. All the compasses bar Faithful Freddie were out. As Blamey and his men worked away the rest of the crew lay still. Breathing was difficult now. Minchenor, sitting by the coxswains, looked dreadful but refused to leave the control room. Telegraphist Jack Pollard sat silently in the radio office. Troup said that with the next pattern he would try to get the boat off the bottom and look for deeper water. But there were no more depth charges.

By late afternoon the air pressure and heat had made ten hours submerged worse than twenty in cooler conditions. The batteries were undamaged, so there was no problem with battery gas, but the air was terrible even so. Some were having vomiting fits. Then Troup asked Blamey to go and help the TGM. One very young seaman torpedoman was rolling about the floor in hysterics, being dangerously noisy, and he was having a bad effect on the others. Blamey, with the advantage of being twice the young man's age, asked him to be quiet. When that had no effect, he grabbed hold of him and 'told him that if he did not pull himself together, he'd have to bear the consequences'. The seaman became quiet and wrapped his head in a large towel so he couldn't hear anything. As the afternoon went on the chasers seemed to go further away. There was no reason for them to lose contact, since *Strongbow* was stationary – unless, perhaps, they thought they had sunk her. Even so, they would probably be waiting and watching.

The crew themselves waited in silence. Blamey was far from sure that any of his machinery would work when it was put to the test, far from sure that they could get off the bottom at all. He prayed for strength, thinking bitterly that after five years of war and so many close shaves, it seemed unfair that things were going to end this way so near the end of hostilities.

At 1715 Troup decided to try to come to periscope depth and take a look around. The high-powered search periscope didn't work at all, while the attack periscope produced a blurred picture of four chasers about two miles away. They seemed to be on the same course, so he headed towards land. An hour later the chasers were seen signalling to each other. The temperature in the motor room had reached 200° and Blamey cleared everyone out except the LTO operating the motors. Troup decided to surface at 2000 and make a dash for it on the main motors.

Before they surfaced Troup checked that the motors would stop and start. The clutches were very stiff but two men could move them. Blamey prayed that the bearings wouldn't overheat. First they ran the low-pressure blower to reduce the pressure within the boat before opening the hatch, so that the person who opened it wouldn't be fired out like a champagne cork. After an hour running southward on the motors they started the main engines. During the night they discovered various serious faults. The high-pressure air compressors were irreparably damaged, the repaired asdic was 120 degrees out of phase. They had to dive to avoid patrol vessels, but they got out of the area, contacted base and were given permission to return.

The Japanese triumphantly announced the sinking of a submarine. Tetsunoke Moriama was awarded the order of Imperial Treasure 3rd Class. The British intelligence summary reported that the Japanese claimed to have sunk *Strongbow* and in London, Jack Pollard's wife Joan, who worked at the War Office, read the report. 'I never knew how I got through the rest of that day and the next few days before I received a telegram from Jack to say that he was safe.'

On the way home Blamey was deciphering signals when he came across a series addressed to *Porpoise*. He decoded them to find it was the familiar, sad, repeated plea to her to report her position. The loss of *Porpoise* 'made me feel so miserable that I could have cried ... one becomes part of a submarine after a while, and I had been with *Porpoise* for a very long time.'

The old, battered *Porpoise* had been betrayed by pools of oil after being bombed. The Japanese followed her and bombed and depth-charged her until she sank. Hubert Marsham had questioned the advisability of 'patrolling this massive submarine in flat calm seas with leaking external fuel tanks' and had been 'summarily relieved of his command'. A young, zealous captain replaced him and paid the price on his first patrol. She had been the oldest submarine on active service and was the last British submarine to be lost in the war.

Marsham was not the only one to be feeling the strain and sensing the futility of taking risks at this stage. Alastair Mars was also increasingly jittery. He undertook a terrifyingly dangerous mission into the unknown to resupply and reinforce with Force 136 commandos an undercover wireless group dropped very close to Singapore by Bill King some months earlier. The passage of the Sunda Strait was alarming enough, without the shallow-water beach landing in an area that was mined and heavily patrolled. After this, *Adamant* and the flotilla left for Fremantle, but *Thule* was retained in Trincomalee for an American clandestine operation in the Malacca Strait. When, having completed this, and on his way to Australia, he was ordered back to Trincomalee for another visit to Johore, Mars fell out sharply with the staff of his temporary depot ship *Wolfe*. He took particular exception to Commander (S) Boggy Bone, who 'seemed to have some idea that he was serving in a battleship in peacetime . . .' Mars was not alone in this. Incensed by being told off by Bone for appearing in the ward room in sandals, Bevis Andrew, now commanding *Subtle*, thereafter wore a white tunic, long trousers, buckskin shoes and medal ribbons.

By the time the British submarines reached Fremantle the Japanese had been driven further back and the Americans had destroyed most of their ships. Targets were still thin on the ground, therefore, and submarines based in Australia did no better than they had done in the Malacca Strait. Only once did a British submarine sight elements of the Japanese battle fleet. Appropriately it was *Tantalus* that was tantalised, because Mackenzie couldn't catch up and could only send on a sighting report. In January the Americans recaptured their old submarine base at Subic Bay in the Philippines and submariners were eager to go there, for American submarines operating in the Pacific nearer Japan were still sinking all kinds of worthwhile targets. But the British arrived there too late to take part in real fighting and found life at the bombed base at Subic Bay quite horrific.

Storm left for Britain at the end of January to be followed by *Telemachus* in April. The 4th Flotilla of T-boats moved from Trincomalee to Fremantle to replace the 8th. Mars landed a party of marines and picked up a motley collection of escapees, part of an American bomber crew (the others had been recaptured and beheaded) as well as guerrilla trainers who needed evacuating from the jungle and went on to Australia. His coxswain was kept busy with a very long sick list. Several evacuees had malaria and one of the ERAs was very ill. Despite his post in the motor room, Jim Thomsett had coped well with the heat, but on the morning they reached Australia he had an accident in which a hatch fell on his big toe and cut the top off. After considering amputation, the coxswain gave him rum and stitched it back on. Thomsett went into the sick bay in *Adamant*, while Mars reported to Ben Bryant, who was now Captain S4.

The extraordinary thing about Fremantle and Perth, to the men arriving in *Thule*, was that there were lights visible ashore. They were so used to darkened harbours that the bright lights of the road leading to Perth were amazing. The crew very much enjoyed Australia and several of them settled there after the war. The Swan Brewery was a very popular blessing after the bottle-a-week ration in Trinco, while the Australians were generous and hospitable. The rest trips were to outback farms. Ben Skeates had quite fallen in love with Australia when he had a long break at a farm.

Jack Casemore had just arrived in Trincomalee, becoming a spare crew coxswain in *Wolfe*. He 'joined the water polo club and went swimming and playing polo daily. One of the men who played water polo with us on *Wolfe*, was Mick Magennis who shortly after, was awarded the Victoria Cross.' In one of the last X-craft adventures of the war, Magennis and Ian Fraser took *XE3* up the Jahore Strait and sank the heavy cruiser *Takao*.

This was not the only cruiser to be claimed. Baldy Hezlet found himself in the right place, along with Guy Clarabut and *Stygian*, to intercept the Japanese cruiser *Ashigara* on her way back from Batavia as she passed through the Banka Strait. Hezlet had to ask the Americans for permission, and was glad that it was James Fife, who had become a friend as an American observer in the Mediterranean, that he was asking. *Trenchant* and *Stygian* took station either side of a minefield laid by *O19*. Clarabut occupied a destroyer that was steaming ahead of *Ashigara*, leaving Hezlet free to attack the unescorted cruiser. He fired a salvo of eight torpedoes from 4000 yards. Hezlet described the attack to the BBC shortly after his return, saying they could just make out the Rising Sun two miles away. Their torpedo tracks stretched towards her like an arterial road. He saw the first torpedo hit sending up a shower of spray higher than the cruiser's mast. A cheer went up in the control room as the explosions were heard, and he allowed about thirty of the crew to watch the blackened ship subsiding into clouds of steam.

According to Peter Wood, Hezlet's running commentary at the time was, 'One hit ... two hits ... three hits ... four hits ... five hits! There you little yellow bastards, where's your Rising Sun now?'

22

COMING HOME

'Sit down Joe and have a drink because I have some very bad news for you,' said Jacky Slaughter. All kinds of horrible possibilities flashed through Joe Blamey's mind. 'After all the work you and your staff have done to bring *Strongbow* back, now she has been ordered to return to the UK.' Restraining himself from draining the gin in one gulp and shouting 'Whoopee!', Blamey managed to blurt out 'Damn it!' in a manner that was far too obviously feigned.

Blamey had refused even to have a drink when the news that 8 May was VE Day reached *Strongbow* while she patrolled off Rangoon, after his strenuous efforts to patch the boat up had made her just about seaworthy. Tony Troup spliced the mainbrace and even the officers had a drink, but Blamey sulked, begrudging 'those at home and on shore their hilarious celebrations; we were still at war out here'. The war had dragged on for over five years 'and all those who had been in from the start were beginning to feel war weary'. Blamey had been on more patrols than just about anybody still around and was 'beginning to grudge the risk of going on another patrol'. With so few enemy targets around, he 'wondered whether it really mattered whether

Strongbow was on patrol or not'. But he was determined to stay with her to the end. Slaughter's bad news was the news he was waiting for.

Bill King found it impossible to relax. VE Day found *Telemachus* at Aden, already travelling home. Hordes of Arab and Indian troops fired their rifles into the air and King warned his men to be careful as they went ashore to celebrate. He found he couldn't follow them. 'Tense as a coiled spring I walked up and down the after casing.' The novelty of safety soon wore off 'and within a week we were taking for granted the unimaginable bliss of being able to charge batteries whenever we wanted'. As he passed through Suez he reflected bitterly that Anita Leslie was now somewhere beyond the Rhine, driving an ambulance for a French armoured division. When *Telemachus*'s crew returned to their various women, Anita was still far away. 'Nearly all my friends had been killed,' King wrote, 'so I did not feel the urge to look people up.' He remained tense, rehearsing over and over in his mind his mistakes and missed opportunities and what had been wrong with the higher direction of the submarine war.

The old hands were tired. The news that *Thule*'s next patrol was yet another commando landing left Alastair Mars jittery and resentful. Then the atom bomb was dropped and the patrol was cancelled. 'V.J. Day in Western Australia became V.J. week and was finally known as the Battle of Perth,' he wrote. 'The Swan brewery threw open its portals to the ship's company and barrels of its strong lager beer were being taxied, carried and even rolled through the streets towards the houses of the hundreds ashore who were entertaining our men.' The submarines were thrown open for the first time to those adventurous enough to go inside them. Mars and Sam Porter held parties in *Thule* and *Tudor*. Michael St John arrived with three new submarines just in time to join in the party. Hugh Haggard was desperately trying to get out of the Far East at a time when transport was chaotic and people were stuck all over the world. By the time he reached Fremantle the war had ended. Ben Bryant, commanding the flotilla, celebrated 'with a feeling somehow of something lost and over, leaving a strange emptiness'.

On 26 August 1945 the Red Cross discovered the existence of Ofuna prison camp and found Don Douglas, Gibbs and Robinson there. Douglas and Gibbs were suffering from beri-beri and malnutrition and the frostbite from which Douglas had suffered during the previous bitter winter had not yet healed. They were shifted to a hospital and liberated by the US Navy on 29 August.

Jack Casemore was on patrol as coxswain of *Vigorous* when the war ended. In September the boat left Trincomalee. At Alexandria the surgeon on an American destroyer gave him a tin of sulphonamide which cured the tropical ulcers that many of his men were suffering from. Next stop was Malta, which was 'still war torn but there was plenty of food now and everybody seemed very happy'. He tried to find Charlie's Bar in Sliema, near the old cinema, but it had been bombed. He did find Charlie and his wife, and their son, young Charlie. At Gibraltar he bought a large bunch of bananas. In November at Dunoon his wife joined him, and they stayed there until he was demobbed.

Skeates went in *Maidstone* to Hong Kong, where he installed a new radio transceiver at the signal station. By then he had consulted Muriel and they had decided to emigrate to Australia. John Gibson witnessed the lowering of the Japanese flag there. Hong Kong exploded with firecrackers as the Japanese departed.

Baldy Hezlet had been sent home and found his way to Northways, where he found the staff packing up to return to Fort Blockhouse. News of the dropping of the atom bomb broke that day. Having learned of a new appointment at the Admiralty, Hezlet went on leave to see his parents at Aghadowy, confirming to his mother that her premonition that he would survive the war had been fulfilled. Joe Blamey had also survived but he remained weary and bitter, feeling over-exploited. 'The whole population except myself celebrated VJ day. I could raise no enthusiasm whatsoever; it all seemed an awful anti-climax. Of course I was glad that it was all finished, but we had lost nearly eighty submarines, and with them so many of my good friends and contemporaries.'

Near Londonderry Max Horton formally accepted the surrender of a token eight U-boats, victor in his own private war against Dönitz. His loyal lieutenant Commodore Shrimp Simpson was with him. Hugh Mackenzie became Commander (S) of the flotilla of captured U-boats at Londonderry and there fell in love with a Wren third officer from Simpson's staff. Joe Brighton was chief petty officer in charge of another collection of surrendered U-boats near Stranraer. Stanley Hawkey, by this stage second coxswain, went with him.

Prisoners of war came home. Many of them, like Michael Kyrle-Pope, had been away for five years or more. He returned from Lübeck after five years to find that the woman who had been his wife for three months before he disappeared had left him. In September 1945 he rang Admiral Layton's daughter Suzanne Parlby from Fort Blockhouse and explained to her that he was still alive. Her marriage also had fallen apart during the war. Eventually, Suzanne divorced John and married Michael.

Anita Leslie wrote to Bill King say that she was on the Moselle and that, with the water supplies contaminated, they were only allowed to drink the wine. He received a Christmas card from Philip Ruck-Keene accompanied by a photo showing his aircraft carrier *Formidable* in action on 4 May, with two Kamikaze planes crashed and burning on the flight deck. Ruckers' message ended, 'Wait till we get to the Alps together'.

The Admiralty was quick to realise that it now had too many boats. *Sealion* had already been scuttled in Scotland to provide an asdic target for destroyer crews in training. The remaining battered veterans were sold for scrap in December 1945 or soon after. Joe Blamey was appointed engineer officer to a reserve group, with *Ursula* as their base ship, that supervised the beaching of the unwanted veterans on Falmouth mud. Blamey had *Shakespeare*, *Strongbow*, *Truant*, *Torbay*, *Thrasher* and *Rorqual* in his charge but left before they were all refloated to be broken up. *Truant* slipped her tow on the way to the scrapyard and disappeared. Syd Hart heard the news over the radio with delight: 'I felt a glowing pride in her. She had still retained her fighting soul . . . and rather than submit to the offered indignity, she had broken loose from control and preferred to take her fate fighting to the last.'

The Navy kept eighty of the newest boats along with twenty-seven that were under construction. As a result of wartime experience, the latest designs included a number of new features. The Admiralty had finally adopted the Dutch *Schnorkel*, which the Germans had incorporated into new boats in 1943. This was a device that could be raised like a periscope to allow in air at periscope depth, so that the engines could be run to charge the battery without surfacing. New A class boats had a 'snort' mast, periscopic radar, longer periscopes and a safe diving depth of 500 feet. The search for greater underwater speed and endurance drove research after the war. Nuclear power provided an answer; although nuclear engines proved noisy they were a significant advance in enabling submarines to move fast under water and to remain submerged for long periods. The British *Dreadnought* was launched in 1960, powered by an American nuclear reactor.

A major new development emerged when the Americans revealed their plans for a submarine-launched ballistic missile system as a nuclear deterrent. They called it Polaris. In 1953 the American *Tunny* launched the first cruise missile to be fired from a submarine. By 1958 the USA had two purpose-built submarine missile launchers, followed by the nuclear-powered *Halibut*. The first submarines equipped with ballistic missiles were brought into service by the USA and Russia in 1959–60. In December 1962 Hugh Mackenzie was given what he called a 'pierhead jump' to direct the British Polaris programme, alongside an Air Ministry that was reluctant to abandon its right to carry the nation's nuclear threat and an Admiralty that was in two minds over the wisdom of accepting the responsibility and expense.

Submarines armed with major nuclear weapons took on a new status within the navy, signalled by their appropriation of names formerly reserved for battleships. The *Valiant* class, fitted with British Rolls-Royce nuclear reactors, was introduced from 1966. From 1968 the *Resolution* class was armed with US Polaris missiles. During the 1990s *Vanguard* class submarines were introduced and armed with the Trident nuclear missile. Eventually submarines carried Britain's only nuclear threat.

Deployment of submarines capable of performing their traditional role against surface ships continued, and increases in speed made their use for convoy or carrier group defence feasible. Submarines became platforms from which to attack land targets with missiles, while hunter-killer submarines were designed to attack enemy submarines, especially ballistic missile carriers. In 1982 HMSM *Conqueror* became the first nuclear-powered submarine to sink a surface ship, her victim being the Argentine cruiser *General Belgrano*.

The wartime submariners watched these developments with interest. Shrimp Simpson married in 1945, became Flag Officer Submarines from 1952–4 and retired to New Zealand to become a sheep farmer. Philip Ruck-Keene led a committee that investigated submarine escape and discovered, among other things, the harmful effect of breathing oxygen under pressure. A new, much deeper escape tank was constructed at Fort Blockhouse. Leslie Bennington worked on Ruck-Keene's committee and later joined the Fleet Air Arm. He married, retiring in 1960 and going into commerce. Ben Bryant retired as a rear-admiral in 1957 and afterwards worked for Rolls-Royce. Before retiring to Bovagh to write a series of books on naval history and future strategy, Arthur Hezlet was Flag Officer Submarines in 1959–61. Hugh Mackenzie succeeded him, before becoming chief Polaris executive. Ian McIntosh rose to be deputy chief of defence staff in 1971–3, at a time when Tony Troup led the Submarine Service for Nato as well as Britain.

Bill King retired from the navy in 1948. The following year he married Anita Leslie, settling down in her castle by the sea in County Galway. In 1973 he completed a singlehanded circumnavigation of the world in his yacht *Galway Blazer*. Teddy Woodward joined Vickers before eventually retiring to Australia. Edward Young had several senior roles in publishing and design, at one time working with Ruari McLean at Rainbird McLean. Alastair Mars lost patience with naval bureaucracy; wishing to leave, he was court-martialled and dismissed on a minor charge and threw himself into writing.

Quite a number of submariners, like Ben Skeates, enjoyed Fremantle and decided to settle in Australia, including several of Mars's crew in *Unbroken* and *Thule*. Joe Brighton retired from the navy in 1948, became a coastguard for a while and then retired to his native south Norfolk. Jim Thomsett, stationed at Chatham, settled into married quarters with Eileen and eventually drove buses for the family firm. Jack Casemore was demobbed in 1946 and eventually retired to Sussex. After finally retiring from the navy after thirty-seven years' service, Joe Blamey worked for the Inland Revenue at Newton Abbot, where he trained a choir with his wife Clare at the organ.

It is difficult to measure the success or failure of the British submarine effort. Figures for the number of vessels sunk by submarines still undergo constant revision. One set for British submarines alone gives 475 merchant ships, 105 warships and 36 submarines sunk. This does not count the contribution of the Polish, Dutch, Norwegian, French, Greek, Yugoslavian and Russian submarines operating under British control. Dutch submarines sank another two U-boats, for instance.

But sinkings are not a realistic measure of success. A tanker that struggled into the wrong port with most of its cargo leaked or burned was a significant victim, but not one that had technically been sunk. Damaged warships that could not take part in an impending major operation such as the invasion of Britain were significant losses to the Kriegsmarine. Similarly, it was valuable to force a convoy to return to port in Italy rather than completing its voyage if its supplies failed to reach the Axis armies in time for an impending attack. How do you measure the value of all those dangerous, stressful operations to land agents, drop commandos or carry out beach reconnaissance? What, if any, was the value of standing in for surface craft or aircraft that were unable or unwilling to keep watch on Norwegian shores or escort convoys? How important was it to transport essential supplies to Malta when nothing else could get through? Instead of being used to sink ships, for much of the war submarines were deployed in various roles like these for which they were ill-equipped but for which no better solution could be found. The effectiveness of British submarines cannot be measured simply in terms of tonnage sunk, in the way that German raids on thinly protected Atlantic convoys could be. They were never going to sink the same tonnage as U-boats: Britain had far fewer submarines than the Germans, while Germany and Italy, with smaller numbers of merchant ships, had less vulnerable lines of communication and were able to guard their far shorter supply lines much more effectively.

For the same reasons it is futile as well as invidious to attempt to create any league table of officers. Admiral Hezlet made this point in 2001, although he did put together separate lists of successful officers classified by 'warships hit', 'U-boats sunk' and 'most tonnage sunk'. The last list was topped by David Wanklyn, followed by Hugh Haggard, Tubby Linton, Lynch Maydon and Rumble Clutterbuck. Some fêted commanders undoubtedly overclaimed during the war and several were awarded medals for ships they didn't sink. It is fair to say that by all measures Wanklyn remains outstanding.

What did submarines achieve? Their impact was attritional, and never easily measurable, and it could certainly have been greater had the Admiralty appreciated their potential. For long periods they operated with significant disadvantages, most of which were the result of having been a low priority in a cash-strapped navy. They had poor radios, poor guns and, most importantly, an inadequate supply of torpedoes, of which the reserve stock was far too small before the war began. Having been trained to fire salvoes of six, commanders were soon asked to fire only one or two in order to conserve a diminishing supply. Those who obeyed the order usually missed the target. The lack of torpedoes was shameful. It was particularly unfortunate because British Mark VIII torpedoes worked, whereas American and German torpedoes often didn't. Using old torpedoes brought the British down to the level of their rivals – dodging duds that circled round and came straight back at them.

The greatest opportunity for British submarines, had they been unleashed, came at the beginning of the Norwegian campaign when Max Horton deployed his submarines in anticipation of a German invasion of Norway that nobody else realised was about to be attempted. Unfortunately, the politicians refused to allow British submarines to attack the merchant ships that were carrying troops and supplies until it was too late. Superior German intelligence, the Admiralty's refusal to believe sound British intelligence and unlucky weather further thwarted their efforts. With better luck, better cipher security and less interference from the Admiralty, the result of Max Horton's dispositions prior to the German invasion might have been truly spectacular. Nevertheless, though no one was fully aware of it at the time, submarines inflicted so much damage on German heavy ships off Norway that, despite enduring mythology, an invasion of Britain in summer 1940 was rendered more or less inconceivable – at least without the total annihilation of the RAF at trifling cost to the Luftwaffe.

In the Mediterranean the role of submarines was crucial, decisive in influencing the outcome of a land campaign that turned on logistics. Their job was to deny supplies to the Axis armies and submarines were chiefly responsible for such denial as occurred. There were brief periods when enemy air forces were sufficiently weak that British surface ships were able to destroy enemy convoys; there were longer spells from autumn 1942 when, as a result of their numbers and convenient shore bases, Ultra-guided aircraft were the most destructive Allied weapon. But only submarines were able to take a heavy toll over the whole three-year campaign in the face of enemy superiority in the air and Axis command of the sea. For a two-month spell in late spring 1942 the loss of their bases caused a virtual cessation in submarine operations, but otherwise they achieved steady attrition.

It was on British submarines that Rommel's brilliant chief of staff, Fritz Bayerlein, blamed the failure of the Afrika Korps' drive to Alexandria and beyond. Rommel was defeated by logistics before the much-lauded Montgomery ever appeared on the scene. Wartime propaganda made much of Montgomery and the myth of the Desert Rats endures, but in the real world disparity in logistical supply continued to be the decisive factor in the campaign. Of total Italian losses of large ships, submarines sank 44 per cent of the number and 43 per cent of the tonnage. Ninety-four British and twenty Allied submarines took part in the campaign, firing 2674 torpedoes and sinking three cruisers, twelve destroyers, twenty-one U-boats and 243 merchant ships of more than 500 tons. Torpedoes damaged a battleship, and another five cruisers, three destroyers and sixty-four merchant ships. Submarine-laid mines and gunfire directed at minor vessels and trains added to the mayhem caused by British submarines in the Mediterranean.

The cost was terrible – 42 per cent of submarines in the Mediterranean were lost. Of fifty-seven boats deployed in 1939, two were still active in 1945. Thirty-four boats had been lost and nearly all the survivors had reverted to their original role as training submarines. Of 206 boats employed in total, 74 did not return from patrols, 46 being sunk in the Mediterranean. There were 3383 men mobilised in 1939. By the end of 1940, 851 were dead and 115 were prisoners, 28 per cent of those serving. About 3100 men were killed in total, being roughly a third of the total of 9316 in the service in March 1945; 425 were captured. Hezlet calculated that whereas in general service in the navy there were 7.6 per cent casualties, in the submarine branch the figure was 38 per cent.

In the defeated German U-boat service losses were much heavier: 785 out of 1205 boats were sunk and some 28,000 out of 39,000 men were killed. American losses were significantly lower – 52 boats out of 288 deployed against Japan and 13 per cent of personnel in the service as a whole. But the wars fought by these three services were different in aim, conditions and risk.

The level of loss in the British Submarine Service was comparable with that in Bomber Command. But in the intimate world of submarines, where many people knew each other, the impact was particularly devastating. Since the worst years for losses were 1940 and 1942, the casualties were heavily weighted towards the beginning. Very few of those in submarines at the start of the war lived to see the end of it, whereas relatively few who joined the service in the later stages of the war were killed. Casualties in 1944–5 were only 3 per cent.

Those who did survive were often to some degree mentally or physically scarred by the experience. Many suffered lasting health problems or at the very least recurrent nightmares, but they remained deeply proud of having served in a service that represented all that was best about the Royal Navy, all that was best about British people acting as a team, improvising in adversity.

Then there are the ghosts, among them some of the best: Edward 'Bickie' Bickford, Ian Anderson, David Wanklyn, Edward 'Tommo' Tomkinson, John 'Basher' Coombe, Guy 'Jumbo' Watkins, John 'Tubby' Linton, 'Harmonica Dick' Cayley, George Colvin and so many others. They remain as memories of energetic young men: Bickie marching along the Dingli Cliffs insisting, 'Drive on! Drive on! There is an eternity of rest to follow.'

Acknowledgements

It was my agent Julian Alexander who first suggested that I might like to write a book about Second World War submariners and so first thanks are owed to him. I had begun to research the subject more than a decade before when working on *Finest Hour*, at a time when it had been intended that that television series should cover the Norwegian campaign. At that time, with the help of Jeff Tall, then curator of the Royal Navy Submarine Museum, I wrote and spoke to a number of prominent submarine officers who were then living – Arthur Hezlet, Ian McIntosh, John Roxburgh, Tony Troup, Ian McGeoch – and I had a most enjoyable lunch with Bill King, after pursuing him by post from Austria to Mexico and finally tracking him down at Wilton House. It was a very enjoyable, instructive and inspiring lunch. I very much regretted it when higher powers decided to exclude submarines from that project and very much welcomed the opportunity to revisit them. Sadly, by the time that I returned to the subject all the officers to whom I had spoken, except Bill King, had died. I am most grateful to Bill King and his daughter Leonie for allowing me to dedicate this book to him and to quote extensively from his own story of his career to the end of the war, *The Stick and the Stars*.

However, thanks to Submariners Association secretaries Jim McMaster, Barry Harris, Bill Apps, Malcolm Douse and Tom

Oates I made contact with Jack Casemore, Jim Thomsett, the late Ben Skeates, and Mark Law. Mark told me the story of Leslie and Margaret Howard and made me copies of documents relating to it. The late Iain Nethercott I already knew as a legendary yarner. Louis de Bernières kindly put me in touch with his mother Jean de Berniere-Smart; Joanna and Jane Martin kindly replied to my enquires about Desmond Martin.

I could easily have contacted more people and apologise to those who made kind offers that I was unable to take up. It is always difficult to choose where to concentrate effort in a book and in this case I was working to a particularly tight schedule. That is why I found myself with insufficient time to take full advantage of generous offers from Peter Schofield, Jeff Tall, Malcolm Llewellyn-Jones of the Naval Historical Branch, Christina Lee, John Featherstone, and a number of other veteran submariners.

Over recent years various websites have become extremely useful and convenient reference resources. I found Hans Houterman's account of British naval officers at unithistories.com very helpful and he kindly published the careers of several submariners at my request. I have made much use of Uboat.net and am also grateful to Geoff Chalcraft of the British Submarines website. For personal accounts I am indebted to the staff of the Imperial War Museum, where the sound archive was especially useful and Roderick Suddaby was as helpful as he possibly could have been, and to George Malcolmson, archivist to the Royal Navy Submarine Museum. The staff of the National Archives were the usual model of efficiency. Debbie Corner, head of photography at the Submarine Museum set aside some days to search for illustrations for me.

Kate Johnson was a great help and encouragement from the beginning of this project. Jane Greenwood very kindly read the text and helped to make it accessible to those who had not just spent twelve months submersed in submarines. Chris Jones translated passages of Italian for me. Julie Smith, Lee Trevail and

Michael Hall very kindly conjured up a CD of an interview with Joe Brighton. I benefited from interesting conversations with Christopher Morgan-Jones and with Jean Baker who answered my questions about Kefalonia. Kostas Thoctarides very generously sent me a copy of his fascinating book on the wreck of *Perseus*. Keith Nethercoate-Bryant kindly gave permission to quote from the *Submarine Memories* series.

Steve Mobbs and Pauline Thomas have once again been extremely generous hosts and loyal friends. Phil Craig has waited patiently for me to get on with the next project. Juliette, William and Lily suffer most from my books – this time it was the summer holiday that went – but they continue to tolerate and even encourage me. It has been a pleasure to work for the first time with Richard Beswick, Iain Hunt, Linda Silverman, Sian Wilson, Rowan Cope, Steve Gove and John Gilkes at Little, Brown.

Notes

PROLOGUE: *PERSEUS*

All quotations from Capes are from 'J. H. Capes' in Nethercoate-Bryant, *Submarine Memories*, pp. 17–41. The debriefer's report (NA, Adm 1/14538) is published in *Submarine Memories*, pp. 31–4. Further details appear in 'John Capes Saga', Nethercoate-Bryant, *More Submarine Memories*, pp. 59–62 and 'Perseus', Nethercoate-Bryant, *Even More Submarine Memories*, pp. 2–6. The fullest account of the dives and the Greek background is in Giatropoulou and Thoctarides.

Several films of the wreck of *Perseus* made by Kostas Thoctarides can be seen among those posted by Planet Blue Dive Center on YouTube. The most detailed interior views are at http://www.youtube.com/watch?v=8wUMYapfBhE& feature=related.

1 FIRST BLOOD

11 *We was dozing*, and the following quotations, Carr, pp. 16–17.

13 *Most conversations*, Chalmers, p. 8.

14 Good *at his boat*, Chalmers, p. 4.

14 *In those early days*, and following quotation, Bernard Acworth quoted in Chalmers, pp. 5–6.

14 *a past master*, E.O.B. Osborne quoted in Chalmers, p. 7.

14 *It was on an old twin-Minerva*, and following quotations, Chalmers, p. 6.

15 *I understand Commander Horton*, Chalmers, p. 19.

16 *[Horton] gets on particularly well with the Russians*, Chalmers, p. 20.

16 *took the view that it was wise*, Chalmers, p. 4.

16 *I call them underhand*, Chalmers, p. 4.

16 *practically blind*, H.G. Wells, 'An experiment in prophecy', *Fortnightly Review* 1901, republished in *Anticipations*, 1901.

17 *the immense impending revolution*, Compton-Hall, *Submarines*, p. 8.

17 *I followed very carefully*, 'Future of the Submarine', *Popular Mechanics*, 6 (June

1904), pp. 629–31. Authorship of this article has been debated but it is currently thought to be Verne's work.

17 *no one seriously contemplated*, Compton-Hall, *Submarines*, p. 19.

18 *as the motor has driven the horse*, Sir Percy Scott quoted in Compton-Hall, *Submarines*, p. 8.

18 *made the world realise*, Carr, p. 92.

19 *When a submarine is submerged*, Bower, p. 291.

19 *In my opinion good handling*, and following quotations, Brodie, pp. 15–16.

19 *In submarines*, Chalmers, p. 27.

20 *There is a Democracy of Things Real*, Bower, pp. 4–5.

20 *the Trade lives in a world*, Rudyard Kipling, 'Tales of the Trade', *The Times*, 21–28 June 1916.

21 *We need no Lead*, Compton-Hall, *Submarines*, p. 123.

21 *Nasmith was one of the most popular*, Carr, p. 31.

21 *I as a humble 'new'*, and following quotation, Brodie, p. 16.

22 *an almost ferocious insistence*, Carr, p. 31.

22 *The voyage was not unusual*, Carr, p. 32.

22 *I consider a man of this type*, and the following quotation, Carr, pp. 32–3.

23 *to loom black and imminent*, Compton-Hall, *Submarines*, p. 266.

24 *apart from destroying*, and the following quotations, Compton-Hall, *Submarines*, pp. 281–3.

2 SENIOR SERVICE

26 *hardly any way out*, Haggard interview, IWM Sound 8991.

27 *The Navy sounded jolly*, King, p. 11.

29 *the discipline and constant rushing*, Mackenzie, p. 21.

29 *was run like a Japanese*, Bill King, interview with the author, 1999.

29 *we were taught to leap*, and following quotations, King, p. 12.

30 *any forgetfulness or a fault*, and following quotations, King, p. 14.

30 *If the sub-lieutenant shouted*, Simpson, p. 26.

31 *What happened to me*, Simpson, p. 22.

31 *the treatment meted out*, Mackenzie, p. 27.

32 *You had your allotted place*, and following quotations, Anscomb, p. 15. Details of Anscomb's background from his interview, IWM Sound 13249.

33 Drury details from interview, IWM Sound 13766.

33 *His first words were*, and following quotations, Buckingham, pp. 9–11.

35 *one desire was to go*, Thomsett, interview with the author, 14 July 2009. The account of the Howard brothers is based on information kindly supplied by Margaret Howard and Mark Law, including their service records.

35 *the two lads detailed*, Ben Skeates, 'My World War II Recollections', sent to the author 2009.

36 *caning is by far*, Roskill, *Naval Policy*, II, p. 35.

36 *soon found that I was nothing*, Anscomb, p. 19.

36 Blamey interview, IWM Sound 17603, and Blamey, pp. 15–18.

37 *Justice is open to all*, and following quotation, Roskill, *Naval Policy*, II, p. 34.

37 For Bennington's background see Trenowden. Hawkey details from Gosport, Royal Navy Submarine Museum, A2007/518 Stanley Hawkey scrapbook. His portrait photograph of Bennington is labelled 'My great skipper, who ten years

previous was an able seaman with me. He deserved everything he got.'
38 *I was learning my job*, and following quotations, Anscomb, pp. 22–4.

3 THE SUBMARINE BRANCH

40 *Tha's not so lung to live*, Hart, p. 22.
40 *During that tedious train journey*, and following quotations, Hart, pp. 13–14.
41 Drury details from his interview, IWM Sound 13766; pay from Gordon Selby IWM Sound 16738.
42 *various personal reasons*, and following quotations, Mackenzie, p. 42.
42 *I did not want to specialise*, King interview, IWM Sound 17832.
42 *no idea*, Mills interview, IWM Sound 9088.
42 *wanted to be a gunnery officer*, Hezlet interview, IWM Sound 12571.
43 *so much happier,* Pook interview, IWM Sound 9167.
44 *it was hard to imagine*, Blamey, p. 21.
44 *cabins had been condemned*, Bryant, p. 13.
44 *an oilskin over one's bunk*, Mackenzie, p. 44.
46 *Uneasy speculation*, Anscomb, p. 25.
46 *Our shining oilskins*, and following quotations, Hart, pp. 14–15.
47 *Cautiously, hearts thumping*, Anscomb, p. 27.
47 *we were due to go down*, and following quotation, Hart, pp. 16–17.
47 *When it came our turn*, Anscomb, pp. 29–30.
48 *In came the water*, Hart, p. 18.
48 *I was scared now*, Anscomb, p. 30.
48 *Imagination worked strange freaks*, Hart, pp. 18–19.
49 *in a bit of a whirl*, Hart, p. 21.
50 *madhouse of brass and steel*, and following quotations, Young, pp. 20–2.
51 *learned to operate the valves*, and following quotation, Anscomb, p. 31.
52 *a curious feeling*, Hart, p. 21.
52 *involved intensive training*, Skeates, 'My World War II Recollections'.
53 Drury interview, IWM Sound 13766; Simpson, pp. 46–7.
54 *The Fourth Submarine Flotilla*, Mackenzie, p. 45.

4 THE CHINA STATION

55 *the total abolition*, Roskill, *Naval Policy*, I, p. 306.
56 *I do not believe*, Brodie, 'Frightfulness – the post-war view', RNSM archive discussed in Compton-Hall, *Submarines*, pp. 312–13.
57 *Japan as the nation*, Roskill, *Naval Policy*, I, p. 278.
58 *turned the fore-ends into a nightmare*, Mackenzie, p. 48.
59 *Sooner or later with all riveted tanks*, Anscomb, pp. 38–9.
59 *Isn't England, the Empire*, Mannering, p. 57.
60 *makee plenty quick*, Blamey, p. 60.
60 *Hong Kong was wonderful*, Philip Francis interview, IWM Sound 18090.
60 *King would end an evening*, King, pp. 17–18.
61 *in best Colvin style*, and following quotations, Anderson diary, IWM Documents 11355 PP/MCR/17.
61 *For engineer Joe Blamey*, Blamey, p. 61.
61 *the inevitable wave of girls*, and following quotations, Capes in Nethercoate-Bryant,

Submarine Memories, pp. 80–1.

64 *in each other's pockets*, Bryant, p. 32.

64 *was 'well in' with the drafting staff*, Mackenzie, pp. 51–2 and 47; Blamey, p. 60.

65 *your fucking first lieutenant*, Izzard, p. 32.

65 *When we won the torpedo-loading*, King, p. 18.

67 *2 Girlie – 1 hour – 15 yen*, Mackenzie, p. 61.

67 *the boat cost £800 . . . Tai-mo-shan* was sailed home by four submariners, 'Red' Ryder, Martyn Sherwood, George Salt and Philip Francis, together with naval doctor Bertie Ommaney-Davis. On the voyage see http://www.coburgbrokers.com/tai2.html and 'Round world trip was daring spy mission', *The Times*, 25 August 2007 at http://www.timeson-line.co.uk/tol/news/uk/article2324103.ece. Quotations are taken from Ryder's papers in the IWM as given in this article or from Philip Francis interview, IWM Sound 18090.

68 *The German ships were the only ones*, Bryant, p. 34.

68 *Two years, Japanese come*, King, p. 22.

68 *Mackenzie left on a liner*, Mackenzie, pp. 62–4.

68 *as the Chinks and Japs shoot up*, and following quotation, Mannering, pp. 70–1.

69 *Such Men as These*, Mars gives a detailed account of training under Barry and Menzies in *Submarines at War*, pp. 40–54; for the 'Colonel's' popularity and a copy of 'Such Men as These' see the Anderson diary, IWM Documents 11355 PP/MCR/17; for Martin see Mannering, pp. 90–1.

69 *an awful stony silence*, Mannering, p. 94.

69 *By this time (and it was 2.30 am . . .)*, and the following quotation, Anderson diary, IWM Documents 11355 PP/MCR/17.

5 WAR CLOUDS

72 *a tall, cool, handsome chap*, Carr, p. 74.

73 *The entrance to Grand Harbour*, Anscomb, p. 41.

74 *cruisers and destroyers appealed*, and following quotations, King, p. 24.

75 *a team of charming and intelligent Wrens*, and following quotations, Young, pp. 116–18.

76 *it was not difficult*, Bryant, p. 36.

77 *I adjudge Hood sunk*, Simpson, p. 58.

77 *I saw a look of horror flash across his face*, Mackenzie, p. 70.

77 *The captains of cruisers*, and following quotations, Hutchinson interview, IWM Sound 9137.

78 *arcane mysteries*, Roskill, *Naval Policy*, II, p. 230.

79 *and I fired four torpedoes*, Hutchinson interview, IWM Sound 9137.

79 *did a day in a submarine*, Piper interview, IWM Sound 13298.

79 *I knew there was going to be a war*, Casemore, in Nethercoate-Bryant, *Even More Submarine Memories*, p. 27. Casemore's story, available in mss in the RNSM and IWM, was published in *Even More Submarine Memories*, from which I take the pagination. Some details come from my conversation with him, 13 July 2009.

80 *He was a huge bull of a man*, King, p. 27.

81 *the most forward-looking submariner*, Bryant, p. 39.

81 *He had a flair for knowing what mattered*, Simpson, p. 79.

81 *It's the greatest fun*, King, p. 28.

81 *we were quite good at firing torpedoes*, Mackenzie interview, IWM Sound 11745.

82 *had read most of the accounts*, Padfield, p. 16.

82 *There were dances at the club*, Bryant, p. 41.

83 *Drive on! Drive on!*, Bryant, p. 42.

83 *a young man of unforgettable charm*, King, p. 29.

83 Exercise story in Simpson pp. 74–6.

84 *a submarine had no business*, Bryant, p. 40.

85 *racing and golf at Smouha*, and following quotations, Bryant, pp. 42–3.

86 *very smooth and attractive*, Kyrle-Pope, pp. 23–5.

86 *we all began cramming*, King, p. 29.

87 *Mackenzie was at a guest night dinner*, Mackenzie, p. 74; Allaway, pp. 49–50.

87 *Any news of the Thetis?*, Hart, p. 22.

87 *we hadn't joined submarines to fight*, Mackenzie interview, IWM Sound 11745.

88 *no medals, no tombstones*, Mackenzie, p. 77.

88 *the climax of all that*, Bryant, p. 45.

88 *where we again embarked our mines*, and following quotations, Simpson, pp. 77–9.

6 TOTAL GERMANY

91 *that my job will be*, Mars, *Submarines*, p. 33.

93 *sitting there with the operator listening*, Drury interview, IWM Sound 13766.

93 *I had just remarked to my first lieutenant*, BBC interview 1939, http://news.bbc.co.uk/olmedia/430000/audio/_430152_commander_eadon.ram

94 *when the chief petty officer telegraphist*, McGeoch, p. 26.

94 *over a whisky and soda*, Mars, *Submarines*, p. 56.

94 *was in the Club having a drink*, Bartlett memoir, IWM Documents, 1459 91/38/1.

95 Piper details from interview, IWM Sound 13298.

96 *Very soon we heard cries for help*, Steel ADM178/194, printed in Hood, p. 137.

97 *The staff had neglected both to tell*, Hezlet, *British and Allied Submarine Operations*, Ch.97

97 Swordfish *had had to alter course*, Trenowden, p. 153.

97 *Meanwhile, a second U-boat*, Compton-Hall, *Underwater War*, p. 49.

97 *The whole ship seemed to spring*, Eaden interview, IWM Sound 9864.

100 *At the end of the month*, Compton-Hall, *Underwater War*, p. 49.

102 *a rucking*, and following quotation, Mars, *Submarines*, pp. 35–6.

102 *It is almost certain*, according to Hezlet, *British and Allied Submarine Operations*, Ch. 2.

102 *Always told you when things*, Chalmers, p. 68.

102 *of national importance*, Simpson, pp. 80–2.

104 *with the object of winging*, Bickford's patrol report, Adm 199/1839, published in Hood, pp. 148–50.

104 *all was happiness*, Mars, *Submarines*, p. 35; *Life*, 29 January 1940.

104 *I itched, I just itched*, King, p. 45. See also Anderson diary, IWM Documents 11355 PP/MCR/17 for reaction of submariners to the press coverage of Bickford.

105 *The Germans announced on Thursday*, Chalmers, p. 69.

106 *We had three submarines at sea*, Drury interview, IWM Sound 13766.

106 *However, it is now known*, Showell, p. 46.

7 FIRST PATROLS

107 *If you're a submarine cox'n,* Anscomb, p. 65.

107 *maybe the drinks were consumed,* Hart, p. 30.

108 *hair-raising stories,* and following quotations, Hart, pp. 32–4.

109 *Open main vents,* and following quotations, Hart, p. 35.

110 *In* Truant *Christopher Hutchinson,* Hutchinson interview, IWM Sound 9137.

110 *begged borrowed and stole,* King, p. 32.

113 *someone had to be found and forced into the galley,* King, p. 42.

114 *Our only change of scenery,* Hart, p. 38.

115 *The position of the lavatory pan,* Casing, p. 93.

116 *made using the heads very unpopular,* and the preceding description of toilet facilities, Brighton, 'Life on the *Porpoise*'.

116 *We grew to know each other's peculiarities,* Hart, p. 38.

117 *wore long woollen pants,* Masters, p. 85.

117 *Once we were secured to moorings,* and following quotation, Hart, p. 39.

118 *Drenched, frozen and unsure of our position,* and following quotation, King, p. 34.

118 *In* Sturgeon *Norman Drury,* Drury interview, IWM Sound 13766; Hutchinson interview, IWM Sound 9137.

118 *In rough weather, the decks,* Bryant, p. 75.

118 *Mopping the spray off,* King, p. 35.

119 *I am not a religious man, Horton,* and following quotation, Simpson, p. 84.

119 *This Officer seems to me,* Churchill papers quoted in Gilbert, p. 169.

119 *down at 100 feet with the sub,* and following quotation, Drury interview, IWM Sound 13766.

120 *She rolls violently sideways,* King, p. 34.

120 *This ghastly see-saw usually ended,* King, p. 36.

121 *She'll fall apart soon,* and following quotation, King, p. 37.

121 *took sickening nose-dives,* Hart, p. 40.

121 *Shut all watertight doors!,* and following quotation, Hart, p. 42.

122 *possessed a small green racing car,* King, p. 47 and interview with the author, 1999.

8 HORTON'S PURGE

123 *He was a tiger to his staff,* Chalmers, p. 70.

123 *people either cared deeply for Sir Max,* Simpson, p. 98.

123 *If a mistake were made,* and following quotation, Chalmers, p. 70.

124 *Just as Simpson,* Simpson, p. 85.

124 *some kind of 'cold cupboard',* and following quotations, RNSM A1941/005.

124 Una*'s gun,* of Boer War vintage, Nethercoate-Bryant, *More Submarine Memories,* p. 8.

125 *so strongly influenced by first impressions,* Simpson, p. 98.

125 *the golf course just outside,* Horton quoted in Chalmers, p. 72.

126 *always went to see him,* Bowhill quoted in Chalmers, p. 73.

126 *The ship claimed to be Estonian,* Piper interview, IWM Sound 13298.

127 *But with Hutchinson, said ERA Jack Pook,* and the following quotations, Pook interview, IWM Sound 9167; see also Brown's diary, RNSM A1992/058.

128 *a high Swedish source,* Gilbert, p. 197.

128 *England must take control*, Chalmers, p. 269.

129 *Recent reports suggest that a German*, Gilbert, p. 213.

129 *But were they transports?*, Bryant, p. 85.

130 *We saw these ships going north*, and following quotations, Hezlet interview, IWM Sound 12571.

131 *According to the torpedo officer*, Gatehouse interview, IWM Sound 12213.

131 *Just in case a landing was planned at Narvik*, Barnett, p. 106.

132 *instruments in those days*, Hutchinson interview, IWM Sound 9137.

132 *the only man I ever knew*, Wilmot mss, f. 86.

133 *Sink . . . all . . . ships . . . at . . . sight*, Masters, p. 96; King, p. 56.

133 *the captain came on the Tannoy*, Pook interview, IWM Sound 9167.

133 *Next day Tarpon attacked Schiff 40, Tarpon's fate is uncertain*. She was possibly lost on 14 April to the minesweeper *M6* in the Skagerrak.

135 *Faces lit up as if illuminated*, Hart, p. 47.

135 *Will the crew be all right, sir?*, Bryant, p. 88.

136 *Captain in the control room*, King, p. 64.

137 *We saw lines of sailors waiting*, King, p. 69.

138 *The refusal of help from the Commander-in-Chief*, Simpson, p. 88.

138 *I had the very difficult task*, Mars, *Submarines at War*, p. 76.

139 *High pressure within a submarine during long dives*, Compton-Hall, *Underwater War*, p. 49; Padfield, p. 84. This was not discovered until January 1942 and was not considered the principal reason for failure by the Germans.

9 HUNTER AND HUNTED

143 *To help him, in this brand new boat*, the recently invented 'fruit machine' was introduced into new boats, gradually replacing the more primitive 'Iswas' disk, which was a sophisticated slide rule. Masters, p. 85, states that *Tigris* had a fruit machine, so *Truant* presumably also had one.

143 *showing a lot of feather*, and following quotations, Hutchinson interview, IWM Sound 9137.

144 *on a 130 degree track*, where track refers to the track of the torpedoes. Submariners habitually spoke of the 'track', when they meant a compass bearing of so many degrees. Similarly, to get 'off track' meant to get away from the track left by the torpedoes in order to escape enemy destroyers that might follow the track to the submarine's firing position.

144 *submarine became slightly heavy*, *Truant's* patrol report, RNSM A1989/164 (NA, Adm 199/1861).

145 *nothing but a very enlarged after-part*, and following quotations, Hutchinson interview, IWM Sound 9137.

147 *saw the water coming in*, and following quotations, Pook interview, IWM Sound 9167.

147 *tried to pump water out*, and following quotations, Hutchinson interview, IWM Sound 9137. The Sperry compass was a gyroscopic compass that found true north rather than magnetic north and was not affected by the submarine's own magnetic fields. It was delicate and rarely survived depth charges.

148 *like gravel dropping on the hull*, *Truant's* patrol report, SM A1989/164. When other submariners heard similar noises it turned out to be the sound of the target breaking up.

148 *If you're in the control room*, stoker George Woodward in Hood, p. 18.

149 *It was possible to hear depth charges*, Hart, pp. 48–9.

150 *I wouldn't say that people showed their fear*, Pook interview, IWM Sound 9167.

150 *in a fifteen-inch turret standing between the guns*, Mills interview, IWM Sound 9088.

151 *This was early on in the days*, and following quotations, Hezlet interview, IWM Sound 12571.

153 *too much dark and damn little light*, Hutchinson interview, IWM Sound 9137.

153 *I crash-dived to 300 feet*, and following quotations, Mills interview, IWM Sound 9088.

10 NIGHTMARE SUMMER

156 *Everybody had faith*, Pook interview, IWM Sound 9167.

156 *a great red flash*, and following quotations, Hutchinson interview, IWM Sound 9137.

157 *sweated every second the periscope was raised*, and following quotation, King, pp. 70–1.

157 *On 5 May* Seal, The story of *Seal* – another epic – is told in full in Warren and Benson, *Will Not We Fear*.

158 *broke into a broad grin*, Bryant, p. 97.

159 *Frossard was subjected to a severe dressing down*, Stevens, pp. 17–18.

159 *one of Britain's most beautiful*, The Times, 8 May 1940.

161 *long introspective walks*, and the following quotation, King, p. 73.

163 *Personally I do not believe it*, Chalmers, pp. 86–7.

164 *Again I state*, Chalmers, p. 90.

165 *very hard going*, Manuscript accounts of Joe Brighton's career are in the RNSM at A1995/444 and the IWM at 2687 94/6/1. My account is based on the RNSM manuscript combined with a compact disk of an interview, 'Life on the *Porpoise*', made for Diss museum and supplied to me through the kindness of Julie Smith, Lee Trevail and Michael Hall.

165 *I packed my gear*, Skeates, 'My World War II Recollections'.

166 *The word 'attack' was hardly necessary*, and following quotations, King, pp. 75–7.

167 *it was no longer a case of whether we could operate*, Bryant, p. 98.

168 *The hours dragged by*, Bryant, p. 103.

 Shark's last fight, Peter Buckley interview, IWM Sound 4759 and Quigley, pp. 108–14.

168 *wrote a letter of sympathy*, for Churchill's letter and an extract from Claude Barry's obituary notice see Gilbert, pp. 686–7. Barry's piece appeared with others in *The Times*, 25 July 1940.

169 Thames *disappeared on her first patrol*, Hezlet suspected that the B-Dienst's code-reading activities lay behind these losses and attacks on the minelayers. Hezlet, *British and Allied Submarine Operations*, Ch. 4; Blamey, p. 100.

169 *Supplies of modern torpedoes*, maximum annual production of torpedoes for ships, aircraft and submarines from Britain's three factories was 2000. In 1937 the reserve of torpedoes had been cut. Having drastically underestimated torpedo expenditure there was not the capacity to replenish stocks fast enough. See Hezlet, *British and Allied Submarine Operations*, Ch. 1.

169 *a miserable few years*, and following quotations, Haggard interview, IWM Sound 8991.

170 *It wasn't a pleasant task*, Blamey, p. 101.

170 *grew to notice the special expression*, King, p. 75.

170 *It was August when our eighth patrol ended*, and following quotation, King, p. 86.

171 *Somehow the horror of that grim summer*, and following quotation, Bryant, p. 107.

172 *He and his wife Somers*, McGeoch, pp. 34–5.

172 *I like that, said Horton*, Simpson, pp. 97–8.

172 *until the end of the period*, Leslie Howard's service record in the possession of Margaret Howard.

173 *Saw three men amidships sitting on a raft*, Wingate, p. 19.

11 NO TEARS!

174 *I hate this finish to everything*, and following quotations, Anderson diary, IWM Documents 11355 PP/MCR/17; Mannering, pp. 125–30.

179 *under water he had only the vaguest*, Mackenzie, pp. 81–5.

179 *She was rather odd*, Anscomb, p. 45.

180 *Rimington sent for him at once*, Anscomb, p. 84.

181 *Tell the captain there is a long*, and following quotations, Anscomb, pp. 59–61.

183 *the withdrawal of the Eastern Mediterranean Fleet*, see Barnett, pp. 209–12.

185 *perfectly groomed*, Thomsett, interview with the author, 14 July 2009, 'He was so perfectly groomed and that's why we called him "Pansy".'

186 *reports of heavy traffic across*, Bartlett memoir, IWM documents, 1459 91/38/1.

186 *The excitement aroused by meeting*, Mackenzie, p. 87.

187 *a special recognition signal*, Compton-Hall, *Underwater War*, p. 62.

187 *his inability to interpret correctly*, Mackenzie, p. 88.

188 *Haggard was met by the chief of staff*, Haggard interview, IWM Sound 8991.

188 *With little to do to the boats*, Hart, pp. 57–8.

189 *Careless lives cause talk*, Bartlett memoir, IWM Documents, 1459 91/38/1.

189 *Good God man, you're supposed to be dead!*, and following quotations, Hart, pp. 60–2.

190 *somewhat icy*, and following quotations, Haggard interview, IWM Sound 8991.

192 *not exactly maudlin*, and following quotations, Hart, p. 68.

12 DRAFTED DOLPHIN

194 *heartened and impressed*, Mackenzie, pp. 89–91.

195 *temperamentally unsuitable for submarines*, Young, p. 28.

196 *He talked endlessly*, and following quotations, Young, pp. 44–5.

197 *Hard a port, shut off*, and following quotations, Mackenzie, pp. 95–7; Derek Curtis in Nethercoate-Bryant, *More Submarine Memories*, p. 98

197 *You bloody bastard*, and following quotations, Young, pp. 49–52.

199 Porpoise *sailed for Canada*, Brighton, RNSM A1995/444, p. 3; Blamey, pp. 110–17.

201 *I had missed Torbay*, Alexander McCulloch in Izzard, p. 43.

201 *Trials off Dunoon had not gone smoothly*, Drury interview, IWM Sound 13766.

201 H31 *lost her fore-planes*, Rawdon 'Banger' Bannar-Martin in Nethercoate-Bryant, *More Submarine Memories*, pp. 119–20.

202 *We need an electrician*, Casemore, interview with the author, 13 July 2009 and in Nethercoate-Bryant, *Even More Submarine Memories*, pp. 32–3.

202 *You the Skipper? I'm Kerr*, and following quotations, Michael St John in Hood, pp. 118–20.

204 *Bertha, I've shit the bed*, Brighton, RNSM A1995/444, p. 3.

204 *Joe Blamey had hoped*, Blamey, pp. 119–22.

205 *After about a week or so*, and following quotations, McIntosh interview, IWM Sound 11950.

206 *it seemed at the time unlikely*, Brighton, RNSM A1995/444, p. 4; Blamey, p. 123.

206 *Mouillez un!*, and following quotations, McLean, pp. 77–90.

209 *There were only three*, King, pp. 88–90; Young, pp. 60–4.

209 *Submarines were the last thing*, and following quotations, Buckingham, p. 69.

210 *started courting*, and following quotations, Thomsett, interview with the author, 14 July 2009.

210 *Arthur Dickison was drafted*, Dickison, pp. ix–xi.

211 *If you were in the control room*, Skeates, 'My World War II Recollections'.

211 *some people . . . who were claustrophobic*, Roy Broome interview, IWM Sound 13367.

212 *grew to like him more*, and following quotations, Young, pp. 65–8.

213 *picturing vividly in his imagination*, Young, pp. 76–7.

213 *One final thing*, Mars, *Unbroken*, pp. 16–17.

13 SINK, BURN AND DESTROY!

214 *In Egypt he had been briefed*, Simpson, pp. 101–2. The figures for sinkings are those given by Simpson, representing what the submariners thought they had sunk. Present estimates suggest rather more had been sunk than was then known: eleven merchant ships, 18,000 tons by Haggard in *Truant*, 13,000 by Dewhurst on *Rorqual's* mines and 13,000 by the rest combined, with three torpedo boats, Linton's French sloop and *Parthian's* submarine.

215 *and more information is obtained*, RNSM A1941/001.

216 *The most serious problem*, see Hezlet, *British and Allied Submarine Operations*, Ch. 9.

217 *Admiral Layton's daughter*, Kyrle-Pope, pp. 36–43.

219 *Truant rose and fell*, Hart, p. 75; Pietro Faggioli, 'Attilio Deffenu', http://www.marcosieni.it/file/DEFENNU.pdf.

219 *No, that's a T-Class – leave it*, Mike Crawford quoted in Allaway, p. 84.

220 *Upright attack*, details from NA Adm 1/11376. The asdic operator was Ray Cook.

221 *three enemy merchant ships*, RNSM A1997/182.

221 *An enormous, fantastical ball of fire*, Coliolo's report (*La Marina Italiana nella Seconda Guerra Mondiale, VI: La difesa del traffico con l'Africa Settentrionale dal 10 giugno 1940 al 30 settembre 1941*, Roma 1978) in Faggioli 'Attilio Deffenu' (trans. Chris Jones).

221 *One got torpedoed and then there were two*, RNSM A1997/182.

221 *Great flames rose from the ship*, Coliolo's report in Faggioli, 'Attilio Deffenu' (trans. Chris Jones).

222 *it took me years*, Jim Murdoch quoted by Wingate, p. 49.

222 *advanced elements of German 15th Armoured*, Winton, *Ultra at Sea*, p. 165.

223 *extremely disappointing*, Allaway, p. 88.

223 *a good few German soldiers*, George Curnall (as anon: his identity can be established by comparison with Curnall's contributions to Wingate) in Quigley, p. 31.

223 *every possible step must be taken*, Cunningham, p. 343.

225 *a tremendous change*, Haggard interview, IWM Sound 8991.

225 *Oh my God!*, Drury interview, IWM Sound 13766; Casemore, interview with the author, 13 July 2009; patrol report in Casemore's possession.

227 *Upholder was on patrol*, Allaway, pp. 104–7; Quigley, p. 30; Mike Crawford interview, IWM Sound 11763; Tullio Marcon, ed., 'In memoria del piroscafo *Conte Rosso*', *Notiziario della Marina*, XXXI no. 7, July 1984.

229 *advance notice of virtually every convoy*, Hinsley, II, p. 284.

230 *The occupants did not appear*, patrol report quoted by Izzard, pp. 50 and 55.

230 *The operation against the caiques*, and following quotations, Izzard, p. 59.

232 *Utmost to S10. Next please*, Wingate, p. 85; Skeates, 'My World War II Recollections'.

234 *two MAS boats*, the abbreviation stands for Motoscafo Armato Silurante. They were small, fast boats with a ten-man crew.

234 *She sank ten minutes later*, Christiano d'Adamo, 'The Sinking of the *Esperia*' http://www.regiamarina.net/detail_text_with_list.asp?nid=51&lid=1 gives the official Italian account from *La difesa del traffico con l'Africa Settentrionale* and extracts from the diary of eyewitness Fabrizio Romano.

235 *My god, everything is lit up*, and following quotation, Casemore in Nethercoate-Bryant, *Even More Submarine Memories*, p. 34.

236 *every submarine that can be spared*, Wingate, p. 109.

236 *the most dangerous British weapon*, and following quotation, Wingate, p. 105.

14 BAND OF BROTHERS

237 *Rum-issue time!*, and following quotations, Hart, pp. 133–5.

238 *he had one finger up his nose*, Casemore, interview with the author, 13 July 2009.

238 *Thank heaven no one*, King, p. 123.

238 *He was short, scruffy*, Casemore in Nethercoate-Bryant, *Even More Submarine Memories*, p. 34.

239 *Generally*, Casemore, interview with the author, 13 July 2009.

239 *Secretly they kept an eye on you*, Izzard, p. 79.

239 *I was pretty shaky*, Quigley, p. 31; Allaway, p. 116.

239 *standing in the galley*, Casemore in Nethercoate-Bryant, *Even More Submarine Memories*, p. 34.

239 *It was claustrophobic*, Sheffield local newspaper article in Margaret Howard's scrapbook.

240 *it was bad enough on patrols*, Dickison, p. 57.

240 *the asdic rating is the ears*, Quigley, p. 53.

240 *got mixed up with women*, Casemore, interview with the author, 13 July 2009.

240 *If something out of the ordinary*, Casemore in Nethercoate-Bryant, *Even More Submarine Memories*, p. 34.

241 *a torpedo fanatic*, and following quotations, Anscomb, pp. 76–9.

241 *always thought they were better*, Casemore, interview with the author, 13 July 2009.

241 *ashore with the lads*, Blamey, p. 133.

242 *the first night out always*, Hart, p. 70.

242 *refrigerator well stocked*, and following, Brighton, 'Life on the *Porpoise*'.

243 *of his daughter Patricia, with her doggie*, Dickison, p. 40.

243 *liked to keep my crew well informed*, Haggard interview, IWM Sound 8991.

244 *given a rendezvous to be at a certain position*, Cleminson interview, IWM Sound 13655.

244 *I don't know where the British*, Drury interview, IWM Sound 13766 (conducted before the existence of Ultra was revealed).

244 *On* Medway *in Alexandria harbour*, Courtney, p. 17.

244 *Getting the mail kept you sane*, Dickison, p. 62.

245 *swimming and croquet*, Bartlett memoir, IWM Documents, 1459 91/38/1.

246 *When Victor Bartlett*, Anscomb, p. 92.

246 *there was an Irish stoker*, and following quotations, Casemore, interview with the author, 13 July 2009.

247 *It's got a terrible reputation*, Casemore, interview with the author, 13 July 2009.

247 *Everybody knew her*, Skeates, 'My World War II Recollections'.

247 *a nice girl, a bit too strict morally*, and following, Buckingham, p. 100.

248 *Pay me any time*, Hart, p. 79.

248 *had drunk our tots when the sirens*, and following, Buckingham, pp. 100–1.

249 *watching a dogfight going on*, Buckingham, p. 97.

249 *I was woken by shells*, John Oakley of *P31* in Wingate, p. 149.

249 *On the outskirts of St Paul's*, and following quotations, Casemore in Nethercoate-Bryant, *Even More Submarine Memories*, pp. 37–8.

250 *We (that is the whole crew)*, Casemore, interview with the author, 13 July 2009.

250 *The Captain had the floor first*, Skeates, 'My World War II Recollections'.

250 *For those who don't fancy being wounded*, Coote, p. 115.

251 *a mathematical genius*, Mackenzie, p. 132.

251 *pleased to be serving under Woodward*, Piper interview, IWM Sound 13298.

251 *The pace he set himself*, Simpson, p. 167.

251 *My best C.O.*, and following quotations, Simpson pp. 126, 164.

252 *one hell of a gent*, and following comments by Murdoch, Skeates to the author by email.

252 *a cool customer*, Coote, p. 2.

253 *Do not hit me, Sir*, Izzard, pp. 137–8.

253 *some of the lads went on shore*, Sheffield local newspaper in Margaret Howard's scrapbook.

253 *Whatever he had wrong with him*, Le Gros in Izzard, p. 128.

253 *Perhaps it was because I was too young*, Troup in Izzard, p. 193.

254 *If you do suffer from this*, Cleminson interview, IWM Sound 13655.

254 *Hearing my story of the patrol*, Mackenzie, pp. 126–7.

254 *For the first time in five patrols*, McGeoch, p. 101.

254 *To sink one ship only*, and following quotations King, pp. 98 and 101–2.

255 *the pride of the submariners*, Fraser, p. 57.

15 NO MARGIN FOR MISTAKES

257 *Pommie bastard*, McIntosh interview, IWM Sound 11950.

257 *We soon learned*, Brighton RNSM A1995/444, p. 5.

257 *I, Boris Karnicki*, Simpson, p. 168.

257 *They were a wild and utterly charming bunch*, Kyrle-Pope, p. 44.

258 *Welcome back to the Mediterranean*, Haggard interview, IWM Sound 8991.

258 *Instead of being snugged up*, and following quotation, Hart, pp. 107–10.

258 *a splendid man*, and following quotation, Haggard interview, IWM Sound 8991.

260 *fleet operation orders and directives*, Mackenzie, pp. 102–3; the daily intelligence reports on the Italian convoy situation are in NA Adm 223/31.

261 *There is no margin for mistakes*, Chalmers, p. 106.

261 *a million pounds*, King, p. 98.

262 *a number of bulkhead fittings*, and following quotations, Skeates, 'My World War II Recollections'. Operational details from NA Adm 1/12320.

263 *German Army Enigma*, Hinsley, II, pp. 285–6.

264 *Malta air forces report two merchantmen*, Fellers' cables in National Archives, Washington, RG 165, 6910 box 759. The fullest account of Fellers is to be found in Clayton and Craig.

265 *All four torpedoes were ready*, Casemore in Nethercoate-Bryant, *Even More Submarine Memories*, p. 36.

266 *The little boat is working very well*, Wingate, pp. 131–2.

266 *each time the vibration*, Skeates, 'My World War II Recollections'.

268 *First lieutenant, see if you can see something*, and following quotations, Piper interview, IWM Sound 13298; for what was learned from the interrogation of Ploch and details of the attack see http://www.uboatarchive.net/U-374INT.htm, 'U374 interrogation of sole survivor'. Other details come from NA Adm 1/12344.

269 *inside, strained and anxious*, and the following quotations, Hart, pp. 137–44; see also Mackenzie, pp. 1–6.

270 *Her steering was light and accurate*, and following quotations, Anscomb pp. 106–7 and 111–14.

271 *That piece of clumsiness*, Anscomb, p. 118; for the episode see Wingate, pp. 144–5.

272 *had the first watch on duty*, and following quotations, Anscomb, pp. 118–25.

274 *Up above, Palmas had decided*, Wingate, pp. 145–6.

274 *the ultimate horror*, and following quotations, Anscomb, pp. 125–8.

276 *Captain Palmas was on the hunt again*, Wingate, p. 150; extracts from Palmas's report can also be read at: http://crusaderproject.wordpress.com/2010/05/22/sinking-of-hm-submarine-p-38-23-february-1942/.

16 COUNT THE DAYS

277 *There was some waste ground*, Casemore in Nethercoate-Bryant, *Even More Submarine Memories*, p. 37.

278 *While standing there doing what comes*, Buckingham, pp. 89–90.

278 *Two parachute mines* Simpson, pp. 198–200.

278 *wave after wave of JU88s*, Buckingham, p. 90.

279 *we were going ashore in seaboots*, Casemore in Nethercoate-Bryant, *Even More Submarine Memories*, p. 38.

279 *On 17 March the Polish* Sokol, on *Sokol* see Baxter, pp. 160–4 and Simpson, pp. 301–4; on *Pandora* see Quigley, p. 18, Wingate, pp. 168–9.

280 P36 *was alongside*, Thomsett, interview with the author, 14 July 2009.

280 *suddenly, red, white, yellow*, Casemore in Nethercoate-Bryant, *Even More Submarine Memories*, p. 39.

281 *Piss off, Tug*, Allaway, p. 161.

281 *count the days*, Allaway, p. 162.

281 *In December the* London Gazette, Allaway, pp. 135–6.

281 *While he was asleep*, Wingate, pp. 130–1.

282 *on 14 April 1942 air escorts*, the mystery of *Upholder*'s destruction has not yet been solved conclusively. Francesco Mattesini's explanation is at http://www.uboat.net/allies/warships/ship/3535.html. He states that *Pegaso*, often said to have sunk *Upholder*, attacked a dolphin. Mattesini's is the most plausible of a number of theories, including Mackenzie's belief that Wanklyn was mined while returning to Malta.

282 *the British government's policy*, Simpson, p. 242.

282 *During April the British decrypted*, Clayton and Craig, pp. 47–8.

283 *when suddenly a flight of aircraft*, Casemore in Nethercoate-Bryant, *Even More Submarine Memories*, p. 41.

283 *It is evident that Commander Miers*, Izzard, p. 119.

284 *We are in the most*, Izzard, p. 125.

284 *After Torbay had tied up*, Casemore in Nethercoate-Bryant, *Even More Submarine Memories*, p. 41.

284 *I didn't want to go*, Drury interview, IWM Sound 13766.

284 *Leslie Howard, meanwhile, went to a party*, Margaret Howard's account courtesy of Mark Law.

285 *Crap was escorted*, Izzard, p. 128.

285 *Prime Minister, I am satisfied*, and the aftermath, Clayton and Craig, pp. 100–1, 115–16, 124 and 151.

286 *went ashore just before*, Brighton, 'Life on the *Porpoise*'.

286 *In Medway* Hart, Hart, pp. 154–60.

288 *H.E. ahead, sir*, Mars, *Unbroken*, pp. 115–26, an account that Simpson (pp. 250–1) found vainglorious.

290 *Ultra had tracked*, Santoni, pp. 162–3; Hinsley, II, p. 419 and Appendix 17.

290 *transmits itself to the human body*, Brighton, RNSM A1995/444, p. 11.

290 *one joker asked us*, Blamey, p. 161.

291 *We were in a hell of a mess*, and the following quotation, Brighton, RNSM A1995/444, p. 11.

291 *state of the rum jars*, Brighton, RNSM A1995/444, p. 9.

292 *Estimated Time of Departure Naples*, Hinsley, II, Appendix 17. For this episode see also Simpson, pp. 261–4.

292 *P.O. Willey came in*, Mars, *Unbroken*, p. 166.

292 *At 1700 on the 17th*, Wingate, p. 222.

293 *The tanker Saturno left Cagliari*, Santoni, p. 181.

293 *18 October. We spent*, Dickison, p. 37.

293 *That night there was a constant hustle*, Mars, *Unbroken*, pp. 166–7.

293 *Next day being Sunday*, Dickison, p. 38.

294 *sat in the ward-room*, Mars, *Unbroken*, p. 167.

294 *At 1153 the mastheads and smoke*, Wingate, p. 222.

294 *Our torpedoes were set*, Douglas in Quigley, p. 82.

294 *the familiar noise of an express train*, and following quotations, Mars, *Unbroken*,

pp. 172–6; for John Jones of *Unbroken* see also Quigley, pp. 46–50.

295 *We started the attack*, Dickison, p. 38.

296 *plunged into a swirling bank*, Wingate in Wingate, p. 226.

297 *walked up the Rock*, and the following quotation, McGeoch, pp. 69–70.

17 SELBY'S LUCK

298 *Selby was in the petty officers' mess*, Selby interview, IWM Sound 16738.

299 *It's abandon ship*, and following quotations, Wright in Quigley, pp. 24–57.

300 *Ben Bryant always went*, Bryant, pp. 105–6.

301 *As ye sow*, Quigley, p. 27.

301 *The Lord is calling us*, W.R. Pierce in Nethercoate-Bryant, *More Submarine Memories*, p. 6.

301 *Shrimp Simpson remembered*, Simpson, pp. 155–6.

301 *Len 'Tug' Wilson*, The bottle is RNSM G24/02/71 and there are several versions of the story on the internet; Coote, p. 141.

302 *the worst I ever experienced*, Piper interview, IWM Sound 13298.

302 *People cut corners*, Michael St John quoted in Allaway, p. 165.

303 *one of the most emotional things*, and following quotations, Casemore in Nethercoate-Bryant, *Even More Submarine Memories*, pp. 33–4.

304 *we used to make our landfall*, Bryant, p. 42.

304 *Of approximately eighty British submarines lost*, the total varies according to whether you include or exclude (as here) midgets and how exactly you define British.

305 *In* Untamed *the transducer got stuck*, see Coote, pp. 31–7.

306 Vandal *had sunk*, the account of the loss of *Vandal* is based on the conclusions of the 2003 expedition leader, Nick Gilbert, available at http://www.deep-image.co.uk/wrecks/vandal/vandal_pages/vandal-sinking_theorypopup.htm

307 *his story remained untold*, according to Shelford who describes these escapes, pp. 129–50.

307 *After the war, Tiny Fell took part*, Fell, *Sea Surrenders*, pp. 51–64.

308 *one out of sixty-one from* Perseus, the story of John Capes's escape from *Perseus* is told in the prologue.

308 *In July 1941 she had her bow blown off*, Abdy in Wingate, pp. 93–7.

309 *you've got the one attribute*, McIntosh interview, IWM Sound 11950.

309 *should you ever find yourself*, Gordon Selby obituary, *The Times*, 5 April 2007; see also *Daily Telegraph*, 20 April 2007.

18 THE MOST IMPORTANT TARGET IN THE WAR AT SEA

310 *Hello Fell! What mischief*, Fell, *Sea Our Shield*, p. 106.

311 *the most important target*, Max Shean in Hood, p. 311.

312 *You seem to have picked the right sort*, Fell, *Sea Our Shield*, pp. 120–1.

312 *A young lady answered*, and following quotations, Skeates, 'My World War II Recollections'.

316 *involved a very primitive*, and following quotations, Skeates, 'My World War II Recollections'.

317 *questions that began 'Where is?'*, Chalmers, pp. 150–1.

317 *How would you like to join us*, Place interview, IWM Sound 10431.

317 *Again, it was on a Sunday*, and following quotations, Coles interview, IWM Sound 13422.

318 *We were on the surface*, Casemore in Nethercoate-Bryant, *Even More Submarine Memories*, p. 43.

319 *not very thrilled*, RNSM A2007/514.

319 *about twelve of the crew*, and following quotations, Casemore in Nethercoate-Bryant, *Even More Submarine Memories*, p. 43.

320 *Raikes turned round*, and following quotations, RNSM A2007/ 514.

322 *The beauty of this*, and following quotations, Coles interview, IWM Sound 13422.

323 *During supper we heard an alarming noise*, Place interview, IWM Sound 10431.

323 *I was the sparker on duty*, Brown, RNSM A2000/024.

324 *I wasn't particularly aware*, and following quotations, Place interview, IWM Sound 10431.

325 *a long, black submarine-like object*, Warren and Benson, *Above Us the Waves*, p. 130.

325 *everybody seemed to be waving pistols*, Warren and Benson, *Above Us the Waves*, p. 132.

326 *But at sixty feet*, and following quotations, Place interview, IWM Sound 10431.

326 *Here goes the last of the Places*, Warren and Benson, *Above Us the Waves*, p. 134.

326 *The firing stopped immediately*, and following quotation, Place interview, IWM Sound 10431.

19 MARE NOSTRUM

329 *An investigation in 1942*, NA Adm 223/46 ff. 20–1 Italian ships carrying prisoners of war, dated 20 November 1942.

329 *Orders to submarines*, Simpson's comments on Bromage's patrol report, NA Adm 199/1839.

330 *On 13 November 'the Mediterranean authorities' were told*, NA Adm 223/46 ff. 20–1: 'Scillin was sunk by HM S/M P212 at 2000A/14/11/42. A QT message passed out at 2241Z/13/11/42 informed the Mediterranean authorities that she carried prisoners.'

330 *The Italians had packed*, NA WO 361/132 (the investigation into what happened) and WO 32/18501 (survivors' reports).

330 *1950 One torpedo*, and following quotation, Bromage's patrol report, NA Adm 199/1839.

332 *the gnawing anxiety*, Simpson, p. 285.

332 *Leslie Howard married*, Margaret Howard's account, supplied through Mark Law.

333 *the effervescent, roly-poly*, Simpson, p. 168.

333 *Gosh, it's good*, Simpson, p. 277.

333 *Our sister ship,* Traveller, Forbes in Quigley, p. 52.

334 *that he had reached that stage*, Simpson, p. 268.

334 *Hezlet, writing his history*, Hezlet, *British and Allied Submarine Operations*, Ch. 18.

335 *It had been worth it*, Warren and Benson, *Above Us the Waves*, p. 83.

335 *in retrospect it is obvious*, Simpson, p. 285.

336 *Dickison found a very beautiful front*, Dickison, pp. 54–6.

336 *John Gibson, arriving in June*, Gibson, pp. 51–2.

337 *Others, who were based at Algiers*, Casemore in Nethercoate-Bryant, *Even More Submarine Memories*, p. 44. Coote, p. 66, described the Sphinx as 'an imposing four-storeyed building with tiny rooms reeking of potassium permanganate leading off the internal verandahs around its covered courtyard. It was a boisterous, sordid production line.'

337 *Tubby Linton was missing*, Linton's death remains unexplained. The explanation usually given – that *Turbulent* was sunk on 12 March after an attack on the *Mafalda* – is likely to be incorrect, since the submarine that attacked the *Mafalda* was almost certainly the French *Casabianca*. My account is informed by research posted on the internet by Platon Alexiades at http://www.uboat.net/forums/read.php?22,65526,77466#msg-77466.

338 *the usual tale*, Forbes in Quigley, p. 56.

339 *Bill Jewell in* Seraph, for the most recent account of 'the man who never was' see Ben Macintyre, *Operation Mincemeat*, London: Bloomsbury, 2010.

339 *If I miss this*, McGeoch, p. 73.

340 *Blow all main ballast*, McGeoch, pp. 13–24. McGeoch occupies twelfth place in Hezlet's table of largest tonnage sunk.

341 *The girls were trained in modesty*, Gibson, p. 104.

342 *extremely nice*, and the following quotation, Jean de Berniere-Smart (née Smithells), interview with the author, November 2009.

342 *another bottle of wine*, Gibson, p. 149.

343 *massacre of 200 Huns*, Sokol's patrol report (TNA Adm 199/1854) in Hood, pp. 333–4.

344 *Well, I don't know*, and following quotations, Roderick Wilmot, manuscript account of his career in *Torbay*.

346 *slipped through the German lines*, Anscomb, pp. 188–97.

20 H FOR HELL

347 *urgent need is submarines*, Hezlet, *British and Allied Submarine Operations*, Ch. 12.

349 *the figures you supply*, Haggard interview, IWM Sound 8991; King, p. 125.

350 *One charge forced open the battery*, and following quotations, RNSM A1992/058, diary of Telegraphist Eddie 'Buster' Brown.

351 *native straw huts with mosquito net*, and following quotations, RNSM A2000/024, letter from Eddie Brown.

351 *The sentry on the next boat*, Pook interview, IWM Sound 9167.

352 *nicknamed him Dillinger*, Mervyn Wingfield obituary, *Daily Telegraph*, 28 May 2005.

353 *a big black hairy man*, and the following quotations, Nethercott interview, IWM Sound 11068.

354 *Gibson of* Taurus *swam and fished*, Gibson, pp. 168–70.

356 *nerve-shattering noise*, and following quotation, King, p. 146.

357 *Young took* Storm *on an operation*, Young, pp. 242–9; RNSM A2007/514 Richard Hodgson.

358 *Around June Hugh Mackenzie arrived*, Mackenzie, p. 145; King, pp. 148–55.

358 *behind that rugged exterior*, and following quotation, Blamey, pp. 222 and 189.

359 *shaved with a mass of soap suds*, and following quotation, Skeates, 'My World War II Recollections'.

361 *met a Wren Second Officer*, Hezlet, *HMS Trenchant*, p. 110.
362 *the thrash of the Japanese destroyer*, and following quotations, official report by Douglas, on the internet at http://www.cofepow.org.uk/pages/ships_stratagem.htm.
364 *to her most welcome air-mail*, Skeates, 'My World War II Recollections'.

21 ONE JUMP AHEAD OF DEATH

365 *Jim Thomsett married*, Jim Thomsett, interview with the author, 14 July 2009.
366 *There seemed to be nothing for it*, Mars, *HMS Thule*, pp. 66–7.
367 *It was a policy I did not like*, Mackenzie, p. 145.
368 *Some of the things we did*, and following quotations, Watters RNSM A.
369 *The worst single disaster*, I have not seen an investigation into the role of Ultra (or the lack of it) with regard to the sinking of the *Junyo Maru* or other POW sinkings in the Far East.
369 *had better give some sort of answer*, and following quotations, official report by Douglas at http://www.cofepow.org.uk/pages/ships_stratagem.htm
370 *a robust, overweight, pot-bellied and scruffy*, and following quotations, Ken Wade in Nethercoate-Bryant, *Submarine Memories*, pp. 124–37.
372 Strongbow *sailed for a patrol*, based on Blamey, pp. 205–15; Jack Pollard in Nethercoate-Bryant, *Submarine Memories*, pp. 44–9; Tony Troup in Nethercoate-Bryant, *More Submarine Memories*, pp. 141–2.
376 *patrolling this massive submarine in flat calm seas*, Coote, p. 142.
377 *seemed to have some idea*, Mars, *HMS Thule*, p. 144.
378 *joined the water polo club*, Casemore in Nethercoate-Bryant, *Even More Submarine Memories*, pp. 47–8.
379 *Hezlet described the attack*, Hezlet interview, IWM Sound 2603.
379 *One hit ... two hits ... three hits*, Peter Wood in RNSM A2007/509. Cf Hezlet, *HMS Trenchant*, p. 175 for Hezlet's enduring dislike of the Japanese.

22 COMING HOME

380 *Sit down Joe*, and following quotations, Blamey, pp. 221–2.
381 *Tense as a coiled spring*, and following quotations, King, pp. 174–5.
381 *V.J. Day in Western Australia*, Mars, *HMS Thule*, p. 226.
382 *with a feeling somehow*, Bryant, p. 45.
382 *Jack Casemore was on patrol* Casemore in Nethercoate-Bryant, *Even More Submarine Memories*, pp. 49–50.
382 *John Gibson witnessed the lowering*, Gibson, pp. 281–2.
382 *The whole population except myself*, Blamey, p. 227.
383 *Wait till we get to the Alps*, King, p. 176.
384 *I felt a glowing pride in her*, Hart, p. 206.
384 *pierhead jump*, for Mackenzie's account of the Polaris project see Mackenzie, pp. 204–42.

Bibliography

GOSPORT: ROYAL NAVY
SUBMARINE MUSEUM

A1941/001 Correspondence regarding flotilla reports and war experience
A1941/003 Italian account of sinking of *Cachalot*
A1941/005 improvements that might be desirable as a result of war experience
A1941/062 John Capes, narrative of escape
A1943/011 John Capes letters
A1984/012 account of sinking of *Karlsruhe* by *Truant*
A1989/164 patrol reports, *Truant* November 1939–April 1940
A1990/182 alleged atrocities committed by *Torbay*
A1992/058 diary of Eddie Brown
A1995/444 Joe Brighton memoir
A1996/059 Eric Fulford note
A1996/168 alleged atrocities committed by *Rorqual*
A1997/182 signals 9 and 12 March 1941
A2000/024 letter from Eddie Brown
A2007/509 Peter Wood memoir
A2007/514 Richard Hodgson memoirs
A2007/518 Stanley Hawkey scrapbook
A R.A. Watters memoir
A Brodie, Charles Gordon, 'Frightfulness – the post-war view and its effect on the navy', lecture to Royal Naval War College, Greenwich, 1 Feb 1928, RNSM archives

LONDON: IMPERIAL WAR MUSEUM

Sound:

2360 Boris Karnicki 1939
2397 Sydney Raw 1941
2412 Anthony Kimmins 1942
2416 Lynch Maydon 1942

2424 Hugh Haggard 1942
2428 Hugh Mackenzie and Thomas Gould 1943
2438 Anthony Mars 1943
2440 Claude Barry 1944
2441 Godfrey Place 1944
2581 Edward Young 1945
2603 Arthur Hezlet 1945
4759 Peter Buckley
4839 Harold Ship
8991 Hugh Haggard
9088 Ronnie Mills
9137 Christopher Haynes Hutchinson
9153 Mervyn Wingfield
9167 William John Pook
9310 John Stevens
9578 Rob Roy McCurrach
9822 Ian Fraser
9858 Ian McGeoch
9864 John Eaden
10188 John Bromage
10431 Basil Charles Godfrey Place
11068 Iain Nethercott
11745 Hugh Mackenzie
11763, 26764 Michael Crawford
11769 Conrad Berey
11881 Alexander Ferrier
11950 Ian McIntosh
12071 Hugh Mackenzie
12213 Richard Gatehouse
12278 Bill Jewell
12317 Edward Young
12336 Tony Troup
12571 Arthur Hezlet
13235 Michael Lumby
13249 Charles Anscomb
13298 Aston Piper
13367 Roy Broome
13392 Paul Chapman
13422 Vernon Coles
13655 Antony Cleminson
13766 Norman William Drury
13922 Alfred Giordan
16738 Gordon Selby
17259 Dick Raikes
17603 Joel Blamey
17832 Bill King
18090 Philip Francis
28642 Maxwell Shean

Documents:

6338 96/22/1 Ehlebracht account of sinking of his caique by *Torbay*
11355 PP/MCR/17 Ian Anderson journal
1459 91/38/1 Peter Bartlett memoir
1461 91/38/1 Christopher Hutchinson memoir
2687 94/6/1 Joe Brighton memoir
4524 Peter Buckley memoir
7176 97/24/1 Joe Blamey memoir
12946 Jack Casemore memoir
13509 05/63/1 G.P. Darling letters

LONDON: THE NATIONAL ARCHIVES

Adm 1/11376, 11378, 12320, 12342, 12344 recommendations for awards
Adm 178/194 loss of *Oxley*
Adm 199/136 report on Red Sea sinkings
Adm 199/1814, 1817, 1819, 1820, 1832, 1839, 1848, 1861, 1865, 1866, 1867, 1868, 1922 patrol reports; 1889 Italian records of attacks on them
Adm 223/31 Italian convoy reports 1941–3
Adm 223/46 ff. 20–1 Italian ships carrying prisoners of war, dated 20 November 1942
Adm 223/89 report of OIC Alexandria
Adm 236/48 contains Simpson's report on *Upholder*'s encounter with *Truant*
Adm 236/54 WW1 experience
AIR 40/2323 use of Ultra in the Mediterranean
HW 1/90 report on losses due to sinking of *Oceania* and *Neptunia*
HW 1/657 damage to *Trento*
HW 1/821 and 822 fate of *Lerici*
WO 32/18501 Ill-treatment of POWs being taken from Tripoli, Libya to Italy on SS *Scillin* and sinking of ship by HM Submarine *P212*
WO 361/132 Casualties at sea: SS *Scillin*
WO 361/133 Casualties at sea: Italian vessels carrying British prisoners of war

OTHER PRIVATE MANUSCRIPT SOURCES

Leslie Howard's copy of Roderick Wilmot's account of *Torbay*'s second commission and other material relating to Leslie Howard, kindly passed to me by Mark Law
Joe Brighton, 'Life on the *Porpoise*', compact disk made for Diss Museum
Ben Skeates, 'My World War II Recollections' and conversations with the author by email
Author's interviews with Jack Casemore, Jean de Berniere-Smart, Bill King, Iain Nethercott and Jim Thomsett

PUBLISHED SOURCES

Allaway, Jim, *Hero of the Upholder*, Shrewsbury 1991
Anscomb, Charles, *Submariner*, London: William Kimber, 1957

Arthur, Max, *The Navy: 1939 to the Present Day*, London: Hodder & Stoughton, 1997

Barnett, Correlli, *Engage the Enemy More Closely*, London: Hodder & Stoughton, 1991

Baxter, Richard, *Stand By to Surface*, London: Cassell, 1944

Beesly, Patrick, *Very Special Intelligence: The Story of the Admiralty's Operational Intelligence Centre, 1939–1945*, London: Hamilton, 1977

Bekker, Caius, *Hitler's Naval War*, London, Macdonald, 1974

Blamey, Joel, *A Submariner's Story: The Memoirs of a Submarine Engineer in Peace and in War*, Penzance, Cornwall: Periscope Publishing, 2002

Bower, John Graham, *The Story of Our Submarines*, Edinburgh: Chambers, 1919

Brodie, Charles Gordon, *Forlorn Hope 1915*, London: Frederick Books, 1956

Bryant, Ben, *One Man Band: The Memoirs of a Submarine C.O.*, London: William Kimber, 1958

Buckingham, Fred F., *The Strife is O'er: Trials and Tribulations in the Long and Varied Career of a Royal Navy Sparker*, Minster Lovell, Oxfordshire: Bookmarque Publishing, 1993

Carr, William Guy, *By Guess and By God: The Story of the British Submarines in the War*, London: Hutchinson & Co, 1930

Casing, James, *Submariners*, London: Macmillan & Co Ltd, 1951

Chalmers, William Scott, *Max Horton and the Western Approaches*, London: Hodder & Stoughton, 1954

Chapman, Paul, *Submarine Torbay*, London: Robert Hale, 1989

Clayton, Aileen, *The Enemy is Listening*, London: Hutchinson, 1980

Clayton, Tim and Phil Craig, *End of the Beginning*, London: Hodder & Stoughton, 2002

Compton-Hall, Richard, *The Underwater War, 1939–1945*, Poole, Dorset: Blandford Press, 1982

—— *Submarines and the War at Sea 1914–1918*, London: Macmillan, 1991

Coote, John, *Submariner*, London: Leo Cooper, 1991

Courtney, G.B., *SBS in World War Two*, London: Robert Hale, 1983

Crawford, Michael L.C., *HM Submarine Upholder*, Warship Profile, 1971

Cunningham, Andrew Browne, *A Sailor's Odyssey*, London: Hutchinson, 1951

Dickison, Arthur, *Crash Dive!: In Action with HMS Safari 1942–43*, Stroud: Sutton Publishing, 1999

Elphick, Peter, *Far Eastern File: The Intelligence War in the Far East, 1930–45*, London: Hodder & Stoughton, 1997

Faggioli, Pietro, 'Attilio Deffenu', http://www.marcosieni.it/file/DEFENNU.pdf.

Fell, William Richmond, *The Sea Surrenders*, London: Cassell, 1960

—— *The Sea Our Shield*, London: Cassell, 1966

Fraser, Ian, *Frogman VC*, London: Angus & Robertson, 1957

Giatropoulou, Rena and Kostas Thoctarides, *H.M. Submarine Perseus: Whispers from the Deep*, Piraeus: Hellenic Maritime Museum, n.d.

Gibson, John Frederic, *Dark Seas Above*, Edinburgh: William Blackwood, 1947

Gilbert, Martin, *Finest Hour*, London: Heinemann, 1983

Greene, Jack and Alessandro Massignani, *The Naval War in the Mediterranean, 1940–1943*, Rochester, Kent: Chatham Publishing, 1998

Hall, Keith, *Submariners*, Stroud: Tempus, 2006

Hart, Sydney, *Discharged Dead*, London: White Lion, 1956

Hezlet, Arthur, *British and Allied Submarine Operations in World War Two*, 2 vols, Gosport, Hampshire: Royal Navy Submarine Museum, 2001, available as a compact disk.

—— *HMS Trenchant at War: From Chatham to the Banka Strait*, Barnsley: Leo Cooper, 2001

Hinsley, F.H., Thomas, E.E. et al., *British Intelligence in the Second World War; Its Influence on Strategy and Operations*, London: HMSO, 1979–88

Hood, Jean, ed., *Submarine: An Anthology of First-hand Accounts of the War under the Sea, 1939–1945*, London: Conway, 2007

Izzard, Brian, *Gamp VC*, Sparkford, Somerset: Haynes Publishing, 2009

Jameson, William S., *Submariners V.C.*, London: Peter Davies, 1962

Jones, Geoffrey P., *Submarines versus U-Boats*, London: William Kimber, 1986

Kemp, Paul J., *British Submarines in World War 2*, Poole, Dorset: Arms and Armour Press, 1987

Kimmins, Anthony, *Half-time*, London: Heinemann, 1947

King, William, *The Stick and the Stars*, London: Hutchinson, 1958

Kyrle-Pope, Suzanne, *The Same Wife in Every Port*, Crook Town, Durham: The Memoir Club, 1998

L'Herminier, Jean, *Casabianca*, Paris: France Empire, 1992

Lipscomb, Frank Woodgate, *The British Submarine*, London: Adam & Charles Black, 1954

McGeoch, Ian, *An Affair of Chances*, London: Imperial War Museum, 1991

Mackenzie, Hugh, *The Sword of Damocles*, Stroud: Sutton, 1995

McLean, Ruari, *Half Seas Under: Seaman, Submariner, Canoeist*, Bradford on Avon: Thomas Reed, 2001

Mannering, Guy, *The Seas Between: Letters from a Submariner*, Geraldine, New Zealand: GM Publications, 2003

Mars, Alastair, *British Submarines at War 1939–1945*, London: William Kimber, 1971

—— *Unbroken: The Story of a Submarine*, London: Muller, 1953

—— *HMS Thule Intercepts*, London: Elek Books, 1956

Masters, David, *Up Periscope*, London: Eyre and Spottiswoode, 1943

Mitchell, Pamela, *The Tip of the Spear*, Huddersfield: Richard Netherwood, 1993

Nethercoate-Bryant, Keith et al. (eds), *Submarine Memories*, Upper Beeding: Gatwick Submarine Archive, n.d.

—— *More Submarine Memories: Some More Lesser Known Facts from the Gatwick Submarine Archive*, Upper Beeding: Gatwick Submarine Archive, 1997

—— *Even More Submarine Memories*, Upper Beeding: Gatwick Submarine Archive, 2005

Padfield, Peter, *War Beneath the Sea*, London: Pimlico, 1995

Parker, John, *The Silent Service: The Inside Story of the Royal Navy's Submarine Heroes*, London: Headline, 2001

Quigley, Dave J., *Under the Jolly Roger: British Submariners at War, 1939–1945*, Portsmouth: Portsmouth Publishing, 1988

Rohwer, Juergen, *Allied Submarine Attacks of World War Two: European Theatre 1939–45*, London: Greenhill Books, 1997

Roskill, S.W., *The War at Sea 1939–1945*, London: HMSO, 1954

—— *Naval Policy Between the Wars*, 2 vols, London: Collins, 1968

Sadkovich, James J., *The Italian Navy in World War II*, London: Greenwood Press, 1994

Santoni, Alberto, *Il vero traditore: il ruolo documentato di ULTRA nella guerra del Mediterraneo*, Milano: Mursia, 1981

Shelford, William O., *'Subsunk': The Story of Submarine Escape*, London: Harrap, 1960

Showell, Jak P. Mallmann, *German Naval Code Breakers*, Hersham: Ian Allen, 2003

Simpson, George Walter Gillow, *Periscope View: A Professional Autobiography*, London: Macmillan, 1972

Skillen, Hugh, *Spies of the Airwaves: A History of Y Sections during the Second World War*, Pinner, Middlesex: H. Skillen, 1989

Sopocko, Eryk K.S., *'Orzel's' Patrol: The Story of the Polish Submarine*, London: Methuen, 1942

Stevens, J.S., *Never Volunteer: A Submariner's Scrapbook*, N.p.: J.S. Stevens, Woodleigh, Emsworth, 1971

Talbot-Booth, Eric Charles, *Ships of the World's Battlefleets*, Sampson Low, Marston, 1936–40, 4th edn 1942

—— *What Ship is that?*, Sampson Low, Marston, n.d.

—— *Merchant Ships*, Sampson Low, Marston, 1942

Tawney, Cyril, *Grey Funnel Lines: Traditional Song and Verse of the Royal Navy 1900–70*, London: Routledge, 1987

Thomas, David A., *Submarine Victory: The Story of British Submarines in World War II*, London: Kimber, 1961

Trenowden, Ian, *The Hunting Submarine: The Fighting Life of HMS Tally-Ho*, [Bristol]: Crecy, 1994

Turner, John Frayn, *Periscope Patrol: The Saga of Malta Submarines*, London: Harrap, 1957

Waldron, Tom and Gleeson, James, *The Frogmen: The Story of the Wartime Underwater Operators*, London: Evans Bros, 1950

Warren, Charles Esme Thornton and Benson, James, *Above Us the Waves: The Story of Midget Submarines and Human Torpedoes*, London: Harrap, 1953

—— *Will Not We Fear: the Story of His Majesty's Submarine 'Seal' and of Lieutenant-Commander Rupert Lonsdale*, London: George G. Harrap, 1961

Wilson, Michael, *A Submariner's War: Indian Ocean 1939–45*, Stroud: Tempus, 2000

Wingate, John, *The Fighting Tenth: the Tenth Submarine Flotilla and the Siege of Malta*, London: Leo Cooper, 1991

Winton, John, *Ultra at Sea*, London: Leo Cooper, 1988

—— *The Submariners: Life in British Submarines 1901–1999*, London: Constable, 1999

Young, Edward, *One of our Submarines*, London: Rupert Hart-Davis, 1952

Index

WP 9/13